Doping and Anti-Doping Policy in Sport

The issue of doping has been the most widely discussed problem in sports ethics and is one of the most prominent issues across sports studies, the sports sciences and their constituent disciplines. This book adds uniquely to that catalogue of discourses by focusing on extant anti-doping policy and doping practices from a range of multidisciplinary perspectives (specifically ethical, legal and social scientific).

With contributions from a world-class team of scholars and legal practitioners from the UK, Europe and North America, the book explores key contemporary issues such as:

- sports medicine
- international doping policy
- the whereabouts system
- the criminalization of doping
- privacy rights, gene doping and ethics
- imperfection in doping test procedures
- steroid use in the general population.

Doping and Anti-Doping Policy in Sport offers an important critique of contemporary anti-doping policy and should be essential reading for any advanced student, researcher or policymaker with an interest in this vital issue.

Mike McNamee is Professor of Applied Ethics in the Department of Philosophy, History and Law in Healthcare, Swansea University, and is also a member of the Clinical Ethics Committee at Cardiff and Vale National Health Service Trust, UK. He is Series Editor of *Ethics and Sport* and Editor of the journal *Sport, Ethics and Philosophy*. He is a former President of the International Association for the Philosophy of Sport and the Founding Chair of the British Philosophy of Sport Association.

Verner Møller is Professor of Sports Science at Aarhus University, Denmark. He is the coordinator of the International Network of Humanistic Doping Research (INHDR) and a leading expert on the cultural and philosophical aspects of doping.

Ethics and Sport

Series editors

Mike McNamee, *Swansea University, Wales, UK*
Jim Parry, *Charles University in Prague, Czech Republic*
Heather L. Reid, *Morningside College, USA*

The Ethics and Sport series aims to encourage critical reflection on the practice of sport, and to stimulate professional evaluation and development. Each volume explores new work relating to philosophical ethics and the social and cultural study of ethical issues. Each is different in scope, appeal, focus and treatment, but a balance is sought between local and international focus, perennial and contemporary issues, level of audience, teaching and research application, and variety of practical concerns.

Ethics and Sport
Edited by Mike McNamee and Jim Parry

Values in Sport
Elitism, nationalism, gender equality and the scientific manufacture of winners
Edited by Torbjörn Tännsjö and Claudio Tamburrini

Spoilsports
Understanding and preventing sexual exploitation in sport
Celia Brackenridge

Fair Play in Sport
A moral norm system
Sigmund Loland

Sport, Rules and Values
Philosophical investigations into the nature of sport
Graham McFee

Sport, Professionalism and Pain
Ethnographies of injury and risk
David Howe

Genetically Modified Athletes
Biomedical ethics, gene doping and sport
Andy Miah

Human Rights in Youth Sport
A critical review of children's rights in competitive sports
Paulo David

Genetic Technology and Sport
Ethical questions
Edited by Claudio Tamburrini and Torbjörn Tännsjö

Pain and Injury in Sport
Social and ethical analysis
Edited by Sigmund Loland, Berit Skirstad and Ivan Waddington

Ethics, Money and Sport
This sporting Mammon
Adrian Walsh and Richard Giulianotti

Ethics, Dis/Ability and Sports
Edited by Ejgil Jespersen and Michael McNamee

The Ethics of Doping and Anti-Doping
Redeeming the Soul of Sport?
Verner Møller

The Ethics of Sport Medicine
Edited by Claudio Tamburrini and Torbjörn Tännsjö

Bodily Democracy
Towards a Philosophy of Sport for All
Henning Eichberg

Ethics, Knowledge and Truth in Sports Research
An Epistemology of Sport
Graham McFee

Exercise and Eating Disorders
An Ethical and Legal Analysis
Simona Giordano

The Ethics of Sports Coaching
Edited by Alun Hardman Carwyn Jones

Doping and Anti-Doping Policy in Sport

Ethical, legal and social perspectives

Edited by
Mike McNamee and
Verner Møller

Routledge
Taylor & Francis Group
LONDON AND NEW YORK

First published 2011 by Routledge
2 Park Square, Milton Park, Abingdon, Oxon OX14 4RN

Simultaneously published in the USA and Canada
by Routledge
270 Madison Avenue, New York, NY 10016

Routledge is an imprint of the Taylor & Francis Group, an informa business

Typeset in Goudy by
Florence Production Ltd, Stoodleigh, Devon
Printed and bound in Great Britain by
CPI Antony Rowe, Chippenham, Wiltshire

British Library Cataloguing in Publication Data
A catalogue record for this book is available from the British Library

Library of Congress Cataloging in Publication Data
Doping and anti-doping policy in sport: ethical, legal and social perspectives/edited by Mike McNamee and Verner Møller.
p. cm.
1. Doping in sports. 2. Athletes – Drug use – Moral and ethical aspects. I. McNamee, M. J. (Mike J.) II. Møller, Verner.
RC1230.D667 2011
362.29 – dc22 2010041523

ISBN13: 978–0–415–61923–3 (hbk)
ISBN13: 978–0–203–09326–9 (ebk)

Contents

Contributors

Rob Beamish has held a joint appointment in the Department of Sociology and the School of Kinesiology and Health at Queen's University, Kingston, Canada, for the past twenty-five years. In addition to numerous articles, book chapters and encyclopedia entries related to social theory and sport sociology, he is the author of *Marx, Method and the Division of Labor* and *Fastest, Highest, Strongest: The Critique of High-Performance Sport* (co-authored with Ian Richie). Beamish has recently published *Sociology's Task and Promise*, an introductory sociology text, and is in the process of completing a forthcoming book entitled *The Steroid Specter in Sport: The Devil is in the Details.*

Ask Vest Christiansen is an Associate Professor in the Department of Sport Science, Aarhus University, Denmark. His research has followed two main branches: doping in elite sport and recreational athletes' use of anabolic androgenic steroids and other performance- and image-enhancing drugs in gyms. His cultural analyses are based partly on qualitative interviews with the athletes involved and partly on literature studies. Among his publications are books and articles on doping, sports policy and ethics in professional cycling, elite sport and recreational sport.

James E. Coleman, Jr. is the John S. Bradway Professor of the Practice of Law at Duke University, where he is Director of the Duke Center on Criminal Justice and Professional Responsibility and Co-Director of the Duke Wrongful Convictions Clinic. As private attorneys in Washington DC, Coleman and his wife, Duke Law Professor Doriane Lambelet Coleman, were instrumental in developing the out-of-competition drug testing program for The Athletic Congress (TAC), the former national governing body for track and field in the United States. They later defended the drug-testing program on behalf of TAC and the United States Olympic Committee in several state and federal lawsuits brought by American athletes. Between 1996 and 2001, they also represented Mary Decker Slaney, the American track star who, they believe, was wrongfully accused of a doping violation as a result of the flawed TE ratio test discussed in Chapter 2. Coleman is a graduate of Harvard University and the Columbia University School of Law.

John Gleaves is a doctoral candidate and instructor in the Department of Kinesiology at Pennsylvania State University. He divides his research between philosophical and historical aspects of sport. His forthcoming doctoral dissertation focuses on a cross-disciplinary approach towards understanding the issues of doping and performance enhancement by incorporating diverse fields such as physiology, medicine, bioethics, legal theory along with philosophy and history. In 2010, his essay 'Doped professionals and clean amateurs: how amateurism shaped modern anti-doping philosophy' won the North American Society of Sport History's Graduate Student Essay Contest. When he is not researching drug use in sport, John can be found training for his local cycling races on the back roads of Pennsylvania.

Dag Vidar Hanstad is Associate Professor and Head of Department of Cultural and Social Studies at the Norwegian School of Sport Sciences in Oslo. His Ph.D. was on the topic 'Anti-doping in sport. A study of policy development since 1998'. He was previously sports editor for the leading Norwegian newspaper *Aftenposten*. He also has a background in handball, as a player in the national team and as trainer. His research interests include anti-doping, media, event and organizational change.

Martin Hardie is a solicitor and a barrister who has acted in matters concerning administrative law and constitutional law for Australian Aboriginal artists in their quest for copyright protection, the challenge to Australian legislation, and in a case concerning legislation legalising euthanasia. He has also been an advisor to various members of the former East Timorese resistance and government, a university lecturer, a cyclist, cycling journalist and team manager. He now teaches law at the School of Law at Deakin University, where he is currently working on a Ph.D. thesis about cycling's doping crisis, in an attempt to find a way forward for the sport.

John Hoberman has been active in sports studies and sports journalism for many years, specialising in the political aspects of sport, the Olympic movement, the racial dimension of sport and the doping crisis in high-performance sport. He is the author of *Sport and Political Ideology* (1984), *The Olympic Crisis: Sport, Politics, and the Moral Order* (1986), *Mortal Engines: The Science of Performance and the Dehumanization of Sport* (1992), *Darwin's Athletes: How Sport Has Damaged Black America and Preserved the Myth of Race* (1997) and *Testosterone Dreams: Rejuvenation, Aphrodisia, Doping* (2005). He was a visiting researcher in doping studies at the University of Southern Denmark (2001–6) and has taught sports studies courses at Harvard University, the University of Chicago and the University of Texas at Austin, where he is a Professor of Germanic Studies.

Bengt Kayser is Professor in the Faculty of Medicine of the University of Geneva, where he directs the Institute of Movement Sciences and Sports Medicine. He is a medical doctor and exercise physiologist, with an interest in endurance performance in hypoxia, as well as the link between physical activity and health. He is also a critic of modern anti-doping policies and has published, together with colleagues, a series of articles and essays on the subject.

Joshua M. Levine is a championship tennis player from Texas with a strong interest in sports performance from the practical, biological, ethical, legal and economic perspectives. He graduated *cum laude* from Vanderbilt University in 2010 and is currently working toward a Masters degree in Public Affairs at the Lyndon B Johnson School of Public Affairs at the University of Texas at Austin.

David McArdle is a Senior Lecturer in the School of Law, University of Stirling, Scotland. He has written extensively on legal issues in sport and recreation and has particular interests in their relationship with anti-discrimination law, human rights and jurisdictional issues. His other research and teaching interests encompass discrimination law, trade union law, and European law more generally. David has contributed over thirty refereed journal articles, book chapters and monographs to the broad field of sport and the law and is frequently a keynote speaker and guest lecturer at academic and professional events worldwide. He edits the *Entertainment and Sports Law Journal* and has carried out research on doping and other sports-related issues for governments, charities and several other stakeholders in the UK and elsewhere.

Mike McNamee is a Professor of Applied Ethics at the School of Human and Health Sciences, Swansea University. He is a book series editor of Ethics and Sport and the founding editor of the international journal *Sport, Ethics and Philosophy*. He is a former President of the International Association for the Philosophy of Sport and the founding chair of the British Philosophy of Sport Association. His books include: *Sports, Virtues and Vices* (Routledge, 2008), *Doping, Elite Sports and Public Health* (with Verner Møller and Paul Dimeo; University Press of Southern Denmark, 2009) and *The Ethics of Sports: A Reader* (Routledge, 2010).

Verner Møller is Professor of Sports Science at Aarhus University, Denmark, and a visiting Professor at the School of Recreation, Health and Tourism at George Mason University, Manassas, Virginia. His main research interest lies in elite sports and body cultural extremes. For more than a decade he has devoted much of his time to the study of doping in sport. His books include: *Doping and Public Policy* (with John Hoberman, University Press of Southern Denmark, 2009) *The Doping Devil* (Gyldendal, 1999, Book on Demand, 2008), *The Ethics of Doping and Anti-Doping – Redeeming the soul of sport?* (Routledge 2010); *The Scapegoat – About the expulsion of the yellow jersey Michael Rasmussen from the Tour de France 2007 and beyond* (People's Press, 2010) and *Doping, Elite Sports and Public Health* (with Mike McNamee and Paul Dimeo, University Press of Southern Denmark, 2009).

Werner Pitsch is a Senior Researcher and Lecturer in the Department of Sociology and Economics of Sport at the Institute for Sport Sciences, Saarland University, Germany. His research in the field of doping in elite sport is divided between sociological, methodological and economic approaches. Among his publications on doping are book chapters and articles on the prevalence of doping in elite sport, as well as articles discussing the methodological shortcomings of doping tests and of the present anti-doping regime.

Angela J. Schneider received her Ph.D. in Philosophy (Ethics), writing her thesis on Doping in Sport in 1993. She is an Associate Professor and a former Assistant Dean, Ethics and Equity, in the Faculty of Health Sciences at the University of Western Ontario. She teaches and researches on ethics in sport and gender issues in sport. Her publications include numerous scholarly articles on ethical and gender issues in sport and the Olympic Games, including *Gene doping in sports: the science and ethics of genetically modified athletes*, co-authored with Theodore Friedmann. She has been Director of the Health Ethics Resource Centre and a member of the Research Ethics Review Board of the University of Western Ontario. Dr Schneider was also an executive member of the International Centre for Olympic Studies at the University of Western Ontario, Chair of the Ethics Committee for Women's Sport International and President of the International Association of the Philosophy of Sport. Dr Schneider has also been the Chair of the Expert Advisory Committee on Education of the Canadian Centre for Ethics in Sport and a member of the Canadian Olympic Association's Education Committee. She competed in the 1984 Olympics (Rowing) for Canada, winning a silver medal.

Justice Lauri Tarasti is an expert in constitutional law, the leading specialist in Finland in electoral and party legislation. He was formerly Permanent Secretary of the Ministry of Environment 1983–94 and the Justice of the Supreme Administrative Court of Finland 1994–2007. He chaired the first ever international sport tribunal, the Arbitration Panel of the International Association of Athletics Federations (IAAF) from 1985–97 and was their member of the Legal Committee of the WADA from 2000–2. Justice Tarasti has taken part in many international sport organisations since being the General Secretary of the First World Championships in Athletics in 1983. He is presently a member of the Sport and Law Commission of the International Olympic Committee, Chairman of the Juridical Commission of the IAAF. His book *Legal Solutions in International Doping Cases* was published in Milano in 2000.

Ivan Waddington is Visiting Professor at the Norwegian School of Sport Sciences, Oslo, and the University of Chester, UK. He is the author of *Sport, Health and Drugs* (Spon, 2000) and a co-author of the British Medical Association report, *Drugs in Sport: the Pressure to Perform* (British

Medical Journal Books, 2002). He has also co-edited *Sport Histories: Figurational Studies of the Development of Modern Sports* (Routledge, 2004), *Pain and Injury in Sport: Social and Ethical Analysis* (Routledge, 2006) and *Matters of Sport: Essays Presented in Honour of Eric Dunning* (Routledge, 2007). His most recent book (with Andy Smith) is *An Introduction to Drugs in Sport: Addicted to Winning?* (Routledge, 2009).

Introduction

Since institutionalised anti-doping began to emerge in the 1960s, the societal importance of sport has increased significantly. Unsurprisingly, economic interests too have increased accordingly, and it appears that the use of doping in sport has increased as well. When, in 1998, a Belgian soigneur from Team Festina was caught by customs officers on his way to the Tour de France with his trunk loaded with doping substances, the reality shockwaves extended well beyond the world of sports. Politicians across the world began to realise that sports leaders might be incapable of solving the doping problem on their own. Hence, they engaged constructively on an international scale to develop, in 1999, the World Anti Doping Agency (WADA). The idea behind this unique development, where sports organisations and governments around the world shared responsibility for anti-doping, was as reasonable as it was inevitable. Its guiding mission was premised upon key ethical ideals:

- athletes have the right to participate on equal terms with respect to doping-free sport;
- anti-doping should be harmonised, and athletes should be treated on a par across nations and sports;
- the health of athletes and fair play should be a main concern of the global governance of sports.

In the early years of WADA's operation, the initiative and its future looked bright. Not only did the governments commit themselves to sharing the economic burden of the enterprise with the International Olympic Committee (IOC), they also accepted the regulatory framework – the WADA code – despite its incorporation of legal principles not always harmonious with those held in high esteem in liberal democratic societies. Of course, not all societies of the international sports world may be described thus. Nevertheless, for practical reasons, anti-doping operates on the basis of a reserved burden of proof. The benefit of the doubt is not given to the athlete but to the prosecuting authority; intent and guilt have been replaced by the strict liability principle. Today, the WADA code has been adopted by almost every government and sports organisation in the world.

Unfortunately, the near univocal support given to anti-doping by governments and sports organisations has not brought sports doping cultures to an end. Doping is still part of the reality of elite sport and widespread recreational sports cultures, in the west at least. At the minimum, two undesirable consequences flow from the increased anti-doping effort. Insofar as educational efforts, or personally held values, ensure the majority of athletes abstain from doping (or cease doping because of fears of being caught), the relative advantage increases to those who dope who are willing to run the risk. Another undesirable consequence of the anti-doping regime is that the market value of experts who know how to dope while minimising the risk of getting caught also increases.

These consequences are, of course, not unknown to the anti-doping authorities. Nevertheless, WADA's general policy response has thus far been to implement more and stricter controls. It is widely thought that in-competition testing was relatively inefficient, catching only careless athletes and their entourage, or those with unsophisticated or outmoded techniques of doping. To this measure has been added more rigorous policies, including out-of-competition testing, the declaration of athletes' whereabouts information and, most recently, blood testing for indirect detection of prohibited substances or methods. These advances in anti-doping policy have not met with universal accord. Athletes, scholars and scientists have begun to comment upon the apparent discrepancy between the moral rights inherited from the Enlightenment, which are still held in high esteem in liberal democratic societies, and the regulatory system elite athletes are now subjected to.

In light of this, the International Network of Humanistic Doping Research found it timely to focus its third conference on the human and legal rights aspects of anti-doping. Hence, a group of world-leading experts from a wide range of disciplines within the human and social sciences were invited to present their thoughts and studies on the topic. From the resulting convention, held at Aarhus University, 20–21 August 2009, it became clear that there were serious reasons for concern coming from both advocates and detractors of general anti-doping postures. Equally, it also became clear that credible alternatives to the current approach were hard to find. After the conference, the speakers were invited to turn their oral presentations into the essays that now comprise this volume. The network consists of independent researchers who share an interest in rigorous and principled debate about ways to improve the situation for the athletes, but who nevertheless hold differing and sometimes opposing views about core questions regarding the ethics of performance enhancement. The result is a rich and diverse body of thinking that is reflected in the present volume.

The book opens with Mike McNamee's and Lauri Tarasti's chapter on 'Ethico-legal aspects of anti-doping legislation'. This chapter sets the scene for the volume by drawing attention to the interface between law, medicine and ethics in the contexts of elite sports and sports medicine. The authors explore arguments concerning the apparent legal idiosyncrasies of anti-doping legislation and their ethically salient features in terms of guilt negligence and liability, punishment, means of legal defence, implications of previous offences when imposing sanctions and, finally, privacy in anti-doping practice and policy. After having pointed out some of the core problems and peculiarities related to the application of legal principles to sport's anti-doping regulations, the authors close the chapter with the reminder that, although finding a firm and justified ethical and legal rationale for anti-doping is of international significance, there are no easy ways to iron out the ethical and legal dilemmas coupled with anti-doping.

In 'The burden of proof in endogenous substance cases: a masking agent for junk science', James E. Coleman, Jr. and Joshua M. Levine launch a sustained critique of one of the cornerstones of anti-doping: the strict liability rule, which puts the burden of proof on the athlete accused of doping after an adverse analytical finding. In doping cases involving endogenous substances, both the governing authorities and accused athletes often must rely on circumstantial evidence to prove or rebut a doping charge. To negate the evidentiary difficulties of not having direct evidence to prove or disprove a violation, they note that WADA relies on two legal moves that pose as standards of proof: first, that indirect or proxy evidence deemed credible by WADA satisfies the authorities' burden to prove doping by clear and convincing evidence; and, second, that, despite this mandatory presumption of doping, the legal rights of accused athletes nevertheless are protected because they are afforded the opportunity to rebut the presumption of guilt under the less demanding preponderance of evidence presented. Taking into account both the current state of the science relating to doping with endogenous substances, and the important interests implicated in the development of any evidentiary standard, this chapter evaluates the merits of these legal strategies and argues that they neither account adequately for the needs of the anti-doping authorities nor adequately protect the legal rights of accused athletes.

David McArdle follows the legal discussion in his chapter on 'Longitudinal profiling, sports arbitration and the woman who had nothing to lose: some thoughts on *Pechstein* v. *International Skating Union*'. He addresses the new challenge athletes face in defending themselves against an accusation based on blood profiling, the so-called biological passport. The conviction of German speed skater Claudia Pechstein – the first ever to be banned on the basis of blood profiling – has been the cause of much debate. The Pechstein case is significant because it involves sanctions against an athlete who had never returned an adverse analytical finding. McArdle uses the case as an opportunity to discuss the jurisdictional scope of the Court of Arbitration in Sport (CAS), based in Switzerland. He addresses legal concerns that come with the incorporation of indirect evidence, as it is the core of this new anti-doping measure. In the course of his essay, McArdle reveals a perceived laxity in the proceedings of CAS and draws attention to powerful arguments that were apparently overlooked by the defence at the CAS. Given the special status of sports law, athletes who are charged under the regulations hold the burden of proof. In light of this, and given the fact that WADA's blood profiling provisions are now in force across all sports, the essay concludes that any athlete wishing to challenge profiling would be advised to consider their options very soon.

Athletes' potential vulnerability under WADA governance is further emphasised in Werner Pitsch's contribution, 'Caught between mathematics and ethics: some implications of imperfect doping test procedures'. In this chapter, Pitsch reminds us that WADA's claim that the core rationale for anti-doping is the protection of athletes' fundamental right to participate in doping-free sport is an ideal. Being an ideal, it is of course unreachable. Insofar as there is always a risk of false positive and false negative results in doping tests, the reality, he argues, is likely to fall too far short of the desired end. Both false positive and false negative results restrict the possibilities of clean athletes to participate in doping-free sport. False positive test results deprive clean athletes of their right to participate. A false negative result affects the integrity of a 'doping-free' sport, as doped athletes are allowed to participate. By application of a mathematical simulation model, Pitsch explores the extent to which doping test procedures are 'fair' and 'effective' and, accordingly, the extent to which WADA reaches its objective of enabling 'doping-free sport' and 'a level playing field'. It concludes that anti-doping agencies are faced with an unachievable task.

Bengt Kayser shares the concern over the athletes' poor protection against doping charges, but for another reason. In his chapter, 'On the presumption of guilt without proof of intentionality and other consequences of current anti-doping policy', Kayser acknowledges that the establishment of WADA has significantly improved the 'fight' against doping. He argues, however, that the advances have not come without side effects. A substantial number of people who have been caught for a doping rule violation are punished for the presence of substances that clearly were not taken with the intent to enhance performances. Kayser addresses the ethical problem that, in the name of the 'spirit of sport' – one of the three criteria for which a substance or process can be banned – the anti-doping agencies apparently consider it justifiable that athletes who were not performance enhanced, or had no intent to enhance their performance, are charged with doping offences. Under present anti-doping policy, he argues, athletes who try to play the game according to the anti-doping rule risk significant harm, while we must presume that there are athletes who dope but get away with it. Cognisant of the use of psychotropic drug use in wider society, Kayser concludes that anti-doping policymakers should become more pragmatic and choose regulation and harm-reduction strategies that can replace the presumption of guilt without proof and other controversial side effects of current anti-doping policy.

The European trend towards the criminalisation of doping offenders is a troublesome matter, which John Hoberman analyses in 'Athletes in handcuffs? The criminalization of doping'. For at least a century, the idea that doping is an unacceptable and unethical practice has been promoted, but a strong, political counter-critique has only existed for two or three decades. The setting-up of WADA, the unique international organisation to fight doping worldwide, was a manifestation of an unprecedented, unified political will to remedy the problem. So far, however, the initiative has largely succeeded in addressing the problem. Nevertheless, a lasting solution to the problem still looks frustratingly far from completion. One fairly drastic policy response from certain countries has been to criminalize doping offences, which, given the 'reversed' burden of proof in doping cases, appears to be a worrying development. Drawing extensively on the German debate, this essay discusses the broader social consequences, including those pertaining to the image of sport itself. The investigation leads to the conclusion that the criminalisation of doping in sport may be taking the fight one step too far, not least in light of the growing medicalisation of the problems of everyday living.

A consequence of progressive medico-technological research is that new drugs and techniques are invented that can be used to enhance athletic performances. In her chapter on 'Privacy rights, gene doping ethics', Angela Schneider adds to the much debated prospect in this field, namely the consequences of advances in gene technology that create a new set of problems for anti-doping. If testing for gene therapy is to have any chance of success, even restraints on athletes' rights may be necessary. Schneider analyses the concept of privacy rights as they pertain to athletes and doping control protocols, in light of the problems gene doping raises. Part of this analysis comprises an examination of whether or not 'privacy' counts as an essentially contested concept. It also addresses the relationship between athletes' privacy rights, rules and sport, before it ends by pointing to the dangers that may face athletes' autonomy when, or if, the prospect of gene doping becomes a reality.

The right to privacy, which athletes claim they should enjoy in liberal democracies, is also a central issue in Ask Vest Christiansen's 'Testing citizens training recreationally in gyms'. Christiansen shows how the anti-doping campaign, run by WADA and targeting achievement sports, has an impact outside the world of elite sport. In Denmark, the WADA strategy has been adopted and adapted as a political tool to remedy the problem of casual drug use in recreational gyms. His essay brings to light the implications of the model of elite sports surveillance for this arena and demonstrates that the application of the WADA standard for out-of-competition testing in gyms may paradoxically give rise to further ethical problems and leave a number of relevant issues unresolved. Moreover, whereas male bodybuilders are tested for use of androgenic anabolic steroids, female athletes' abuse of medicines for slimming purposes, which are on the banned substance list, are not targeted.

Following the analysis of the political impact of the anti-doping campaign outside the sphere of elite sports, Rob Beamish focuses, in his chapter on 'Steroids in the court of public opinion: Roger Clemens versus the

Mitchell Report', on the politicisation of anti-doping in America. In a thorough and highly evocative account of the Senate hearing arising from Senator George Mitchell's report on steroid use in the Major Baseball League, Beamish demonstrates that one consequence of the moral panic surrounding doping has been that ordinary legal principles have been neglected in the attempt to remedy sport's doping problem. He queries whether athletes have been given sufficient legal protection and whether, therefore, they risk being judged in 'the people's court' of public opinion, before they are ever found guilty in a legal court. Because the current system of detection is perceived to be failing, there are, according to Beamish, influential people who opt for a more aggressive approach, where the end, in and of itself, justifies the means. In analysing the treatment of star baseball pitcher Roger Clemens, Beamish argues that it is a matter of serious concern when athletes have their names slurred, without being granted the opportunity to contest the evidence brought against them, and he finds it criticisable that cases sometimes are taken directly to the public without proper concern for the rule of law.

In 'It's not about the blood! *Operación Puerto* and the end of modernity', Martin Hardie offers a similarly thorough account of the doping scandal that hit Spain in 2006, which occurred in the wake of a police investigation into the illegal importation of medicine from Australia. Similarly, in this case, the public was informed about suspected athletes before a formal lawsuit had been presented. He argues that the Spanish doping case known as '*Operación Puerto*' exists within the framework of the abandonment of old, modernist notions of law and the construction of a new functional global system. Hardie uses *Operación Puerto* as a vehicle to show how law (related to anti-doping at least) is constructed or performed in the media as much as it is constructed and enacted in the law courts. *Operación Puerto* is an example par excellence of the distance that exists between the rhetoric of the media crisis surrounding doping and professional cycling and the actual reality of the material processes that are occurring as cycling goes through the process of global structural readjustment and the construction of the new cycling cartography. Legitimation occurs through the management of crisis and events – exception, functionality and spectacle – under the guise of the just war against the evil of doping.

One of the most controversial initiatives WADA has invented to combat doping is the whereabouts information rule, which Ivan Waddington measures in '"A prison of measured time"? A sociologist looks at the WADA whereabouts system'. Taking inspiration from the French Marxist Jean-Marie Brohm's classic *Sport – a prison of measured time* (1978), Waddington addresses the WADA whereabouts rule, which has been the subject of ethical and legal challenge since it came into effect in 2004. Through the revision of the code in 2009, the rule became even stricter, and athletes themselves began to speak out against its requirements. The author does not argue that the whereabouts system either can or cannot be justified. He restricts himself to the more limited aim of locating the whereabouts system within the context of broader social processes, including changing practices and ideas concerning surveillance and control, personal liberty, privacy and democracy. Furthermore, he examines the impact of the introduction of the whereabouts system on the relationship between elite athletes and WADA. In doing so, he aims to increase the understanding of some of the opposition to, and the major difficulties associated with, the whereabouts system. In this respect, Waddington creates a sounding board for the following two chapters, which are both specific case studies of the inconsistent management of the whereabouts rule.

Verner Møller's case study, 'The expulsion of Michael Rasmussen from the Tour de France 2007 – Or what happened to the level playing field?', explores and, to a certain extent, exposes the biggest *anti*-doping scandal in the history of the Tour de France. The 2007 event of the world's most famous cycling race underwent a dramatic and completely unexpected outcome when the leader, Michael Rasmussen, was expelled from the race just hours after he had won the most gruelling mountain stage, which would have effectively sealed his overall victory. This was the end result of an active and noisy media campaign that boiled up around him when it was revealed that he had received warnings for whereabouts failures from the Danish anti-doping authorities. Møller presents the facts behind the turmoil and demonstrates, on one reading of the rules at least, that the expulsion was not strictly justified by the violation of sporting regulations. It also shows how inconsistent international management of the whereabouts rules played a crucial role in the development of the situation. Accordingly, he draws attention to the need for evaluation of the legal procedures behind the sanctions system.

Dag Vidar Hanstad's case study, 'Governance and the whereabouts system', is another example of the arbitrariness with which the whereabouts rules are applied. The central object is to draw attention to the managerial difficulties and problems that national anti-doping organisations (NADOs) face in implementing the whereabouts system. This is exemplified by the disciplinary action that was taken against the Norwegian beach volleyball player Vegard Høidalen by Anti-Doping Norway (ADN), the Norwegian Olympic and Paralympic Committee and the Confederation of Sports (NIF). In 2008, Høidalen was judged by the NIF to have violated the anti-doping regulations regarding whereabouts information. During Høidalen's appeal, he revealed operational errors committed by the doping control officers, poor procedures followed by ADN and other discriminatory procedures. He was finally cleared by the NIF's appeals committee. Based on the analysis of the case, it is argued that the complexity of the WADA rules creates difficulties for NADOs. By highlighting the problems created for ADN – generally regarded as one of the most effective NADOs – the managerial problems with the WADA's whereabouts rule facing NADOs in general are brought into focus.

Since the beginning of anti-doping in the 1960s, the approach has been rather univocal: some education, more testing and increasingly severe punishments. With the forming of WADA, pressure for tougher sanctions has intensified, and, although one of the founding ideas for WADA was harmonisation, the agency now accepts that individual sports organisations may add extra sanctions, e.g. huge fines, in addition to the WADA rules. In the final chapter, 'A critique of the contemporary trend towards severe anti-doping sanctions: changing directions', John Gleaves argues that the current state of affairs is ethically problematic. He offers a novel approach to the issue predicated on a clear philosophical account of the nature of sports contests. Gleaves provides three reasons for the rejection of the current trend towards harsher doping punishments that support a new approach towards sanctions for anti-doping violations. Moreover, he suggests that imposing sanctions for doping in the same manner as other rule infractions may generate punishments that better preserve fairness and accomplish their goal of deterring doping. In rethinking the problem and considering what anti-doping wants to achieve, he advocates a reconfiguration of the conventional anti-doping policy, paving the way for the conclusion that, by replacing the current approach with a sport-specific, game-based punishment strategy, sports can continue to impose sanctions on users who violate anti-doping rules while preserving the integrity of their contests.

The volume in full leaves little doubt that there are tough challenges and serious issues to be solved in anti-doping for those who wish to preserve sport as an ideal, non-doping arena for the cultivation of human excellences. Neglecting the problems that arise in what is a notoriously difficult policy area does not, of course, make them go away. Until now, WADA has enjoyed overwhelming backing and support from athletes, their sports organisations and politicians around the world. As anti-doping has moved forward and become more advanced and aggressive, athletes, organisations and, increasingly, politicians have begun to voice their concerns. It is true that these voices are both few and far between compared with the mainstream. Yet they are not merely crying wolf, nor are they the product of some sporting Cassandra. The volume then, taken as a whole, is an attempt to bring together key actors in the anti-doping debate to challenge critically the present orthodoxy in order to enhance the governance of sports with respect to doping and anti-doping practices.[1]

Note

1 We are grateful to Klavs Madsen, Dean of Sports Studies at Aarhus University, for his support of the original conference. Moreover, we register a special thanks to Jonas Havelund, whose publishing expertise saved us a lot of time in the final preparation of the manuscript.

1 Ethico-legal aspects of anti-doping policy

Mike McNamee and Lauri Tarasti

Doping: ethical and juridical responses

Over the last 30 years, there has been steady and growing scepticism with regard to the justification of anti-doping policies. It has arisen in a variety of academic and professional milieus, from sports medicine (Kayser and Smith 2008), medical ethics (Foddy and Savulescu 2007) and sports technology (Miah 2005; Magdalinski 2009). Sometimes it has been motivated by a philosophical scepticism regarding the internal coherence of anti-doping, whereas, at other times, it has focused on the apparent inconsistencies between anti-doping postures and analogous practices that are permissible in sports. Although debates have typically focused on the legitimacy of the use of steroids, genetic manipulation and other forms of illicit performance enhancement, little discussion has been had of the interface between law, medicine and ethics as they converge in elite sports and sports medicine.

Doping continues to achieve greater levels of sophistication. It might be that there are reasons for employing a looser and less intrinsically negative term than doping. Certainly, sceptics may argue that the term is so pejorative that those engaging in behaviours that potentially fall under it are already cast in negative terms, if not condemned. Occasionally, it is used to capture any form of physical enhancement, which is scarcely conducive to subtle or complex debates. Clearly, there are a wide variety of uses of medicines, vitamins, health pills, additional nutrients, hormones, steroids, the manipulation of blood products (referred to as 'blood spinning' by those sceptical of the legitimacy of the technique, and 'platelet rich therapy' by advocates), in the future possibly gene technology, and other means aimed at improving results or performance ability by changing the biochemical systems of the body. Any of these techniques might, under given conditions, be called doping, and this is just a conceptual problem we may have to live with in policy debates. Given, however, the focus on doping in this book, we shall refer to it throughout using that term and use what we take to be uncontentious examples.

Doping is not a phenomenon restricted to elite 'athletes'. Rather, it is widespread throughout the world of sports and beyond, especially among those who merely engage in activities such as physical conditioning for aesthetic or lifestyle reasons (Monaghan 2003). This development corresponds roughly to the general change in social attitudes to pharmacological products in the West, which in turn depends partly on the equally emergent attitudes that are accepting of non-therapeutic goals of medicine. The markets are seemingly flooded with medical products for the prevention of psychological and societal ills, from ageing, alcoholism and depression, to the prevention of pregnancy. As Parens (1988) has argued, better is not always good. Athletes provide role models for society, and their better performances are not good when their record-breaking feats are not the product of what Murray calls the 'virtuous perfection of our natural talents' (Murray 2008).

Developing authoritative ethical and legal responses to the use of doping is not easy, not merely because of the theoretical heterogeneity of ethics, but because of the challenges ethical postures have traditionally created for the law. In this chapter, we explore some original arguments concerning the legal peculiarities of anti-doping legislation and their ethically salient features in terms of:

- guilt and related concepts;
- aspects of punishment;
- un/ethical means of legal defence;
- the taking into account of previous offences when imposing sanctions; and
- the issue of privacy in anti-doping practice and policy.

The ethics of doping and the rise of harmonized policy

Even sports devotees understand that many, and perhaps most, of their sporting heroes enjoy their elevated social and economic status, not merely for their extensive physical and psychological preparation, but also as a result of chemically assisted training, whether in terms of legitimate nutritional supplements or doping products and processes. It is only what is referred to as 'doping', a pejorative term that emerged from descriptions of those who were addicted to opium (Fost 2008), that is considered illegitimate in the vast majority of elite sports. One cannot say that this is true of all sports. Notably, for example, professional baseball in the USA does not disallow the use of steroids for performance enhancement. Much ink has been spilt over the status of Barry Bonds, who broke the all-time record for home runs while openly using steroids, which would be banned in any sport signed up to the World Anti-Doping Code (WADC). Even Barack Obama (Obama 2009) has joined the public debate, decrying their use in the same sport. Not only athletes but also the general sports-viewing public understand that the risks to health are high in elite sport, whether performances are procured within or without the rules. In general, however, we can say that elite athletes and those who perform at more modest levels are not in favour of a libertarian approach per se.

There have been several sceptical challenges (Tamburrini 2000; Foddy and Savulescu 2007; Kayser and Smith 2008) to the legitimacy of the anti-doping position arising from philosophers working in the fields of both medical ethics and sports ethics. They argue, typically, that the bans on certain performance-enhancing processes and substances rest on principles that are inconsistently applied (Brown 2007; McNamee 2008: 177–93). Sport, it is widely canvassed, is about healthy, natural and ethically regulated activity. WADA itself employs three criteria, of which at least two must apply, in order for a product or process to be proscribed: it should be performance enhancing; it should present an actual or potential health risk; and it should violate the spirit of sport (WADA 2009: Article 4.3). Although there is no objection to performance enhancement per se, it is the latter two problematic means that are the object of prohibition in conjunction with the former. In response, sceptics typically argue,

1 that doping is no more unnatural than the muscle-bound and technologically saturated athletes and their equipment, prostheses, stadia and so on;
2 that doped athletes no more coerce their opponents than do their training-mad, but non-doped, competitors;
3 that doping is no more harmful than other behaviours that are legimited, such as punching in boxing, or brutal tackling in rugby or American football; or
4 that doping confers no more of an unfair advantage than is enjoyed by athletes or teams from economically or technologically superior countries or sports clubs/systems.

A more passive case made by the anti-doping lobby is that, by failing to proscribe socially undesirable behaviours, it would celebrate bad role models and promote undesirable lifestyles. Such a stance is consistent with widely shared public health policies against smoking or the use of marijuana, even though it only (potentially) harms the users themselves.[1] To this, the sceptics' rebuttal is that the undesirability of doping would be chimerical if anti-doping rules were repealed and not forced wrongfully upon athletes seeking only to enhance their performance and optimize their own athletic potential, while only (potentially) harming themselves. It is, of course, true that each of these sceptical challenges has some merit. In addition, it is possible in the future that the ethical legitimacy of doping control may partly collapse if undetectable gene technology comes into widespread use. It could be argued, however, that these sceptical challenges are largely redundant because, most importantly, the sporting practice communities (MacIntyre 1981)[2] themselves have rejected doping through their engagement in the processes of the formulation of anti-doping policies and practices. Whether the official decisions made by international sports federations democratically reflect the views of practitioners in the field is not something known in any detail, though we assume here, in the absence of wholesale outcries from athletes themselves, that this is a reasonable assumption. Certainly, there has been a large and voluble lobby, across sports (especially individual sports such as athletics), of sportsmen and women castigating doped athletes who have been caught.

In addition to athletes, as well as national and international sports organizations, governments too have taken a strong position against doping. Although it is true that we wish to endorse anti-doping postures and policies, for present purposes we merely note the inter-governmental legitimacy of the World Anti-Doping Code, signed up to by 186 nations and 570 national and international sports organizations. We proceed to draw out the ethical and juridical peculiarities of their legislation, having set out its general contours. The goal of harmonization achieved by WADA in their 2009 code does not meet with universal approval, of course.

Nevertheless, nearly all international sports federations have signed up to the WADC. Concerning doping, therefore, WADA and the WADC enjoy a hegemonic position with respect to medical, policy, scientific as well as juridical matters. The WADC is predicated upon the evidence of sports medicine and sports science experts, who determine which substances or processes are to be classified as doping and thus prohibited. The determination of the list of prohibited substances and methods in connection with the WADC is juridically final. This position is the default, as it has never been challenged in any court. Anti-doping rules are juridical norms and belong to the area of sports law (Houlihan 2002; Blackshaw *et al.* 2006; Siekmann and Soek 2007), the relationship of which with public legislation is not always clear.

Between the WADC and state legislation

Subtle and complex relations hold between WADA and international agencies such as UNESCO and INTERPOL, with whom they have formal agreements. Nevertheless, WADA is a private foundation, although it is administrated and financed on an equal footing by governments and sports federations (SFs) alike. One consequence of this status is that the juridical norms of the WADC are not generally binding, but rather have governance only over those sports organizations that are signatories to the WADC. This being the case, it is no surprise then that WADA itself does not enforce the WADC nor punish athletes who commit offences. This is carried out by the SFs, though WADA has in the past challenged rulings by SFs where these were thought to be lenient. National SFs typically fall under the jurisdiction of international sports federations (ISFs) and, where relevant, the IOC.

Although nearly all major SFs today have their own anti-doping rules, the WADC nevertheless obliges them to apply the obligatory articles of the

WADC as such and also, more generally, to follow the principles of the WADC. In this way, the juridical norms of the WADC concern, not only the athletes, but also other people taking part, in one way or another, in the sport concerned under the jurisdiction of a signatory of the WADC. This development is a response to the palpable fact that the athlete is thought to engage in doping as part of a systemic effort between coaches, masseuses, physicians, physiotherapists, team management and so on. The clearest uncovering of this systemic sports medicine and sports science development has been in the Tour de France 2006, where it is widely thought that the majority of professional teams were engaged in doping practices to some degree.[3]

A sports organization may impose a sanction for this violation in accordance with its rules. This is not a punishment in the same sense as in the criminal code, but is better thought of as a disciplinary consequence. These sanctions are limited to the powers of a private organization.[4] So, if these doping rules are broken, the question is not typically one of a crime being committed, but rather the lesser one of a violation of the rules of a private organization.

Doping has been criminalized in many countries, especially in Europe, but only seldom outside Europe.[5] A special, legally enforceable Act on doping has been issued in some countries of the member states of the Council of Europe, and in other member states some forms of doping are punishable as drug abuse or smuggling of medicines, or in some other way. A criminal court imposes sanctions in these cases. The most common form of punishment is a fine and, in some cases, imprisonment. It is important to note that doping has not, however, usually been defined in criminal codes exactly in the same way as in sport. Doping in criminal law is often more limited in scope than in sports legislation. For example, the WADC bans certain substances that have no unhealthy impact, simply because they act as masking agents that prevent the detection of banned doping substances.

In the WADC, a doping offence is referred to as an anti-doping rule violation. The validity of a violation is established by a sports tribunal that is convened by a national or international SF. Sanctions normally take the form of ineligibility and the loss of medals, prize money and so forth. These are rights to compete and reward that are internal to the sport and its governance. In cases of dispute, and in accordance with the WADC, the CAS will arbitrate between the parties. It is noteworthy that this is obligatory in cases of anti-doping under the auspices of the WADC, whereas in other disputes both parties must normally consent for the case to be heard there and to abide by its rulings.

Anti-doping rules of sports organizations have emerged within the sphere of private law and, in most cases, remain there. The state gives its norms by legislation. Only public authorities have the power to issue generally binding norms. If somebody breaks these binding norms, they will be sentenced in a state criminal court, if the violation of the norms is considered a criminal act.

State authorities have the right to use coercive powers, such as search and seizure, as well as Internet investigations in accordance with law when it is necessary for the detection of crimes, to prosecute the case by hearing whomever they call, and so on. State authorities can also execute the punishments with force, for example by collecting fines or denying the liberty of those prosecuted through the execution of their laws.

The differences between public law and private law and their respective procedures keep them juridically distinct in principle. On the one hand, sports organizations or their tribunals apply their anti-doping rules with disciplinary sanctions, whereas, on the other hand, criminal courts apply the state law concerning doping punishments. One significant consequence of this dual legal economy has been that the same anti-doping violation can today be, and often is, punishable both as a crime in a criminal court and as a disciplinary offence in a sports organization or its tribunal (or a surrogate, such as the CAS (Tarasti 2007)). The incidence of these cases has increased greatly in recent years, for many reasons. More countries have included doping offences in their criminal legislation, the supervision of doping offences has expanded, and, where previously only athletes were punished, now the focus is also on the elite sports support system, including sports physicians. This dual legal economy – the processes in accordance with state legislation and in accordance with the sports organization's anti-doping rules – has sometimes seen the processes become mixed with each other.

A cursory examination of this confluence can be found in the following recent and high-profile examples. The Tour de France doping scandal in cycling, in 1998, which started from police investigations,[6] and the Chinese doping scandal in swimming, in 1998, which started from Australian customs officers' seizure of human growth hormones being taken into Australia for the world championships of that year.[7] Similarly, in Spain, *Operación Puerto* was conducted by the Spanish authorities looking into doping practices following the seizure of prohibited substances and other material by the Spanish police in 2006 (Waddington and Schmidt 2009: 134–5). It should be noted here, however, that tax evasion legislation initially uncovered an illegal pharmacology trade, and the fallout led to the revelations that led to UK sprinter Dwayne Chambers' ban from international athletics competition for 2 years and (controversially for some) his lifetime ban from representing Britain at the Olympic Games.[8] In the Athens Olympic Games in 2004, two Greek sprinters, Kenteris and Thánou, escaped from doping control.[9] The sports ruling body, the International Amateur Athletics Federation, waited as long as possible for the results of police investigations, with the purpose of obtaining better evidence before imposing sanctions. Perhaps the most recent example of the confluence was the investigation in the USA into the Balco laboratory, where tax investigations uncovered widespread doping, which saw the former world champion and Olympic medal winner and record holder, Marion Jones, being imprisoned. We shall comment on this below. These high-profile cases seem to reinforce the idea that there is a certain dependency (when push comes to shove) on the powers of states' authorities if anti-doping rules are to be efficacious. In the following section, we probe this dual legal economy between sports anti-doping legislation and criminal law.

Principles in anti-doping rules and criminal law

When cases of the dual prosecution of athletes and their medico-scientific support systems become more common, the question of whether the principles of criminal law, at least in some degree, should be applied also to the disciplinary process of a sports organization or its tribunal cannot be avoided. There are, in particular, ethical and legal dimensions of doping prosecution that deserve further critical scrutiny. We shall consider these as follows:

1. guilt, negligence and liability;
2. aspects of punishment;
3. un/ethical means of legal defence;
4. previous offences that might be taken into account when imposing sanctions; and
5. privacy.

Guilt, negligence and liability

Rule-breaking in sport typically exhibits degrees of intentionality. It also typically, though not necessarily, elicits feelings of guilt. In reality, matters are not so clear-cut. The rugby player who stretches a foot out to trip an opponent and the football player who swears at the referee in response to a perceived poor judgement fully intend their acts and may or may not feel any associated guilt. Equally, players may feel guilty about career-ending injuries they inflict accidentally on another professional (McNamee 2002). Moreover, there are many instances during a game when the official decides that a pattern of rule-breaking behaviour, though it does not appear premeditated, shows intentionality by virtue of the repetitive or habitual nature of the act (cf. Anscombe 1957). Aside from these cases, there are others where a rule is determined to have been broken where the athlete fails in some other duty. So, the relay runner who steps on or over the inside lane marking is deemed not to have completed a minimum of 400 m thereby and is disqualified, irrespective of the absence of *mens rea* (guilty mind). Equally, the athlete who takes a short cut in cross-country running or uses underweight throwing equipment will be disqualified, regardless of their culpability. This also extends, for example, to Formula 1 racing, where the driver may unwittingly win a race with equipment that fails to conform to exacting technical standards (e.g. relating to turbulence), or to a racing jockey in a handicap race, who is found to weigh less than (s)he ought to according to the system of handicapping.

The establishment of an offence without *mens rea* is not without precedent in sports rules, but a particularly strong variant is found in the case of an anti-doping rule violation when a prohibited substance is found to be present within an athlete's body tissue or fluids. This is also the most common type of doping offence. Article 2.1 in the WADC states that offence is merely 'The presence of a Prohibited Substance or its Metabolites or Markers in an Athlete's Sample', which occasions an anti-doping violation. The wording of this violation indicates that this type of doping offence can include wider liability (often referred to as 'strict liability') than in other types of doping offence, where the liability is estimated in accordance with normal juridical principles (Soek 2006). Wide liability is justified in doping cases, as the standards of criminal proof would be unreasonably high to establish against athletes who necessarily dope in private. The accusing party, typically the sports organization, may have no means to show intention or the culpability of the athlete.

In its judgement of 15 March 1993, concerning the juridical nature of the awards pronounced by CAS, the Swiss Federal Tribunal pointed out that,

> as for the opinion of the CAS, whereby it is sufficient that the scientific analyses performed reveal the presence of a banned product for there to be presumption of doping and, consequently, a reversal of the burden of proof, this relates not to public policy but to the burden of proof and the assessment of evidence, problems which cannot be resolved, in private law matters, in the light of notions proper to criminal law, such as the presumption of innocence and the principle '*in dubio pro reo*', and corresponding guarantees which feature in the European Convention on Human Rights.[10]

When, therefore, prohibited substances have been detected, the athlete has demonstrated their negligence with respect to their active duty to avoid doping. This interpretation arises from, and focuses upon, the assiduousness and prudence of the athlete. Athletes are advised by relevant sporting bodies as to which substances may or may not be ingested. They are expected to be educated as to the products that may contain illicit substances and to use only approved supplies, usually purchased and audited by their team or SF. The application of these powers of self-surveillance is experienced as burdensome or anxiety-provoking. Yet elite athletes are necessarily creatures of habit, by virtue of the need to adhere to strict training regimes. Some athletes seem to accept it as a necessary evil. We discuss the matter further below. Nevertheless, the requirements in this respect are indeed strict, for liability is not merely limited to the intention of the athlete to use doping products or processes.

Ought then the principle of *nulla poena sine culpa* (no punishment without guilt) to be applied in doping offences without intention. It is important to note that *culpa*, guilt, may be constituted either by act or omission. The common omission is that of negligence. Guilt *may* indeed be relatively blameless in the case of accidental or unwitting ingestion of banned substances provided by other parties.[11]

Yet, beyond the legal sphere, it could be argued that this strict liability is in conflict with the more general presumption of innocence. It might be argued that doping offences ought not be considered as an exception to the general ethical norm of establishing culpability. The manoeuvre is not as exceptional as might first be thought. There exist numerous other examples where the level of care demanded is as strict when imposing sanctions, for example in the transport of radioactive substances and wastes, or in dealing with hazardous chemicals or medicines, in dangerous building works and so on. Here, the sanction operates to prevent harm to others and the self when engaged in dangerous practices. Moreover, the CAS 95/142 has held that:

> The use of the term 'strict liability' in the context of doping could be misleading: under the term 'strict liability', one should understand a concept of liability similar to that of civil liability, without fault in tort, or comparable to product liability cases.
>
> (Honsell 1995)

It does not raise the issue of guilt, or the 'presumption of guilt', with respect to the applicability of disciplinary sanctions. The concept of 'strict liability', as it has been used in doping cases, as we have argued does not entail intentionality. The sanction is an inevitable consequence, if a doping offence has been established. Whether a severe sanction such as a 2-year ban may be imposed on an athlete without examining the issue of guilt is a point worthy of further consideration.

Finally, the Court of Arbitration for Sport (CAS 95/141) holds, in more stark terms, that,

> too literal an application of the principle '*Nulla poena sine culpa*' could have damaging consequences on the effectiveness of anti-doping measures. Indeed, if for each case the sports federations had to prove the intentional nature of the act (desire to dope to improve one's performance) in order to be able to give it the force of an offence, the fight against doping would become practically impossible.

In summary, without strict liability, anti-doping legislation would not so much be impotent as it would be inoperable.

One crime, one punishment?

One of the leading principles in criminal law is that, in one and the same crime, only one punishment can be imposed: *ne bis in idem* (not twice for the same). To what extent can or ought it to be applied also in the context of doping sanctions?

Theoretically speaking, the answer is clear and generally accepted. A punishment in a criminal court and a doping sanction in a sports organization or its tribunal are not against the principle of *ne bis in idem*. The question is of two separate matters: the punitive measures are qualitatively different. Only the punishment by a criminal court is a punishment in the sense of criminal law, whereas the other is better conceived of as a sanction. Thus, the doping sanction by a sports organization or its tribunal is a disciplinary measure. The first one belongs to the area of public law, the latter to private law.

Many examples of this distinctness, both in nature, procedure and purpose, exist with regard to sports. In the contexts of sports, monetary fines and imprisonment have been measures taken by legal courts, whereas measures relating to ineligibility and loss of prize money have been levied by sports organizations or their tribunals. It might be thought that, for example, a loss of prize money or financial sanction might function to reduce an ineligibility ban. Such a view is explicitly rejected in Article 10.12, Imposition of Financial Sanctions, of the revised WADC, which came into force in 2009. In accordance with this Article:

> Anti-Doping Organizations may, in their own rules, provide for financial sanctions in response to anti-doping rule violations. However, no financial sanction may be considered a basis for reducing the period of Ineligibility or other sanction which would otherwise be applicable under the Code.
>
> (WADA 2009)

It is interesting to ask, though, what additional lattitude is given by the phrase 'other sanction', and whether this latitude offends the principle of *ne bis in idem*? One such other sanction, and a fairly obvious one at that, is a financial penalty. If this Article is enacted, there can be, in one and the same doping offence, two fines, one imposed by a criminal court and another imposed by a sports organization or its tribunal. The first fine goes to the state, and the latter to the sports organization according to its rules. Can the separateness of these two sanctions still stay, without offending the principle of *ne bis in idem*? It seems not. Rather, the athlete merely has to pay twice for one act; only the recipient is separate. From the athlete's point of view, there is no difference in fines between public and private law, because the consequence is the same. The *ne bis in idem* principle has been valid as a part of human rights only in criminal processes, and is not related to disciplinary sanctions. If this kind of situation were to arise, the civil court or the execution authority would be obliged to deal with and to resolve whether the *ne bis in idem* principle shall or shall not be applied. We hold that it would be both intrusive and wasteful of public resources if the province of public law were to start to determine ineligibility in sport, given the quasi-autonomous nature of sport's own regulatory frameworks.

Nevertheless, the same result or better, from the point of view of doping control's effectiveness, can be obtainable purely by means of private law. Very often, elite athletes have made or make an agreement with their SF for different kinds of economic and other benefits and rights. In these agreements, it is possible for athletes to commit themselves to compensate their federation for the loss to their image and/or economic losses in the case of any doping offence of which the athlete is found guilty. This kind of a contractual penalty need not be insignifcant; indeed, it can be quite high. Contractual penalties are normal in business contracts, such as those for actors regarding the avoidance of certain drugs, and there is no reason to suppose that athletic contracts (especially lucrative ones) ought be considered an exception. We can say, therefore, that there can be, for one and the same doping offence, three different sanctions: punishment according to criminal law, disciplinary sanction according to the SF's anti-doping rules and contractual penalty (financial compensation) according to private law and the agreement between the athlete and his/her SF.

Finally, it should be noted that sanctions may come in forms other than official. Consider the recent case of Dwain Chambers, who served a 2-year ban for the use of growth hormone contrary to the WADC. Following his 2-year ban, he won the right to represent the UK in the 2008 World Indoor Championships 60 m sprint. The British Olympic Association is unusual, though not alone, in having a by-law that precludes any British competitor convicted of a doping offence from representing them at an Olympic Games. The former head of WADA (and barrister), Richard Pound, has suggested it is unlikely to be upheld in a court of law.[12] To his cost, however, Chambers unsuccessfully challenged the ruling against him in the High Court in 2008. Whether other courts would follow this precedent is not clear, nor is it clear that, if challenged, the ruling could not be repealed, but Chambers has decided (almost certainly on financial grounds) not to appeal.[13] Legal frameworks, and sports regulatory ones too, are not the only mechanisms of power in sports. Although commonly derided for their pathological intrusion into sports, there are times when commercial agencies can intervene. In the case of Chambers, the leading athletics events organizers, taken aback by some of Chambers ill-advised comments in his 2-year sojourn, simply would not invite him to participate in their televised track and field meetings, thus depriving him lawfully of the ability to earn income.

Un/ethical means of legal defence

A general principle in criminal law is that the accused person can defend him/herself with all lawful means. Article 2.5 of the WADC states that tampering or attempted tampering with any part of doping control is itself a doping offence. In its 2009 revision, Article 2.5 includes one new sentence, according to which providing fraudulent information to an anti-doping organization (ADO) should also be punishable. This has the result that, for example, when an athlete denies that he/she has taken a prohibited substance, but is sanctioned regardless of this information, he/she is also guilty of tampering.

The rationale for this new revision is, we argue, ethically defensible. Until now, all witnesses (including an athlete's support personnel, such as the team physician) could give fraudulent information to an ADO without any fear of consequences. The revised WADC may permit greater latitude for sanctions: the athlete or other person can be given a sanction of 2 years' ineligibility for fraudulent information. However, this would not be extended to the accused athlete or another person. It is no reason to impose two sanctions on him/her, one for prohibited substances, for example, and one for not admitting taking them (because he/she has given fraudulent information). Marion Jones, the multi gold-medal-winning American athlete, received 6 months' imprisonment as the consequence of her perjury with respect to the use of doping products, but she was a witness, not the accused before the court in the Balco Laboratory case. This differs from the normal procedure in a criminal case. The accused person will not be punished separately if he/she does not tell the truth when defending himself/herself. Instead, witnesses must tell the truth. This is why Marion Jones received 6 months' imprisonment. She was a witness in the Balco Case, not an accused person. It is, of course, a serious crime when a witness lies before the court, but that is another matter.

Previous offences that might be taken into account when imposing sanctions

It is an open question in the WADC whether a conviction for a doping crime by a criminal court has to be taken into account when estimating multiple violations in another sports-driven tribunal, in accordance with the WADC. If the answer is positive, the sanction is much stronger. The WADC itself gives no clear answer. It might be thought, in accordance with the dual sports and legal frameworks noted above, that these two systems impose separable, and not duplicate, penalties or sanctions.

Normally, the requirements for a doping crime to be established in a criminal court are somewhat higher than for a doping offence in a sports organization or its tribunal. This makes it easier for the sports organization or its tribunal to accept the results achieved in a criminal court than for the criminal court to accept the decision and its arguments presented by the sports organization or its tribunal.

In accordance with Article 3.1 of the UNESCO International Convention Against Doping in Sport, States Parties undertake to adopt appropriate measures at the national and international level that are consistent with the principles of the Code (WADC) and, according to Article 4.1, the States Parties commit themselves to the principles of the code, as the basis for the measures provided for in Article 5 of this convention. Thus, it seems to be sufficient basis to accept higher sanctions against repeat offenders when a previous violation in another doping case has been shown in the decision of a criminal court. This can have significant impact in the deliberations of SFs and ISFs regarding the imposing of sanctions.

Privacy

In the WADC, there are also processes that might be considered unique to private organizations. Effective doping control evidently requires such measures as are otherwise unknown, sometimes even forbidden, in private organizations.

The conditions for police to undertake bodily searches have been forbidden in law except in serious criminal cases. By contrast, in doping control, all athletes have an obligation to give a urine or blood sample, in any place, at any time, upon request. These samples have to be given under the supervision of a doping control officer, so that he/she can observe urination at all times. This ruling was established in order to prevent athletes using a catheter to provide 'clean' urine samples that were produced at a time when they were not on a doping cycle. Clearly, there is no privacy in this operation, and this is confounded in the case of athletes who are legally minors, where a further chaperone is required to avoid criticisms of failure to protect a member of a vulnerable population.

In liberal democracies, one may move freely without being obligated to announce where one is or is going. However, top athletes belonging to a doping testing pool in each sport are, according to Article 14.3 of the WADC, required to give whereabouts information, i.e. accurate and current location information (Hanstad and Loland 2009). Typically, this means nominating, 3 months in advance, their daily whereabouts between 6 a.m. and 11 p.m., but specifying a location for one hour of each day therein when they must consider it their duty to be present in order to give a sample if requested. If they refuse to give a sample or if they fail to be present at their stated location – at the specified time – three times within an 18-month period, they are deemed to have committed an anti-doping rule violation. The consequent sanction will be ineligibility from athletic competitions for between 1 and 2 years. Variations in discretion and compliance appear to cause some concern among anti-doping officers, who range from the empathetic to the zealous. Ought an officer to accept an athlete's phone call at 55 minutes into the allotted hour, when he/she claims to be caught in a traffic jam and will arrive 15 minutes late? Or, for the sake of formal equality (understood as identical treatment), ought the officer to depart the designated location exactly as the hour tolls?[14] Moreover, at an anti-doping hearing or indeed upon appeal, various mitigating circumstances may be heard and upheld by SFs. Clearly, there are issues raised here that merit further discussion, which is not possible here.

Although the WADC attempts to prosecute any athlete using a banned doping substance, it nevertheless recognizes a prior right for athletes to receive therapeutic treatment. Given that the side effects for certain pharmacologies are performance enhancing, WADA recognizes a potential and potentially unjustifiable conflict in a central platform of their stated rationale for anti-doping, namely the promotion and preservation of the health of athletes. Article 2.6 of the WADC forbids the possession, by an athlete in competition, of any prohibited method or substance and the possession, by an athlete in out-of-competition testing, of any prohibited method or substance that is prohibited in out-of-competition testing, unless the athlete establishes that the possession is pursuant to a therapeutic use exemption (TUE), in accordance with Article 4.4, or other acceptable justification. While recognizing the right of the athlete to receive healthcare treatment, the use of TUE is heavily qualified, and the athlete and their sports medicine team must supply evidence in advance of the condition, its proper therapeutic application and the unavailability of other relevantly efficacious pharmacologies that do not have performance-enhancing side effects.[15] A substantial number of these prohibited substances are used also as normal medicines.

The surrender of certain freedoms of movement free from surveillance is an interesting issue (Kreft 2009).[16] Recent UK anti-terrorism policy has used surveillance to a degree that many civil liberties associations argue against. Although there may be a justification for such expanded surveillance in terms of public safety, the case for its application in anti-doping seems less obvious. The privacy limitations on athletes in competitive sport have been justified by saying that the athletes have agreed to apply them when putting themselves forward to compete. But, in fact, they have no other choice if they want to take part in organized competitive sport. It may well be thought that this is a coercive offer: that elite sportsmen and women can only ply their trade effectively in one arena, and thus that the controls undermine voluntary assent.

From a more philosophical perspective, the whereabouts case might be seen as a classic problem of liberal theory: how to allow individuals to share a social space while holding conflicting values, under a system of equity that enables the pursuit of individual goals while preventing the degradation of social practices such as sports. A minority of elite athletes want to dope, the majority do not wish to. Surrendering an aspect of privacy from their private lives appears to be the price. Is that compulsory foregoing of privacy justifiable? Nagel writes (2002: 4), 'The boundary between what we reveal and what we do not, and some control over that boundary, is among the most important attributes of our humanity.' His particular target is the apparent collapse of the distinction between the public and private lives of politicians in American politics under the gaze of intrusive investigative journalism. He argues that the mere holding of a public office ought not force upon the occupant of the role a relinquishment of that boundary. He argues that some reticence or concealment of aspects of our inner lives is a central aspect of civilization and a critical function of social relations. Nevertheless, while we might wish to keep certain aspects of our lives away from the public gaze (for fear of our shame, or its disgust at our inner wickedness, meanness, egoism or whatever), it is far from clear that this general argument can be pressed into the service of whereabouts dissenters. Of course, there will be athletes who say, 'I'm not trying to be deceptive, I just don't think you are entitled to know my whereabouts'. In such a case, their concealment need have nothing to do with deception. Against such a view, we must recognize, with Nagel, that, 'The public–private boundary faces in two directions – keeping disruptive material out of the public arena and protecting private life from the crippling effects of the external gaze' (2002: 15). While acknowledging this, however, we can agree that *some* data regarding our personal lives have no such effect. It can be argued, quite reasonably, that entitlement to privacy is not strongly overridden by declaring dates and locations that are themselves kept private and accessed by very few, if at all. In being thus concealed from nearly all, one is hardly open to some corrosive external gaze. To only a very limited extent is a principle of privacy ever overridden in practice. If one leaves all the data unobserved, because of intelligence testing, just how egregious can the invasion really be?

It is true that the compulsory element of the whereabouts policy is an exercise of institutional power. To that extent, it is important to require those institutions charged with effecting anti-doping policy to act with a close eye upon equality of treatment. To the extent that inequalities exist, whether because of national resources or the sheer geography of vast nations, the justification for demands for private information may be seriously challenged and their legitimacy potentially undermined. There are many examples of athletes who have 'disappeared' for an extended period between competitions. We might say that the greater the intrusion, the higher the demands for equality of treatment. Without it, however, it is difficult to envisage any foundation for efficacious anti-doping testing.

Concluding remarks

We have attempted to show how anti-doping legislation and rules variously cohere with, and differ from, other areas of law, and how they are related to very general ethical notions such as guilt, negligence, privacy and responsibility. The principles in criminal law discussed above are applied as such in many areas of doping control. We have shown how anti-doping violations are not typically related to criminal law (with the exception of certain European countries) but to the disciplinary measures of private organizations. Nevertheless, doping rules do not remain outside general juridical principles. It can sometimes be difficult to articulate differences between general juridical principles and those principles existing only in criminal law. The tensions between the two are important to consider, as the conflation or merging of the two spheres of regulatory frameworks is not without its problems, as we have argued.

The nearly unanimous decision of sports organizations to battle against doping has been a response to a genuine crisis in the representation of the values of sports themselves. Given their function as global vehicles of ethical development, finding a firm and justified ethical and legal rationale for anti-doping is of international significance. Nevertheless, we are aware that neither the juridical peculiarities in the doping rules presented here nor the legitimacy of the interpretations we have offered are without their problems.

Notes

1 An argument similar to this is put forward by Miah (2005), among others.
2 We mean by this, following MacIntyre's classic thesis about the malaise of liberal modernity and the dominance of economically driven bureaucratic institutions therein, the players, spectators, officials and aficionados committed to the internal values of the game – as opposed to those involved in sporting institutions (such as the International Olympic Committee, the Federation of International Football Associations and so on), whose task it is to administer, market, organize and promote sports in order to regulate their commodity and distribute external rewards, such as prize money or titles and so on.
3 See Hardie's discussion of *Operación Puerto* (Chapter 10).
4 Sport organizations do not have such coercive powers as authorities do. Their powers are limited within their sport. Thus, for example, they can prevent the athlete from competing in official competitions or tournaments. Similarly, the execution of the sanctions is limited.
5 Thus, for example, there are countries who have made such offences a criminal act(s), such as France (in the wake of perennial Tour de France cycling doping incidents), and also Italy and Slovenia.
6 For a chronology of the event, please see: http://sportsillustrated.cnn.com/cycling/1998/tourdefrance/news/1998/08/02/drug_chronology/ (accessed 16 February 2009).
7 See: http://news.bbc.co.uk/1/hi/sport/47684.stm (accessed 16 February 2009).
8 See: http://news.bbc.co.uk/sport1/hi/olympics/athletics/7503792.stm (accessed 16 February 2009).
9 See: http://news.bbc.co.uk/sport1/hi/olympics_2004/athletics/3571944.stm (accessed 16 February 2009).
10 Strictly speaking, we could say that there is no presumption of guilt here: the mere presence of the doping product renders the athlete guilty of a doping violation.
11 The newly revised WADC includes a more flexible sanction system than the previous system to allow for this fact.
12 See: http://news.bbc.co.uk/sport1/hi/olympics/athletics/7277322.stm (accessed 16 February 2009).
13 It has been suggested, however, that the ruling was in part motivated by the lateness of the appeal by Chambers. It was thought by some that this was a deliberate (though ultimately unsuccessful) tactic employed to pressurize the Courts into a quick and favourable decision.
14 In a recent ESRC symposium in Swansea (Wales), the former anti-doping officer of the Australian Anti-Doping Agency, Gavin Dovey, offered 'testimony' of chasing Australian weightlifters who had had attempted to train under the radar in Fiji, only to be apprehended by officers who – in an effort to post the violation notice – had to chase the athletes through a car park and indeed jump onto the bonnet (hood) of a moving car in order to do so.

15 There are exceptions in the prosecution of this rule: see, for example, the recent Scottish rugby union player Scott Macleod, who received only a caution when found using an inhaler with a prohibited product.

16 See also http://news.bbc.co.uk/sport1/hi/olympics/athletics/7503792.stm (accessed 16 February 2009).

Bibliography

Anscombe, G.E.M. (1957) *Intention*, Oxford: Blackwell.

Blackshaw, I.S., Siekmann, R.C.R. and Sock, J.W. (eds) (2006) *The Court of Arbitration for Sport 1984–2004*, The Hague: T.M.S. Asser Press.

Brown, W.M. (2007) 'Paternalism, drugs, and the nature of sports', in W.J. Morgan (ed.), *Ethics in sports* (2nd edn), Champaign, IL: Human Kinetics Publishers.

Foddy, B. and Savulescu, J. (2007) 'Ethics of performance enhancement in sports: drugs and gene doping', in R.E. Ashcroft, A. Dawson, H. Draper and J.R. McMillan (eds), *Principles of healthcare ethics*, West Sussex: Wiley.

Fost, N. (2008) '"Doping" is pejorative and misleading'. Available online at: www.bmj.com/content/337/bmj.a584.extract/reply (accessed 2 December 2010).

Hanstad, D.V. and Loland, S. (2009) 'Elite athletes' duty to provide information on their whereabouts: justifiable anti-doping work or an indefensible surveillance regime?', *European Journal of Sport Science*, 9(1): 3–10.

Honsell, H. (1995) *Schweizerisches Haftpflichtrecht*, Zürich: Schulthess Verlag.

Houlihan, B. (2002) *Dying to win: doping in sport and the development of anti-doping policy*, London: Routledge.

Kayser, B. and Smith, A.C. (2008) 'Globalisation of anti-doping: the reverse side of the medal', *BMJ*, 337: a584, 4 July.

Kreft, L. (2009) 'The elite athlete – in a state of exception?', *Sport, Ethics and Philosophy*, 3(1): 3–18.

MacIntyre, A.C. (1981) *After virtue*, London: Duckworth.

McNamee, M.J. (2002) 'Is guilt a proper emotional response to the causing of an unintentional injury?', *European Journal of Sport Science*, 2(1): 1–10.

McNamee, M.J. (2008) *Sports, virtues and vices: morality plays*, London: Routledge.

Magdalinski, T. (2009) *Sport, technology and the body*, London: Routledge.

Miah, A. (2005) 'From anti-doping to a "performance policy": sport technology, being human and doing ethics', *European Journal of Sport Science*, 5(1): 51–7.

Monaghan, L. (2003) *Bodybuilding, drugs and risk*, London: Routledge.

Murray, T. (2008) 'Deepening the debate around bioethics'. Available online at: www.fondazionebassetti.org/en/ubois/2008/07/deeping_the_public_conversatio.html (accessed 16 February 2009).

Nagel, T. (2002) *Concealment and exposure*, Oxford: Oxford University Press.

Obama, B. (2009) 'Alex Rodriguez steroids admission "tarnishes an entire era"'. Available online at: www.telegraph.co.uk/sport/othersports/baseball/4577838/Barack-Obama-Alex-Rodriguez-steroids-admission-tarnishes-an-entire-era.html (accessed 16 February 2009).

Parens, E. (1998) 'Is better always good?', in E. Parens (ed.), *Enhancing human traits*, Washington, DC: Georgetown University Press.

Siekmann, R.C.R. and Soek, J.W. (eds) (2007) *The Council of Europe and sport: basic documents*, The Hague: T.M.S. Asser Press.

Soek, J.W. (2006) *The strict liability principle and the human rights of athletes in doping cases*, The Hague: T.M.S. Asser Press.
Tamburrini, C. (2000) 'What's wrong with doping?', in T. Tännsjo and C. Tamburrini (eds), *Values in sports*, London: Taylor & Francis.
Tarasti, L. (2007) 'Interplay between doping sanctions imposed by a criminal court and by a sport organisation', *The International Sports Law Journal*, 3(4): 15–18.
WADA (2009) *World Anti-Doping Code*. Available online at: www.wada-ama.org/rtecontent/document/code_v2009_En.pdf (accessed 16 February 2009).
Waddington, I. and Schmidt, A. (2009) *An introduction to drugs in sport*, London: Routledge.

2 The burden of proof in endogenous substance cases

A masking agent for junk science[1]

James E. Coleman, Jr. and
Joshua M. Levine

Introduction

In 1996, the International Amateur Athletic Federation (IAAF), the international governing body for track and field athletics, charged Mary Decker Slaney, one of the most accomplished American runners in the history of track and field, with a doping violation based solely on what it characterized as a testosterone to epitestosterone (TE) ratio above the level that the IAAF deemed to be natural.[2] Under IAAF rules in effect at the time, Ms. Slaney could have avoided a doping violation only if she could prove by a preponderance of evidence that her TE ratio was due to a "physiological or pathological condition," and not the use of exogenous testosterone, as the IAAF presumed in prosecuting anti-doping policy. Ms. Slaney prevailed in the initial hearing before her national federation only by convincing the hearing panel that, under American law,[3] the United States Olympic Committee (USOC) (which prosecuted Ms. Slaney on behalf of the IAAF) had to prove by clear and convincing evidence that Ms. Slaney *in fact* had committed a doping violation; the panel could not presume Ms. Slaney's guilt, based solely on the level of her TE ratio. The USOC could not satisfy that burden.

The IAAF appealed against the hearing panel's decision and assigned the case to a panel of three, handpicked international arbitrators. At the beginning of the arbitration proceedings in Monte Carlo, Ms. Slaney's representatives asked the three arbitrators to decide, in advance of hearing any evidence, whether the IAAF would be required to prove by clear and convincing evidence that Ms. Slaney *in fact* had committed a doping violation. In challenging the mandatory presumption of guilt based on her TE ratio, Ms. Slaney relied on several published studies conducted by the Olympic Laboratory in Cologne, Germany, which found that unidentified factors other than doping also caused the TE ratios of some women to rise above the level deemed natural under the IAAF rule.[4] Based on such studies, Ms. Slaney argued that, to prove she had committed a doping violation, the IAAF had to present clear and convincing evidence that Ms. Slaney's "elevated" TE ratio was not due to innocent factors.

The IAAF's representative responded with two points: First, he argued that the arbitration panel did not have the authority to ignore the IAAF's rule, which presumed a doping offense based solely on a TE ratio above a certain level. Second, he admitted that, if the IAAF had to prove that Ms. Slaney's "elevated" TE ratio in fact was due to doping, it would fail, because the science underlying the TE ratio was inadequate to identify the precise cause(s) of an apparent spike in an athlete's TE ratio.

The panel of IAAF arbitrators rejected Ms. Slaney's argument and held that the IAAF satisfied its burden of proof by presenting analytical evidence that Ms. Slaney's TE ratio was above the level set by IAAF rules; to avoid being found guilty of a doping violation, Ms. Slaney had to prove by a preponderance of the evidence that she was innocent. For the same reason that the IAAF could not prove that Ms. Slaney had ingested testosterone, Ms. Slaney could not identify the innocent factor that had caused her TE ratio to appear elevated. In light of that, Ms. Slaney withdrew from the arbitration and filed a lawsuit in federal court in the United States, challenging the IAAF's burden-shifting rule. Although Ms. Slaney lost her claim, the court acknowledged that, without the burden-shifting rule, the IAAF could not prove that Ms. Slaney had ingested a prohibited substance. The system is purely utilitarian:

> Reduced to its essence, Slaney contends that the burden-shifting approach adopted by the IAAF violates United States public policy. We disagree. According to the parties, proving the presence of exogenous testosterone in the body by scientific tests is not possible at the present time. Therefore, the IAAF has adopted the rebuttable presumption of ingestion from a high TE ratio in an athlete's urine [. . .] Were the IAAF not to make use of the rebuttable presumption, it would be nearly impossible, absent eyewitness proof, to ever find that an athlete had ingested testosterone.[5]

Since the decision in the Slaney case in 2001, much has changed in the effort to combat doping in sports. But the easy "burden" that WADA assigns to ADOs under its jurisdiction to prove a doping violation has not changed. The elaborate system that WADA has established appears fair and scientifically based, but, in doping cases involving the suspected use of endogenous substances, that appearance is illusory.

In the last 10 years in the United States, an alarming number of innocent individuals have been wrongfully convicted in criminal cases (Huff 2003; Cox and Bratina 2007). Many of these wrongful convictions were discovered through DNA analyses of biological evidence left at crime scenes by the real perpetrators of the crimes. These cases bring to light several factors that contribute to wrongful convictions, including the use of "junk science" and forensic science techniques and processes that have little scientific validity. According to a recent report of the National Academy of Sciences, contrary to claims routinely made in criminal courts, many forensic methods have not been shown consistently and reliably to connect evidence taken from crime scenes to specific people or sources: "The simple reality is that the interpretation of forensic evidence is not always based on scientific studies to determine its validity" (National Research Council of the National Academies 2009: 8).

The same criticism, we claim, can be made about the rules under which WADA prosecutes cases of alleged doping with endogenous substances. These rules have not been shown reliably to connect the standard of proof for a doping violation involving endogenous substances to the actual ingestion of such substances. As a result, the rules neither create a level playing field nor protect innocent athletes from false claims of doping.

The World Anti-Doping Agency rules governing endogenous substances

Under the WADC, "it is not necessary that intent, fault, negligence or knowing use on the athlete's part be demonstrated to establish an anti-doping violation [under the Code]" (WADA 2009b: Article 2.1). Athletes are strictly "responsible for any Prohibited Substance or its Metabolites or markers found to be present in their bodily Specimens" (WADA 2009b: Article 2.1). Accordingly, "the detected presence of any quantity of a Prohibited Substance or its Metabolites or Markers in an Athlete's Sample shall constitute an anti-doping violation" (WADA 2009b: Article 2.1.2). Before the imposition of sanctions, however, the code permits anti-doping agencies to take into consideration how the prohibited substance got into the athlete's specimen. According to the Code, this approach "provides a reasonable balance between effective anti-doping enforcement for the benefit of all 'clean' Athletes and fairness in the exceptional circumstance where a Prohibited Substance entered an Athlete's system through no fault or negligence on the Athlete's part" (WADA 2009b: Comment to Rule 2.1).

One exception to this general rule of strict liability is reflected in the manner in which endogenous substances such as testosterone are defined as "prohibited substances." Under the code, a doping offense with such substances is not based on their presence in the athlete's specimen, but on some proxy thought to indicate the prohibited use of the substance. For example, the prohibited list may provide that a TE ratio greater than some value (currently 4:1) is doping, unless a longitudinal analysis of prior or subsequent test results by the ADO demonstrates a naturally elevated ratio, or the athlete otherwise establishes that the elevated ratio is the result of a "physiological or pathological condition" (WADA 2009b: Article 2.1.4).[6] This is the formulation that ADOs such as the United States Anti-Doping Agency use to determine when a specimen contains an exogenous "prohibited substance." In the case of testosterone, this is based on a hypothesis about the natural relationship of testosterone to epitestosterone in the human body. The hypothesis, however, has changed over time, as predictions about the stability of the relationship between testosterone and epitestosterone proved more complex than first thought, based on repeated observation and testing. Such trial and error inevitably result in some unknown number of innocent athletes being wrongly found guilty of doping. But, as one concern for anti-doping effectiveness increases, a similarly important concern about the protection of innocent athletes appears to diminish.

Detection of the prohibited use of common endogenous substances

The most common anabolic androgenic steroids (AASs) that athletes use to enhance their performance and to recover from injuries are testosterone, erythropoietin (EPO), and recombinant human growth hormone (rhGH).

Testosterone

Testosterone was probably the first AAS used by athletes to improve performance and promote rapid development of lean muscle mass (Bashin et al. 1996).[7] Although scientists began studying the importance of the hormone to normal sexual function as early as 1849, they did not recognize its use as a performance enhancer until about a century later.[8]

In the late 1940s, the United States weightlifting team, led by athletes from the Philadelphia-based York Gym, was the best in the world. But these athletes were surprised when their records were shattered in losses to weightlifters from the Soviet Union in 1953 and 1954. After the 1954 defeat, the York team doctor, John Ziegler, met with the Soviet team doctor and learned "the secret" of the Soviet success: the Soviet athletes had been using synthetic testosterone to improve their training and increase their strength. This led Ziegler to experiment with testosterone as a performance-enhancing substance (Yesalis and Bahrke 2002). Later, he formed a partnership with a pharmaceutical company to create a synthetic substance that would duplicate the benefits of testosterone without the hormonal side effects. By 1958, the top American weightlifters began using the new substance, called Dianabol, and resumed their dominance of the sport. This was the beginning of the anabolic steroid era (Hickoksport.com 2009).

The IOC and other international federations (IFs) felt increased pressure to combat the rise of doping in sport after the death of a Danish cyclist in the 1960 Olympic Games in Rome. By 1967, the IOC had created a Medical Commission to monitor the use of performance-enhancing drugs (Catlin et al. 2008). However, this initial effort was not very successful, especially given the overwhelming dominance of East German athletes, in the 1970s and 1980s, fueled by a zealous, centralized doping program (Harding 2005). Although anti-doping science improved greatly throughout the 1980s and 1990s, there was not a systematic international effort against performance-enhancing substances until 1999, when the WADA was formed (Gudjónsson n.d; Catlin et al. 2008).

As anti-doping agencies developed more sophisticated tests to combat more wisdespread steroid use in international competition, athletes found alternatives to drugs such as Dianabol that could be taken without being detected in in-season urine samples. One of the most popular and effective options was recombinant testosterone, which is synthesized from plants (Catlin et al. 2008). As testosterone is produced naturally in the testes (men), ovaries (women), and adrenal gland (men and women), it is difficult for tests to distinguish synthetic from endogenous testosterone (WebMD n.d.: 'Testosterone'; Houlihan 1997).

Professor Manfred Donike, who ran an IOC drug-testing laboratory in Cologne, Germany, was one of the first scientists to identify this threat to the IOC's anti-doping efforts (Todd 1992). Adding to the difficulty involved in testing for exogenous testosterone was the fact that the concentration of testosterone found in urine samples could not be reliably measured for anti-doping purposes. This is because the actual amount of testosterone in the body constantly varies, owing to factors such as age, weight, time of day, level of activity, and gender (Guay 2002; Diver 2006). However, Dr. Donike and Dr. Don Catlin of the UCLA Olympic laboratories concluded, based on observation of thousands of urine samples, that the ratio of testosterone to a hormone called epitestosterone (which is excreted in tandem with testosterone and has a slight moderating effect on testosterone's anabolic effects) is relatively stable in normal, healthy individuals, apparently at a ratio of about 1:1 (Havlikova et al. 2002). Donike discovered that doping with synthetic testosterone would cause this ratio to increase, because the body apparently did not produce additional amounts of epitestosterone to account for the testosterone exogenously administered. Thus, he concluded that a urine sample that had a higher than normal TE ratio could be taken as evidence of a testosterone doping violation.

Based on the work of Dr. Donike and Dr. Catlin, testosterone was added to the IOC list of banned substances in 1982, with the maximum TE ratio set at 6:1, which was chosen based on sample data from Donike's laboratory and the desire to avoid false positives (Todd 1992). As more data became available, however, anti-doping authorities found that some individuals had naturally high TE ratios, above the doping threshold of 6:1. As a result, the level for a doping violation was increased to 10:1. Later, when the concern about widespread use of testosterone became greater than the concern about false positives, the federations lowered the ratio back to 6:1, and finally, in 2005, WADA lowered the ratio to its current 4:1 (Catlin et al. 2008: 106). The result is that the test is set at a level where the anti-doping officials, especially the scientists, assume there will be some unknown number of false positives. Occasionally, athletes who had been found guilty of using testosterone were later determined to have been innocent, but not before their careers had been destroyed, often without official vindication.[9]

Although the TE ratio has been a permanent fixture in anti-doping efforts since the first athlete was tested with this method in 1983, its fluctuation reflects serious scientific uncertainty about the validity of the ratio as a proxy for the exogenous use of testosterone. The first problem that the Olympic testers discovered was that, contrary to their original belief, TE ratios do vary from athlete to athlete. Whereas some people have naturally high ratios, for reasons unknown to anti-doping authorities, others (apparently including 66.7 percent of Asians) have naturally low TE ratios, because they apparently do not excrete testosterone into their urine at the same rate as they excrete epitestosterone. This apparently is owing to differences in the gene that controls the excretion of testosterone into the urine (Schulze et al. 2008). Authorities also found that athletes could defeat the TE ratio test by balancing exogenous testosterone with exogenous epitestosterone, thereby keeping the TE ratio below the suspicious level (Houlihan 1997).

Finally, anti-doping officials have found that it is more difficult to detect testosterone doping in women than in men, because women produce a significantly lower amount of the hormone. This means that it takes less testosterone to obtain its performance-enhancing effect, allowing women to administer significantly less exogenous testosterone while avoiding testing positive using the TE ratio (Kolata 2008). Dr. Donike and his colleagues also discovered, from studies involving women, that, under some inexplicable circumstances, some women who had not used doping agents had TE ratios that fluctuated sometimes above the level set for a violation.[10] Mary Decker Slaney relied on these tests in her challenge to the IAAF's claim that she had used testosterone. As part of her representatives' investigation, they contacted the Cologne Olympic Laboratory and requested its assistance in trying to identify the factor or factors that might have caused Ms. Slaney's TE ratio to exceed the suspicious level. Yet, because the IOC does not permit its accredited laboratories to assist athletes in doping cases, the scientists were not able to work openly with Ms. Slaney. Nevertheless, they agreed that urine samples taken from Ms. Slaney over time did not appear to indicate that exogenous testosterone had been the cause of her suspicious test. This evidence, however, could not be used in Ms. Slaney's defense.

In the mid 1990s, Don Catlin, head of the Olympic Analytical Laboratory at UCLA, developed a new method for detecting synthetic testosterone that was supposed to solve many of the problems of the TE ratio test (*USA Today* 2007). This test, called the carbon isotope ratio test, compares the amount of carbon-13 (an isotope of carbon comprising about 1 percent of all carbon in the world) in the athlete's sample and the amount of carbon-12 (the most abundant form of carbon). As synthetic testosterone is manufactured from plants, it has a slightly different level of carbon-13 than the body's natural testosterone. The test purportedly detects the actual presence of synthetic testosterone based on small shifts in the ratio of carbon-13 to carbon-12 noted in an athlete's sample (Catlin et al. 2008). Although this test purportedly is an accurate method to identify the presence of synthetic testosterone in a sample, it is very difficult to perform. According to Dr. Catlin, "if the extraction and . . . tests are not perfectly executed to provide complete baseline separation of the steroids, the results will be unintelligible" (Catlin 2001). This was one of the grounds on which Floyd Landis, the American cyclist, challenged the result of the carbon isotope test performed on the urine sample taken from him after Stage 17 in the 2006 Tour de France (Blackledge 2009).[11] Although the CAS found that no breach of protocol had occurred in collecting, handling, or testing the sample, several credible experts called the findings of the test "completely unreliable" (DeSimone 2007). In 2010, however, Mr. Landis admitted that he had used performance-enhancing substances during the 2006 Tour de France, perhaps implicitly conceding that the carbon isotope test had been reliable in his case (Ford 2010).

In addition to the carbon isotope test being difficult to perform, there also is evidence that the results of the carbon isotope test may vary according to the ethnicity of the tested athlete (Aguilera et al. 2001). Finally, the test is expensive and performed only at selected WADA-certified laboratories. As a result, it is generally used only to confirm a doping violation after the initial screening of the athlete's sample is deemed suspicious under the TE ratio test (Catlin et al. 2008). This means that athletes who are administering exogenous epitestosterone as a way to avoid producing a suspicious TE ratio are not caught with the arguably more accurate carbon isotope test. It also means that an unknown number of athletes whose suspicious samples are not subjected to the carbon isotope test undoubtedly are innocent. It is not known whether WADA or its certified laboratories are generating data from the carbon isotope tests to determine what the error rates are for both the carbon isotope test and for the TE ratio test. Without such analyses, claims about the efficacy of both tests lack the scientific credibility demanded, given the irreparable harm caused by a false positive.

Endogenous rEPO

Endogenous EPO is a hormone that regulates the production of red blood cells in the body. It increases naturally in response to anemia (not enough red blood cells) or hypoxia (not enough oxygen). Ninety percent of the body's EPO is produced by the kidneys and liver. EPO stimulates the production of red blood cells in bone marrow. In some cases of chronic kidney disease, the loss of the main production site of endogenous EPO can lead to severe anemia. Before the development of artificial or recombinant EPO (rEPO), patients whose kidneys could not adequately produce EPO needed blood transfusions to keep their blood volume and hemoglobin at a normal rate (WebMD n.d: 'Erythropoietin stimulators'). The creation of rEPO to stimulate red blood cell growth helped eliminate the need for blood transfusions for patients undergoing hemodialysis (WebMD n.d: 'Erythropoietin stimulators'). Pharmaceutical companies such as Amgen found that, by transfecting the DNA sequence for human EPO into Chinese hamster ovarian cells, they could produce an effective and useable form of human EPO, which then could be injected into patients to stimulate the production of red blood cells (WADA n.d).

Although this new form of recombinant EPO has been especially effective for medical treatment, it also has been useful to athletes seeking to enhance their performance by increasing their blood volume and hemoglobin (Levine 2008). Several studies have shown that increased blood volume and hemoglobin lead to a higher maximal oxygen uptake (VO_2 max), which translates into a higher oxygen-carrying capacity and ability to do aerobic work (Stray-Gundersen et al. 2003; Williams et al. 1981). This is particularly beneficial for athletes in endurance sports such as cycling, running, and cross-country skiing, which place a premium on an athlete's ability to carry and use large amounts of oxygen over long periods of time (Williams et al. 1981). For example, a 2003 study found that 50 percent of cross-country skiers receiving medals in the competitions reviewed had highly abnormal hematologic profiles strongly suggestive of doping; in contrast, only 3 percent of the bottom 50 percent of finishers had such profiles (Stray-Gundersen et al. 2003).

The use of rEPO by athletes is a widespread concern for anti-doping authorities. Generally, rEPO is relatively safe when administered properly; the principal concern is improper use of the substance for its performance-enhancing effects. For example, there are health risks for athletes who use rEPO to increase their hematocrit to extremely high levels. When there are too many red blood cells in the body (generally when the hematocrit is above 60 percent), the viscosity of the blood increases, and the flow of blood becomes problematic. If the viscosity gets too high, the blood can stop flowing smoothly through blood vessels, and clots can develop, leading to heart attack, stroke, and pulmonary embolism. Some suspect that excessive use of EPO was a factor in the death of several Belgian cyclists in the 1980s (Fotheringham 2004).

During the early days of its use by athletes, anti-doping agencies were unable to detect the presence of rEPO in athletes' samples, and the substance was not banned. However, the apparent widespread use of rEPO led WADA to declare rEPO a banned substance in 1990 on account of "health concerns." The approach taken was to set upper limits for what the anti-doping authorities considered natural hematocrit or hemoglobin levels. These levels varied from sport to sport. For example, the International Cycling Union (ICU) set a maximum hematocrit level for competition of 50; the International Skiing Federation (FIS) set upper limits for hemoglobin of 18.5 for men and 17.5 for women. Under this system, any athlete whose hematocrit or hemoglobin level exceeded the maximum set by his or her federation was banned from competition, unless the athlete proved that his or her level was normal. This test led to problems similar to those encountered with the TE ratio test. Anti-doping authorities could not detect the actual presence of rEPO in the athletes. This meant it was impossible, in many cases, to say with certainty that an athlete in fact was guilty of a doping offence. In addition, authorities also found (again similar to the TE ratio problem) that some athletes have naturally high hematocrit levels, discovered only after long-term data were available for the individual. In addition, the suspicious levels were high enough that some athletes were able to use rEPO without concern about detection, simply by keeping their levels under the maximum levels set by the authorities. Thus, the test undoubtedly has resulted in an unknown number of both false positives and false negatives.

Since the early days of indirect testing for rEPO, WADA developed a urine test using isoelectric focusing, which, like the carbon isotope test for testosterone, purports to detect the prohibited substance itself in the urine sample. This test is designed to distinguish between endogenous EPO created in the body and recombinant EPO from external sources. Currently, recombinant EPO is produced under a patented process from Chinese hamsters (Catlin et. al 2004). Although the amino acid sequence coding for EPO is identical in both humans and other mammals, isoelectric focusing allows anti-doping authorities to distinguish between the two sources. This is made possible because the final EPO molecule is a complex combination of amino acids and carbohydrates that are attached to the proteins in a process called "post-translational modification." This process is species-specific. Therefore, an EPO molecule made in a human cell will have a different carbohydrate coating than one made in a hamster cell, or the cell of any other species of animals (Lasne and de Ceaurriz 2000; Lasne et al. 2009). WADA's isoelectric focusing technique thus is able to identify the carbohydrate coating of any EPO molecule found in a urine sample by transferring the glycosylated (complexed with carbohydrate) proteins onto a membrane on which traces of EPO appear as dark bands. Endogenous EPO molecules and any recombinant EPO molecules appear in two different areas of the membrane, because they have different electric charges (Jelkmann 2007). This isoelectric focusing technique does not rely on any arbitrary ratio of red blood cells, EPO, or hemoglobin-to-blood volume in order to catch cheaters. As a result, it avoids the legal and ethical concerns associated with indirect tests of endogenous substances, such as the TE ratio and the early indirect test for EPO.

There are limits to the test, however, even when it is properly administered. First, the test is capable of detecting rEPO made in non-human mammalian cells for only 2–3 days after it is injected, beyond which the test is highly insensitive and ineffective (Catlin et al. 2008). In addition, the test is apparently difficult to administer. In a study published in the *Journal of Applied Physiology*, a group of Danish investigators found serious problems with this testing method (Lundby et al. 2008). In the study, researchers injected individuals with rEPO and subsequently sent their samples to WADA-certified laboratories for testing. Using the isoelectric focusing technique, the laboratories had a remarkably high rate of failure in identifying the samples that contained the rEPO. Although testers were able to identify the "cheaters" during the initial "boosting" period, in which the subjects were injecting significant amounts of rEPO to augment their red cell mass, they were successful in only two of forty-eight cases in identifying the individuals injecting EPO during the maintenance period, during which the athletes took smaller doses of EPO to maintain their blood volume and hemoglobin at a high but stable level (Lundby et al. 2008). Such a high rate of error undermines the deterrent effect the test has. Not only will cheaters reap the benefits of illegal performance enhancement, but athletes who otherwise would not use performance-enhancing drugs are faced with a stark dilemma: cheat, or risk losing to people who are cheating (Stray-Gundersen et al. 2003). Finally, the patent protecting the process of making rEPO using Chinese hamster ovarian cells has expired in Europe and Asia. As a result, it is likely that the number of new producers of the substance will proliferate, using the previously protected process to put increasing amounts of the substance on the market at lower and lower prices. Some of these producers undoubtedly will create cell lines for producing EPO that are obtained from other animals, making it more uncertain whether a test designed to detect rEPO made from Chinese hamsters will similarly detect rEPO from other cell lines (Jelkmann 2007).

There are other promising developments that may help to detect the prohibited use of rEPO. One such development was revealed at the 2008 Tour de France, involving collaboration between anti-doping authorities and the pharmaceutical industry. Before EPO can stimulate the bone-marrow to make more red blood cells, it first must bind with a special EPO receptor. Studies have found genetic mutations in this receptor that result in very high hematocrit levels. This mutation was found in the great Finnish cross-country skier Eero Mantyranta, who won several Olympic and World Championship gold medals in the 1960s (Juvonen et al. 1991). Recently, researchers have developed a drug called continuous erythropoiesis receptor activator, or CERA, that can stimulate this receptor pathway directly. In the 2008 Tour, Italian cyclist Richard Ricco was caught using CERA because testers detected a molecule implanted in the drug by the manufacturer of the drug, Roche Pharmaceuticals. This approach offers a method of detection that overcomes some of the limitations of the isoelectric focusing method, requiring only detection of the implanted molecule, which reduces the margin of error for the test, because an athlete who tests positive for the substance almost definitely is doping (*Sydney Morning Herald* 2008). Nevertheless, the approach raises a number of questions. For example, is there any way the marker implanted in the CERA could enter an athlete's body under any other circumstance (diet, legal supplements, etc.)? More seriously, how difficult would it be for other companies to make CERA without the marker and sell it to athletes on the black market? If a black-market version of the drug becomes available, cheaters would be much more difficult to identify.

Although the current isoelectric focusing test for rEPO avoids some of the "junk science" concerns raised by the indirect ratio tests, serious limitations remain. First, the test is effective only during a small window after rEPO is injected. Second, it may be ineffective altogether during the maintenance period of use, when the athlete uses smaller doses of EPO for the purpose of stabilizing the high levels of red blood cells and hemoglobin that were built up using larger doses in the previous weeks.

Human growth hormone

Endogenous rhGH is the most abundant hormone produced in the anterior pituitary gland. When released (primarily) by the liver, hGH binds to receptors in targeted cells to stimulate an increase in the levels of insulin growth factors (IGFs), which stimulate growth and development of the cells. The amount of hGH secreted into the body's cells varies with age. Although women generally have a slightly higher level of secretion than men, both men and women experience peak levels of hGH during puberty, after which the level of secretion decreases by about 14 percent per decade (Melmed 2004).

When this system functions properly, and the correct amount of hGH is produced in the body, people grow and develop at a normal and healthy rate. Nevertheless, there are serious consequences for individuals who produce either too much or too little hGH. Individuals who have hGH deficiency fall short of population norms for height. Exogenous growth hormone was first developed to treat such people. Conversely, patients who have an excess of growth hormone are unusually tall. This results in a syndrome called acromegaly, characterized by large body size (particularly head, hands, and feet), and is complicated by diabetes, arthritis, and heart disease, often leading to premature death. The complications from chronic elevations of growth hormone are much more severe and more clearly documented than those from other anabolic agents, such as testosterone and its analogues (Melmed 2004).

Recombinant hGH was developed in 1983. Before that, patients with hGH deficiency were treated with growth hormone extracted from the pituitary glands of cadavers. Although this method is less expensive than producing recombinant hGH, patients using cadaver growth hormone face the risk of contracting a deadly virus called a "prion," which causes brain degeneration (Saugy et al. 2006).

Athletes who use rhGH believe its anabolic action will promote lean muscle growth, which explains its appeal to athletes who wish to enhance muscle growth and performance. Scientific studies, however, do not support general claims of its effectiveness for that purpose. Although it might be reasonably expected that hGH would provide the same benefits as anabolic steroids, such as accelerating muscle recovery and preventing muscle–tendon failure, it is noteworthy that studies have not consistently documented that hGH actually produces muscle growth (Doessing and Kjaer 2005).

After normal growth and development are complete, the body's ability to use growth hormone by itself to stimulate growth is greatly decreased. Also, although it is likely that hGH causes a decrease in body fat and an increase in lean body mass, it is difficult to prove that hGH actually stimulates the protein synthesis needed for muscle growth more than regular training. Some studies suggest that increased girth resulting from hGH does not necessarily lead to relative increases in strength (Hoffman et al. 2008). On the other hand, there are not many studies that have specifically examined the benefits of rhGH as it is used by athletes to enhance performance. Thus, one cannot discount athletes' claims that rhGH is beneficial for their training, even though current scientific research does not corroborate the claim. This state of affairs is not uncommon. Anti-doping authorities frequently try to detect, and prevent the use of, many substances that have not actually been proven to enhance performance (e.g., precursors to testosterone, such as DHEA).

There are two principal tests used to detect the prohibited use of rhGH. Both tests are problematic. The test most commonly used by WADA quantifies actual hGH in the athlete's urine sample and relies on differences in the assays (testing measurements) of hGH and rhGH. The assay for endogenous hGH is comprised of 22 kDa hGH, acidic hGH, modified hGH, and fragmented hGH, reflecting the variety of forms in which it occurs naturally in the body. In contrast, rhGH occurs only in the 22 kDa hGH form. Therefore, the prohibited use of hGH can theoretically be determined by measuring the amount of 22 kDa hGH in the sample and its ratio to the other types of endogenous hGH. These results can then be compared with predetermined normal values for these assays (Saugy et al. 2006). This test suffers from the same deficiencies as the TE ratio test. Because it relies on a ratio that may be affected by unknown factors, it is possible that athletes with relatively high natural amounts of 22 kDa hGH will be unfairly labeled as cheaters. This is likely because the levels of all types of hGH vacillate constantly, making it difficult to establish an accurate baseline measurement for standard (i.e. "natural") hGH values and ratios. For example, hGH levels are affected by such factors as gender, age, exercise, body composition, time of day, and stress. Finally, as with tests for rEPO, the effectiveness of this method of detection is limited by the short half-life of hGH; the test is effective only if it is administered between 24 and 36 hours after rhGH is taken (Bidlingmeier and Strasburger 2007).

The second test involves measuring hGH-dependent factors, such as IGF, IGF-binding proteins, and markers of bone turnover, rather than attempting to test for the hormone itself. There are many different hGH-dependent "markers" that could be measured this way, but the most effective combination of markers is IGF/insulin-I and an hGH-dependent marker of bone turnover called PIIIP, which is an amino-terminal extension peptide of type III procollagen. This combination also provides the largest possible window of time for testers to catch cheaters; studies have shown that, using this method, suspected rhGH use can be detected as many as 14 days after its administration (Bidlingmeier and Strasburger 2007). Moreover, although hGH-dependent markers vary significantly among individuals owing to age and exercise, their abundances are more stable than hGH itself. Although this indirect approach has some advantages over the direct method of detection, it still suffers from deficiencies similar to the ones that plague other indirect ratio tests (Saugy et al. 2006).

WADA has made heroic efforts to devise tests that will consistently and reliably detect the prohibited use of endogenous performance-enhancing substances. Nevertheless, many of these tests suffer from a lack of reliable and valid scientific knowledge about factors other than doping that might affect the relationships upon which the tests rely. Anti-doping authorities do not know when a defective gene or a suppressed system will cause a change in the ratio. They do not know under what circumstances a physiological or pathological factor will affect the ratio. They do not know what innocent factors may cause the ratio to fluctuate in women, compared with men, or whether there are natural circumstances that might affect the secretion of one of the substances key to the ratio.

Despite the lack of significant knowledge about factors that might innocently cause a ratio to become suspicious, WADA and the anti-doping authorities under its jurisdiction proceed as if the results of these tests are established facts, rather than hypotheses that frequently have to be adjusted as they learn more from observation and study. Based on that assumption, WADA deems proof of the suspicious ratio to be clear and convincing proof of the prohibited use of the substance, whether in fact that is true or not. Then, it creates the illusion of fairness by providing that the athlete can rebut the presumption of guilt by actually proving why his or her ratio is suspicious. It seems obvious that, if WADA and the anti-doping authorities cannot prove to a sufficiently high scientific standard what caused the ratio to be suspicious, that an athlete, without WADA's extensive network of laboratories and resources, cannot prove it was not due to doping. The result is that WADA's burden-shifting scheme masks the unreliability of the ratios on which the athlete's guilt rests. And, because courts in the United States and elsewhere appear to have placed the scheme beyond serious substantive judicial review and instead focus only on procedural issues, little attention is paid to the resulting unfairness to athletes who are innocent, but cannot explain a suspicious test.

The WADA Burden of Proof Rule

With ratification of the WADA code in 2003, the Olympic Movement established a uniform burden of proof regime for anti-doping cases. Under the code, WADA consolidated all the disparate rules and procedures used by different IFs and ADOs into a single set of standards, applicable at every level of administrative proceeding, before both national and international tribunals (Gudjónsson n.d).

In form, the WADA burden of proof regime appears similar to those used regularly in state and federal court systems in the United States and other countries. It appears initially to place the burden of persuasion on the ADO to prove an anti-doping violation has taken place "to the comfortable satisfaction of the hearing panel" (Article 3.1). The level of proof required to satisfy the ADO's burden appears comparable with the "clear and convincing evidence" standard often used in American administrative proceedings involving professional misconduct, such as legal and medical malpractice. Article 3.1 explains, "this standard of proof in all cases is greater than a mere balance of probability but less than proof beyond a reasonable doubt." This burden, however, is modified for any anabolic androgenic steroid that is capable of being produced endogenously.

The 2009 Comment to the list of prohibited anabolic androgenic steroids stated that,

> when an anabolic androgenic steroid is capable of being produced endogenously, a Sample will be deemed to contain such Prohibited Substance and an Adverse Analytical Finding will be reported where the concentration of such prohibited substance or its metabolites or markers and/or any other relevant ratio(s) in the Athlete's Sample *so deviates from the range of values normally found in humans that it is unlikely to be consistent with normal endogenous* production.
>
> (WADA 2009a: Comment to Class S1.1b; emphasis added)

Notwithstanding the foregoing, however, a sample will not be deemed to contain a prohibited substance if the athlete proves by a preponderance of the evidence that the concentration of the substance or its metabolites or markers, and/or any other relevant ratio(s) in the sample "is attributable to a physiological or pathological condition" (WADA 2009a).[12] Stated differently, the athlete is exonerated if he or she affirmatively proves there was no prohibited substance in his or her sample. This is not a typical affirmative defense. If there was a significant doubt about what caused the concentration or ratio found in the sample, under the ordinary burden to provide proof of wrongdoing, the case against the athlete would fail. Under the WADA regime, therefore, the ADO's burden is not to persuade the hearing panel that a prohibited substance was taken exogenously, but to produce evidence that creates an issue whether that may have happened. At that point, the athlete has to persuade that panel, by a preponderance of the evidence, that something other than a prohibited substance caused the suspicious concentration or ratio. This turns the traditional burden of proof regime on its head. The ADO has no burden to carry, because it does not have to persuade the hearing panel what precisely caused the suspicious analytical result. In light of this, one might reasonably ask how an athlete can ever refute a case by a preponderance of the evidence, when proof of the case itself appears unachievable by current scientific standards.

Once endogenous steroids are present in the body, their source generally cannot be determined by direct testing in the way that exogenous steroids or their metabolites can be detected. The various institutions of the

International Olympic Movement have gone to great lengths to find a reliable analytical means to prove when an athlete has exogenously administered an endogenous AAS, such as testosterone, but they have largely failed. To mask that failure, WADA and the international governing bodies under its jurisdiction rely on the burden of proof shift described above.

Traditional principles of burden of proof

Historically, the legal concept of a "burden of proof" has encompassed two distinct responsibilities in legal proceedings: the "burden of persuasion" and the "burden of production."[13] The "burden of persuasion" ordinarily determines which party in a dispute must convince the decision-maker, while the "burden of production" determines which party has an obligation to produce evidence for its position at various points in the proceeding.[14] In 1923, the Supreme Court of the United States held that the "burden of proof" would henceforth refer only to the "burden of persuasion," and the "necessity of producing evidence to meet [evidence] already produced [by the opposing party]" would be considered a completely separate concept.[15] This obligation is referred to as the "burden of going forward with the evidence"[16] or the "burden of production."[17]

In non-criminal legal proceedings, the default rule is that the party making the claim has the burden of proof—i.e. the burden of persuasion—as well as the initial burden of production.[18] Once that party has met its initial burden of proof sufficient to establish a prima facie case, however, the burden of going forward with evidence might shift to the opposing party to negate the evidence produced by the claimant.[19] This may occur formally by rule or as a practical matter inherent in the defense against a claim.[20] This process, in which the claimant produces convincing prima facie evidence, and the respondent presents evidence to rebut it, may repeat itself several times, as the two parties attempt to produce a clearly persuasive case that will permit the decision-maker to resolve the disputed claim.[21]

The result of this default approach is that the legal burden of proof—the duty to persuade the decision-maker that an asserted claim is true—usually remains with the claimant throughout the proceeding.[22] From beginning to end, it is the claimant's obligation to prove that his or her claim is true, and that the respondent is liable.[23] If, at the end of the proceeding, the evidence produced by the parties is insufficient to tilt the decision of the dispute to either side, the status quo ante will be maintained, because the claimant failed in his or her obligation to persuade the decision-maker that the current situation should be changed.[24]

There is one important exception to the general rule that the burden of proof will remain with the claimant throughout a proceeding. If the respondent answers a claim with an affirmative defense, the respondent will bear the burden of proof in asserting that defense.[25] An affirmative defense is raised, for example, when the respondent asserts that, even if the facts underlying the claim are true, there are relevant circumstances that the respondent will prove legally relieve the respondent of liability. Under such circumstances, the decision-maker must deny relief to the claimant.[26]

Importantly, these default rules are not set in stone, and, before a dispute arises, the rules can be altered or overridden by agreement of the parties, by legislation, or by fundamental principles, such as those reflected in constitutions or treaties. In such cases, the agreement, legislation, or fundamental law identifies which party will bear the burden of proof in any given dispute.[27] When passing legislation in any area of law, for example, the United States Congress is free to assign the burden of proof to either side—claimant or respondent—by statute.[28] Athletic doping cases are examples of proceedings in which the "burden of proof" and "burden of production" rules have been altered to accommodate the interests implicated by the perception of widespread doping in sport and the corrosive impact it has had on the economic and social status of athletic competition.

As a general matter, if an athlete challenges a suspension in a doping case under the ordinary burden of proof standard applied by U.S. courts, he or she would bear the burden of convincing the court that the totality of evidence weighed in his or her favor. Nevertheless, the athlete would retain a significant advantage: many of the tests used to detect illegal performance enhancers are plagued by serious flaws that may undermine the weight of evidence against the athlete, theoretically making it easier to rebut a doping charge (Catlin et al. 2008). The greater challenge in doping cases takes place before athletic federations or other administrative regimes set up and controlled by them, where the rules often require the athlete to rebut doping charges by proving that the analytical result deemed clear and convincing proof of a doping violation *in fact* was "attributable to a pathological or physiological condition."[29] The result is that, once an athletic tribunal has carried its burden of presenting a prima facie case of a doping violation, the real burden of persuasion shifts to the athlete to demonstrate that he or she is innocent, a burden that, scientifically, he or she likely cannot meet.[30]

If the athlete challenges the administrative decision in court, the issue generally will not be whether the athlete in fact engaged in doping, but whether the administrative agency followed its own rules, a significantly easier position for the agency to defend. If the agency has followed its own rules, the court ordinarily will defer to the decision of the agency on the merits of the doping claim. The result often is that evidence that merely shows a suspicion of doping is treated as conclusive proof that the athlete used a prohibited substance.

The interest-balancing concerns raised by anti-doping rules

Because it is difficult to prove when an athlete has used a prohibited endogenous substance, arbitration decisions made by bodies that are part of the

Olympic Movement generally reflect a judgment that the benefits of catching cheaters outweigh the acknowledged risk of imposing sanctions on an innocent athlete based on a false positive test result. American courts have endorsed this approach by refusing to interfere with sports arbitration decisions in most cases, notably even when the science necessary to prove doping is inadequate. In the Mary Decker Slaney case, the United States Court of Appeals for the Seventh Circuit, based in Chicago, wrote that, "were [sports bodies] not to make use of the rebuttable presumption [that a highly suspicious test result constitutes doping], it would be nearly impossible, absent eyewitness proof, to ever find that an athlete had ingested [a performance enhancer]."[31]

To express this in terms of "interest balancing," the traditional mainstay of American criminal jurisprudence, that a defendant is "presumed innocent until proven guilty"—in the interest of maximum fairness to the accused—is sacrificed to the sports world's interest in trying to eliminate doping. The primary concern is not to protect innocent athletes, but to deter athletes from cheating; conviction of an innocent athlete serves that utilitarian goal just as well as conviction of a guilty athlete.

International courts take the same approach to these issues as American courts have. Most international sports federations that have adopted WADA's doping policies and rules are incorporated in Switzerland, making Swiss law pivotal in anti-doping disputes.[32] In doping disputes brought before Swiss courts, athletes have based their claims on the Swiss law concept of "personality rights," which is similar to the American law concept of "due process" (protecting against the unwarranted invasion of a person's "life, liberty, or property").[33] Like due process, Swiss "personality rights" protect the fundamental rights of an individual, including "the right to life, to physical integrity, to profess a religion or to exercise the trade or profession of one's choice." Athletes have turned to this last right, along with the related right to personal economic fulfillment, in Swiss doping cases, arguing that, absent the existence of irrefutable evidence against them, these constitutionally guaranteed interests supersede the sports world's interest in trying to eliminate doping.[34]

Swiss decisions have settled this argument in favor of the sports federations by holding that, in becoming members of their sports' professional associations, athletes "consent to a possible infringement of their personality rights due to the strict application of [their governing body's] rules."[35] Moreover, the Swiss Federal Supreme Court has held that the public policy interests of the "war" against doping justify infringing an athlete's interest in his personality rights:

> The fight against doping aims at maintaining an equal playing field among competitors, to ensure the fairness of competitions . . . to fight against the use of dangerous substances, to keep the practice of sports

> clean and to preserve its educational function for young people. These objectives are unanimously recognized [and justify] the infringement of the appellant's personality rights . . . by an overriding public interest.[36]

The WADA has identified four central interests allegedly served by its anti-doping policies (Rigozzi 2008):

1 to ensure a level playing field;
2 to protect athletes' health;
3 to preserve the social (and economic) standing of the sport;
4 to preserve the athletes' status as role models.

One might debate whether all of these interests justify the deference accorded the rules and policies of sports administrative bodies, even at the expense of innocent athletes, or whether any of the four interests really matter in most cases, except the economic and social status of the sport. No one doubts that performance-enhancing substances undermine the integrity of athletic competition. But, before any sports federation labels any athlete a cheater, it should have credible scientific evidence on which such a claim is made. Despite sometimes heroic efforts by IOC and WADA scientists to find it, such evidence is largely unavailable in most cases of suspected doping with steroids that are also endogenously produced. Thus, to WADA's list of four interests served by its anti-doping policies, there should be added a fifth overarching one: to preserve the integrity of the anti-doping enterprise itself.

Notes

1 Coleman and Levine would like to thank Doriane L. Coleman, Rick Auchus of the University of Texas Southwestern, Olivier Rabin of the World Anti-Doping Agency, and Samuel de Villiers, Duke Law School, Class of 2011, for their valuable assistance.
2 One of the co-authors of this chapter, James E. Coleman, Jr., along with his wife, Doriane Lambelet Coleman, both professors at Duke University School of Law, represented Ms. Slaney in the proceedings described herein.
3 See: Ted Stevens Olympic and Amateur Sports Act, 36 U.S.C. §§ 220503(6), (11) (2000 & Supp. 2005), available online at: www.usoc.org/12699_12720.htm.
4 In a November 17, 1997, letter to Gabriel Dolle, Doping Control Officer of the International Amateur Athletic Federation, Wilhelm Schanzer of the Koln Germany Olympic Laboratory wrote in connection with the Slaney case,

> The TE ratio is indeed an important and helpful tool in detection of testosterone misuse. But the method is only an indirect proof and serious criticism from scientists outside the doping filed has been given, especially to TE ratios in women.

See also, H. Geyer, W. Schanzer, U. Mareck-Engelke, and M. Donike, "Factors influencing the steroid profile"; U. Mareck-Engelke, H. Geyer, and W. Schanzer, "The interpretation of female steroid profiles"; U. Mareck-Engelke, H. Geyer, and M. Donike, "Stability of steroid profiles: The circadian rhythm of urinary ratios and excretion rates of endogenous steroids in females and its menstrual dependency." These articles were all published as part of the Proceedings of the Donike Workshop series on Doping Analysis.

5 *Slaney* v. *Int'l Amateur Athletic Fed'n*, 244 F.3d 580, 593 (7th Cir. 2001).

6 But see Note 10 in this chapter.

7 See also "History of steroids." Available online at: www.steroid.com (accessed 15 July, 2010).

8 See "Classical period." Available online at: www.uwyo.edu/wjm/Repro/classica.htm (accessed July 15, 2010); "History of steroids." Available online at: www.steroid.com (accessed July 15, 2010).

9 During the 1984 Olympics in Los Angeles, Japanese volleyball player Eiji Shimomura was banned from the Olympics and sent home after testing positive for testosterone under the recently adopted 6:1 TE ratio test for exogenous testosterone. Shimomura had a TE level of 7:1. This was one of the first times the TE ratio test had been used during the Olympic Games to ban an athlete for using exogenous testosterone. After further testing in Japan, however, Olympic officials determined that Shimomura had a natural TE ratio above 6:1; they had banned an innocent athlete in 1984.

10 See Note 4, *supra.*

11 *Landis v United States Anti-Doping Agency*. No. 1394. Court of Arbitration for Sport. June 30, 2008.

12 Id. The 2010 version of the Prohibited List eliminates the Comment to Class S1.1b steroids. WADA, "The 2010 Prohibited List," at p. 3 (effective January 1, 2010). A summary of major modifications made in the 2010 Prohibited List states, "Comment S1.1b, including revisions, is addressed in another WADA document (Technical Document MRPL)." WADA, 2010 Prohibited List, Summary of Major Modifications, at 1 (September 19, 2009). However, it does not appear than any such technical document has been adopted. WADA Technical Document—TD2009EAAS (October 1, 2009), entitled "Endogenous anabolic androgenic steriods: testing, reporting and interpretive guidance," which deals generally with reporting adverse findings based on TE ratios, apparently has not been adopted: the effective date is "TBD." In any event, however, it does not incorporate the substance of the deleted Comment. The minutes for the September 19, 2009, WADA Executive Committee Meeting, at which the Comment to Class S1.1b was deleted, state only that "some portions [of the 2009 Prohibited List] had been moved to other documents." Minutes at p. 16.

13 *Schaffer ex rel. Schaffer* v. *Weast* 546 U.S. 49, 56 (2005). Involving a dispute between the parents of a child with special needs and his school district. The parents challenged the district's assessment of their child's special needs, and, as it was a close call as to which category the child belonged in, the case turned on which party bore the burden of proof. In a series of appeals, the courts went back and forth between finding for the parents and finding for the school district, depending on which side the burden of proof was assigned by each court. Finally, the Supreme Court held that, as the parents had brought the suit, they bore the burden of proof as the party seeking relief. Thus, the borderline call went to the school district.

14 *Director, Office of Workers' Compensation Programs* v. *Greenwich Collieries*, 512 U.S. 267, 272 (1994).

15 *Hill* v. *Smith*, 260 U.S. 592, 594 (1923).

16 See, e.g., *Commercial Molasses Corp.* v. *New York Tank Barge Corp.*, 314 U.S. 104, 111 (1941); *Webre Steib Co.* v. *Commissioner*, 324 U.S. 164, 171 (1945).

17 Greenwich Collieries, 512 U.S. at 272.

18 Id. at 273 (quoting *Powers* v. *Russell*, 30 Mass. 69, 76–77 (Mass. S.C. 1833)).

19 Id.
20 Greenwich Collieries, 512 U.S. at 273.
21 *Lilienthal's Tobacco* v. *United States*, 97 U.S. 237, 266 (1877).
22 Schaffer, 546 U.S. at 56 ("we have usually assumed without comment that plaintiffs bear the burden of persuasion regarding the essential aspects of their claims").
23 Id. at 56–7.
24 Id. at 56.
25 See, e.g., *FTC* v. *Morton Salt Co.*, 334 U.S. 37, 44–5 (1948).
26 *Black's Law Dictionary*, 430 (8th edn. 2004) (defining an "affirmative defense" as: "A defendant's assertion of facts and arguments that, if true, will defeat the plaintiff's or prosecution's claim, even if all the allegations in the complaint are true.").
27 Schaffer, 546 U.S. at 56–8.
28 Id.
29 *Slaney* v. *International Amateur Athletics Federation*, 244 F.3d 580, 587 (7th Cir. 2001).
30 Id. ("The implementation by the IAAF of a burden-shifting approach to proving ingestion of testosterone damaged Slaney in that, as a result, she was unable to disprove that she had committed the offense—resulting in her suspension.")
31 Id. at 593.
32 Id. at 10, FN. 13.
33 Id. at 10, Sec. 30.
34 Id. at 10–11.
35 *Fédération Suisse des Courses des Chevaux (FSC)* v. *Shafflutzel and Zollig*, para 5 e), p. 12, unreported. (High Court of the Canton of Vaud, 2006).
36 *Shafflutzel and Zollig* v. *Fédération Suisse des Courses des Chevaux (FSC)*, ATF 134 III 193, 200 (Swiss Federal Supreme Court, 2008).

References

Aguilera, R., Chapman, T.E., Starcevic, B., Hatton, C.K., and Catlin, D.H. (2001) "Performance characteristics of a carbon isotope ratio method for detecting doping with testosterone based on urine diols: Controls and athletes with elevated testosterone/epitestosterone ratios," *Clinical Chemistry*, 47: 292–300.

Bashin, S., Storer, T.W., Berman, N., Callegari, C., Clevenger, B., Phillips, J., Bunnell, T.J., Tricker, R., Shirazi, A., and Casaburi, R. (1996) "The effects of supraphysiologic doses of testosterone on muscle size and strength in normal men," *New England Journal of Medicine*, 335: 1–7.

Bidlingmaier, M. and Strasburger, C.J. (2007) "Technology insight: Detecting growth hormone abuse in athletes," *Nature Clinical Practice*, 3: 769–77.

Blackledge, R.D. (2009) "Bad science: The instrumental data in the Floyd Landis case (Editorial)," *Clinica Chimica Acta*, 406(1–2): 8–13.

Catlin, D.H. (2001) "Pharmacokinetics of pharmaceutical testosterone and T/Es in subjects with low and high baseline T/Es: Assessment of the ethnic differences and of the sensitivity of various carbon isotope ratio methods relative to T/E." Available online at: www.wada-ama.org/rtecontent/document/c2_2001.pdf (accessed July 14, 2010).

Catlin, D., Howe, C., Lasne, F. Nissen-Lie, G., Pascual, J.A., and Saugy, M. (2004) "WADA Technical Document TD2004EPO." WADA. Available online at: www.wada-ama.org/rtecontent/document/td2004epo_en.pdf (accessed July 14, 2010).

Catlin, D., Fitch, K., and Ljungqvist, A. (2008) "Medicine and science in the fight against doping in sport," *Journal of Internal Medicine*, 264(2): 99–114.

Cox, A. and Bratina, M. (2007) "Wrongful conviction in the United States." Paper presented at the Annual Meeting of the American Society of Criminology, Atlanta Marriott Marquis, Atlanta, Georgia, November 13, 2007.

DeSimone, B. (2007) "Landis grilled on final day of testimony." Available online at: http://sports.espn.go.com/oly/cycling/columns/story?columnist=desimone_bonnie&id=2879160 (accessed July 14, 2010).

Diver, M.J. (2006) "Analytical and physiological factors affecting the interpretation of serum testosterone concentration in men." *Annals of Clinical Biochemistry*, 43: 3–12.

Doessing, S. and Kjaer, M. (2005) "Growth hormone and connective tissue in exercise," *Scandinavian Journal of Medicine and Science in Sports*, 15(4): 202–10.

Ford, B.D. (2010) "Landis admits doping, accuses Lance." Available online at: http://sports.espn.go.com/oly/cycling/news/story?id=5203604 (accessed May 21, 2010).

Fotheringham, W. (2004) "Inquiry into Belgian cyclist's death raises new fears over EPO," *The Guardian*. Available online at: www.guardian.co.uk/sport/2004/feb/16/cycling.cycling1 (accessed July 14, 2010).

Guay, A.T. (2002) "Screening for androgen deficiency in women: Methodological and interpretive issues," *Fertility and Sterility*, 77(suppl. 4): S83–8.

Gudjónsson, B. (n.d) "Drugs in sport." IAAF Medical and Anti-Doping Commission Medical Manual. Available online at: www.iaaf.org/mm/Document/imported/42026.pdf (accessed July 14, 2010).

Harding, L. (2005) "Forgotten victims of East German doping take their battle to court: Athletes who were given drugs to compete in the name of communism seek £8 m compensation," *The Guardian*. Available online at: www.guardian.co.uk/sport/2005/nov/01/athletics.gdnsport3 (accessed July 14, 2010).

Havlikova, H., Hill, M., Hampl, R., and Stárka, L. (2002) "Sex- and age-related changes in epitestosterone in relation to pregnenolone sulfate and testosterone in normal subjects," *Journal of Clinical Endocrinology and Metabolism*, 87(5): 2225–31.

Hickoksports.com (2009) "Weightlifting 3: Weightlifting in the U.S." HickockSports.com. Available online at: www.hickoksports.com/history/weightlifting03.shtml (accessed July 14, 2010).

Hoffman, A.R. et al. (2008) "Systematic review: The effects of growth hormone on athletic performance," *Annals of Internal Medicine*: 747–58.

Houlihan, B. (1997) *Sport, policy, and politics: A comparative analysis*, New York: Routledge.

Huff, C.R. (2003) "Wrongful conviction: Causes and public policy issues," *Criminal Justice Magazine*, 8(1).

Jelkmann, W. (2007) "Recombinant EPO production—Points the nephrologist should know," *Nephrology Dialysis Transplantation*.

Juvonen, E., Ikkala, E., Fyhrquist, F., and Ruutu, T. (1991) "Autosomal dominant erythrocytosis caused by increased sensitivity to erythropoietin," *Blood*, 78(11) (Dec. 1): 3066–9.

Kolata, G. (2008) "Men, women and speed. Two words: Got testosterone?" *The New York Times*, Aug. 21. Available online at: www.nytimes.com/2008/08/22/sports/olympics/22women.html (accessed July 15, 2010).

Lasne, F. and de Ceaurriz, J. (2000) "Recombinant erythropoietin in urine," *Nature*, 405: 635.

Lasne, F., Martin, L., Martin, J.A., and de Ceaurriz, J. (2009) "Detection of continuous erythropoietin receptor activator in blood and urine in anti-doping control," Letters to the Editor, *Haematologica*, 94(6): 888–90.

Levine, B.D. (2008) "VO_2 max: What do we know, and what do we still need to know?" *Journal of Physiology*, 586(1)(Jan. 1): 25–34.

Lundby, C., Achman-Andersen, N.J., Thomsen, N.J., Norgaard, A.M., and Robach, P. (2008) "Testing for recombinant human erythropoietin in urine: Problems associated with current anti-doping testing," *Journal of Applied Physiology*, 105: 417–19.

Melmed, S. (2004) "Pituitary." WebMD.

National Research Council of the National Academies (2009) *Strengthening forensic science in the United States: A path forward*, Washington, DC: The National Academies Press.

Rigozzi, A. (2008) "Legal opinion on the conformity of the exclusion of 'team athletes' from organized training during their period of ineligibility with Swiss law, including the general principles of proportionality and equal treatment," WADA, 6–7. Available online at: www.wada-ama.org/rtecontent/document/Rigozzi_Legal_Opinion_July_2008.pdf (accessed July 14, 2010).

Saugy, M., Robinson, N., Saudan, C., Baume, N., Avois, L., and Mangin, P. (2006) "Human growth hormone doping in sport," *British Journal of Sports Medicine*, 40(July, Suppl. 1): i35–9.

Schulze, J.J., Lundmark, J., Garle, M., Skilving, I., Ekström, L., and Rane, A. (2008) "Doping test results dependent on genotype of uridine diphospho-glucuronosyl transferase 2B17, the major enzyme for testosterone glucuronidation," *Journal of Clinical Endocrinology and Metabolism*, 93(7): 2500–6.

Stray-Gundersen, J., Videman, T., Penttilä, I., and Lereim, I. (2003) "Abnormal hematologic profiles in elite cross-country skiers: Blood doping or?" *Clinical Journal of Sports Medicine*, 13(3)(May): 132–7.

Sydney Morning Herald (2008) "Ricco busted at Tour with help of planted molecule: Fahey." Available online at: www.smh.com.au/news/tourdefrance/ricco-busted-at-tour-with-help-of-planted-molecule-fahey/2008/07/23/1216492496759.html (accessed July 14, 2010).

Todd, T. (1992) "Anabolic steroids in sport," in *Sports and exercise science*, Chicago: University of Illinois.

USA Today (2007) "Milestones in Don Catlin's career." Available online at: www.usatoday.com/sports/olympics/2007–02–28-catlin-timeline_x.htm (accessed July 14, 2010).

WADA (2009a) "The 2009 Prohibited List." Available online at: www.wada-ama.org/Documents/World_Anti-Doping_Program/WADP-Prohibited-list/WADA_Prohibited_List_2009_EN.pdf (accessed July 14, 2010).

WADA (2009b) *World Anti-Doping Code*. Available online at: www.wada-ama.org/rtecontent/document/code_v2009_En.pdf (accessed July 15, 2010).

WADA (n.d) 'Clarification about the EPO detection method." Available online at: www.wada-ama.org/rtecontent/document/EPO_QA.pdf (accessed July 14, 2010).

WebMD (n.d.) "Testosterone." Available online at: http://men.webmd.com/testosterone-15738 (accessed July 14, 2010).

WebMD (n.d.) "Erythropoietin stimulators." Available online at: www.webmd.com/a-to-z-guides/erythropoietin-stimulators (accessed July 14, 2010).

Williams, M.H., Wesseldine, S., Somma, T., and Schuster, R. (1981) "The effect of induced erythrocythemia upon 5-mile treadmill run time," *Medicine and Science in Sports and Excercise*, 13(3): 169–75.

Yesalis, C.E. and Bahrke, M.S. (2002) "History of doping in sports," in M.S. Bahrke and C.E. Yesalis (eds), *Performance-enhancing substances in sport and exercise*, Champaign, IL: Human Kinetics.

3 Longitudinal profiling, sports arbitration and the woman who had nothing to lose

Some thoughts on *Pechstein* v. *International Skating Union*

David McArdle

Introduction

The juridical field's (Bourdieu 1987) willingness to recognise that sports disputes are often best resolved by sporting organisations themselves, rather than by the courts, is perhaps the most important aspect of the relationship between sport and the law. Sports that have been willing to develop impartial and transparent disciplinary mechanisms, where both parties are given the opportunity to present their case before appropriately qualified decision-makers, in proceedings not tainted by bias or impropriety, can ordinarily expect to carry out their functions without attracting judicial intervention. It does not, however, follow that there is no potential for judicial oversight, and sports-specific dispute resolution systems such as the Court of Arbitration for Sport (CAS) may thus be regarded as an aspect of the juridification (Cowan 2004) of sports. Parties are obliged (or at least afforded the opportunity) to seek resolution through a forum that may be cheaper, quicker and more responsive to the peculiarities of sport than are the 'ordinary courts', but those bodies still need to abide by legal principles and they are not 'above the law'.

However, a common factor among arbitral bodies is that, historically, there has been no expectation that their decisions will be explicitly and consistently informed by the rulings of earlier arbitral bodies in a manner akin to judicial precedent. Moreover, this has been the case even when a dispute shares marked factual similarities with the subject-matter of an earlier arbitral award. There is no system of binding authority in arbitration, and

> each award stands on its own; it may well happen that an arbitral tribunal . . . will arrive at a different conclusion from another tribunal faced with the same problem. The award of the first tribunal . . . may be of persuasive effect, but no more.
>
> (Blackaby *et al.* 2009: para 1.1113)

Although this 'traditional' approach to arbitration can certainly be discerned in many decisions of sports dispute resolution panels that defy both logic and legal norms, some of the CAS's determinations have been explicitly informed by both its earlier rulings and by wider legal principles. This comparative legal sophistication, together with the CAS's robust procedures (Mangan 2009), the ever-increasing scope and importance of its jurisdiction and its potential to safeguard competitors against the procedural ineptitude, mendacity or sheer incompetence on the part of decision-makers (McArdle 2009), have contributed to 'the recognition and enforcement of CAS awards domestically and internationally. There is a growing body of private international sports law which some claim might soon be seen to override national law' (Anderson 2010: para 3.01).

This potential for sports law to override national law is susceptible to exaggeration, but this increased juridical sophistication on the part of the CAS is certainly to be welcomed. The application of a coherent corpus of arbitration principles to sports dispute resolution, if underpinned by appropriate reference to its own earlier determinations and wider legal authority, will help locate the CAS in the same firmament as other prominent arbitral systems[1] that, for the most part, inspire confidence among those who either choose to, or are compelled to, submit to their jurisdiction. That, in turn, would represent a pivotal feature of what some will inevitably continue to describe as the *lex sportiva* – a dreadful cod-Latin phrase ('the law of little buckets') that, notwithstanding its lexical shortcomings, has come to connote that body of statutory and judicial authority, secondary sources and procedural rules which comprises what others prefer to call simply 'sports law'.

How striking, then, to note that in *Claudia Pechstein* v. *International Skating Union* CAS 2009/A/1912, 1913, the CAS was able to determine the matter without any consideration either of previous CAS judgments or of the wider legal principles that one would have expected to be raised, given that this was the first CAS judgment to deal with the problematic use of longitudinal profiling as a means of detecting doping violations. There is little discussion of *Meca-Medina and Majcen* v. *FINA* CAS 99/A/234, the subsequent ruling of the European Court of Justice's (ECJ) seminal ruling in *Meca-Medina* v. *The Commission* (2006) ECR I-6991, or indeed any other decisions of the CAS or the courts. But longitudinal profiling is legally problematic, and the doubts concerning its legality are not going to disappear simply because they were not advanced on this occasion. Detailed consideration of those issues must wait until another occasion, but this chapter uses *Pechstein* as an opportunity to discuss the scope of the CAS's jurisdiction, to reflect on some of the arguments that were raised (although they fell ultimately on stony ground) and briefly to highlight some of those legal issues that might arise in the future.

Party autonomy and sports arbitration

It would be wrong to suppose that arbitral bodies that may be called upon to resolve sports disputes are somehow immune from legal principle. The putative autonomy of the parties is vitiated by the arbitrators' need to ensure compliance with the *lex loci arbitri* – the laws and rules that are applicable to arbitral proceedings under the law of whichever state the parties have decided (whether by choice or by default) is to govern the process. The CAS is based in Switzerland, and Swiss law provides less potential for intervention than is the case with other jurisdictions (see, for example, the attempted use of 'long-arm' statutes by the state of Ohio in *Reynolds* v. *IAAF* (1992) US Dist LEXIS 8625, or the judgment of the English court in *Gasser* v. *Stinson* (1988) unreported, 15 June (Queen's Bench Division)). In the case of the CAS, Switzerland's Federal Code on Private International Law is the provision that deals with the relationship between it and the *lex loci arbitri*.[2] The code gives the parties considerable freedom on such matters as choice of law, composition of the arbitral panel and so forth, and, under Article 190, there are very limited grounds upon which the decision can be challenged,[3] but grounds do exist, and there is still a role for judicial oversight. Indeed, there have been occasions where the Swiss court has corrected a CAS determination, on the grounds that it conflicts with the code. In *Gundel* v. *FEI* CAS 1992/A/63, for example, the court stated that the relationship between the CAS and the IOC was such that the former could not truly be regarded as independent of the latter. The CAS thus had to be reconstituted as an independent entity in order to give validity to any decisions it reached in cases where the IOC was a party.

Furthermore, in *Meca-Medina* v. *FINA*, the CAS noted that it was obliged additionally to consider European competition law if there was a close connection between the subject-matter of the dispute and the European Union (para 4.9, citing *AEK Athens and Slavia Prague* v. *UEFA* CAS 98/200), and it would be open to the European courts to intervene if the CAS failed to do so. Meca-Medina hailed from an EU member state (Spain), while Majcen, who was Slovenian, also had certain rights under EU law by virtue of that country's then Association Agreement with the EU.[4] Accordingly, in that case, the panel proceeded 'on the premise that the same protection [Meca-Medina] enjoys can be derived in respect of [Majcen]' (paragraph 4.8). In the present case, Pechstein's German nationality clearly gave rise to a sufficiently 'close connection' between the EU and the subject-matter of her dispute, and even the relatively hands-off approach of the Swiss courts in the exercising of their supervisory jurisdiction does not defeat the relevance of European law. Pechstein's decision to argue neither European Union law nor the European Convention on Human Rights (ECHR) seems remiss in retrospect, but time was of the essence and Pechstein played a tactical game in her search for a ruling that would allow her to compete at the Winter Olympics. However, the complexities of longitudinal profiling demand a far more robust legal scrutiny than occurred here: her arguments were weak, and the CAS had little difficulty in rebutting them but, when a similar case arises in the future (as it surely will), legal advisers may well decide that there is little merit in the *Pechstein* approach, preparing their client for a long haul through the domestic or European courts if their overtures are rejected by the CAS.

Blood profiling

Claudia Pechstein's case centred on blood profiling, which has been developed over the past decade in response to the use of a synthetic version of recombinant human erythropoietin (rHuEPO), which accelerates red blood cell production in bone marrow. This can be beneficial to athletes because rHuEPO can increase the number of red blood cells in circulation and 'dramatically improve[s] the oxygen-carrying capacity of the blood and therefore endurance performance' (Parisotto *et al.* 2001: 128). Other studies have documented the benefits of moderate rHuEPO use on the quality of life among the wider populace, including life satisfaction and happiness in patients with chronic renal failure, heightened libido and improved sexual 'performance' (Ninot *et al.* 2006). From a sporting perspective, rHuEPO use is generally associated with endurance sports (hence, the high-profile involvement of those disciplines' governing bodies in the development of blood profiling), but it has also been shown that,

> an enhanced oxygen carrying capacity can bestow a marked advantage in events lasting as little as 45 seconds, as well as recovery from intermittent efforts and general training drills. It is prudent to consider most sports (individual and team) at risk of blood doping.
>
> (Ashenden 2002: 225)

In the late 1990s, haematologists started to develop ever more sophisticated procedures that could be used to detect the illicit use of rHuEPO. These procedures focused on the role of reticulocytes (rather than on other haematological parameters such as haemoglobin) 'because of their particular sensitivity in identifying bone marrow stimulation, especially when recombinant human erythropoietin is fraudulently used' (Banfi 2008: 188). In addition to helping identify illicit substance use, reticulocyte evaluation has a significant role in protecting the health of professional athletes (many of whom have an increased risk of anaemia (Banfi 2008: 189), but earlier research had revealed that the manner in which reticulocytes were counted, the time and manner in which blood samples were drawn and stored, and the influence of training, competition, altitude and haematological or genetic abnormalities all presented considerable barriers to the development of an effective 'test' that could be used in anti-doping.

Athletes can experience a performance benefit for several weeks after ceasing to use rHuEPO, but, upon cessation, there will be a significant reduction in reticulocyte count because the body reduces both endogenous erythropoietin production and reticulocyte release until the red cell count returns to normal (Banfi 2008). In long-distance cycling and other endurance sports, athletes who return an abnormally high red cell mass in haematocrit testing can be prohibited for competing for more than two weeks on medical grounds (high haematocrit levels are particularly associated with an increased risk of deep vein thrombosis), but up to 5 per cent of athletes may exceed the 'safe' threshold because of genetic factors. Hence, there is patently a risk that many athletes could be unfairly prevented from competing (Banfi 2008), and, in turn, this means than any attempt to use haematocrit levels as an evidential basis for a doping offence is untenable. It had also been noted that testing athletes' urine samples for the presence of rHuEPO was of limited utility, because,

> although a small amount is detectable unchanged in the urine for 24–96 hours after each injection, once the red cell mass has been boosted, the athlete can substantially reduce their dosage of rHuEPO. During this maintenance phase, it is difficult to discern the hematologic profile of a maintenance user from that of a non-user.
>
> (Ashenden 2002: 225–6)

Establishing an effective test for rHuEPO was thus undermined by the concern that 'altitude/training/genetic factors (which) may also be associated with a transient increase in erythropoiesis (albeit of a much smaller magnitude) might lead to mistakenly accusing an athlete when no drug was taken' (Ashenden 2002: 228). There was also a clear need to combine any effective in-competition test with reliable out-of-competition random testing, given the need for rHuEPO users to engage in the prohibited activity for several weeks prior to a competition. However, by 2002, the practicality of using a mobile blood testing facility that 'could relocate to a remote competition site and would make place-getters subject to blood testing immediately after competition' (Ashenden 2002: 229) had been established: the technology to allow many samples to be taken and analysed quickly was in place, and a similar facility could be used for random testing too. Moreover, the same machine could be used consistently across all sports to eliminate any technical variations that might skew the results.

Procedures that would allow an athlete's blood profile to be monitored over a period of time were also being developed around the same time, and the International Cycling Union (UCI) seems to have been the first international governing body to develop a procedure under which competitors were required to give blood samples as part of the regular medical examinations they were obliged to undergo as a condition of their participation in UCI events. Since 2008, this has been a central aspect of their 'biological passport', alongside the results of the urine and other tests.

The UCI website states that:

> Blood and urine samples may be collected during a race, during preparation/training periods or during the non-competitive season. Riders should expect to be required to provide a blood or urine sample at any time of the year and in any place. All samples will be collected by authorised UCI sample collection officers. Blood collectors will have appropriate qualifications approved by the UCI.
>
> (UCI 2007)

The International Skating Union's (ISU) Communication No. 1520, which makes provision for blood testing, is in broadly similar terms. It provides that:

> The ISU will conduct Blood Testing at various ISU Championships, World Cup Events and other International Events as deemed necessary by the ISU. Blood screening or Testing is conducted by a specialist Anti-Doping Agency appointed by the ISU under the direction of the ISU Medical Advisors. Out-of-Competition Blood Tests may be carried out at any time by specialist Anti-Doping Agencies, appointed by the ISU or WADA.
>
> (ISU 2008)

This communication lays down the detail of the procedures that were at issue in *Pechstein and Deutsche Eisschnellauf Gemeinschaft (DEFG)* v. *International Skating Union* CAS 2009/A/1912, 1913.

Pechstein *v.* International Skating Union: *the arguments*

Claudia Pechstein is one of speed skating's most successful exponents, having won five Olympic gold medals and two bronze medals between 1992 and 2006. Between 2000 and April 2009, she underwent many doping control tests, both in and out of competition, and she gave over ninety blood samples under the ISU's blood profiling programme. The last twelve of those were given between January and April 2009. The ISU asserted that 'during the months of January and February 2009 the Athlete changed her whereabouts on numerous occasions rendering it especially difficult, if not impossible, to organise any out-of competition testing on her' (CAS judgment, paragraph 68). The implication was that, during those months, Pechstein had changed her whereabouts in order to facilitate her use of rHuEPO and thus artificially stimulate 'her body's capacity to produce red blood cells that carry oxygen to muscles and organs, with the evident purpose of reducing fatigue and attaining an unfair advantage over her competitors. In short, blood doping' (paragraph 191).

Pechstein is thus significant because it involved sanctioning an athlete who had never returned an adverse analytical finding but was condemned on the basis of her blood values and profile. 'The Panel (was) thus mindful that this case involves issues that have not previously had to be decided by CAS Panels' (paragraph 78), although there were some parallels with the American Arbitration Association's ruling in *USADA* v. *Michelle Collins*.

The ISU's regulations provide for a blood profile that monitors participants' haemoglobin, haematocrit and percentage of reticulocytes (hereafter '%retics'). The last of these was of particular relevance to this case, because it serves as an indicator of potential blood doping (paragraph 7), and, although the upper end of the 'normal' %retics level is deemed to be 2.4, many of Pechstein's readings had been considerably in excess of that level. In particular, on 6 February 2009 – the day before a 2009 World Championship event at Hamar, Norway, commenced – all participants gave blood samples, and Pechstein's %retics value was measured at 3.49. She was tested twice more on 7 February, and her readings were 3.54 and 3.38, respectively. These findings were communicated to Pechstein's domestic governing body (the DEFG), which took the decision to withdraw her from the competition, even though her haemoglobin and haematocrit levels were not so high as to provide a 'no-start' situation, where the ISU prohibits the athlete from competing for the next 18 days in order to safeguard their health status (ISU 2008: paragraph 4.2).

On 18 February 2009, another test showed that her %retics had declined to 1.37. Such high readings being followed by a much lower-level reading ten days later give rise to a suspicion that the athlete had been engaging in some form of blood doping, and, on 5 March 2009, the ISU's Disciplinary Commission duly held that Pechstein has violated its new anti-doping policy (which had come into force on 1 January 2009 and accorded with the terms of the new WADA code) and imposed a 2-year ban (CAS judgment: paragraphs 12, 13).

In July 2009, the athlete and her domestic governing body appealed to the CAS (as they were entitled to do under the ISU's rules and Article R47 of the CAS Code). In the interim, she sought a stay of the decision until the CAS ruled on the matter or, failing that, the right to use appropriate skating facilities in order to assist her training for the 2010 Winter Olympics. Pechstein was duly granted leave to train, but not to compete, and, after much procedural wrangling (paragraphs 16–32), the hearing took place on 22–23 October 2009, the parties agreeing that Swiss law would apply to the proceedings (paragraph 76).

Pechstein's defences were wide-ranging, but rather than include the legal arguments that one might have anticipated had time not been of the essence or if the case had been fully argued before the courts, they concentrated on sample collection and testing and the propriety of the ISU's regulations – arguments that are the staple fare of athletes' appeals but that are doomed to failure unless it can be shown that the agreed procedures had not been followed. She contended that, because the ISU had only allowed blood profiles to be used as evidence of a doping violation since 1 January 2009 (when its new provisions came into effect), only blood samples collected after that date could be used in evidence against her (paragraph 47). She also contended that ISU blood profiling rules provided that the blood samples had to be analysed in WADA-accredited laboratories, and that WADA's standards governing collection and chain-of-custody applied (paragraph 48); that the upper limit of 2.4 %retics was not generally accepted in sports medicine (paragraph 49); and that, for several reasons, the blood screening data were unreliable and not appropriate for statistical analysis (paragraph 50). Pechstein also challenged the accuracy of the machine used to analyse her samples (paragraph 51), stressed that her haemoglobin and haematocrit levels had always been within ISU limits and asserted that her high %retics values were 'likely' due to a hitherto-undiagnosed chronic blood disorder and/or a genetic abnormality (paragraph 52). Finally, she argued that, with regard to the burden and standard of proof, the ISU 'must convince the Panel to a level very close to "beyond reasonable doubt" that all alternative causes for the increase in %retics can be excluded and that, additionally, the Athlete had an intention to use blood doping" (paragraph 53). The CAS summarily dealt with this matter by asserting that there was no need to show intent or fault, because the putative strict liability principle applied in doping cases (paragraph 120), and the 'comfortable satisfaction' test, which applied under the ISU's rules, was well known in CAS practice, had withstood the scrutiny of the Swiss federal tribunal in several previous cases (paragraph 124), and would consequently be applied in this case (paragraph 126).

Pechstein's domestic governing body, the DESG, 'contends that it has a neutral role in the proceedings (but) essentially supports most of the arguments raised by the Athlete' (paragraphs 55, 56). In addition, the DESG argued that any violation must have occurred before 30 January 2009 and, because the ISU made reference to the blood profiling results obtained prior to 6 February 2009 (rather than just relying on the Hamar figures), the ISU had breached its Rules of Procedure, Article 8.1, which provides that complaints have to be lodged within 30 days of it learning about the alleged offence (the complaint was lodged with the ISU's Disciplinary Commission on 5 March). The DESG said that, in effect, the ISU had used the Hamar tests as an opportunity to 'buy time', and that its case had actually been built upon Pechstein's earlier test results.

In rebuttal of the athlete's arguments, the ISU stated that it had implemented its own procedures for blood profiling in July 2008 and was not obliged to wait for WADA to draft specific rules for blood doping (which it was in the throes of doing at that time) before it could develop such rules for its own sport; it also drew an important distinction between the blood profiling programme – which 'focuses on measuring blood parameters rather than on detecting prohibited substances' – and anti-doping controls, which have far more complex testing and analysis procedures and were accompanied by stringent rules and procedures that were unnecessary in the context of blood profiling. There was no evidence that any of the procedures regulating blood profiling had been departed from, and that 'the use of a longitudinal (blood) profile as evidence of doping is legally admissible since it is an evidential/procedural rule to which the prohibition against the retroactive application of the law does not apply' (paragraph 65). The ISU also said that intent was relevant only in cases of 'attempted use' (rather than occasions where use had actually occurred); that it could not provide evidence relating to possible blood diseases, because Pechstein had refused to cooperate in its enquiries into that possibility; but that in any event the significant fluctuations in her %retics could not be explained by any known blood disorder.

The CAS judgment

The CAS determined that, under the ISU rules, the 30-day period began to run only once the ISU 'learned about' the alleged offence – a phrase which,

> must be properly understood as the moment at which the ISU had reasonable suspicion of the alleged offence. Unlike allegations based on an adverse analytical finding, doping charges based on longitudinal (blood) profiling require a series of tests and evaluation of the results by the anti-doping organisations experts. For this reason, the ISU had not 'learned' about the offence and was not in a position to raise charges until its medical advisors had determined that Ms Pechstein's blood profile constituted – in their opinion – sufficient proof of the use of a prohibited method.
>
> (Paragraph 91)

The CAS stated that the Hamar competition tests were 'at the core' of the case, and there was no evidence of the ISU using them in order to 'buy time' as the DESG had suggested (paragraph 92). Further, Pechstein's contention that she had never consented to the ISU using her blood profile as evidence of blood doping was summarily rejected on the grounds that, under its regulations, any person taking part in the ISU's 'international activities' is bound to comply with all its provisions, and the anti-doping rules cited 'conclusions drawn from the profile of the skater's blood or urine samples' as a specific example of a reasonably reliable means by which an anti-doping rule violation could be established (paragraph 101). 'In willingly registering for international skating competitions sanctioned by the ISU, she obviously expressed her acceptance of ISU rules and regulations, including the [anti-doping rules] . . . When they accede to competition, athletes cannot pick and choose the rules they like' (paragraphs 98, 99). This clearly gives rise to concerns about how much credence should be attached to the athletes' putative acceptance of the rules, given that one either signs up to the anti-doping regime or one does not compete at the international level; but if athletes wish to voice their opposition to anti-doping regimes (and there is no evidence that Pechstein or the wider firmament of skaters had opposed them beforehand), this has to be done long before the disciplinary hearing or subsequent application to the CAS. In any event, the CAS noted that the ISU's rules stated that profiling was just an 'evidentiary means' by which a doping offence could be demonstrated, and so,

> the only relevant issue is whether longitudinal blood profiling can be regarded as among the 'reasonably reliable means' to prove the use of a prohibited method . . . its utilisation for anti-doping purposes does not constitute a retrospective application of a substantive anti-doping rule.
>
> (Paragraph 108)

The CAS further asserted that, 'even in cases of adverse analytical findings, departures from WADA international standards do not invalidate per se the analytical results, as long as the ADO establishes that such departure did not cause the adverse analytical finding' (paragraph 117). It stated that the WADA draft Biological Passport Guidelines could not be regarded as setting down 'minimum standards' (as Pechstein contended), and, even when they were finalised (which occurred on 1 December 2009), the Biological Passport Guidelines would not become mandatory. However, this stands in clear contradiction to WADA's own position: the introduction to the WADA Guidelines states that the Athlete Biological Passport

> includes mandatory requirements for collection, transportation, analysis of blood samples and results management that anti-doping organisations wishing to adopt WADA's model will have to follow in order to ensure consistency of application and to comply with the WADA Code and the International Standards. These mandatory technical documents will be incorporated into WADA's International Standard for Testing and International Standard for Laboratories.

For the avoidance of doubt, it is now clear that governing bodies would be very well advised to ensure their blood profiling provisions replicate those laid down by WADA. If they do not, a governing body must be able to advance very strong, clear arguments as to why it has departed from what WADA has laid down, and it ought not expect too sympathetic a hearing from either the CAS or the courts if its decision to do so is subsequently challenged.

The CAS reiterated that Pechstein had been accused of a doping offence in respect of the %retics findings at Hamar, in early February 2009, and the sample taken on 18 February. Consideration of her earlier results

> may help in understanding and interpreting the Athlete's blood values as found on 6, 7 and 18 February 2009 but it is strictly a question of considering the evidence on record and its scientific reliability, not involving retrospective application of any new anti-doping rule to old facts.
>
> (Paragraph 107)

It continued:

> The Panel would have no hesitation in holding that new scientifically sound evidentiary methods, even not specifically mentioned in anti-doping rules, can be used at any time to investigate and discover past anti-doping rule violations that went undetected, with the only constraint deriving from the eight-year time limitation and the timely initiation of disciplinary proceedings. As long as the substantive rule sanctioning a given conduct as doping is in force prior to the conduct, the resort to a new evidentiary method does not constitute a case of retrospective application of the law.
>
> (Paragraph 109)

With regard to the athlete's allegations that the collection, administration and storage of her blood samples had not complied with the provisions of the WADA code, the CAS asserted that, because this was not a case of adverse analytical finding, the ISU was not obliged to follow WADA's provisions on those matters. Instead, 'in the Panel's opinion, any reasonably reliable practice of sample collection, post-test administration, transport of samples, analytical process and documentation would suffice' (paragraph 116). With that in mind, the CAS engaged in a long analysis of the collection, storage and sampling procedures that had been adopted by the ISU in July 2008 and utilised at the Hamar event. It found that Pechstein had never challenged the procedure, nor asserted a desire to have the samples taken by her own doctor rather than an ISU official, and that she had never protested against any of the sampling procedures nor been able to point out any of the material flaws in the process as applied to her (paragraph 137). It highlighted the distinction between the procedures for blood testing for screening purposes and those for post-event anti-doping control (paragraphs 133, 134) and stressed that:

> The analytical process followed by the [testing] laboratories does not require any person from the laboratory personnel to open the [sample], since it is placed directly . . . into the analysing machine . . . Unlike in anti-doping where the laboratory (by means of a complex and costly investigation) looks for prohibited substances yielding an adverse

> analytical finding, in blood screening the laboratory simply measures (by means of an automated machine) certain hematological parameters.
>
> (Paragraph 146)

The CAS had no reservations about the chain of custody ('the Panel has heard and examined evidence that does not leave any reasonable doubts as to the transportation conditions' (paragraph 144)). Pechstein further contended that physical stress due to cold temperatures, altitude, intense exercise, pressure on the foot cause by her skates and blades, menstrual bleeding, infection or the fact that the tests were unequally distributed throughout the year could have caused her adverse profile. Nevertheless, the panel was not swayed:

> The Panel has not found the above-mentioned justifications, nor the few others that the Appellants have thrown in during the course of the proceedings, to be convincing . . . The athlete's multifarious explanations imply that all of a sudden a perfectly fit athlete incurred all sorts of unlikely situations and misfortunes that in some way affected her blood values; it appears to the Panel to be too astonishing a coincidence to be reasonably credible.
>
> (Paragraph 197)

Medical tests carried out in advance of the hearing had returned no untoward results, and the panel was comfortably satisfied that Pechstein's abnormal %retics values 'must derive from the athlete's illicit manipulation of her own blood, which remains the only reasonable alternative source of such abnormal values' (paragraph 210). It upheld the FIS's original sanction of a 2-year ban.

The initial CAS hearing did not herald the end of the affair. On 9 December 2009, the Swiss Federal Tribunal granted Pechstein an injunction that partially prevented the imposition of that 2-year ban, pending a full hearing of her application. The injunction was granted under the extraordinary 'super provisional' (*superprovisorisch)* power under Article 104 of the Federal Supreme Court law (*Bundesgerichts gesetz*), but it was partial to the extent that it only allowed her to train for, and compete at, one specific 3000 m event (to be held in Salt Lake City on 11 December), rather than allowing her to compete at other distances and in any forthcoming events through which she might secure qualification. Salt Lake City thus represented her last opportunity to qualify for the Winter Olympics, but she failed to achieve the top-eight finish that she needed (Krouse 2009). Undaunted, in the two weeks after Salt Lake City, Pechstein made repeated efforts to obtain further injunctive relief that would allow her to participate in various 1500 m competitions, in team events and in two upcoming World Championship races in Norway and Holland, prior to the full hearing of her appeal,[5] but all to no avail. On 26 January 2010, the Tribunal refused to grant her the opportunity to try out again at events in the last weeks before Vancouver and, on that occasion, intimated that her appeal was unlikely to succeed when it was finally heard in full (Knoblauch 2010). Consequently, when the Federal Tribunal heard her appeal on 10 February 2010, it asserted that Article 190 provided no grounds for reviewing the factual determinations of the CAS, and neither could it entertain new evidence.[6]

Less than a week later, the redoubtable Pechstein appealed to the CAS's ad hoc division at Vancouver, delivering herself of a wide-ranging application that, in effect, invited the ad hoc tribunal to overturn the CAS's November ruling and force the IOC and the German Olympic Committee to allow her to compete (*Pechstein* v. *Deutscher Olmpischer Sortbund and the IOC* CAS No OG 10/04). Her application was rejected on the grounds that there had been no 'decision' at the Winter Olympics (or in the 10 days prior to the opening ceremony) that the ad hoc tribunal could entertain under the terms of the CAS Arbitration Rules for the Olympic Games, Article 1, and that, even if it did have jurisdiction to hear the case, the ad hoc tribunal was not a competent tribunal for the purpose of challenging her ineligibility (paragraph 4.13). Prior to that, the Swiss Tribunal's willingness to grant her injunction in December, albeit to a very limited extent, simply reinforced that the CAS is indeed subject to its supervisory jurisdiction (as discussed above), whereas the February judgment provides some guidance on the limits of that jurisdiction and is consistent with the Tribunal's earlier case law on CAS appeals.

Future developments?

At the time of writing, it is unclear if Pechstein will choose to pursue the matter through the courts, but, if she does, any arguments will have to be far more legally robust than what has been advanced hitherto. Conduct of the case thus far suggests that one can expect further arguments to the effect that the CAS panel erred in adopting a 'comfortable satisfaction' test or in its application of it, or that it had erred in departing from WADA guidelines. In the alternative, maybe new scientific evidence will indicate Pechstein's hitherto-undiagnosed medical condition does indeed exist, or she will be able to adduce new scientific evidence that casts doubts on the accuracy of longitudinal profiling in general, or testing for synthetic rHuEPO in particular.

Aside from these last two areas, it is difficult to discern anything that either the CAS or the testing authorities might have done that could amount to so egregious an error that it could be regarded as fatal to the whole process and, as per *Meca-Medina*, there would still be the difficulty of showing that any alternative scientific explanations for her %retics undermined the strong evidence that she had engaged in blood doping. But perhaps there are more fundamental legal issues that will be argued, either as well as or instead of these. It is at least arguable that the sheer number of blood tests that are taken for the purposes of longitudinal profiling is excessive and contravenes Article 8 of the ECHR. Between 2000 and April 2009, Pechstein gave over ninety blood samples under the ISU's blood profiling programme, and, to those of us who do not fully understand the scientific basis of blood profiling, that may seem a disproportionate interference with athletes' privacy rights and requires justification.

There is little in the case law that discusses the interference with Article 8(1) ECHR that a compulsory medical intervention undoubtedly entails (*Peters* v. *The Netherlands* (1994) 77-A DR 75), but that infringement has to be balanced against Article 8(2) ECHR, which allows for such interference where it is necessary for, inter alia, the protection of health. Analogy with the Privy Council decision in *Whitefield* v. *General Medical Council* (2003) HRLR 9 suggests that maybe the blood tests can be regarded as pursuing the legitimate aim of protecting the health of participants, for it is true that athletes are at a greater risk of anaemia than the general population (Banfi 2008: 189), and there is evidence that use of rHuEPO 'may cause a dangerous hedonic effect linked to endurance training . . . [our] findings suggest a clinical increase in global self-esteem with rHuEPO, which can have a euphoric effect on global self-perception' (Ninot *et al.*, 2006: 390). Ergo, perhaps the Article 8(2) justification can indeed be made – but, even if blood testing is justifiable in principle, the sheer number of tests to which athletes are subjected needs to be explained by reference to cogent medical grounds. The more nebulous arguments that concern 'fair play' and 'cheating' in sport have little relevance to human rights jurisprudence, although (in the wake of *Meca-Medina*) they might strike a chord if it is argued that longitudinal profiling contravenes European competition law. An alternative argument would be that Article 8 also states that there shall be no unwarranted interference by 'a public authority', and perhaps one might argue that the CAS itself is a court or tribunal that is a public authority and thus under an obligation to act consistently with ECHR rights; but it is hard to discern anything in the CAS's disposal of this case that may amount to a breach of that obligation.

She is now 38 years of age, and one wonders whether Claudia Pechstein will really see any merit in dragging out this sorry saga still further. If she feels her future work aspirations (media commentator, high-profile governing body member, sporting 'ambassador') depend upon her being exonerated, then perhaps she will advance the EU law and ECHR provisions that have hitherto been untested. If she does throw in her hand, then it will simply fall to others to make those arguments, but, either way, WADA's provisions on longitudinal profiling – and the CAS's support of it – do not sit easily with European law. Other possible arguments might include the EU laws on working time, health and safety law and data protection, in addition to the Article 8 Convention rights discussed above, and, while this author is not convinced that any of those arguments would be successful, one might also consider, in passing, the situation of the athlete who challenges longitudinal profiling on the grounds that any blood test cannot be reconciled with their religious beliefs and thus contravenes their right to freedom of thought, conscience or religion, as established under Article 9 ECHR (or the equivalent provisions that exist in other parts of the world). However, those athletes need to be raising their voices now if they are to have any credibility. That aside, the lesson to learn from *Pechstein* is that the complex legal issues that undoubtedly arise here are far more relevant than the essentially procedural matters that underpinned her appeal, and, although that inevitably means the timeliness of the remedy will have to be sacrificed upon the altar of legal certainty, such an approach will be necessary if those applicants are going to achieve more success than Pechstein has hitherto.

Finally, the ECJ's ruling in *Meca-Medina* clearly illustrates its willingness to accommodate the specialist knowledge of decision-makers such as the CAS, sports scientists and sports governing bodies, rather than substitute its own limited expertise – but it also demonstrates its obligation to oversee whether those bodies' use of their powers is necessary and proportionate when they have a negative impact on citizens of the European Union. Notwithstanding the arms-length approach of the Swiss courts in their supervision of the CAS and the balanced approach of the ECJ in *Meca-Medina*, the legal and scientific complexities of longitudinal profiling will doubtless ensure it represents a new dimension of the relationship between the sporting and juridical fields. Claudia Pechstein may go away, but the issues her case has raised will certainly not.

Notes

1 For example, those that deal with construction contracts or Internet domain name disputes.
2 See: www.tas-cas.org/en/arbitrage.asp/4–3-292–1023–4-1–1/5–0-1023–3-0–0/.
3 The grounds for challenge are restricted to: (i) that the tribunal was not properly constituted; (ii) its jurisdiction was incorrectly drawn; (iii) its decision went beyond the claim submitted to it or did not deal with all parts of the stated claim; and (iv) breach of one of the parties' rights to equal treatment and a fair hearing; incompatibility with public policy.
4 That status became otiose when Slovenia fully joined the EU in 2004.
5 See: http://jensweinreich.de/?p=6169.
6 See: www.bger.ch/mm_4a_612_2009_d.pdf.

References

Anderson, J. (2010) *Modern sports law*, Oxford: Hart.
Ashenden, M. (2002) 'A strategy to deter blood doping in sport', *Haematologica*, 87: 225.
Banfi, G. (2008) 'Reticulocytes in sports medicine', *Sports Medicine*, 38(3): 187.
Blackaby, N., Partasides, C., Redfern, A. and Hunter, M. (2009) *Redfern and Hunter on international arbitradion* (5th edition), Oxford: Oxford University Press.
Bourdieu, P. (1987) 'The force of law: towards a sociology of the juridical field', *Hastings Law Journal*, 38: 814.

Cowan, D. (2004) 'Legal consciousness; some observations', *Modern Law Review*, 67(6): 928.

ISU (2008) 'ISU procedures for blood testing'. Communication no. 1520. Available online at: http://isu.sportcentric.net/db//files/serve.php?id=1007 (accessed 29 June 2010).

Knoblauch, A. (2010) 'German speedskating champion loses doping ban case', *Los Angeles Times*, 26 January. Available online at: www.latimes.com/search/dispatcher.front?Query=Pechstein&target=article&sortby=display_time+descending (accessed 1 December 2010).

Krouse, K. (2009) 'Germany's Claudia Pechstein tries to restore reputation', *New York Times*, December 12, p. D3.

McArdle, D. (2009) 'Elite athletes and disability discrimination', *Cambrian Law Review*, 40: 49.

Mangan, M. (2009) 'The Court of Arbitration for Sport: current practice, emerging trends and future hurdles', *Arbitration International*, 25(4): 591.

Ninot, G., Connes, P. and Caillaud, C. (2006) 'Effects of recombinant human erythropoietin injections on physical self in endurance athletes', *Journal of Sports Sciences*, 24(4): 383.

Parisotto, R., Wu, M., Ashenden, M., Emslie, K., Gore, C., Howe, C., Kazlaukas, R., Sharpe, K., Trout, G., Xie, M. and Hahn, A. (2001) 'Detection of recombinant human erythropoietin abuse in athletes utilising markers of altered erythropoiesis', *Haematologica*, 86: 128.

UCI (2007) 'Information on the biological passport'. Available online at: www.uci.ch/Modules/ENews/ENewsDetails.asp?MenuId=&id=NTQzOA&LangId=1 (accessed 29 June 2010).

4 Caught between mathematics and ethics

Some implications of imperfect doping test procedures

Werner Pitsch

The first objective of WADA and, accordingly, of the many different NADOs according to the WADA code (WADC) is:

> To protect the Athletes' fundamental right to participate in doping-free sport and thus promote health, *fairness and equality for Athletes* worldwide.
> (WADA 2009b: 11)

This objective is frequently, if colloquially, referred to as the function of providing a "*level playing field*" with respect to non-doped performances between competitors. The objective, as it is formulated in WADA policy, is not defined with sufficient precision to enable researchers to investigate rigorously whether or not the objective in question has ever been reached, nor even to answer the question if this goal can ever be reached in principle. This shortcoming is scarcely unique to WADC, but seems typical for many programs and policies (e.g. Rossi et al. 2004). For the purpose of the present argument, it is important to notice that the WADA has not specified special objectives for the different anti-doping strategies, such as doping tests, educational programs or the anti-doping program harmonization. Therefore, we may assume that the objectives to be reached by the testing program are not different from the overall objectives of the WADA.

A different interpretation of the objectives of the WADA's doping test procedures, which is sympathetic to empirical investigation, was provided by Faber (2009), who translated the objective into the postulation that doping tests should be "fair" and "efficient." He defines:

> A minimum requirement for a doping test . . .
>
> - . . . to be considered *fair* is that the risk of a *false positive* be well defined and acceptable.
> - . . . to be considered *effective* is that the risk of a *false negative* be well defined and acceptable.
>
> (Faber 2009: 224)

This definition of "fair" and "effective" testing implies already a fact that is often omitted in public discussions on anti-doping testing procedures, namely that there is always a risk of false positive and false negative results of doping tests (Gleason and Barnum 1994; Berry 2008; Pitsch, 2009). For this reason, "fairness" and "effectiveness" are not absolute qualities that can be reached. To the contrary, there is always only the chance to approximate "fairness" and "effectiveness" by construing newer and better doping tests. Moreover, the anti-doping officials themselves must decide what levels of approximation are acceptable.

In technical terms, the "fairness" of a single doping test refers to the specificity (*sp*), which describes the probability that a doping test will give a negative result if a negative sample is analyzed. The counter-probability (1-*sp*) is the "false positive" probability: the probability that the test has a positive result, if a negative sample is analyzed. Doping tests need to be specific in order to avoid false accusations of clean athletes. The "effectiveness" of a doping test refers to the sensitivity (*se*) of the test. This parameter describes the probability that the test has a positive result if a positive sample is analyzed. The counter-probability (1-*se*) describes the probability that the analysis of a positive sample has a negative result. Doping tests need to be sensitive in order effectively to ban doped athletes from competition.

It is important here that the direct relationships between "fairness" and specificity, as well as between "effectiveness" and sensitivity, hold only for a doping test of one sample for one single substance or method. The discussion of the two concepts concerning an anti-doping strategy as a whole will be described in the subsequent sections.

The relation between Faber's postulates and the WADC is rather straightforward. Both fairness and effectiveness of doping tests refer to the first objective in WADC to "protect the Athletes' fundamental right to participate in doping-free sport and thus promote health, *fairness and equality for Athletes* worldwide." Both classes of false test results (false positive as well as false negative) restrict the possibilities of clean athletes to participate in doping-free sport: False positive test results (and thus false accusations of non-dopers) deprive clean athletes of their right to participate. A false negative result affects the integrity of a "doping-free" sport, as doped athletes are allowed to participate. Thus, the question to what extent doping test procedures are "fair" and "effective" in Faber's sense and the question to what extent doping tests are specific and sensitive in technical terms both refer to the question to what extent the WADA reaches the objective to provide a "doping-free sport" with respect to "a level playing field."

Thus, the central research question is: "to what extent are WADA/NADOs' doping test procedures well suited to reach their defined objectives?" It will be explored in what follows. The discussion will be based on a mathematical simulation of different outcomes of testing procedures. These simulations will start from different assumptions concerning the most important model parameters, thus simulating, not only the actual state of anti-doping work, but also the possible outcomes of activities within this field. As there may be readers who are unfamiliar with both the utility and the limitations of mathematical simulations, the benefits of a mathematical formalization as well as the restrictions of this technique will be discussed in brief methodological interim conclusions.

Modelling the WADA doping testing procedure

When modelling any social system, we must start by identifying the relevant variables that influence the outcome of the activities within the system under study. When simulating the WADA doping testing procedure in order to estimate its levels of effectiveness and fairness, we are not interested in the simulation of single (individual) doping tests and their results. Rather, we must focus on modeling the outcome of a large number of tests, with samples from many athletes all over the world, in many different sports, and with analyses for a huge number of doping substances.

The variables necessary to model the WADA anti-doping system are:

- the mean sensitivity (*se*): the mean probability that a test for one single substance results positive if a positive sample is analyzed;
- the mean specificity (*sp*): the mean probability that a test for one single substance results negative if a negative sample is analyzed;
- the number of substances each sample is being tested for: actually, the list of prohibited methods and substances contains about 200 items, some of them mentioning classes of substances with unknown extension;
- the prevalence of doping in the collective of tested athletes (*pre*);
- the mean number of substances used by a mean doper.

Because we must try to model the whole system of doping tests, rather than the results of series of tests for certain substances (Berry 2008; Pitsch 2009), we can work with estimated mean values of many parameters. This abstraction (or "preteration" in Stachowiak's (1973) general theory of models) enables us to take a step away from investigating the quality parameters of every single doping test. Furthermore, we do not need to simulate the single steps of a doping sample analysis, which typically consists of a screening test for whole classes of substances, an A-sample analysis to identify a certain prohibited substance or method, and a confirmatory B-sample analysis. Doping tests are only modeled with the help of the quality parameters of the whole testing procedure, while the analysis itself is treated as a black box. Nevertheless, with this approximation, the model may as well be used to calculate for the expected effectiveness, although it does not allow this estimation for special classes of substance or for special events.

So, for the following discussion, it is important that the term "specificity" refers only to the quality of the biochemical testing procedure, whereas the term "sensitivity" refers to the whole anti-doping regime. This implies that

ADOs can influence the specificity of tests only indirectly, by defining threshold values for the accreditation of tests. At present, even this possible attempt at securing a high specificity is not made. The specificity of doping testing procedures will only be provided by the necessity of consistently obtaining the results of A- and B-sample analyses in order to substantiate a doping allegation and by the obligation of the laboratories to use the best available techniques for analyzing the samples. Furthermore, the laboratories, as well as the testing procedures, must be accredited by the WADA prior to a doping test being conducted. Interestingly enough, the accreditation of a test does not build on the proof that its specificity exceeds a defined minimum threshold value.

In contrast, the sensitivity of the system can be influenced, not only by the development of newer and better tests, but also by the use of better laboratory equipment or the better protection of samples from adulteration. The sensitivity of a doping test depends heavily on the probability of testing an athlete who has used any doping substance or method in the short period of time when the usage can be detected, and on the opportunities for the athlete to cheat when he or she is selected for sampling. Attempts at providing a high sensitivity therefore rely on parameters such as the number of tests conducted per athlete and the general conditions of sampling from athletes. In recent years, there has been a great effort to increase the sensitivity by targeted, out-of-competition tests before important events, by reducing the opportunities to cheat during the sampling process, or by a decreased ability to miss a test without being sanctioned. The intense discussions on some of these means have shown, nevertheless, that NADOs cannot use anti-doping procedures without (social) costs and without threatening their own legitimacy. Furthermore, it is worth noting that the rate of adverse analytical findings apparently was not heavily influenced by these changes to the anti-doping policy.

Interim conclusion 1

The identification of the relevant variables shows that an optimization strategy of an ADO must take into account that the solution of the problem has at least five dimensions, and:

- only one can be manipulated directly by the organization, namely the number of substances each sample is tested for;
- the sensitivity and the specificity of the tests can be affected only indirectly (see above); and
- the remaining two dimensions are defined by the athletes, namely the number of substances an average doper uses and the doping prevalence.

Defining the model equations

After having identified the relevant dimensions (variables) of the problem, it is necessary to define the relations between the parameters and to formalize these relations mathematically in order to perform the relevant objective evaluation. In our case, the definition of the relations is rather straightforward. Using Faber's terms, we have to calculate the probability of false positive and false negative decisions of doping tests. These probabilities can be directly derived from the aforementioned variables:

1. the mean positive predictive value of the test procedure (*ppv*): the probability that an athlete is doped if his doping test resulted positive;
2. the mean negative predictive value of the test procedure (*npv*): the probability that an athlete is clean if his doping test resulted negative.

Both of these parameters depend on the sensitivity and the specificity of the tests, but they must be sharply distinguished from these aforementioned variables. The positive predictive value can be interpreted as the level of security when we infer, from a positive doping test result, that the athlete is a doper. In addition to the quality of the test, much depends also on the doping prevalence. This can easily be shown from two brief examples.

Consider the outcome of doping test analyses in anti-doping laboratories. Among the positive results, there will be true and false positives. If we assume that nearly every athlete is doped (e.g. 95 or even 99 percent; see, for example, the results of many game theoretical analyses, such as Breivik (1992) and Bird and Wagner (1997)), there are only a few samples from clean athletes and many samples from doped athletes that arrive at the laboratories. One part of the positive samples will be analyzed as positive (= true positives), and another part of them will be analyzed as negative (= false negatives), which are not observed in this discussion. Owing to the high number of positive samples, there will also be a high number of true positive results, no matter what the sensitivity of the test is. Additionally there will be a certain number of negative samples that are analyzed as being negative (true negatives), but there might also be some negative samples that give a positive result (false positives). As there are only a few negative samples, the number of false positives will also be very low. If we look at the sum of true and false positive results, we find a large number of true positives and a low number of false positives. Drawing the conclusion from a positive test result that the athlete is doped is therefore nearly perfectly secure.

Let us now assume that there are very few dopers (e.g. 2 percent (WADA 2009a)). In this case, there will be very few positive samples and many negative samples that arrive at the testing laboratory. Because of this ratio (even with a perfect sensitivity), there will be few true positive results. Nevertheless, even with a very high specificity, which implies a very low false positive probability, there will be false positive results because of the high number of negative samples. Drawing the conclusion from a positive result that the athlete is doped is therefore much more insecure than in the case discussed above.

These close interrelations between positive predictive value, sensitivity, specificity, and prevalence are often subject to discussions on the effects of biomedical testing procedures. Even with very sensitive and very specific HIV screening tests, there would be very many falsely unsettled true negatives and very few true positives, even with a very high specificity, owing to the low incidence rate of this disease.

At this point in the development of the model, we do not need to assume certain values for the different parameters, because these steps are solely conceived of in analytical terms. In mathematical terms, for a single doping test, *ppv* is calculated as follows:

$$ppv = \frac{pre^{*}se}{pre^{*}se + (1 - pre) * (1 - sp)}$$

This formula is easy to understand for the non-mathematically inclined: The top number (the numerator) describes the rate of true positive doping tests. It is calculated by multiplying the doping prevalence (*pre*) by the sensitivity (*se*), which equals the true positive probability. The bottom number (the denominator) describes the total rate of positive doping test results. It consists of the rate of true positives (the prevalence of doping multiplied by the sensitivity (*pre*se*)) and the rate of false positives (the prevalence of non-doping (1 – *pre*) multiplied by the false positive probability (1 – *sp*)). The parameter *ppv* refers directly to Faber's construct of "fairness," as it describes the probability of drawing correct conclusions about the behaviour of an athlete from the test results. Apparently, the counter-probability (1 – *ppv*) describes the "risk of a false positive." Translated into Faber's terms, an anti-doping strategy is seen to be "fair" if the positive predictive value of the tests is "well defined and acceptable" (Faber 2009: 224).

Comparably, the second important construct, the "effectiveness," is defined by the negative predictive value. It can be understood as analogous to the positive predictive value, described above. The negative predictive value describes the probability that a negative test result stems from a true negative sample. It is calculated as follows:

$$npv = \frac{(1 - pre)^{*}sp}{(1 - pre)^{*}sp + pre^{*}(1 - se)}$$

Analogously to the formula for the positive predictive value, we find in the top number (the numerator) the rate of true negative results, calculated by multiplying the prevalence of non-doping (1 – *pre*) by the probability of a negative test result when a negative sample is analyzed (the specificity, *sp*). In the bottom number (the denominator), we find the sum of the true negative rate (as in the numerator) and the false negative rate. For the latter, the doping prevalence (*pre*) is multiplied by the probability of falsely analyzing a positive sample as being negative (1 – *se*).

When conducting this translation of natural language notions to mathematical formulae, it is important to notice that, for the calculation of the total positive and negative predictive values for all prohibited substances and methods, we must bear in mind two factors: (1) the number of substances each sample is analyzed for (see Gleason and Barnum 1994; Pitsch 2009); and (2) the number of prohibited substances an average doper uses. Both parameters influence the total probability of being falsely accused and of being falsely exonerated. It is easy to see that, for each substance that is added to the list of prohibited substances, the probability of a false negative result rises, because of the rising number of tests that will be conducted. A similar logic accounts for the influence of the average number of substances used by dopers. If a doper uses more than one substance or method simultaneously, the probability of being tested positively increases with every additional substance, as only one positive A- and B-test for one substance is enough to substantiate a doping allegation. Accounting for these parameters changes the numerical results of the calculations, but it does not change the logic of the calculation. Thus, a basic understanding of the concepts of *the positive* and the negative predictive value is sufficient for us to understand the logic of formulating the objective functions of the WADA (i.e. formalizing them) in order to test them.

One problem in the formulation of the appropriate goal function of anti-doping is that the aims of anti-doping are not well defined in the WADC and in other related policy and research papers. In mathematical terms, there are several possible ways to express the objective of maximizing the positive and the negative predictive value simultaneously. All these ways are consistent with the objective—expressed in natural language—to "protect the Athletes' fundamental right to participate in doping-free sport." In the following, I will present several objective functions that shall be read as examples of how this natural language objective can be translated into mathematics. For the overall objective, I will use the abbreviation "*tpv*," which stands for the "total predictive value":

Function 1: $tpv_1 = ppv * npv$

Using this function means that both parameters are seen as equally important and that it is important to reach at least a mediocre level for each parameter, as the equation approximates zero fast, as soon as one of the two parameters declines. Furthermore, the maximum value of the function is delimited by the smallest value of these two parameters.

Function 2: $tpv_2 = k^*ppv + npv$

This function can be named the "valued sum" function: Positive and negative predictive values can have different levels of importance, expressed by the factor *k*, which defines the relative weight of the positive predictive value (*ppv*) compared with the weight of the negative predictive value (*npv*). If *k* exceeds 1, then *ppv* is more important than *npv*. This implies that the risk of a false allegation (the objective of being fair) is valued more strongly than the risk of wrongly allowing dopers to participate in a competition (the objective of being efficient). If *k* is smaller than 1, then *npv* is more important than *ppv*. With this function, an approximation to the overall objective is possible, even if one of the parameters *npv* and *ppv* approximates or equals zero.

This attempt at translating the objective of the WADA to a mathematical function shows us that the question whether the objective can be met at all cannot be answered unless the objective is defined in more precise terms. For the following simulations, it is nevertheless important to note that the two functions do not differ very much qualitatively: For both functions, the result (the level of approximation to the objective) increases with an increasing *ppv* and with an increasing *npv*. As long as the aspects fairness (modelled as the *ppv*) and effectiveness (modelled as the *npv*) reach at least an acceptable, even if mediocre, level, both functions result in an approximation to the total objective but differ, first and foremost, in terms of the numerical results.

In order to select the most appropriate objective function, we must refer to further information on how WADA and the different NADOs try to reach their objectives, as we can infer from these strategies an interpretation of the objectives within these organizations. There is a strong suggestion that the probability of false positive and false negative test results are understood, and also valued, differently within NADOs. The most important hint stems from the regulations of the double-blind proficiency-testing program of the WADA (2004). In this program, the laboratories must prove that they correctly distinguish between substances with similar chemical structures (one aspect of the specificity) and that they can detect prohibited substances at very low concentrations (i.e. sensitivity). The norms of the proficiency-testing program contain exact steps that have to be taken as soon as a laboratory delivers a false positive report, whereas false negative reports are not mentioned at all. This shows that the present anti-doping regime is constructed in order to avoid false positive results but does not care, or cares insufficiently, about false negatives.

The difference between the two possible objective functions presented before was that, with the tpv_1 function, both the positive predictive value (reflecting "fairness") and the negative predictive value (reflecting "efficiency") are weighted equally. The tpv_2 function allows for the two parameters to be weighted differentially, which seems more suitable to reflect present anti-doping strategies. For this reason, the simulations will be run using the

tpv_2 function, the "valued sum function." In what follows, we can show that—contrary to current practice—NADOs should consider that false negative results may also be critical for the anti-doping movement.

Interim conclusion 2

The problems in finding the appropriate objective function of the WADA shows one important benefit of a mathematical simulation compared with natural (everyday) language discussions of the same topic: It can easily be seen if the objectives of a program need to be defined more clearly in order to enable a rational strategy selection. The term "well defined" shall refer to the question of whether the objectives are defined in a manner that allows the finding of parameters that can be empirically observed and measured. Only with objectives that are "well defined" in this special sense of the words can stakeholders of the (anti-doping) program, as well as researchers, analyze whether the activities within the program are sufficiently well designed in order for the objectives to be reached, or if resources should be used differently in order to perform better doping tests.

Can the anti-doping objective be reached at all? A mathematical discussion

The question of whether the objective of a "level playing field" can be reached in principle can now be answered by using the classical tools of mathematic optimization theory (cf. Nocedal and Wright 1999; Boyd and Vandenberghe 2004). Applying these methods to the model equation shown above leads to an analytical solution. This means that the problem of finding an optimal strategy to achieve the objective of the WADA *can* be solved in principle. Unfortunately, the complexity of the problem (with the five dimensions noted above) makes an easy interpretation of the solution problematic. The proposed solution can be expressed by five equations, each having four parameters. The proposed solution holds that there are optimal values for the sensitivity and the specificity for every possible combination of the number of substances each sample is tested for, prevalence rates, and numbers of prohibited substances an average doper uses. Nevertheless, the solution is much too complex to be expressed in natural language. Thus, the proposed analytical solution is only a hypothetical possibility. It may be actualized in real life, but, owing to the complexity of the problem, nobody will ever be able to recognize if it is actualized. Beyond this limitation, the high complexity also inhibits a rational control of means in order better to approximate the objective.

Interim conclusion 3

The analytical solution of the optimization problem shows that, in everyday life, there may be problems that are highly complex. These complex problems may have analytical "solutions" if they are translated into mathematical optimization problems. These "solutions" may nevertheless be too complex to be useful as a guide for decisions in everyday life. Nevertheless, these real-world problems must be dealt with somehow in everyday life.

Simplification of the model

Besides the question of whether there are solutions to such problems by principle, mathematical optimization can also help to discuss the question of whether the decisions of agents concerning such "real-world" problems lead to an approximation to the overall objectives, or if they are counter-productive in these terms. The first step in this task is to simplify the model and to restrict the solution to values of the parameters that are plausible in order to find a solution that is practicable.

There are several different methods of simplification. The first method that is used here increases the abstractness of the problem by excluding variables that are not of great interest to the actors in the field and replacing these variables with constant values. Thus, the dimensionality of the problem is reduced, and the model and solutions to the optimization problem become easier to understand.

We may exclude the variable that consists of the number of substances each doper uses. This variable can be omitted without restricting the value of the model, as this variable cannot be influenced by national and international anti-doping authorities. For the following simulations, we assume that each doper uses two different doping substances or techniques. Any value we select here is selected arbitrarily, solely based on a subjectively assumed plausibility. We must keep in mind here that the reason for the selection is simply a technical one, namely to simplify the model in order to make its results more understandable.

A second technique to simplify the model by another dimension builds on empirical knowledge about the phenomenon under study. The present anti-doping strategies reveal a rate of approximately 2 percent of adverse analytical findings (*aaf*). This 2 percent of *aaf* reflects the sum of true positive (*tp*) and false positive (*fp*) findings:

$$aaf = tp + fp$$

Replacing *tp* and *fp* shows that the *aaf* rate depends on the sensitivity, the specificity, and the prevalence:

$$aaf = se * pre + (1 - sp) * (1 - pre)$$

When using the model described above to estimate the quality of the current anti-doping regime, this formula and the knowledge of the rate of adverse analytical findings can help further in the simplification of the model. It shows that, for any estimated prevalence and specificity, the sensitivity of the tests can be determined, and vice versa. These dependencies can be used to simplify the model by one more dimension as far as we are able to find a semblance of the present doping prevalence and of the specificity of the tests.

Pitsch et al. (2005; 2007) have measured the prevalence in elite sport in Germany using the randomized response technique. This technique has often been shown to lead to more reliable results when measuring hidden deviant behavior (cf. Lensvelt-Mulders et al. 2005). The survey covered German squad athletes of both sexes who were supported in the national sport development system in all kinds of sport. The range of dopers in the 2005 season was estimated to be between 20.4 and 38.7 percent. In a recently published replication study, with a different sampling technique in order to ensure a representative sample (Pitsch et al. 2009), the rate of dopers was estimated to range between 9.6 and 35.0 percent. Based on the results of the second study, the doping prevalence is set at 20 percent for the following simulations. With this prevalence, any estimated specificity directly defines the respective sensitivity, and vice versa.

Bearing in mind the great importance of false positives (of what are, in reality, non-doping or clean athletes, or simply athletes against whom a doping violation case cannot be made) in the double-blind proficiency-testing program, we will use this parameter as a variable for the simulations and calculate the respective sensitivities. It is plausible that anti-doping laboratories attempt to ensure high specificity in their tests, resulting in a very low false positive rate. For the following simulations, we will use a specificity of at least 0.999, which means that, at maximum, one in a thousand tests of truly clean athletes will produce a false positive result. Under the assumption of totally independent methods for the analysis of the A- and B-samples, the probability of a false sanction will then be 0.000001, equaling one false accusation deriving from A- and B-sample analyses producing consistently false positive results in 1 million analyzed clean samples for one substance.[1]

After these simplifications, the remaining model variables for the simulations are (1) the number of substances on the list and (2) the mean sensitivity of a doping test. This allows a further interim conclusion.

Interim conclusion 4

Real-life phenomena (such as the quality of the anti-doping testing regime) may be too complex to be simulated analytically. By reducing the complexity, the model itself, as well as any solution derived from it, then becomes more abstract. Nevertheless, the simplification of the model by replacing intangible variables with plausible values and by accounting for empirical interdependencies between the model parameters leads to a model that cannot be used to generate general solutions for any set of parameter values, but can be used to evaluate the current status of the phenomenon under study.

Simulations

Starting from these parameters, the quality of the current anti-doping regime in terms of its level of approximation to its objectives can be calculated. The results are shown in the subsequent figures. The figures display the level of approximation to the objective defined by objective function tpv_2—also named the "valued sum"-function. For the simulations, a value for $k = 3$ was used (also selected arbitrarily), meaning that the importance of false positives equals three times the importance of false negative results. In these three-dimensional figures, the two axes defining the bottom area show the values of the two variables.

In Figure 4.1, the vertical axis shows the value of the objective function, reflecting the level of approximation to the objective. The values on this axis are normalized to the co-domain [0;1], where 1 reflects that the objective is maximally achieved, and 0 means that the objective is maximally missed. The surface displayed shows for any combination of the number of substances each sample is tested for and of the average specificity of the respective value of the objective function. The area where this surface is not shown reflects constellations of values where the objective function leads to results that are impossible in the real world, e.g. a negative number of true positive test results.

The interpretation of the results shown in Figure 4.1 is quite straightforward. The shape of the surface shows that the solutions to the optimization problem are solely defined by marginal maximum values of tpv_2: the extremes are that doping tests achieve either a perfect specificity—which cannot be reached by principle—or that they miss perfectly (i.e. no doping tests at all—a solution that is, at least politically, impossible). The former would guarantee a maximum efficiency and fairness of the anti-doping regime. Besides this, the shape of the surface also shows that anti-doping agencies cannot increase the efficiency and fairness of the testing system massively, as nearly all values range between 0.95 and 0.97. However, these absolute values of the objective

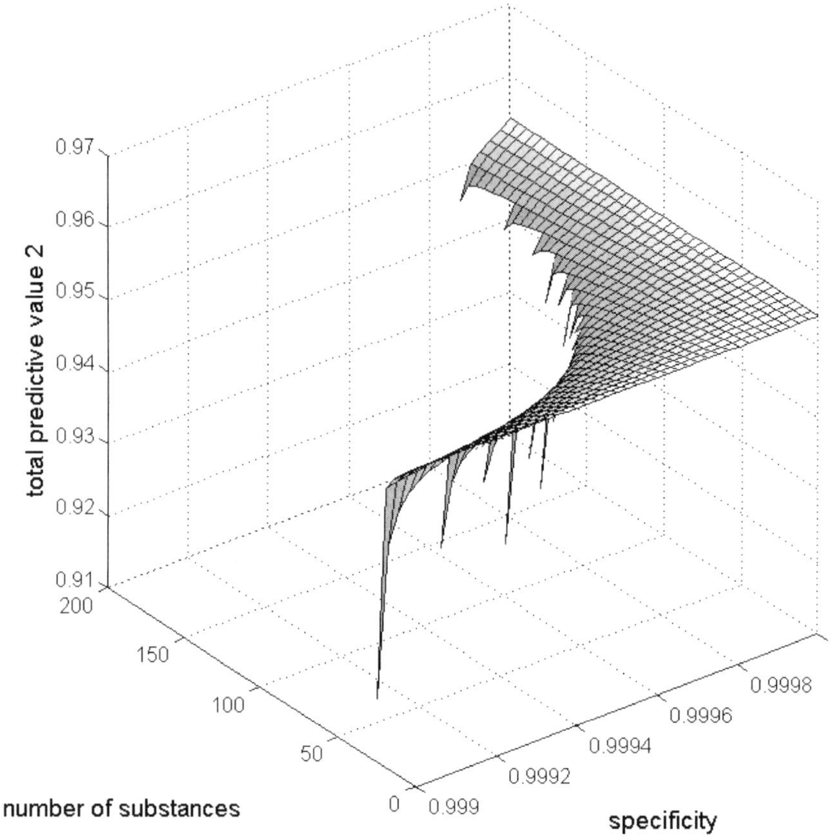

Figure 4.1 Level of approximation to the objective of fair and efficient doping tests by average specificity and the number of substances and methods on the list

function may not be misunderstood in the sense of a good approximation, as they are heavily influenced by the parameter k (here, $k = 3$), reflecting the relative importance of false positives compared with false negatives. A lower level of k indicates a greater importance of the right of the undoped athletes in competition to be protected against doped competitors and would result in lower values of the objective function.

Figures 4.2 and 4.3 show the results of the simulations in terms of the estimated number of false positive doping accusations (Figure 4.2) and of false negative doping tests (Figure 4.3). In economic terms, Figure 4.2 can be understood as the estimation of variable costs to the athletes. Besides the diminution of the athletes' privacy caused by the sampling procedure and of their liberty rights by the whereabouts system, there are variable costs in terms of the risk of being falsely accused. Bearing in mind that there are more than 200,000 doping test samples analyzed per year, the maximum value of 0.5 false

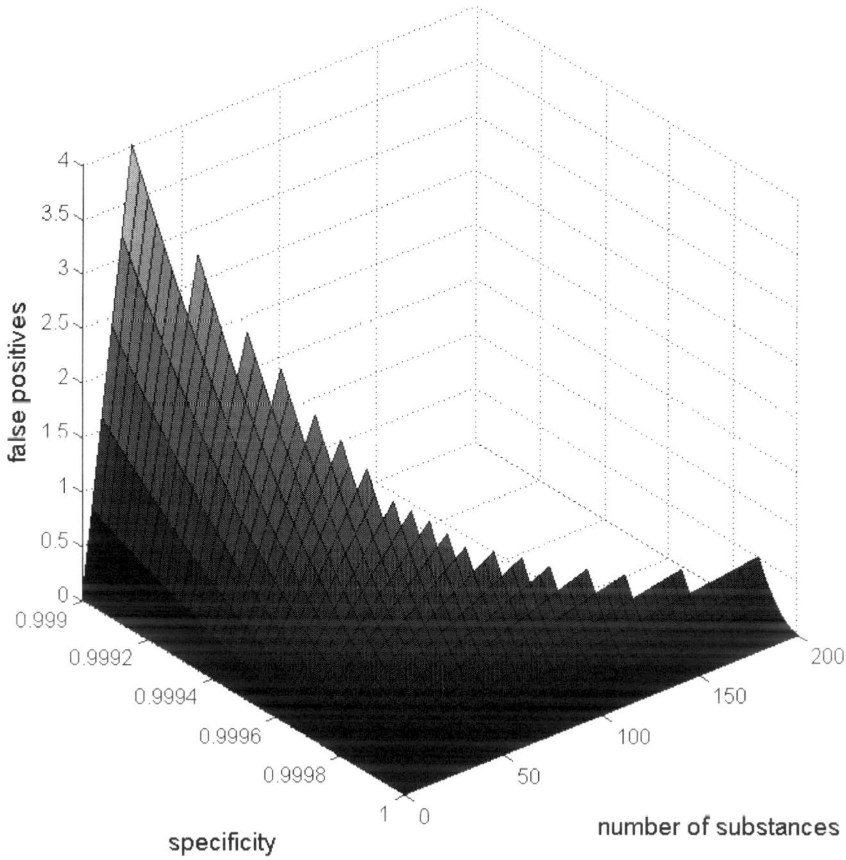

Figure 4.2 Estimated number of false doping accusations per year

accusations per year with 200 substances on the list might be what Faber named "that the risk of a *false positive* be [. . .] acceptable". This result differs largely from the result presented by Pitsch (2009), who had estimated a number of forty false positive results per year. The differences result from the fact that, in the simulations published in 2009, the dependency between prevalence, sensitivity, and specificity was not used as a restriction to the model parameters. This "acceptable" low number of false positive results is nevertheless reached at the expense of the false negative rate (see Figure 4.3).

The estimated number of false negative doping test results ranges between 36,000 and 40,000 among 200,000 doping tests per year. This equals 90–100 percent of the estimated number of true dopers, calculated from the prevalence estimation of 0.2.

For clean athletes, these results mean that they are well protected against false doping accusations deriving from false positive doping test results.

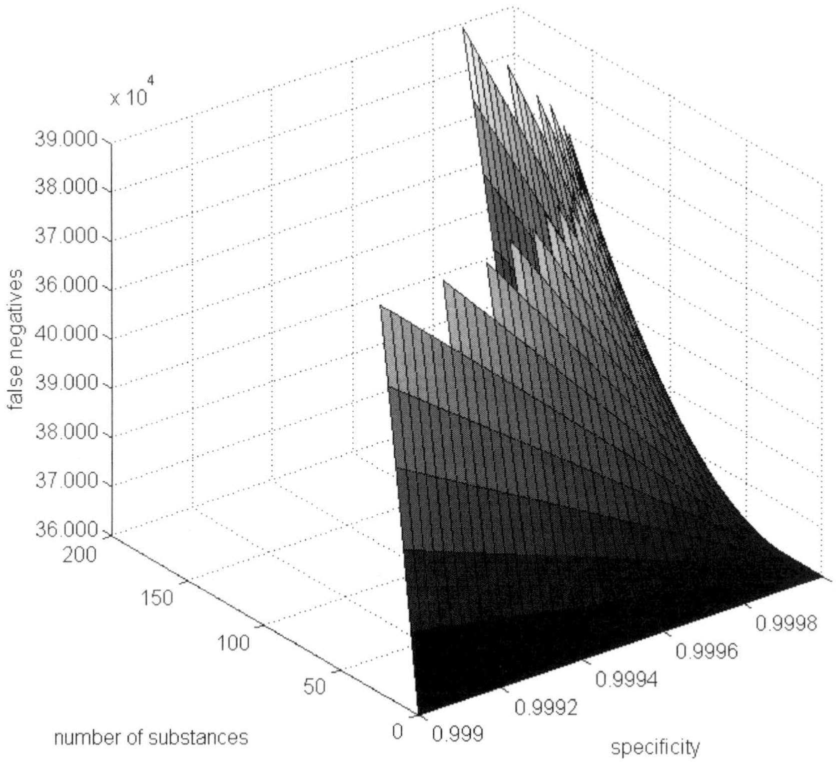

Figure 4.3 Estimated number of false negative doping test results per year

Nevertheless, the protection against doped competitors is very weak, owing to the high estimated number of false negative results. This latter effect is first and foremost a benefit to the undiscovered dopers, as the vast majority of them are labelled as "clean" after having passed a doping test. This enables them to participate in competition at increased chances of winning.

Discussion

The translation of the objectives of ADOs from natural language to mathematical equations reveals several advantages of this technique compared with a social scientific or philosophical discussion, typically expressed in natural-language terms. Mathematical models can only be identified by employing unambiguous terms with respect to well-defined problems that have to be solved. The attempt at reformulating a "real-world" problem in mathematical terms reveals whether the problem is sufficiently well defined. Furthermore, this reformulation is valuable in that it reveals whether the problem can be solved in principle. One consequence of this investigation is the recognition that ADO actors deal with highly complex and high-dimensional problems that could be shown to be solvable by principle, but that have incomprehensible general solutions. Notwithstanding this inherent complexity, a simplification of the model could be developed in order to evaluate how close the current anti-doping regime is to its objectives.

Conclusions

For less abstract implications of this analysis, it is important to note that these implications work in principle, and that they are not affected by arbitrary decisions on the values of the different model parameters (such as the average number of substances used by dopers or the relative importance of false positive results compared with false negative results in ADOs). This means that, if we accept the "valued sum"-function (tpv_2) as an objective function of an anti-doping agency, we must accept the following implications.

With plausible assumptions for some parameters, the anti-doping system seems rather close to its objective. Nevertheless, the proximity to its objective is affected by arbitrary decisions on the relative meaning of the rights of clean athletes to be protected from false accusations and their right to be protected from doped competitors. For the current anti-doping regime, this means that the achievement of a low risk of false accusations is reached at the expense of the chances of clean athletes in competition, who "pay" for the anti-doping efforts by accepting the injury to their rights, without getting the pay-off of a "level playing field."

In order to evaluate the reality of the current anti-doping regime, this means that, if we accept the measurement of the doping prevalence among German elite athletes to be more reliable than an estimation based solely on the results of doping tests, and if we take this value as an average value of the doping prevalence all over the world, then at least 36,000 samples from dopers are analyzed and returned as false when they ought not to be. This would mean that the vast majority of dopers are unfairly allowed to participate in competition.

For the policy of anti-doping agencies, the results of the simulations present a significant dilemma. It seems that the two aspects of fair and effective doping tests cannot be reached simultaneously by principle:

1 Any decision to make an effort to reach one of these goals entails a reduction in the chance of reaching the other goal, and vice versa. As the objective is defined as a preservation of the rights of honest athletes to compete against athletes who are similarly dope-free, this means that any decision damages their rights—either their right to be protected against false accusations or their right to be protected against dishonest competitors. It is an ironic consequence that, at present, in protecting athletes against false accusations, we have correspondingly increased the chances of the dishonest dopers in competition.

2 Additionally, a doping athlete who has not been caught in testing, owing to the weak sensitivity of the doping test regime, increases the doper's economic chances, as his or her increased performance and thereby higher probability of being successful are "honored" by the anti-doping test as conforming to the rules.
3 Furthermore, the low test sensitivity may lead to a learning effect in the population of dopers. If many dopers are perceived not to be detected, the deterrence effect of doping tests decreases.
4 Finally, any decision to increase the sensitivity of the doping test regime by increasing the number of tests per year would also lead to a higher probability of falsely accused non-dopers. In other words, anti-doping agencies must choose between a moral hazard on the one hand and ineffectiveness on the other. Moreover, even if policymakers decide to choose the morally hazardous route, there seems to be little space for such decisions, as the current whereabouts system is already subject to intensive discussion (see several chapter in this book).

As an aside, the only parameter not discussed so far is the number of doping substances and methods each sample is tested for. Decreasing this number would allow anti-doping agencies to approach their overall objective (see Figure 4.1) by decreasing the estimated number of false positives as well as false negatives for any given average specificity, but this only holds as long as the list includes all potential doping methods or substances. A deletion of substances and methods with weak effects on the athletic performance might be a rational step in the struggle for a better anti-doping regime. This may not be an acceptable political or symbolic maneuver. Nevertheless, the simulations have shown that the organizations themselves can only marginally influence the fairness and the efficiency of their policy.

Note

1 For a discussion of limitations regarding this calculation, see Pitsch (2009).

References

Berry, D.A. (2008) "The science of doping," *Nature*, 454: 692–3.

Bird, E.J. and Wagner, G.G. (1997) "Sport as a common property resource. A solution to the dilemma of doping," *Journal of Conflict Resolution*, 41(6): 749–66.

Boyd, S. and Vandenberghe, L. (2004) *Convex optimization*, Cambridge: Cambridge University Press.

Breivik, G. (1992) "Doping games. A game theoretical exploration of doping," *International Review for the Sociology of Sport*, 27: 235–55.

Faber, N.M. (2009) "Towards more fair and effective doping tests based on chromatography with mass spectrometric detection," *Accreditation and Quality Assurance*, 14: 223–6.

Gleason, J.M. and Barnum, D.T. (1994) "A probabilistic analysis of multiple-drug testing procedures in sports doping control," *International Transactions in Operational Research*, 1(4): 395–407.

Lensvelt-Mulders, G.J.L.M., Hox, J.J., van der Heijden, P.G.M., and Maas, C.J.M. (2005) "Meta-analysis of randomized response research. Thirty-five years of validation," *Sociological Methods and Research*, 33: 315–48.

Nocedal, J. and Wright, S.J. (1999) *Numerical optimization*, Berlin: Springer.

Pitsch, W. (2009) "'The science of doping' revisited: Fallacies of the current anti-doping regime," *European Journal of Sport Science*, 9: 87–95.

Pitsch, W., Emrich, E., and Klein, M. (2005) "Zur Häufigkeit des Dopings im Leistungssport. Ergebnisse eines www-Surveys," *Leipziger Sportwissenschaftliche Beiträge*, 46(2): 63–77.

Pitsch, W., Emrich, E., and Klein, M. (2007) "Doping in elite sports in Germany: Results of a www survey," *European Journal of Sport and Society*, 4(2): 89–102.

Pitsch, W., Maats, P., and Emrich, E. (2009) "Zur Häufigkeit des Dopings im deutschen Spitzesport—eine Replikationsstudie," in W. Pitsch and E. Emrich (eds), *Sport und Doping: Zur Analyse einer antagonistischen Symbiose*, Frankfurt am Main: Peter Lang, pp. 19–36.

Rossi, P.H., Lipsey, M.W., and Freeman, H.E. (2004) *Evaluation: A systematic approach* (7th edn), Thousand Oaks: SAGE.

Stachowiak, H. (1973) *Allgemeine Modelltheorie*, Wien: Springer.

WADA (2004) *The world anti-doping code. International standard for laboratories, Version 4.0.* Available online at: www.wada-ama.org/rtecontent/document/lab_aug_04.pdf (accessed January 15, 2010).

WADA (2009a) "2008 adverse analytical findings and atypical findings reported by accredited laboratories." Available online at: www.wada-ama.org/Documents/Science_Medicine/Anti-Doping_Laboratories/WADA_LaboStatistics_2008.pdf (accessed March 30, 2010).

WADA (2009b) "The world anti-doping code." Available online at: www.wada-ama.org/Documents/World_Anti-Doping_Program/WADP-The-Code/WADA_Anti-Doping_CODE_2009_EN.pdf (accessed July 20, 2010).

5 On the presumption of guilt without proof of intentionality and other consequences of current anti-doping policy

Bengt Kayser

The globalisation of anti-doping

The use of performance-enhancing substances has been endemic in elite sports since the very beginnings. In the first half of the twentieth century, sports organisations such as the IOC and the IAAF responded little to doping practices among athletes, probably because of the limited pressure from public opinion and the limited means available at that time to impose a ban and to control athletes for the use of doping. In the second half of the twentieth century, increasingly powerful biomedical inventions with potential performance-enhancing effects were quickly adapted to and adopted by elite sports (for example, recombinant human EPO[1] in the 1980s and 1990s). Following a series of widely publicized doping scandals and public outrage, in the last decades of the twentieth century an increasingly strong movement advocating doping-free sports has developed. One probable reason for the increasingly negative public opinion of athletes who dope is the similarity between the image of the doped athlete and the negative image of the illicit psychotropic drug user. Anti-doping accelerated with the inception of the World Anti-Doping Agency (WADA), which celebrated its 10-year anniversary at the end of 2009. WADA aims at harmonizing anti-doping practices worldwide and is helped by the fact that an increasing number of UN member states now have signed a UNESCO anti-doping convention (UNESCO 2005).

The symbolism of harmonized anti-doping

The objective of anti-doping efforts is to rid elite sports of the use of doping. Anti-doping policy at the international level is typically punitively focused. Mainly based on surveillance, in-competition testing and unannounced out-of-competition testing for substances in urine or blood, the objective is to identify all cheats and to exclude them from competition for the benefit of the 'clean' athletes and the spectators. For the system to be successful, it needs to catch all offenders and to exclude false accusations of 'clean' athletes. In the end, the IOC, which is a main driving force behind this globalization of anti-doping efforts, wants to be certain that the public only admires 'clean' athletes winning Olympic medals.

At first glance, the objective of doping-free sports seems rather noble, and the globalization of anti-doping policy governed by WADA the appropriate means to reach that objective. But, as Amos concludes:

> Anti-doping policy is fraught with confusion and ambiguity, even in the most basic and fundamental issues. To look at anti-doping policy today, with its universal code and a level of governmental agreement and cooperation not often seen, it is easy to assume that no such problems exist. The degree of consensus is largely a result of unity in public opinion regarding the issue of performance enhancing substances in sport. This unity of public opinion is, in turn, largely a result of the power of symbolism in doping discourse.
>
> (Amos 2009: 316)

Amos argues, then, that the public validation of anti-doping is in part skewed by the public's grasp of the issues, which are themselves mediated by WADA. The symbolism of harmony has its roots in the strong negative image that public opinion has of the user of illicit psychotropic substances, which has been transferred on to that of the doping athlete. One problem that threatens to undermine this symbolism of harmony is that current anti-doping policy has a number of operational problems that lead to unintended negative side effects. As Amos shows, the definition of doping in public discourse is different from the operational definition of doping by WADA in the World Anti-Doping Code. The code defines doping in a much broader way. One consequence of this arises when, for example, WADA punishes athletes found to have doping substances in their body, regardless of whether they had intended to improve their performance via the forbidden substances. In contrast, it is reasonable to suppose that public opinion would not condemn athletes in such circumstances.

The application of the code is sufficiently problematic that it warrants critical analysis of the reasons for current anti-doping policy and reflection on possible alternatives. In previous publications, I have, with co-authors, developed arguments undermining the basis for present anti-doping policy in elite sports, and the reader is referred to those papers (Kayser et al. 2005, 2007; Kayser and Smith 2008; Kayser 2009). The aim of the present essay is to further highlight some limits and side effects of present anti-doping policy rarely discussed in the extant literature.

Consequences of current operational doping and anti-doping definitions

At first glance, developing and implementing anti-doping policy in elite sports seem simple. All that is required is a definition of doping, a no-doping rule, methods to make athletes obey that rule, and the imposition of sanctions when they do not. However, there are difficulties in defining what doping is, and the methods used to impose the rule are inherently limited in what they can achieve. As Møller commented, in its main document, the code, WADA uses a circular definition of what doping in sports is:

> Doping is defined as the occurrence of one or more of the anti-doping rule violations [. . .] Doping is simply defined as infringement of WADA's doping regulations. In other words, doping is whatever WADA at any moment assesses it to be.
>
> (Møller 2009: 4)

Methods and substances that are not allowed are listed on the Prohibited List, which is updated on an annual basis by WADA. WADA uses three criteria, of which at least two must be met, for inclusion on the prohibited list: the method or substance must have performance-enhancing effects; it must pose a health risk or at least have the potential for such; and it must be against the 'spirit of sport'. These criteria lack clear-cut boundaries, and especially the 'spirit of sport' argument is heavily influenced by time-dependent cultural specificity. For instance, if these three criteria had been used at the beginning of sport in Victorian times in England, physical training would not have been allowed, because it was at that time against the 'spirit of sport' (training was considered cheating: a form of ungentlemanly conduct), it has performance enhancing effects and, if used in excess, it potentially poses a health risk. The inclusion of the 'spirit of sport' criterion allows WADA the flexibility to include substances on the list that do not, or only partially, comply with the two other criteria, such as, for example, derivatives of cannabis (marihuana, hashish).

An illustrative example of what the consequences of present anti-doping policy can be for athletes is the story of Zach Lund, an American skeleton athlete (head-first sleighing), who was prevented from participation in the 2006 Turin Winter Olympics when finasteride was found in a urine sample in late 2005. On the basis of scientific evidence from WADA-funded research published later (Thevis *et al.* 2007), early in 2005, WADA put finasteride on the list of forbidden products as it was thought to be useful in masking anabolic steroid use. Lund had been using finasteride since 1997 because of hair loss (alopecia) and had always informed the doping control officers of his use of this compound. He was not aware of the inclusion of finasteride on the list of forbidden substances in 2005. Interestingly, he was repeatedly tested in 2005 after the inclusion of the drug on the list and never found positive, but, in November 2005, he was. When the USA anti-doping agency decided to treat Lund leniently because there was clearly no intention to dope, WADA appealed and asked the international Court of Arbitration in Sport (CAS) in Lausanne in Switzerland to judge the case just prior to the beginning of the Turin Winter Games, where Lund was a likely medal contender, in order to exclude him from participation. The CAS judgment stated that it was unlikely that Lund had intended to use finasteride to hide steroid use and that Lund was not in any way 'performance enhanced' because of his use of finasteride. The CAS nevertheless declared Lund guilty of a doping offence, even though it expressed its own uneasiness with this ruling (CAS 2006). Lund was sent home on the very opening day of the Turin Games with his name tarnished. In 2008, WADA then decided to take finasteride off the list again, stating that new laboratory techniques had rendered finasteride useless as a masking agent. Lund's request that his record be cleared was refused, leaving the possibility that, upon a second offence, he could be banned from sport for life. This case shows how the strict application of anti-doping policy can cause harm to athletes who did not intend to dope. Even though WADA, in a document published a posteriori, regrets this aspect of its fight against doping, it prefers to remain firm:

> While WADA can understand the discomfort of those athletes who neglected to obtain a TUE [therapeutic use exemption] and consequently were sanctioned for taking alpha reductase inhibitors [e.g. finasteride], one has to keep in mind that the List is prepared on existing science and that anti-doping science progresses quickly for the benefit of clean athletes worldwide [. . .] As in every area of society, one has to abide by the rules in force at the time of the particular event.
>
> (WADA 2009a: 2)

This case is not an isolated one. Similar cases happen regularly. Pluim (2008) analysed doping cases over a 5-year period (2003–7), published by the International Tennis Federation. WADA uses the principle of 'strict liability', where an athlete is responsible for the presence of a forbidden substance in her/his urine or blood, no matter how the substance came into the body. In this way, there can be no excuses, and the procedure of accusation of doping is greatly simplified. On the other hand, this simplicity comes at a price: it may lead to damage to what will widely be conceived of by public opinion as innocent athletes. For the majority (68 per cent) of the forty doping cases in tennis over that period, it was ruled by the sanctioning bodies that there was no intent to enhance performance or no (significant) fault or negligence (Pluim 2008). Nevertheless, sanctions were applied, with significant negative impact for the players with regard to their notoriety, income and career.

These examples show how the operational definition of doping by WADA, which includes the principle of strict liability, regularly leads to the conviction of athletes who had no intent to improve their performance by using forbidden substances or methods. These are athletes who are punished who are not 'guilty' (in the sense of actually being performance enhanced) and without direct intentionality (in the sense that they willingly used forbidden substances to improve their performance). It thus seems as if, in the name of the 'spirit of sport', the sports establishment considers it justified to sacrifice in principle innocent athletes (innocent in the sense that they were not performance enhanced, nor had any intent to become performance enhanced). Furthermore, today's anti-doping policy tends to reverse the 'innocent until proven guilty' rule, as presumption of innocence is replaced by suspicion of doping for any extraordinary athletic achievement.

Surveillance in sports

Another controversial aspect of present anti-doping policy is the obligation of elite athletes to inform the anti-doping authorities for one hour a day, 365 days a year, where they will be, to allow unannounced out-of-competition testing. Athletes have to inform four times a year, for three months in advance of their plans, and use electronic and paper-based means to inform the authorities of any changes. According to WADA, this 'whereabouts' rule is an essential cornerstone of anti-doping, as it prevents out-of-competition doping in preparation for competition. In order to force athletes to comply, a rule states that three missed tests within an 18-month period consitute a doping offence. Athletes regularly have problems keeping the authorities well informed, and cases of suspension because of three missed tests are not uncommon. The case of Yanina Wickmayer, a talented young tennis player from Belgium, is an example of the problems that may arise. At the end of 2009, she was suspended for a year when she failed three times to inform about her whereabouts when she entered the Women's Tennis Association Top 50 and thus became obliged to inform about her whereabouts. She was able to defend herself in a Belgian court, pointing out the shortcomings and administrative errors of the official bodies overseeing her whereabouts obligations and had the ban overturned, allowing her to play again, but her image was probably tainted forever (BBC 2009). There are other examples of athletes who were judged to have committed a doping offence because of three missed tests, some of whom probably tried to escape doping controls but others were athletes who just failed to be sufficiently meticulous. The whereabouts rule may now also apply to non-adult athletes. In 2009, in the Netherlands, a talented 13-year-old girl speed skater, Dominique Lommers, was told to enter the Dutch whereabouts programme when her 15-year-old brother was provisionally found guilty of a doping offence. The parents refused to enter the whereabouts programme, while accepting regular doping controls, but Dominique Lommers was nevertheless excluded from participating in junior-level competitions, a decision that was later overturned (NRC 2009).

Generally, the whereabouts rule seems accepted by athletes, although they obviously have no choice. In fact, many athletes agree with the principles behind the rule, even if they do not like it (Hanstead and Loland 2009). Critical voices are regularly heard, as in early 2009, when several high-level athletes such as Rafael Nadal publicly voiced their discontent about the whereabouts rule, complaining about its excessive intrusion into the athlete's private sphere and the practical difficulties of keeping one's information up to date. WADA's reasoning is pragmatic, arguing that it is a free choice for the athlete either to abide by the rules or to choose another activity. However, since being an athlete has become a profession, its regulation should also abide by general law regulating other professional activities. Currently, discussions are underway between the European Commission and WADA to study the whereabouts rule's potential incompatibility with European law.

The limits of laboratory testing technology

A further problem of current anti-doping policy concerns the testing for forbidden substances in bodily specimens. The ideal situation would be black and white: the forbidden substance is present or is not present. Those two extreme cases exist, but there is, depending on the substance, often a large area of uncertainty. This is true for most biomedical tests in general, including those used for clinical reasons. A test can be positive (showing the presence of a substance) when it is indeed present (true positive) or not present (false positive); conversely, a test can be negative when there is indeed no substance present (true negative) or when in fact the substance is present (false negative).

The basic descriptors of a test are, hence, sensitivity (proportion of actual positives that are correctly identified as such) and specificity (proportion of negatives that are correctly identified, e.g. the percentage of samples without the substance that are identified as not having the substance present). Anti-doping policy enforcers need to keep false positives as low as possible, while striving for the highest sensitivity possible. The problem is that the probability for false positives rises with the number of tests performed, as well as with a drop in prevalence of actual doping (Pitsch 2009; see also Chapter 4). It is very likely possible that false positives have already occurred, even though there is animated debate between scientists on the level of certainty for that statement (Beullens *et al.* 2006; Berry 2008; Lundby *et al.* 2008). WADA does not want to publish the results of the quality of the tests used by the WADA-accredited laboratories. It argues that this would permit athletes to tailor their doping practices to the available testing technology. At first sight, this seems reasonable, but, at the same time, it leaves room for doubt about the impartial nature of anti-doping testing. The absence of transparency is not a good gate-keeper for quality assurance.

In order to overcome some of the limits of the single tests that just compare the findings to some pre-set level based on cross-sectional population data, individualized longitudinal blood analysis has been introduced under the name 'blood passport' (Sottas *et al.* 2010). The idea is that doping can be recognized from certain patterns of change in blood values over time. In late 2009, the first case of an athlete accused of doping on indirect evidence from her blood values was announced. Claudia Pechstein, a very successful German speed skater, was frequently tested throughout her career, but never failed a test. On the basis of fluctuations in the number of young red blood cells in her blood, she was declared guilty of doping (CAS 2009). This case is interesting because it is the first time that an athlete has been considered guilty of doping on indirect evidence indicating the use of a substance that, in itself or its metabolites, was not identified, even though there remains quite some scientific doubt on the probability that Pechstein did indeed use forbidden substances or methods. Although the blood passport approach will certainly add to the pressure on athletes not to dope, there probably will also be athletes who find ways to get away with it. In any case, the blood passport will also, by definition, be limited in what it can detect. Recent findings indicated, for example, that the measurement of total haemoglobin mass with CO rebreathing[2] is unable to detect 50 per cent of those on EPO maintenance treatment (Lundby and Robach 2010), making it a questionable means of surveillance or detection. As EPO testing in urine also poses quite some challenges, leaving leeway to get away with a well-dosed regime (Lundby *et al.* 2008), it remains uncertain how much can be gained with the longitudinal testing, while it may, at least in theory, further expose athletes to the risk of false accusations.

As one can see, with present anti-doping policy, athletes who try to play the game according to the anti-doping rule risk significant harm, whereas there very likely still are athletes who dope but get away with it. Of course, today's anti-doping policy has certainly changed doping practices. Certain types of doping cannot be used anymore because they would be uncovered, but other types can still remain undiscovered. The purpose of anti-doping, the celebration of 'clean' athletes with a strong degree of confidence or even certainty, thus remains an unreached objective. Rather perversely, then, one is forced to question still whether the champions are 'clean'; a question that will unfortunately remain unanswered. It could be argued that public opinion has become even more sceptical about the 'cleanliness' of today's champions, which would be contradictory to WADA aims.

How many dopers are actually caught? According to WADA statistics, about 1–2 per cent of tests are positive, a proportion that has not changed much over the last 10 years. A recent study, however, indicates that prevalence might be much higher (Striegel *et al.* 2009). That paper reported data from Germany indicating less than 1 per cent of doping, according to official test results, but an actual prevalence of doping eight times higher when estimated by using a randomized response technique, which allowed the bias introduced by ordinary questionnaires on sensitive issues to be circumvented.

Anti-doping advocates thus find themselves in a difficult position with regard to the efficient achievement of their goals. The objective of present policy is to be certain that winners are 'clean', but this objective cannot be fully reached. Because of the limits of surveillance and laboratory testing, one cannot be sure that winners are 'clean'. The fact that it is impossible to be sure that the winners are 'clean' sets doping apart from other transgressions in society. Society can accept transgression as long as it continues functioning, the prevalence of transgression remains limited, the cost of repression is acceptable, and the rule is generally accepted by the population. Drunk driving is repressed, and rightly so, but not totally eradicated. The cost of alcohol for society can be considered high, but a pragmatic approach, with a strong harm-reduction component, allows that cost to the individual and society to remain as low as possible.

The claim that the 'war on doping' is increasingly successful is likely to be correct in elite sports. Even if we accept this proposition, however, it remains problematic that the possibility that, among the winners of competitions, there may still be dopers who were simply not discovered can never be fully excluded. In fact, the media and the public increasingly suspect that any extraordinary performance is not just the result of rule-abiding training and 'clean' competitive effort. Indeed, being a successful top athlete today often implies bearing a lasting burden of potential guilt. However, being forced to doubt the 'cleanliness' of our champions directly undermines the goal of elite sports, the celebration of 'clean' champions, a central tenet of the 'spirit of sport'.

Elite sports and general society

WADA and the IOC continuously try to find ways to increase the pressure on athletes not to dope. The whereabouts rule was one such way. Another way being used now is to oblige countries that would like to host the Olympics to comply with a series of conditions that include the introduction of specific doping laws. In some countries, doping has become a transgression of criminal nature that comes with law enforcement practices including house visits, searches, stiff fines and imprisonment. Present anti-doping policy is centred on zero-tolerance and repression. According to anti-doping policymakers, a combination of information, education and repression will lead to drug-free, elite sports competition.

> WADA believes that a long-term solution to preventing doping is through effective values-based education programs that can foster anti-doping behaviours and create a strong anti-doping culture.
>
> (WADA 2009b)

One problem for the creation and maintenance of a strong anti-doping culture anchored in anti-doping legislation and law enforcement is the gap that comes to exist between this specific social practice (elite sports) and what happens elsewhere in society.

In general, in society performance enhancement is becoming rather common. For example, a poll in 2008 by the premier scientific journal *Nature* reported that one in five of the 1,400 readers who participated in the poll used or had used performance enhancing drugs (Maher 2008). The drug methylphenidate (Ritalin) was the most popular, with 62 per cent of users, while 44 per cent reported taking modafinil (Provigil). Reasons advanced were focus, attention, long working hours or jet lag. To illustrate the variation in how society views performance and other enhancement behaviour, Table 5.1 lists several common examples. With the exception of the cyclist, who is clearly transgressing the current no-doping rule in his sport, the other cases are more complex. Concepts such as fairness v. cheating, natural v. unnatural, or healthy v. unhealthy are not easily applied to several of these examples to classify them as either acceptable or unacceptable. As it is very likely that biomedical searches for new therapies will yield more substances and technologies also having extra-therapeutic potential, their extra-therapeutic use is to be expected, especially if the side effects were to remain limited (Cakic 2009). It is both simplistic and illusory to declare that all extra-therapeutic use of substances is illegitimate. Rather, a pragmatic approach is needed, based on regulation of use at the lowest cost to the individual and to society.

Zero-tolerance for doping in sport is thus in contrast with the rather lenient position of general society with regard to cognitive and other types of performance enhancement outside sport. In this regard, it is of interest that the scope of anti-doping policy does not appear to remain restricted only to elite sports and may have consequences outside elite sport. Anabolic steroid use has risen over recent decades but was forced underground with the criminalization of its trade and dangerous practices, akin to what can be observed for psychotropic illicit drug use (Kayser 2009). Anti-doping also leads to excessive surveillance practices, it may be causing more (unintended) harm to society than it prevents, and it might present a slippery slope towards the generalization of anti-doping practices in society at large. Perhaps it is useful to underline that those involved in anti-doping are full of good intentions and driven by positive ideals. To strive for utopia *is*, of course, to act in a wonderful cause. The problem is that it may well be possible that, in the context of present anti-doping policy, striving for a (utopian) cure may turn out to be worse than the disease and lead to dystopia.

Doping is cheating

On a final note, one of the arguments often made is that doping is cheating and therefore cannot be permitted. Apart from the fact that rules can change, and the anti-doping rule can therefore change too, the cheating argument would seem valid, as sport involves playing by rules, and not playing according to the rules undermines the very nature and purposes of the game. However, the moral outcry over doping offences is in great contrast to how sports organizations and the public deal with other forms of cheating in sports. In fact, cheating is also part of sport. Good examples are the famous 'hand of God' goal of Diego Maradona in 1986 and the control of the ball using his hand by Thierry Henry, which allowed France to qualify for the 2010 Football World Cup in South Africa at the expense of Ireland. In both cases, the players got away with it, as the referee did not see the hand-ball, and the rule

Table 5.1 Performance enhancement in and outside sport: some examples

Case	*Evidence for performance enhancement*	*Evidence for health risk*	*Against the spirit (of sport)*	*Comments*
Jane, 21 yrs, medical student, active life style, takes methylphenidate when preparing for difficult exams.	Methylphenidate may have a slight effect, more in those who are somewhat limited.	Occasional use of methylphenidate is probably without much health risk.	Forbidden in competitive sports, not outside sports. But in some countries voices are heard asking for compulsory testing in students.	Jane is an example of a modern achiever, conscious of her limits, eager to succeed; she has adopted a healthy life style with a balanced diet and regular physical activity. She is a coffee drinker, aware of its performance-enhancing effects. She is an informed occasional user of a performance-enhancing drug. The effectiveness of methylphenidate is probably limited, especially in the intellectually gifted, and placebo effects are likely to play a role.
Daniel, 23 yrs, Professional cyclist, takes multivitamins, magnesium, iron, caffeine, and low-dose EPO, to keep an edge and be at the front.	Multivitamins are probably not a good idea, magnesium is probably unnecessary, iron is possibly necessary, caffeine and EPO both have a proven performance-enhancing effect.	It is not well known what the effects are of long-term use of any of these compounds. Iron can be dangerous. High-dose EPO is very dangerous; risk of long-term use of low dose in healthy subjects is unknown.	Any use of a compound on the list of forbidden substances is a breach of the no-doping rule and hence a violation of the spirit of sport.	Daniel is not an exception but rather quite a typical example of a sub-elite cyclist. The actual prevalence of doping in cycling is unknown, but anecdotal and indirect information indicates that doping continues, albeit at 'lower' intensity now that regular testing prevents certain classic 'gross' types of practice.

Continued

Table 5.1 Performance enhancement in and outside sport: some examples, *continued*

Case	*Evidence for performance enhancement*	*Evidence for health risk*	*Against the spirit (of sport)*	*Comments*
Joseph, 32 yrs, commercial, fitness club member, takes anabolic steroids for appearance purposes.	Anabolic steroids amplify training-induced muscle growth.	Excessive use of anabolic steroids can potentially be dangerous but this risk has been exaggerated. It is possible that low-dose use comes with acceptable risk.	Not as long as users do not participate in competitions falling under WADA anti-doping rules. However, there are frequent calls to test for anabolic steroid use in students and fitness clients. Anti-doping Denmark has already introduced testing of fitness clients.	The use of anabolic steroids is frequent in the body-building milieu. The main problem is its medically unsupervised nature and the uncertain origin of the substances that are used. Present ways to deal with the potential health problems related to anabolic steroid use vary between exclusion from health services to special steroid clinics and syringe exchange programmes.
Harry, 45 yrs, manager, inactive, obese, takes sildenafil, for his sex-life.	Sildenafil (Viagra) is a success. It clearly helps men with erectile problems.	Sildenafil has systemic effects and can be very dangerous in subjects with under-lying cardio-vascular disease.	WADA is currently observing sildenafil because of its potential performance-enhancing effects for endurance exercise in hypoxia but it is not on the list of forbidden substances yet.	Harry has an unhealthy lifestyle which probably is a reason for his need for sildenafil. Because of his unhealthy lifestyle he is at increased cardio-vascular risk and sildenafil exacerbates this risk. The best for Harry would be to change his lifestyle.

Catherine, 52 yrs, scientist, takes modafinil when needing to work hard and concentrate on papers or grants.	Modafinil is used to treat narcolepsy but helps healthy subjects to stay awake.	Modafinil has few side effects and is generally well tolerated.	Modafinil is forbidden in competitive sports.	Catherine is an achiever. As a successful scientist she is under continuous pressure to produce high-level science. Regular deadlines for grant proposals have led her to integrate some controlled use of modafinil into her life. She thinks it helps her more than drinking coffee, also because coffee makes her tremble and induces arrhythmia. She is an informed user.
Paula, 65 yrs, retired, takes female hormones, for menopause symptoms.	Hormone replacement therapy is effective for many of the symptoms of menopause.	Hormone replacement increases the risk of breast cancer, heart disease and stroke and regular medical control is necessary.	The hormones used here are not forbidden.	Hormone replacement therapy is mostly for the comfort of women who go into menopause and experience hot flashes and vaginal dryness. It also helps against osteoporosis. Its use is prevalent in affluent society. It is an example of the use of medication where it is not so obvious to distinguish between therapeutic v. non-therapeutic use and natural v. unnatural.
John, 75 yrs, retired, amateur athlete, takes testosterone, growth hormone, and EPO, to continue competition in good shape, participates in the world masters games.	At his age the use of testosterone, GH and EPO certainly has an important performance-enhancing effect.	There is not enough known about such use at an advanced age.	Yes. The world masters games adhere to the WADA anti-doping code and some testing has been introduced in 2009.	This case is rather exemplary of what the evolution of performance enhancement in society may look like in the future. On balance it would seem that a combination of regular physical training, a healthy diet and well-chosen and medically supervised pharmacological anti-ageing treatments is probably a better scenario than that of the general behaviour of the ageing population, the majority of whom have an inactive lifestyle, an unhealthy diet and suffer from associated chronic disease such as diabetes and cardio-vascular disease.

is that the referee has the last word. Cheating in sports as such thus seems not to be such morally reprehensible behaviour. But doping cases are treated much more aggressively, probably because of the strong emotional value of the image of the doping athlete and its similarity with that of the drug addict (Amos 2009). Indeed, it seems as if the 'war on doping' and the 'war on drugs' are, in fact, part of the same endeavour, anchored in a public opinion strongly condemning any behaviour that looks similar to using illicit psychotropic drugs. However, the most successful way of dealing with psychotropic drug use in society is not to strive for full eradication but rather employ harm-reduction approaches and regulate use (Wood *et al.* 2009). By contrast, current anti-doping policy, punitively conceived, is in danger of becoming so radical that it appears justifiable to use any means to reach its goals. It would be a terrible setback for the pragmatic regulation of illicit psychotropic drug use in general society if the anti-doping approach were to become an inspiration for the control of drug use in society in general. This prospect is not as far-fetched as it may seem. One can think of urine controls for students, to check for cognitive-enhancement drugs, or for fitness clients, for anabolic steroids. I doubt that this is the best way to go. I call on anti-doping policymakers to become more pragmatic and to choose regulation and harm-reduction strategies to replace the presumption of guilt without proof and other side effects of current anti-doping policy.

Notes

1 EPO: erythropoietin, a pleiotropic hormone that stimulates the production of red blood cells by the bone marrow.
2 CO rebreathing: by having a subject inhale a known small amount of carbon monoxide, a gas that strongly binds to the oxygen-carrying molecule in the blood's red cells, i.e. haemoglobin, one can calculate total haemoglobin mass from the resulting relative amount of CO–haemoglobin measured in a blood sample.

References

Amos, A. (2009) *Anti-doping policy: rationale or rationalisation?*, Sydney: Faculty of Law, University of Sydney.
BBC (2009) 'Belgian court clears Yanina Wickmayer & Xavier Malisse'. Available online at: http://news.bbc.co.uk/sport2/hi/tennis/8412855.stm (accessed 30 May 2010).
Berry, D.A. (2008) 'The science of doping', *Nature*, 454(7205): 692–3.
Beullens, M., Delanghe, J.R. and Bollen, M. (2006) 'False-positive detection of recombinant human erythropoietin in urine following strenuous physical exercise', *Blood*, 107(12): 4711–13.
Cakic, V. (2009) 'Smart drugs for cognitive enhancement: ethical and pragmatic considerations in the era of cosmetic neurology', *Journal of Medical Ethics*, 35(10): 611–15.
CAS (2006) '*WADA vs. USADA, USBSF and Zach Lund 2006*'. Available online at: http://jurisprudence.tas-cas.org/sites/CaseLaw/Shared%20Documents/OG%2006-001.pdf (accessed 31 May 2010).

CAS (2009) '*Pechstein vs. International Skating Union* and *Deutsche Eisschnelllauf Gemainschaft vs. International Skating Union* 2009'. Availabe online at: www.tas-cas.org/d2wfiles/document/3802/5048/0/FINAL%20AWARD%20PECHSTEIN.pdf (accessed 31 May 2010).

Hanstad, D.V. and Loland, S. (2009) 'Elite athletes' duty to provide information on their whereabouts: justifiable anti-doping work or an indefensible surveillance regime?', *European Journal of Sport Science*, 9(1): 3–10.

Kayser, B. (2009) 'Current anti-doping policy: harm reduction or harm induction?', in V. Møller and M. McNamee (eds), *Elite sport, doping and public health*, Odense: University Press of Southern Denmark.

Kayser, B. and Smith, A.C. (2008) 'Globalisation of anti-doping: the reverse side of the medal', *British Medical Journal*, 337: a584.

Kayser, B., Mauron, A. and Miah, A. (2005) 'Viewpoint: legalisation of performance-enhancing drugs', *Lancet*, 366(Suppl. 1): S21.

Kayser, B., Mauron, A. and Miah., A. (2007) 'Current anti-doping policy: a critical appraisal', *BMC Medical Ethics*, 8: 2.

Lundby, C., Achman-Andersen, N.J., Thomsen, J.J., Norgaard, A.M. and Robach, P. (2008) 'Testing for recombinant human erythropoietin in urine: problems associated with current anti-doping testing', *Journal of Applied Physiology*, 105(2): 417–19.

Lundby, C. and Robach, P. (2010) 'Assessment of total haemoglobin mass: can it detect erythropoietin-induced blood manipulations?', *European Journal of Applied Physiology*, 108(1): 197–200.

Maher, B. (2008) 'Poll results: look who's doping', *Nature*, 452(7188): 674–5.

Møller, V. (2009) *The ethics of doping and anti doping*, London: Routledge.

NRC (2009) '*KNSB schorst jeugdige schaatster*'. Available online at: www.nrc.nl/sport/article2414248.ece/KNSB_schorst_13-jarige_schaatsster (accessed 31 May 2010).

Pitsch, W. (2009) '"The science of doping" revisited: fallacies of the current anti-doping regime', *European Journal of Sport Science*, 9(2): 8.

Pluim, B. (2008) 'A doping sinner is not always a cheat', *British Journal of Sports Medicine*, 42(7): 549–50.

Sottas, P.E., Robinson, N. and Saugy, M. (2010) 'The athlete's biological passport and indirect markers of blood doping', *Handbook of Experimental Pharmacology*, (195): 305–26.

Striegel, H., Ulrich, R. and Simon, P. (2009) 'Randomized response estimates for doping and illicit drug use in elite athletes', *Drug and Alcohol Dependence*, 106(2–3): 230–2.

Thevis, M., Geyer, H., Mareck, U., Flenker, U. and Schanzer, W. (2007) 'Doping-control analysis of the 5alpha-reductase inhibitor finasteride: determination of its influence on urinary steroid profiles and detection of its major urinary metabolite', *Therapeutic Drug Monitoring*, 29(2): 236–47.

UNESCO (2005) 'International convention against doping in sport'. Available online at: http://unesdoc.unesco.org/images/0014/001425/142594m.pdf (accessed 31 May 2010).

WADA (2008) *Q&A: status of finasteride*. Available online at: www.wada-ama.org/rtecontent/document/QA_Finasteride.pdf (accessed 31 May 2010).

WADA (2009a) World Anti-Doping Code. Montreal, p. 19. Available online at: www.wada-ama.org/Documents/World_Anti-Doping_Program/WADP-The-Code/WADA_Anti-Doping_CODE_2009_EN.pdf (accessed 12 December 2010).

WADA (2009b) *Education & awareness*. Available online at: www.wada-ama.org/en/Education-Awareness/ (accessed 31 May 2010).

Wood, E., Werb, D., Marshall, B.D., Montaner, J.S. and Kerr, T. (2009) 'The war on drugs: a devastating public-policy disaster', *Lancet*, 373(9668): 989–90.

6 'Athletes in handcuffs?'
The criminalization of doping

John Hoberman

Introduction: doping, ethics, and the law

The idea that the doping of athletes is unethical has existed for about a hundred years (Hoberman 1992: 103–4, 133–4; Dimeo 2007: 26–9). Although the earliest objections to athletes' use of performance-enhancing substances, dating from the latter part of the nineteenth century, were based on concerns about medical harm, the primary objection to doping for most of a century has been that doping is unethical behavior because it violates ideals of sportsmanship that require fair competition and thus honorable self-restraint on the part of competitors. From this perspective, doping practices violate sport-specific norms that regulate personal conduct within the subculture of elite sport.

The development of elite sport into an enormous and influential global phenomenon has profoundly altered its status as a self-regulating subculture. The symbolic potency of national teams, athletic superstars, and Olympic ritual has projected elite athletes into global public space. What is more, these performers are officially required (if not always expected) to adhere to traditional norms that include "drug-free" status. At the same time, the unwillingness of countless elite athletes to live up to this standard has become all too evident over the past 25 years. Mega-scandals such as the Ben Johnson affair of 1988 and the 1998 Tour de France fiasco finally made it clear to sporting publics around the world that drug-taking had become an integral part of high-performance sport. In these circumstances, and given the symbolic roles assigned to elite athletes, it is not surprising that the unending series of doping scandals in recent years has produced a growing number of demands that athletes who engage in doping be regarded and prosecuted as criminals, on account of their purported status as "role models."

The transformation of doping athletes into criminals represents a radical incursion into a sports world whose ostensible, or imagined, autonomy from the rest of the world has long been one of its principal attractions. The depth of the resistance to turning doped athletes into lawbreakers became evident in Britain in January 2010, when Colin Moynihan, chairman of the British Olympic Association, proposed a new bill in the House of Lords calling for unusually stringent anti-doping measures during the 2012 London Olympic Games. The proposal called for police to be granted the right to raid the athletes' village and search athletes' rooms under a warrant.[1] One response to the Moynihan bill came from Peter Gardner, chief executive of the British Athletes Commission, who predicted that "stop and search" actions and room searches "would be utterly disastrous for the London Olympics." "It's one thing," he said, "for us to be seen to be taking a tough stance on doping but quite another to make athletes feel like criminals."[2]

The official identification of doping with criminality can be dated to the French and Belgian anti-doping laws that were enacted in 1965. Since that time Italy, Austria, and Slovenia have also passed laws that make sports doping a crime. But there is a crucial difference between enacting a law and enforcing it. For example, the 1965 French anti-doping law and the 1989 law that succeeded it remained essentially irrelevant for decades, until riders were imprisoned and interrogated during the great Tour scandal of 1998. The French law passed in 2008 calls for a 1-year prison sentence for a self-doping athlete and a 5-year sentence if trafficking of banned substances is involved. The important distinction between these two types of offense is evident in the large discrepancy between the penalties for personal use versus those for the distribution of banned drugs. Given the expanding use of various performance-enhancing drugs by the general population, there is something counter-intuitive about identifying a self-medicating athlete as a criminal, and this uncertainty about his or her status is expressed in the provisions of the 2008 law. We will return to this issue in the concluding section of the chapter.

Interest in the criminalization of doping has gained momentum in recent years, as the intractability of the doping crisis has become clearer to the sports officials and politicians who are charged with doing something about it. The markedly limited success of doping control programs intended to curb the performance-enhancing drug crisis of recent decades has created a great deal of frustration among national and international sports officials charged with bringing this public relations problem under control. One consequence of this frustration, both inside and outside of official circles, has been a rising chorus of demands that an athlete's use of a banned performance-enhancing drug be made a criminal offense involving the risk of a prison sentence. In 2004, to take one example, the former Australian miler Herb Elliott identified 1–2 percent of elite athletes as people "who break the law [sic] and are cheats and enter into what I call criminal behaviour, because I consider drug taking criminal." In 2006, Dr. Helmut Digel, the sports sociologist and honorary president of the German Athletics Association (DLV), stated: "The athlete who dopes is a criminal who is not criminalized." Dr. Arne Ljungqvist, the chairman of the medical commission of the IOC, argued in 2007 that: "Doping is unacceptable, a social crime." All of these statements (and similar remarks from other commentators) demonstrate the current confusion that reigns concerning whether athletic doping is to be regarded as genuinely criminal behavior, or whether it merely resembles or is somehow analogous to criminal conduct.

Two contrary impulses are at work here. On the one hand, France, Italy, Austria, and Slovenia have criminalized the doping athlete. What is more, this policy can also be applied to non-elite athletes. In 2007, for example, the Danish minister of culture, Brian Mikkelsen, recommended that recreational athletes who dope be criminalized and sent to prison, a position that defines sport as a wholesome communal activity rather than, for example, raising the question of whether the doped athlete has cheated his or her competitors out of money or medals. Expanding the target population in this way to criminalize non-elite athletes points to the authoritarian potential of the anti-doping campaign. The opposing view, while disapproving of doping, expresses a reluctance to dissolve the important boundary between "cheating" and "crime." The prominent IOC member Richard Pound, for example, has distinguished between what he has called "sports crime" and traditional crime. This reluctance to fully criminalize doping practices can be traced to varying motives, such as the kind of sportive nationalism that views doping as a regrettable but necessary competitive advantage, or a determination to preserve sport as a human activity that somehow transcends the social reality within which good and evil are dealt with by criminal law. The criminalization of elite athletic doping becomes even more problematic when seen in the context of a productivity-obsessed modern civilization that is bent on boosting a broad range of human performances by means of performance-enhancing drugs.

How does one justify the criminalization of the doped athlete? One strategy is to portray the doped athlete as a deviant who has betrayed and besmirched the community of honest athletes. Former superstars such as Herb Elliott and Carl Lewis maintain that the vast majority of athletes resist the temptation to dope. "I think it's a tragedy," says Elliott, "that 98 per cent [of athletes] are tainted by the two per cent that are involved in what I think is criminal activity."[3] In 2008, Carl Lewis argued that doping should be a criminal offense in every country. "The reality," he claims, "is that most athletes are clean, most athletes do it right and good athletes don't take drugs. People who don't have talent take drugs." Nor is doping immanent in the system: "The problem is that people choose to cheat."[4]

In both cases, the argument for criminalization is based on the familiar "bad apples" model of elite athlete doping. The emphasis is on stigmatizing the allegedly deviant individual athlete, while ignoring or rejecting the structural model that emphasizes the pressures and incentives to dope that are built into the sports world that has been created by the international sports federations and the governments and commercial interests that fund them. Lewis's implied claim that people who do have talent don't take drugs is contradicted by decades of evidence to the contrary.

Doping and criminalization in Germany

Public discussion about the criminalization of doping among elite athletes has been especially prominent in Germany owing to specific historical and political factors that have made German athletes important public figures. Postwar limitations on the role of the German military have made elite athletes primary representatives of national identity and self-assertion; this special responsibility has intensified public scrutiny of their integrity and moral fitness to represent the nation. The German federal government's funding of elite sport means that doping issues have been debated in the Parliament (Bundestag) for many years; this long process has accentuated ideological differences among the major political parties, with the left-of-center parties usually taking the harder line against the doping of German athletes (Hoberman 1992: 237–65). Finally, the enormous success, and eventual notoriety, of the East German doping program (State Plan 14.25) has played a major role in linking Germany to the doping crisis in elite sport; indeed, the doping trials of former East German sports officials, trainers, and doctors that took place in Berlin during the period 1998–2000 associated "German" doping practices with criminal medical practices in a way that has had no counterpart in any other country.

The conflict in Germany between the factions that either favor or oppose the criminalization of doping has produced many interesting commentaries, thanks in no small part to the "Law to promote the struggle against doping in sport" (*Gesetz zur Verbesserung der Bekämpfung des Dopings im Sport*) that finally became law on November 1, 2007. The passage of this law followed years of passionate debate about whether German society was prepared to accept the spectacle of "athletes in handcuffs" as part of the price to be paid for the anti-doping effort, and the final version of the law made it clear that the coalition of politicians and sports officials that runs the elite sports establishment in Germany was not prepared to tolerate such scenes.

The Social Democratic Party (SPD) had proposed a law against doping in its campaign program as early as 1998, shortly before Gerhard Schröder (SPD) succeeded the conservative Helmut Kohl (Christian Democratic Union (CDU)) as German chancellor. Moreover, in recent years, SPD spokespersons, such as Peter Danckert and Dagmar Freitag, have argued for a strong anti-doping law.[5] In 2006, Danckert, the sports spokesman of the SPD, said that he favored a German doping-law to deal with "athletes who stand at the center of this criminal enterprise . . ."[6] In 2007, he dismissed the idea that German sports federations were really interested in the anti-doping campaign, commenting sardonically that, "organized sport doesn't really want it, they just say they do."[7] In 2007, Dieter Wiefelspütz, the domestic political spokesman of the SPD, also called for the prosecution of athletic consumers as well as dealers of doping drugs.[8] This hard line within the SPD was not, however, unanimous. Otto Schily, who served as federal minister of the interior from 1998 to 2005, made it clear, in 2005, that, like some members of the opposition CDU, he favored leaving the disciplining of athletes to sports officials, while giving the state the assignment of prosecuting doctors, coaches, and support personnel who promoted doping.[9] The German Greens have also taken the harder line, calling, in 2007, for legal penalties against what they called the "distortion of economic competition in sport (sports fraud)" [*Verfälschung des wirtschaftlichen Wettbewerbs im Sport (Sportbetrug)*], involving prison terms of up to 5 years.[10] Winfried Hermann, the sports-political spokesman of Bündnis 90/Die Grünen, declared that: "In the last analysis, doping should be punished as a legally indictable form of sports fraud [*Sportbetrug*]."[11] Or, as the sports attorney Jens Adolphsen put it in 2007: "It makes a difference to an athlete whether it is an investigator from a federation or a state prosecutor who is standing at his door."[12] Conspicuous opposition to doping by these left-of-center politicians reaffirmed an anti-doping position they had supported in the Bundestag during the 1980s, when Social Democrats went so far as to challenge the claim that the production of successful elite athletes was a self-evident national priority for the German nation.

German political conservatives have generally opposed aggressive administrative or legal measures against doping, ever since the Ben Johnson scandal at the 1988 Seoul Olympic Games turned the doping issue into a public relations nightmare for the IOC and its affiliates around the world. As Germany's principal sportive nationalists, who regard the production of internationally competitive athletes as important evidence of national vitality, the conservatives of the CDU and its Bavarian sister party the Christian Social Union (CSU) have tacitly tolerated doping on the grounds that Germany must remain competitive at a world-class level in certain sports. As Manfred Kanther, a CDU minister of the interior in Helmut Kohl's government (1993–8), once put it, Olympic medals are "a German national priority" [*ein nationales Anliegen*], a "demonstration of a people's competitive ability" [*Ausweis des Leistungsvermögens eines Volkes*].[13] This organic model of the nation's relationship to its athletes is not unique to Germany; on the contrary, it remains a powerful stereotype around the world. An important difference is that the historical factors cited above have compelled postwar German politicians and sports officials to debate the national significance of elite sporting success in greater detail and at greater length than anywhere else in the world. It is, therefore, German conservatives who have specialized in articulating the sportive nationalist premise that the production of elite athletes is a matter of national security.

The German political conservatives who oppose targeting doping athletes for prosecution do not, of course, offer the candid argument that the conservative politician, Wolfgang Schäuble (CDU), made to the German parliament (Bundestag) back in 1977:

> We advocate only the most limited use of these [anabolic steroid] drugs and only under the complete control of the sports physicians . . . because

> it is clear that there are [sports] disciplines in which the use of these drugs is necessary to remain competitive at the international level.
>
> (Berendonk 1991: 243)

As federal minister of the interior, first for Helmut Kohl (1989–91) and later for Angela Merkel (2005–9), Schäuble has been responsible for sports–political issues that include doping. Three decades of doping scandals after his endorsement of doping to the Bundestag, this sort of candor has become politically unacceptable. Far more politically acceptable are conservative doubts about the competence of the state to assume certain kinds of authority. This argument may strengthen the hand of those who insist on sport's so-called "autonomy" from the state, a position that denies the state the authority to criminalize athletes.

When the debate over the anti-doping law began in earnest in 2001, the CDU/CSU position was articulated by their sports–political spokesman, Klaus Riegert: "We do not want to criminalize athletes," he said. "Once again the state is taking on an assignment it cannot fulfill."[14] In a similar vein, the position of the Free Democratic Party (*Freie Demokratische Partei*, FDP), in keeping with its emphasis on individual responsibility and the autonomy of the market, was to allow "autonomous sport" to pursue its own dopers.[15] As Wolfgang Bosbach (CDU) argued in 2007: "It is better to rely on sport's capacity to purge itself" [*die Selbstreinigungskräfte des Sportes*]. Dopers, he said, should be motivated to publicly confess and be offered a second chance.[16] In his remarks, Bosback, willfully or otherwise, ignored the accumulated evidence that the only experience that ever motivates elite athletes to confess to doping is being caught. Still, faith in the "educational" approach to doping reform remains standard rhetoric among sports federation and anti-doping officials, including the occasional medical commentator. For example, Klaus Steinbach, a physician and high-ranking German sports official, recommended in 2006 that education [*Aufklärung*] replace punishment. "The anti-doping campaign," he said, "should be taught in school."[17]

Underlying the conservative objection to criminalizing dopers is the idea that drug-taking athletes possess enough good character traits and intentions to make possible their rehabilitation by means of a "second chance." This idea of the athlete as a decent person who has somehow lost his way, rather than a manipulative consumer of illicit drugs, remains influential, even in the face of much evidence to the contrary. For example, Thomas Bach, a member of the FDP and the current president of the German Olympics Sports Association (DOSB) and thus Germany's highest sports functionary, stated in 2006 that state prosecutors should go after the shady characters who run the doping system, rather than the athletes who take the drugs.[18]

The presumed dichotomy between athletes and criminals that Bach invokes here underlies the argument against criminalization. Manfred von Richthofen, a CDU member who is president of the German Sports Association, formulated this point as follows in 2004: "The athlete does not want to be put in the same category as criminals; this is not someone who steals, murders or rapes."[19]

These implicitly exculpating comparisons between doping athletes with consciences and "real" criminals who lack them are misleading. The evidence of many years demonstrates that the genuinely repentant doper is a rarity; in fact, athletes feel entitled to their doping drugs, because they believe that doping is necessary to continue their careers. This is the "sociopathic" logic denounced by the anti-doping leader Dick Pound (see below). Some of these athletes do experience moral qualms, but they are neither bold nor numerous enough to challenge the doping ethos that has prevailed in some sports. Anti-doping and other sports officials publicly embrace the idea of rehabilitation and its "education" mantra, because the intolerable alternative would be to concede that the brutal psycho-physiological requirements of a professional sport such as cycling cannot be addressed by the moral education of the athletes who are hired to undergo these ordeals. No athlete can be "educated" out of inferior performance or the physical suffering of a Tour, but this unhappy fact cannot be acknowledged by people whose administrative (or anti-doping) careers depend on the idea that elite sport can be saved from the scourge of doping by prophylactic "education" and the "rehabilitation" of drug-taking athletes. The other interest group that can be expected to endorse the education model, and oppose criminalization, comprises the conservative politicians who want elite athletes to serve as role models for the national community.

Not all German conservatives, however, oppose criminalization. The Bavarian premier, Edmund Stoiber, declared in 2006 that the state should not abandon sport to deal with its doping problem. "What we need in Germany is a zero-tolerance policy against doping, the way it's done in the other major sports nations."[20] In 2009, the Bavarian minister of justice, Beate Merk, asked:

> Why is there so much anxiety about the legal system? Laws exist for a reason, they are not a form of state interference in the autonomy of sport. It is obvious that sport is not going to rid itself of this problem on its own.[21]

The minister of justice also raised the issue of economic crime: "When an athlete tries to earn more money in such an unfair way, then he is attempting to commit fraud [*betrügen*]."[22] These statements are striking, because conservative officials have effectively abandoned their traditional allegiance to the autonomy of the sports federations. Their endorsements of state action result from the perceived urgency of the doping crisis, which now outranks the principle of autonomy from the state. In this sense, the doping emergency has produced significant ideological change within conservative ranks.

These endorsements of criminalization from CSU conservatives illustrate the important point that positions on the criminalization issue do not always dichotomize neatly along political ideological lines. At the other end of the ideological spectrum, left-of-center European politicians do not always favor criminalization. "Doped athletes are not criminals," the Social Democratic Austrian chancellor, Alfred Gusenbauer, said in 2007. He argued that the abrupt end of their careers was punishment enough.[23] One can also point to apparent differences within the ideological camps themselves. For example, one might have expected the center-left SPD to put less emphasis on punishment and more emphasis on the predicament of the worker–athlete, who practices what is, in effect, workplace doping. Many doped athletes (and many of their competitors) regard this workplace as an ethics-free zone, where the first priority is keeping one's job by using performance-enhancing drugs.

The sports sociologist Helmut Digel, who is better known as the former reformist head of the DLV, favored a German anti-doping-law and criminalization in 2006 to protect what he called "the clean athlete." At the same time, Digel the sociologist pointed to the structural dimension of doping that involves primarily financial incentives to dope:

> Above all we must get rid of the dependence on setting records. We want to provide the spectator with sensational experiences that for the most part no longer exist. We must understand that this struggle requires a very tight system of sanctions and controls.[24]

The question here is whether Digel has taken seriously enough his own emphasis on the problematic commercial arrangement within which high-performance sport takes place. Why would he want to criminalize doping athletes who, in the most demanding sports, are performing under extreme physical and mental duress? Another German sports sociologist, Karl-Heinrich Bette, has offered an alternative perspective that effectively rules out the moralizing approach: "From a sociological standpoint, anti-doping work cannot exclusively or even primarily concentrate on measures that focus on the individual . . . *Because doping results from a social context, the context that produces doping must be changed*" (Bette 2004: 110).

On the political right, one might reasonably have expected a greater degree of moralizing severity about doping on the part of political conservatives, who tend to emphasize individual responsibility and the need to respect and preserve law and order. In this sense, it is striking that Edmund Stoiber's "zero-tolerance policy against doping" is the exception rather than the rule among German conservatives who have addressed the criminalization issue. Why are they so reluctant to seize upon the issue of ethical failure and make an example of the doping athlete as a failed citizen? Perhaps a deep-seated fear of losing the pharmacological arms race to foreign competitors still haunts some of the conservative sportive nationalists. There may also be a concern that criminalization humiliates and devalues the elite athlete as a national resource. Why make a point of inflicting such disgrace on these traditional representatives of the nation? Even in the face of the doping crisis, these conservatives refuse to relinquish their idealized image of elite athletes as inspirational figures who serve the nation as its most dynamic representatives. The choice for conservatives is thus between preserving the heroic status of the elite athlete, even amid the disgrace inflicted on sport by doping, or following Stoiber down the road of "zero-tolerance" and the moral absolutism that leads to a policy of criminalizing doped athletes.

Conclusion: "Criminal" pharmacology and everyday life

The ideological complications of the criminalization issue point to a societal lack of consensus about performance enhancement that deserves close examination. Indeed, some of the notable features of the criminalization debate concerning doped athletes are the private definitions of criminal conduct and the inventive terminology connoting moral failure and criminality that various participants have come up with in order to legitimize their arguments for or against the criminalization of doping. Herb Elliott is satisfied with a category he describes as "what I think of as criminal activity." Arne Ljungqvist, an IOC member and chairman of its Medical Commission, defines doping as "a social crime." Richard Pound, the Canadian tax lawyer who is still on the IOC and was for years the head of WADA, has devised other variations on the concept of what a crime is. "You have a right to work," he said in 2004, "but if you're cheating you do not have the right to work as a cyclist. It is an economic crime as well as a sports crime." At the same time, he emphasized that, "I don't think it's a criminal offense" to be charged with a doping offense. For the athlete, the cost of being decriminalized is that, in Pound's view, "you don't have the benefit of having someone have to prove a case 'beyond all reasonable doubt'."[25] At a conference in Toronto in May 2009, Pound confirmed that he still makes the distinction between "a sports crime" and a crime in the more traditional sense of that term. The U.S. Anti-Doping Agency's (USADA) CEO, Terry Madden, made the same distinction in 2006: "When we're talking [about] an athlete, or a few athletes testing positive, we don't believe that belongs in the criminal area. It's a sporting crime."[26] A year later, however, his successor at USADA, Travis Tygart, said that he and his colleagues at the USADA would be "thrilled" to see Major League Baseball players serving time in prison for felony convictions on doping charges.[27] In February 2010, Pound intensified his verbal assault on doping athletes by calling them "sociopathic cheats," alluding once again to criminality without calling doped athletes criminals in the legal sense of the term.[28]

What the German Greens call the "distortion of economic competition in sport (sports fraud)" [*Verfälschung des wirtschaftlichen Wettbewerbs im Sport*

(Sportbetrug)] is another problematic concept. How can one measure this offense in relation to other offenses as a potential crime and calculate the presumed injustice it inflicts on "clean" competitors? As Gernot Scharr, the chairman of the Austrian anti-doping agency's legal commission, put it in April 2010: "No one has been able to explain to me the difference between a normal cheater [*Betrüger*] and an athlete who makes a profit by winning."[29] Terminological confusion of this scale reveals profound uncertainties about the status of doping as a form of illicit behavior.

What we are dealing with here is what, in English, we call 'cheating', a type of behavior that has traditionally been regarded as distinct from (more serious) criminal offenses. What is more, there are major as well as minor forms of "cheating" or "fraud" that extend across a broad spectrum of human misbehaviors. Many, and perhaps the majority, of these offenses are not covered by criminal law and injure feelings rather than our legal rights. This is why Jürgen Gehb of the CDU considers, "a finding of fraud an inadequate basis on which to call doping athletes to account. The purpose of the criminal law is not to protect sponsors, spectators and athletic competitors from moral disappointment."[30] This is an essential point, in that criminalizing the sources of "moral disappointment" in our lives would vastly expand the "criminal" population, to the point of bringing our private and social relationships to a state of paralysis. So how can we distinguish between cheating and crime? The answer to this question is of crucial importance, because it will determine whether we will choose to criminalize the many forms of dishonesty that inhabit important sectors of human experience but have not been regarded (and punished) as criminal behavior.

Doping is a particularly charged form of misbehavior, in that it involves the consumption of "drugs." For there is no question but that the notoriety of sports doping derives in part from its association with other forms of drug abuse that have provoked moral disapproval, disgust, and criminal charges in Western societies since the nineteenth century. In this sense, there is not a great deal of difference between criminalizing narcotic drugs and criminalizing doping drugs, which have often required the same hypodermic needles that are used by heroin addicts. The consigning of many "drugs" to a single disreputable category has thus served as an important precondition for the criminalization of doping by athletes.

Finally, the criminalization of sports doping requires us to confront a fundamental question regarding life in an era when a wide variety of performance-enhancing drugs are producing what might be called the doping of everyday life: super-caffeinated and other "energy" drinks, along with stimulants such as Adderall and Ritalin, for vast numbers of workers and students; amphetamines for military pilots and truck drivers; anabolic steroids for thousands of police officers; Provigil (Modafinil) for night-workers; and testosterone, growth hormone, and erectile dysfunction drugs for a large population of aging males who want to preserve physical and sexual functioning. Given the growing use of these and other pharmacological aids, how can the criminalizing of doping by athletes be reconciled with this relentless march toward performance enhancement for the masses?

Notes

1 At the 2006 Turin Winter Olympic Games, Italian police carried out an operation of this kind and found illicit doping drugs, as well as blood doping equipment in the living quarters of the Austrian team.

2 "Concern over 2012 athletes village drug searches," news.bbc.co.uk (January 4, 2010). Available online at: http://news.bbc.co.uk/sport2/hi/olympic_games/london_2012/8440088.stm (accessed July 15, 2010).

3 "Jail sport's drug cheats: Elliott," *Herald Sun* (July 19, 2004). Available online at: www.theage.com.au/articles/2004/07/18/1090089027784.html?from=storylhs (accessed July 15, 2010).

4 Matt Slater, "Make doping a crime, says Lewis," BBC Sport (May 7, 2008). Available online at: http://news.bbc.co.uk/sport2/hi/olympics/athletics/7381115.stm (accessed July 15, 2010).

5 Michael Reinsch, "Sportler in Handschellen?" FAZ.NET (May 25, 2005). Available online at: www.faz.net/s/Rub906784803A9943C4A3399622FC846D0D/Doc~E84A4F058CCB94D9D958D9DDC1DED71F7~ATpl~Ecommon~Scontent.html (accessed July 15, 2010).

6 "Ruf nach Anti-Doping-Gesetz" (August 18, 2006). Available online at: www.focus.de/sport/mehrsport/sportausschuss_aid_113856.html (accessed July 15, 2010).

7 "Innenminister Schäuble setzt Sportverbände unter Druck" (June 15, 2007). Available online at: www.welt.de/welt_print/article947528/Innenminister_Schaeuble_setzt_Sportverbaende_unter_Druck.html (accessed July 15, 2010).

8 "Attacke gegen Schäubles Pläne" (May 24, 2007). Available online at: www.focus.de/politik/deutschland/anti-doping-gesetz_aid_57195.html (accessed July 15, 2010).

9 Michael Reinsch, "Sportler in Handschellen?" FAZ.NET (May 25, 2005). Available online at: www.faz.net/s/Rub906784803A9943C4A3399622FC846D0D/Doc~E84A4F058CCB94D9D958D9DDC1DED71F7~ATpl~Ecommon~Scontent.html (accessed July 15, 2010).

10 "Bundestag verabschiedet Anti-Doping-Gesetz" (July 5, 2007). Available online at: www.focus.de/sport/mehrsport/sportpolitik-sportpolitik-bundestag-verabschiedet-anti-doping-gesetz_aid_277976.html (accessed July 15, 2010).

11 Marco Pecht, "Anti-Doping-Gesetz oder nicht, das ist die Frage," *Das Parlament* 21 (May 19, 2008). Available online at: www.bundestag.de/dasparlament/2008/21/Themenausgabe/20529246.html (accessed July 15, 2010).

12 "Innenminister Schäuble setzt Sportverbände unter Druck" (June 15, 2007). Available online at: www.welt.de/welt_print/article947528/Innenminister_Schaeuble_setzt_Sportverbaende_unter_Druck.html (accessed July 15, 2010).

13 Thomas Kistner, "Eine Verschwörung auf breiter Ebene," *Süddeutsche Zeitung* (August 17, 2000).

14 "Führende Sportpolitiker für Anti-Doping-Gesetz" (June 24, 2001). Available online at: www.netzeitung.de/entertainment/people/149216.html (accessed July 15, 2010).

15 Marco Pecht, "Anti-Doping-Gesetz oder nicht, das ist die Frage," *Das Parlament* 21 (May 19, 2008). Available online at: www.bundestag.de/dasparlament/2008/21/Themenausgabe/20529246.html (accessed July 15, 2010).

16 "Attacke gegen Schäubles Pläne" (May 24, 2007). Available online at: www.focus.de/politik/deutschland/anti-doping-gesetz_aid_57195.html (accessed July 15, 2010).
17 "Sport-Funktionäre gegen Anti-Doping-Gesetz" (March 8, 2006). Available online at: www.handelsblatt.com/magazin/sonstiges/sport-funktionaere-gegen-antidoping-gesetz;1046204 (accessed July 15, 2010).
18 "Doping vor Gericht" (September 29, 2006). Available online at: www.taz.de/1/sport/artikel/1/doping-vor-gericht/ (accessed July 15, 2010).
19 Michael Reinsch, "Der Widerstand weicht auf," FAZ.NET (March 23, 2004). Available online at: http://m.faz.net/Rub906784803A9943C4A3399622FC846D0D/Doc~E09DC5DA4E6AD4B9EBCB86D4BAF21EBF2~ATpl~Epartner~Ssevenval~Scontent.xml (accessed July 15, 2010).
20 "Stoiber schiebt Anti-Doping-Gesetz an" (July 24, 2006). Available online at: www.focus.de/sport/tour2006/politik_aid_112431.html (accessed July 15, 2010).
21 "Gesetz gegen Doping?" *Der Spiegel*, 14/2009 (March 30, 2009): 153.
22 "Österreich profitiert von neuem Antidoping-Gesetz" (April 5, 2009). Available online at: www.welt.de/wams_print/article3505010/Oesterreich-profitiert-von-neuem-Antidoping-Gesetz.html (accessed July 15, 2010).
23 "Gedopte Sportler sind keine Verbrecher," www.news.at (June 5, 2007). Available online at: www.news.at/articles/0723/10/175280_s3/gedopte-sportler-verbrecher-antidoping-gesetz-parlament (accessed July 15, 2010).
24 "Der dopende Athlet ist kriminell," sueddeutsche.de (August 4, 2006). Available online at: www.sueddeutsche.de/sport/leichtathletik-em-der-dopende-athlet-ist-kriminell-1.734375 (accessed July 15, 2010).
25 Interview with Richard Pound, *VeloNews* (December 2004).
26 "USADA not interested in criminalizing routine doping cases," AP (August 5, 2006).
27 "Jail may be only deterrent to steroid use," *Daily News* (New York) (November 18, 2007).
28 Steve Merti, "Canadian IOC member Dick Pound calls doped athletes 'sociopathic cheats'," *The Canadian Press*, cp.org (February 9, 2010). Available online at: http://news.ca.msn.com/canada/cp-article.aspx?cp-documentid=23421058 (accessed July 15, 2010).
29 "Vom Kuschelkurs abgekommen," Wiener Zeitung.at (April 2, 2009). Available online at: www.wienerzeitung.at/DesktopDefault.aspx?TabID=4913&Alias=sport&cob=406330&Page16277=11 (accessed July 15, 2010).
30 "Das geplante Anti-Doping-Gesetz verschont die Sportler," www.welt.de (May 26, 2007). Available online at: www.welt.de/sport/article899403/Das_geplante_Anti_Doping_Gesetz_verschont_die_Sportler.html (accessed July 15, 2010).

References

Berendonk, B. (1991) *Doping-Dokumente: Von der Forschung zum Betrug*, Berlin, Heidelberg, New York: Springer-Verlag.

Bette, K.-H. (2004) "Biographical risks and doping," in J. Hoberman and V. Møller (eds), *Doping and public policy*, Odense: University Press of Southern Denmark.

Dimeo, P. (2007) *A history of drug use in sport 1876–1976*, New York: Routledge.

Hoberman, J. (1992) *Mortal engines: The science of performance and the dehumanization of sport*, New York: Free Press.

7 Privacy rights, gene doping, and ethics

Angela J. Schneider

Introduction: gene doping and the concept of privacy rights

This chapter is a conceptual analysis of privacy rights as they pertain to athletes and doping control protocols in light of gene doping and genetic research advances. Part of this analysis comprises an examination of whether or not "privacy" counts as an "essentially contested concept" (Gallie 1955–6). It also sets out an analysis of the relationship of privacy rights, rules, and sport. The conclusion suggests further research questions to aid the progression of future discussion and research on athletes' rights to privacy and genetic doping.

Gene doping and gene doping detection

Doping techniques often develop from medical advances, and gene doping is simply the use of gene therapy to enhance physical performance in a manner proscribed by the anti-doping authorities. The World Anti-doping Agency (WADA)'s 2009 prohibited list includes the transfer of cells or genetic elements or the use of cells, genetic elements or pharmacological agents to modulate expression of endogenous genes having the capacity to enhance athletic performance.[1]

A number of genes have been proposed as potential gene doping agents.[2] The potential benefits range from increasing power to enhancing endurance and to minimizing pain. Some of these genes are being considered for, or evaluated as, treatments for medical disorders such as myopathies, anemias, and growth disorders, while others have been proposed as gene doping candidates based on the effects of manipulation in animals or known functions in humans. Perhaps the most likely candidate for gene doping in the near future is erythropoietin (EPO) (Schneider and Friedmann 2006). The performance-enhancing capabilities of EPO are well known to athletes: the gene produces a circulating hormone and so does not have to be targeted into a specific tissue to function, and the medical need is present—EPO is a commonly used treatment for anemia caused by kidney failure (where EPO is naturally produced) and anemias due to chemo- and radiation therapies.[3]

Testing for gene doping may well be difficult but involves technical issues that are thought to be solvable by WADA through improved research and technology development. Methods for detection and testing could be aimed at both the primary genetic modification and secondary indicators (Schneider and Rupert 2009). As doping control becomes increasing litigious,[4] direct evidence for doping agents, rather than evidence of their effects or secondary consequences, is much preferred by the doping control authorities.[5]

The principal (and principled) difficulty is that current genetic modifications are, in practical terms, untestable, as the therapeutic genes are often identical to the normal human gene. There exists, however, the possibility that genetic markers, for which there could be tests, could accompany modifications. For example, it is possible that all therapeutic genes could be "tagged" with an easily detected DNA sequence. The addition, though, of medically unnecessary markers in a therapeutic construct raises serious ethical and scientific problems. An ethical problem arises in that the presence of an unnecessary marker carries with it additional potential risks of harm. Because these risks are unnecessary from the perspective of treatment, and only necessary for the purpose of detecting doping in sport, they pose an unacceptable risk to patients or clinical trial participants (Schneider 2005). In scientific terms, the addition of unnecessary markers provides an additional risk of compromising the research with the addition of potentially confounding variables (Schneider and Rupert 2009). The incorporation of markers or tags into foreign therapeutic genes to make them more readily detectable may help in doping control programs but would be contrary to best principles of drug design, in which only therapeutic efficacy should be relevant. If, however, the gene constructs were tagged in some manner to allow clinical monitoring of dose, duration of incorporation, and distribution of the constructs, the same assays could be used for doping control.[6]

One of the best ways to protect athletes (and patients) in regard to these issues, as outlined above, is to ensure that their privacy rights are maintained and that proper consent has been appropriately collected. Let us now turn to the concept of "privacy" to gain a good grounding in our interpretation of privacy rights.

The concept of privacy rights

Ethical issues relating to sport, and indeed many other areas, are often tied to conceptual and definitional issues and how they are interpreted in given contexts. Therefore, these issues can turn on how key terms are understood. Discussion about issues in regard to gene doping may be confused when different parties work from different understandings and assumptions. This can happen with the concept of "privacy," a concept that can be ambiguous, multifaceted and contested (Yeo 2004).

Many definitions of privacy can be drawn from the scholarly literature. For example, early on, Warren and Brandeis defined privacy as based on the "right to be let alone" (1890: 278), asserting it as a right specifically grounded in "inviolate personality" similar to "self-determination" and "autonomy." This kind of grounding is pervasive in the literature.[7] Not surprisingly, there are many views about why privacy should be valued. For some, its importance is overrated; for others, it is not rated highly enough. Whether it is intrinsically valuable or valued as a function of other interests is also debated. But, for the purposes at hand, most view its importance with reference to autonomy and respect for persons. Other concepts, including, at least, "ownership," "autonomy," "dignity," "trespass," "intrusion," "intimacy," "anonymity," "secrecy," "security," and "solitude," arise in discussions regarding the relationship between them and privacy. Disagreements center around at least three points: (1) what would count as reasonable expectations that follow from privacy; (2) what should count as private; and (3) what is the boundary between public and private. As a result of these disagreements, it follows that there is much debate about how to protect privacy: (1) by an individual's choice and vigilance; (2) by voluntary codes and self-regulation; (3) by law; (4) by privacy-enhancing technologies; or (5) by some combination of these four possibilities (Yeo 2004: 4).

Importantly, with respect to gene doping and its control, the concept of "group privacy" must also be considered. Tests for genetic manipulation may involve comparative genetic analysis of the athlete's intrinsic genome—for example, athletes could be genotyped for all known performance-affecting genes early in their career and then routinely tested for the appearance of new variants, which would be indicative of genetic manipulation. Information about an athlete, genetic information in particular, may also reveal, or be taken falsely to reveal, information about others (Münthe 2005). This information may contribute to an overall description of a group to which that particular athlete belongs or has been mistakenly thought to belong. The description may adversely affect the interests of others in that group, whether the particular athlete, from which the information was gathered, is adversely affected or not.

There are at least two primary aspects of privacy that have been distinguished (Yeo 2004), each grounded in different values, which can be usefully applied to the discussion in this paper. The first aspect, one most connected to current research on the matter, has been called "self-determination privacy." It has been argued that the value on which self-determination privacy is grounded is tied to respect for persons, namely, autonomy. The second aspect of privacy is referred to as "security privacy" and it is grounded on security from adverse affects resulting from access to, or use of, personal information. These two have been selected from the literature based on their relevance to the genetic doping issues. For the purpose of this chapter, it can be argued that it is important that each of these aspects of privacy be discerned as operative in discussions of ethical issues concerning privacy and issues in gene doping (i.e. doping control, biobank research, etc.). This is not only because distinguishing between the two aspects of privacy can help us better to understand the issues emanating from gene doping and doping control by making explicit the values at stake. Moreover, the failure to recognize this distinction results in confusion and/or obfuscation, which, in turn, undermine the validity of subsequent discussion and policy. Another source that is helpful when dealing with concepts that tend often to be confused or obfuscated is that of Gallie's seminal work on essentially contested concepts. We will briefly turn to this source to shed some light on the matter.

Privacy: an "essentially contested concept?"

Conceptual confusion has long been a source of difficulty in some studies in the area of the humanities. W.B. Gallie's analysis of "essentially contested concepts," published in 1956, stands as the *locus classicus* of the issue. One can consider the concept of "privacy" as one of these essentially contested concepts, as defined by Gallie. This section of the chapter will underscore some major aspects of Gallie's approach, as well as briefly mention some of the controversies it has generated. It is important, for the purpose of this chapter, to address this issue, because discussions of "athletes' rights" (such as they are) will have a greater significance in genetic debates.[8] Gallie explores the normative component of these concepts and offers seven criteria for evaluating their "contestedness." In the present discussion, an examination of Gallie's framework may well help to develop an extended application, focused on "privacy" as it may be applied to issues regarding gene doping in sport.[9] One of the purposes of this chapter is to try to achieve one of Gallie's most difficult goals, namely promoting the reasoned discussion of these concepts (in this case, privacy), given the sharply contrasting normative and analytic perspectives that can be brought to bear on them. Yet his framework, as briefly applied and explored here, may open promising avenues for addressing the challenges around the use of the concept of privacy as it relates to the sports realm, and in particular to gene doping issues.

In 1956, Gallie was very specific about the limits of his enterprise: it dealt exclusively with abstract, qualitative notions, such as *art*, *religion*, *science*, *democracy*, and *social justice*. He proposed a set of conditions for the existence of an essentially contested concept. The important point is that of looking at the features that have come to be accepted as being those which distinguish Gallie's "essentially contested concepts" from merely contested ones. The meaning of many concepts is contested, but it is Gallie's position that some contestedness of certain concepts is part of their essence. Therefore, in this case, we would try to determine if the words that denote "privacy" are used in ways that instead conceal a diversity of distinguishable concepts. If the latter is the case, then, according to Gallie's theory, "privacy" can be shown by use of analysis or experiment to be a radically confused concept, as opposed to an essentially contested one.

The first condition that Gallie identifies is that essentially contested concepts are *evaluative*, and they deliver *value-judgments*. In the case of "privacy," the evaluation is negative if people's rights to it have been violated, and positive if they have been supported. It is also the case that essentially contested concepts denote comprehensively evaluated entities that have an *internally complex* character. As identified above, "ownership," "autonomy," "dignity," "trespass," "intrusion," "intimacy," "anonymity," "secrecy," "security," and "solitude" arise in discussions regarding the relationship between them and "privacy," thus suggesting an internally complex character. Another component of Gallie's definition is that the evaluation must be attributed to the internally complex entity *as a whole*.[10] So, with privacy, if it is to be essentially contested, as opposed to radically confused, when it is violated, it must affect the other concepts listed above as part of the internal complexity.

Another important condition for Gallie is that these different *constituent elements* (namely, "ownership," etc.) of that internally complex entity (i.e. "privacy") are initially variously describable. It is also the case, according to Gallie, that the different users of the concept will often allocate substantially different orders of relative importance and/or interpretations to each of those constituent elements. This does seem to be the case in regard to the literature on privacy. It is also true that, for the concept of "privacy," psychological and sociological causes influence the extent to which a particular consideration is: (a) salient for a given individual; (b) regarded as a stronger reason by that individual than by another; and (c) regarded as a reason by one individual and not by another, thus fulfilling Gallie's next condition for an essentially contested concept.

Further, it would also seem that, when "privacy" is disputed, the related concepts are vague and subject to modification with a change in circumstances, another of Gallie's conditions being thus satisfied. Related to this point, further modification is difficult to predict in advance. Gallie also expresses the stipulation that, although there is no *best* instantiation of an essentially contested concept (or, at least, none knowable to be the best),[11] it is also obvious that some instantiations will be considerably *better* than others; and, even if one particular instantiation seems best at the moment, there is always the possibility that a new, better instantiation will emerge in the future. This particular stipulation also seems to be true in the case of the concept of "privacy," particularly as new technology arises in the area of gene transfer research.

That each party knows and recognizes that their own peculiar usage/interpretation of the concept is disputed by others, who, in their turn, hold different and quite incompatible views, is also a condition of an essentially contested concept for Gallie and seems to apply to "privacy." A related condition is that each party must (at least to a certain extent) understand the criteria upon which the other participants' (repudiated) views are based, thus revealing some common denominators in the debate and discussion. It is in the latter conditions laid out by Gallie that one may find that "privacy" does not fit the definition of an essentially contested concept, but may rather be radically confused. For example, Gallie claims that disputes that are centered on essentially contested concepts are: (a) "perfectly genuine"; (b) "not resolvable by argument"; and (c) "nevertheless sustained by perfectly respectable arguments and evidence." Although "privacy" disputes do seem to be genuine and sustained by respectable arguments and evidence, it may be argued that they can, in fact, be resolved by argument. In opposition to Gallie's position, in the latter part of this paper, I will attempt to explain why resolution of some of the disputes regarding athletes' privacy and gene doping issues are so important.

Finally, it is argued that, often, each party's use of their own specific usage/interpretation of an essentially contested concept is driven by a need to uphold their own particular (*correct*, *proper*, and *superior*) usage/interpretation against that of all other (*incorrect*, *improper*, and *irrational*) users. In the case of the concept of "privacy," it does not seem that this is always the case, thus indicating that it is radically confused and not essentially contested. Nevertheless, it may be argued that it is sometimes the case, and particularly so in regard to athletes' rights to privacy and gene doping. Another related point where the concept of "privacy" does not seem to meet the criteria for an essentially contested concept is that the use of an essentially contested concept is always the application of one use against all other uses, and thus any usage is intentionally aggressive and defensive. In this case, it may well be that we have evidence that "privacy" is a "radically confused concept," because if it were to be essentially contested, rather than "radically confused", the continued use of the essentially contested concept is justified by the fact that, despite all of their ongoing disputation, all of the competitors acknowledge that the contested concept is derived from a *single common exemplar*. This does not seem to be the case with "privacy." It is further argued that the continued use of the essentially contested concept also helps to sustain and develop our understanding of the concept's original exemplar(s). This point does seem to apply to "privacy." Thus, although helpful in better understanding the concept of privacy, this analysis tends to lead one to side with the concept being radically confused, as opposed to truly essentially contested. Let us turn to another perspective to gain a bit more clarification on the matter. The matter of rights and the interrelationship with the rules of sport can be instructive.

Privacy rights and sport

To return to the two primary aspects of privacy identified above, we need to place the discussion within the context of sport. Sport is partly constituted by its rules, and it is thus important to understand the context of the rule-governed nature of sport to identify differences in access demands that form the basis for the invasion of privacy. Rules are often categorized into four types: constitutive rules, regulative rules, auxiliary rules, and rules of skill.

The "constitutive rules" are invented to create a unique conceptual framework and define exactly what it means to play a particular sport.

In addition, the constitutive rules specify the dimensions of the playing area, time for play, approved equipment, what counts as a run, goal, or point, and impose limitations on the means available to score. "Regulative rules" control play by specifying the penalties, when a constitutive rule gets broken. "Auxiliary rules" determine eligibility of players—for instance, by sex, weight, status, or nationality. Rules against doping can be seen to fall into this category, as they specify that players—who have trained using certain substances or practices, such as gene doping—are ineligible to compete. The final category is that of "rules of skill." These are only loosely called "rules," for no penalty attaches to breaking them, and a skilled player may well ignore many of the rules taught to improve the skill of lesser players. Of these four sets of rules, auxiliary rules are the most problematic for the purposes at hand. Whereas the other sorts of rule are intended specifically to make the game a better game, it is not clear that auxiliary rules have the same intention. They have, in the past, been used to discriminate against certain groups of people by excluding them from participation. For example, rules about gender or race have nothing to do with making a game a better game. Thus, auxiliary rules require a justification that must pass a higher level of moral scrutiny, in a way that the others do not.

Many critics believe that we do not need this moral scrutiny of the auxiliary rules and the potential tensions with privacy rights of athletes, because "sport is different" from other practices in society where privacy rights have greater import. Thus, the limitations imposed by the requirements of consent do not apply. Participation in high-performance sport is a privilege, not a right, so the argument goes, and so the imposition of otherwise unjustifiable conditions is acceptable as a precondition of participation in sport. A serious consequence of this sport-is-different argument is that it could allow the imposition of any rules, no matter how absurd, without justification, requiring athletes to give up their rights to privacy just to participate in the activity.

Rights, rules, and sport

One may counter that athletes do not leave their rights to privacy, or even their moral obligations, in the locker room, when they play sports. Sport, then, is not that different. Some bioethicists have argued that there is currently a range of access threats to privacy through extensive demands such as, "workplace monitoring, drug-testing, locker searches, surveillance cameras, databases, identify theft, data-mining, racial profiling, retinal scans, bar codes, microchip implants, radio frequency identification tags, identification numbers, biometrics, hacking, surveys, spyware, personalized marketing, cookies, Web bugs and so on" (Yeo 2004: 9).

This kind of excessive access is sought for such diverse things as crime prevention, administration of justice, the war against terrorism, drugs, poverty, disease, selling or providing products or services, ensuring accountability, security and public safety, the right to know, transparency, sexual prurience, public health, and so on. This access is pursued for various persons and organizations interested in information about us, for example: insurers, employers, marketers, police, criminals, government agencies, statistical agencies, charities, religious groups, and so on. These access demands create genuine concerns about: discrimination, identity theft, denial of insurance, loss of rights, autonomy, and the conversion of persons or communities into bits of data (Yeo 2004).

Of specific relevance, for the purposes of this paper, are the health context and biobanking, which is defined as "a collection of physical specimens from which DNA can be derived, the data derived from the DNA samples, or both" (Yeo 2004: 12). Developments in genetics and genomics have lead to increased interest in access to genetic information and samples. Information linkages pieced together from diverse "data sources" or "silos" have resulted in the formation of revealing composites of individuals and populations. Research into population health, including population genetics, and research on broad determinants of health exemplify this trend. Often, such research relies upon the extensive collection of information that is not health information as such, but may be as sensitive, as it pertains to lifestyles, financial situations, and personal relationships.

The resultant tension between the access need, desire, or demand for information on the one hand, and the interest or right of patients, citizens, communities, and athletes on the other, in controlling the collection, use, and disclosure of their information has lead some bioethicists to argue that, "the norms of research ethics . . . do not adequately capture privacy-related issues concerning research and biobanking"(Yeo 2004: 12). To ensure oversight and accountability due to: (1) the nature of biobank contents; (2) the enhanced ability to reveal biological secrets; (3) the scale of biobanking; and (4) research and access demands, it has been argued by Yeo that business ethics and fair information principles for organizations and databases are needed.

Security privacy, in connection with biological secrets that could be identified and revealed from biobanks collected from athletes, directs our attention to the potential for adverse affects or harm. The problem of the potential for discrimination or denial of insurance cover can be managed relatively easily by restricting access to the information. (Some would argue that this is true only in theory; in practice, however, insurance companies do all they can to find this out.) However, the potential for the information to affect adversely a group or community is more difficult to quantify and manage. Further risks are indirect and speculative and are virtually impossible to assess with any precision. For example, precedents arising in biobank research regarding commercialization or intellectual property could adversely impact society. Another example could come from medical advances enabled by this research that could diminish the health system or lead to greater inequalities. Thus, the risks enabled by the extensive and concentrated collection of genetic information of athletes can be very great, even if their probability of harm is very low.

Inevitable questions arise about who should assess these risks and whether athletes and sport communities should be empowered to assess and decide whether to bear these risks for themselves, or whether others should make that decision for them. It could be further asked how these risks should be communicated to the athletes and others who might bear them. What risks should be communicated? How should they be framed? There are questions regarding individual consent and informed public choice. Further, risks of an entirely different order, such as the potential for the communication of risks and benefits to degenerate into manipulation, come into play.

Yeo (2004) has argued that the distinction between *self-determination privacy* and *security privacy* intends to show that access, collection, or use is problematic, if it occurs in a manner disrespectful of persons and their moral rights or claims over their information. Therefore, consent is an important aspect of privacy. Accessing, using, or sharing information without consent—or doing so under a consent given as a result of manipulation, deceit, or fraud—wrongs athletes, even if only indirectly. A good question one might ask is, "Are all data private data?". One possible answer, as a starting point, is that any data that could potentially harm the individual, if it is released to others, should be considered private.

Privacy and doping control

Information of interest to biobank research has been collected in sport for doping control. When consent for the original purpose—in this case, doping controls—does not authorize desired secondary research access, the requirement for consent is obviously an impediment. Also, grouping these two consents together is problematic, because one is required to compete in sport, and the other is not. In some instances, it may be feasible to obtain a new consent to authorize the new research purpose. In others, this may be deemed impractical or even impossible. In the latter event, either the secondary research collection does not occur, or it occurs without consent. If it were to occur without consent, the athletes whose data are in question may never know. Thus Harry et al. write:

> The immortalized cell lines can be stored in various gene banks around the world. Control and monitoring of samples is a critical issue, and it is very difficult to prevent abuses such as samples being used beyond the original intent. It is almost impossible to tell who is using them and for what purpose. Additionally, DNA can be extracted from tissues and blood. Once the DNA is extracted, it is frozen and is stored for years. Again, these samples can be transported to several different labs without the consent of the donor and used for studies beyond their original intent.
>
> (Harry et al. 2000: 23)

The issues and concerns discussed above are relevant to the issues emanating from the potential for gene doping, but presumably they would apply generically to genetic research involving all humans. One point useful in this regard is the distinction of "washed data"—that is, data cleansed of any identifying characteristics. The ability to facilitate the collection, sharing, and manipulation of personal information through computerization and genetic technology, coupled with the increased demand for it from research, constitute a significant challenge to privacy. Athletes are particularly vulnerable to this challenge. Genetic technology, research, and biobanking are developing at a rapid pace. At present, there is insufficient scrutiny of, and public debate on, them. Some, though not all, would argue that the pace and magnitude of change exceed the capacity of those charged with ethical oversight thereof. Many issues arise, including issues about who should decide which issues should be discussed. The challenge lies in determining what kind of moral constraints should be put in place. Yeo (2004) has argued that the quality of the process for social debate is largely a function of how well it expresses respect for persons and for communities.

It is easy to see from the history of sport that this kind of respect has been less than ideal. Respect of athlete consent is one such issue. That the default for information flow is skewed in a privacy-invasive direction indicates that athlete consent may well be insufficient for protecting privacy. However, from a privacy perspective, it has also been claimed that the problem arises from the design of the system. Information is increasingly a valuable commodity or resource. In the commercial sector, there are strong fiscal incentives to design information systems to ensure access to desired information. Yeo (2004) has argued that the greater the information requirement of the protocol, the greater the incentive there is to skew the system design in a privacy-invasive direction.

Careful attention to consent requirements for collection of biological samples from athletes can help to mitigate these concerns. With respect to the quality of the consent, for example, provisions could exist to ensure that the consent is informed, or that dubious models of consent that effectively bypass autonomy to secure access to the information are ruled out. However, even assuming that consent is as respectful of autonomy as it can be (because one could have consent that is not informed and would not be fully respectful of autonomy), there may yet be reasons to limit which athletes are, and are not, permitted to consent. Following Yeo (2004), we need to rule out research that is privacy-invasive beyond a certain threshold or, at least, ensure that it is brought within that threshold. This may indicate that there are data that are not properly considered to be private. If so, the problem becomes a bit less about consent and more about drawing the line.

Although it is beyond the scope of this chapter to present a detailed assessment of the existing regulatory framework for privacy, doping control, and biobank research, there would seem to be reason to think that the existing framework is inadequate to protect athletes. In particular, consent issues are not adequately resolved in the existing regulatory framework. One's focus here ought also to extend to issues of accountability. This applies to consent issues and other issues, to the extent that the question whether these issues have been framed, debated, and resolved in a transparent, explicit, and public way is a question of accountability. The extent to which doping-control governance may allow the migration of samples collected for doping control to research (and other) contexts without specific informed consent (evaluated in the light of athletes' self-determination) is questionable.

Standardized practices are a part of any comprehensive privacy framework for biobank research on doping-control samples. However, from the standpoint of accountability, this approach is insufficient to resolve ethical issues concerning athlete consent and ownership of the biological samples that athletes are required to give in order to compete in sport. What should be "standard" is precisely what needs to be adjudicated, and what is best from the perspective of privacy for the athlete, or relevant others, may well not be best from the perspective of research access. These issues are of great enough social importance that they require broader public debate than has hitherto been the case.

Yeo (2004) has noted that, in the broader research community, ethical oversight may be, and often is, invoked reassuringly to assuage concerns about privacy and biobank research. He also thinks that ethics review is a very important safeguarding provision. However, he thinks that such reassurances are not very comforting if, or to the extent that, one does not believe that the policy guidance the reviewers will use to adjudicate the issues is adequate. Moreover, he argues that the protocols for research and gene banking are very complex and strain both the capacity and competence of research ethics boards. Thus, the issue is not only one of capacity, but also one of competence. He claims that, distinct from both capacity and competence, there are issues of independence with respect to various interests—particularly given the extensive range of interests that may be involved in biobank research. For Yeo, protocol review does not, and cannot, capture all the features of research and biobanking that may be of a privacy concern. Finally, even supposing that all of the issues identified above were addressed, an important, larger question would remain: What is the right locus of responsibility and authority for resolving unresolved societal questions of this nature? Some might argue that it is not restricted to ethics review boards.

What is most at issue regarding the right locus of responsibility and authority is accountability. The answers to the following questions need to be debated and publicly addressed in the doping-control protocols. What provisions are in place to ensure that information flows only as authorized? Who has the right to do this authorizing? How transparent is the system? What oversight is there by which to hold data stewards accountable? Finally, we need to ensure that public processes exist to ensure that initiatives develop with due regard for the interests *and* rights of the athlete community.

Because of the international nature of elite-sport competition, there are myriad legal issues that differ in different countries. Not all countries are democratic. Not all countries value human rights. The athletes are even more vulnerable in these settings. The information that can be gained from the human genome and genetic research has been called "The book of life" (particularly if one assumes genetic exceptionalism). The athletes expose their individual books of life when they submit a biological sample for doping control. Outside of sport, some ethicists are currently advising that, because no sufficient protection against discrimination (for instance, for eligibility for life insurance) exists for people who have a genetic predisposition to a disease, prudent people are likely to decline consent to research that identifies their genetic makeup.

Conclusions

From an ethical perspective, gene doping does not appreciably differ from other forms of doping, although the possibility of permanent, irreversible, and ongoing enhancement would complicate sanctioning. Whether it should be prohibited and, if it is, how the prohibition should be enforced are subject to the same debate and raise the same issues of privacy, autonomy, and authenticity as other forms of doping. If testing for gene doping involved the use of the athlete's genetic information, then extra privacy safeguards would have to be in place, as such data can be informative about the athlete's kin-group. As well, provisions for post-test genetic counselling would be necessary, as genotyping could identify the athlete as a carrier for deleterious mutations or late-onset genetic disorders.

Few technologies are free of the possibility of abuse. Fears of "gene doping" should not blind us to the potential of gene therapy in the treatment of sports injuries or in abrogating medical conditions that may have otherwise precluded an individual from participating in elite sports. Ultimately, the challenge to sports ethicists may come, not from "gene dopers," but from athletes who have achieved high levels of performance by virtue of legitimate therapeutic interventions—people in whom therapeutic correction may lead to near perfection.

Research and biobanking are proceeding at a rapid pace in many countries. They are often interlinked with developments in health information systems, networks, and databases. Even in the realm of the broader general public, there has been insufficient scrutiny or public debate, let alone in sport. Given the magnitude of change, it could be argued that this discussion challenges our capacity for ethical reflection and social debate. Many issues arise, including even issues about who should decide which issues should be discussed, and with what input. The quality of the process is largely a function of how well it expresses respect for persons and for communities. With respect to athletes, the salient consent questions are as follows:

1 Is the information provided about the biobanking, future testing, and research sufficiently complete for them to know what they are getting into?
2 Is information that could be relevant to the athlete's consent omitted or hard to access?
3 Is the information that is provided to the athlete accurate or misleading?
4 Is there undue inducement that compromises the voluntariness of the athlete's consent by combining things needed (doping control) with other things that would not be agreed to, but for their association with things needed (future testing and research)?
5 Is the process itself sufficiently independent of those with an interest in a given outcome to ensure its integrity and the integrity of its results or conclusions?

One of the greatest dangers is that doping control and biobanking processes will be designed, not to obtain athlete input that truly expresses their considered views—an authentic and autonomous expression of their will, so to speak—but rather to provide support for a predetermined end.

Notes

1 This broad definition restricts the use of modified cells (e.g. following *ex vivo* genetic manipulation), gene therapy using traditional protein-coding genes, as well as other genetic entities, such as anti-sense RNAs and siRNAs, or DNA-targeted drugs (the last clause is somewhat problematic, as many drugs act by modulating gene expression, and the exclusion of drugs intended to activate or modulate transgene (i.e. exogenous gene) function should have been included, even if the drug itself had no performance enhancing capacity).
2 For a fuller discussion of this topic, see Schneider and Rupert (2009).
3 In 2006, investigators in a doping case against German athletics coach Thomas Springstein found an e-mail from 2002 in which Springstein refers to the difficulties in obtaining Repoxygen, an EPO-gene-based therapy that was going through clinical trials by Oxford Biomedica as an anemia treatment at the time. The drug was slated to enter clinical trials in 2002. However, as of 2009, the company has stated that Repoxygen is no longer under development and/or the subject of clinical trials. Ironically, Repoxygen may not have been suitable as a doping agent—similar to the natural EPO gene, the therapeutic EPO gene was regulated by blood oxygen levels, and the treatment may have worked to raise low blood cell counts to normal levels, but not to raise normal levels to supernormal levels.
4 See the increasing number of cases being initiated by athletes that are heard by the Court of Arbitration for Sport.
5 As of 2007, WADA had funded twenty-one research projects designed to investigate possible tests for "gene doping."
6 One reason WADA maintains close contacts with pharmaceutical companies is to assess any assays that companies develop during research and development of new, potential ergogenic drugs for future testing strategies.
7 Gavison rejects "self-determination" or "control" as the definition of privacy, defining it in normatively neutral terms as non-accessibility to others. She breaks

this down into three elements: "the extent to which we are known to others, the extent to which others have physical access to us and the extent to which we are the subject of others' attention" (1984: 347). These three, she claims, correspond to "secrecy," "solitude," and "anonymity." Thus, why non-access (i.e. privacy) in any of these three should be valued, and whether the ability to exercise control over access is a good thing, are independent of the definition of privacy. Yeo points out that, whether Gavison's definitional point is correct or not, normative questions about privacy must necessarily move in the arena of values, as she is fully aware.

8 This point depends on the idea generally referred to as "genetic exceptionalism"—the idea that genetic data are somehow special in kind. This is, of course, also disputed.

9 Some of those controversies are based on claims that his criteria are too narrow. Although the purpose here is not a full-scale analysis of Gallie's approach, it may be suggested that these criticisms fail to recognize that Gallie offers both a restrictive and broader definition of these criteria, and that reconciliation of these criticisms may be achieved with his alternative definitions. It is also the case that some accuse Gallie of naively promoting conceptual relativism by undermining standards for evaluating concepts, and others argue, more sympathetically, that perhaps Gallie is too optimistic about the prospects for resolving conceptual disputes.

10 McNamee (1995) discusses whether sport itself should be viewed as an essentially contested concept.

11 McNamee (1995) has suggested the point is here captured by Ernest Gellner (and later by Nagel), in that there is no way of stepping outside of any framework to determine which might be analytically superior. Each of the instantiations is part of a "form of life" and must be evaluated as such, and only from within. This general move is widely attributed to the later Wittgenstein: one ought not to look for an essential meaning of concepts but rather to their use in "language games/practices."

References

Gallie, W. (1955–6) "Essentially contested concepts," *Proceedings of the Aristotelian Society*, 56: 167–98.

Gavison, R. (1984) "Privacy and the limits of law," in F.D. Schoeman (ed.), *Philosophical dimensions of privacy: an anthology*. Cambridge: Cambridge University Press, pp. 346–402.

Harry, D., Howard, S., and Shelton, B.L. (2000) *Indigenous peoples, genes and genetics: what indigenous peoples should know about biocolonialism*. Indigenous People's Council on Biocolonialism. Wadsworth, Nevada. Available online at: www.ipcb.org/pdf_files/ipgg.pdf (accessed June 30, 2010).

McNamee, M.J. (1995) "Sport: relativism, commonality and essential contestability," in S. Eassom (ed.), *Sport and values*, Bedford: Casper, pp. 86–119.

Münthe, C. (2005) "Ethical aspects of controlling genetic doping," in C. Tamburrini and T. Tännsjö (eds), *Genetic technology and sport: ethical questions*, London and New York: Routledge, pp. 107–25.

Schneider, A.J. (2005) "Genetic enhancement of athletic performance," in C. Tamburrini and T. Tännsjö (eds), *Genetic technology and sport: ethical questions*, London and New York: Routledge, pp. 32–41.

Schneider, A.J. and Friedmann, T. (2006) "Gene doping in sports: an opening scenario for genetic enhancement of normal 'human traits'," *Advances in Genetics*, 51: 37–48.

Schneider, A.J. and Rupert, J.L. (2009) "Constructing winners: the science and ethics of genetically manipulating athletes," *Journal of the Philosophy of Sport*, 36(2): 182–206.

Warren, S.D. and Brandeis, L.D. (1890) "The right to privacy," *Harvard Law Review*, V.IV(5): Boston. Available online at: http://faculty.uml.edu/sgallagher/Brandeis privacy.htm (accessed June 30, 2010).

Yeo, M. (2004) *Biobank research: the conflict between privacy and access made explicit*, Her Majesty the Queen in Right of Canada: Canadian Biotechnology Advisory Committee.

8 Bodily violations

Testing citizens training recreationally in gyms

Ask Vest Christiansen

One of the more controversial issues surrounding the use of steroids in the general population is drug testing of citizens who train recreationally in fitness centres and gymnasia. Although known to be liberal, Norway and Denmark are two among very few countries in which drug controls in gymnasia and fitness centres take place as part of the overall fight against doping in sport. Whereas, however, Norwegian anti-doping officers are only allowed to perform tests on individuals who have given written consent for them to do so and who cannot be sanctioned if they do not give their consent, officers from Anti Doping Denmark (ADD) may choose to test any individual training in a fitness centre or gymnasium that is part of the national anti-doping testing scheme, irrespective of their consent. The Danish scheme for testing recreational athletes training in gymnasia is probably the most comprehensive control scheme of this sort in the world. Despite the uniqueness of the regime, the other Nordic countries have shown interest in the system and acknowledged the potential of the unannounced tests to function as a preventive tool for the use of performance- and image-enhancing drugs in the general population.[1]

In 2010, the system had its 5-year anniversary, and so it is timely to develop a thorough analysis of the foundation and the consequences of such a system for testing for drugs outside organised sports. Thus, in the first part of this chapter, the legal foundation for testing recreational athletes in gymnasia and fitness centres is discussed, along with an examination of whether the purpose of the relevant Danish legislation is realised by the present testing scheme. In the second part, the actual testing procedure is analysed in relation to the question of whether, and to what the extent, the testing in fitness centres and gymnasia can be said to violate Danish citizens' fundamental privacy rights.

Before proceeding, however, a remark concerning terminology is necessary. In accordance with Verner Møller's analysis of the conceptual confusion in the Danish anti-doping campaign, I too consider it misleading to use the term 'doping' in reference to the use of performance- and image-enhancing drugs that takes place in connection with people's training in fitness centres and gymnasia (Møller 2009). Given, however, that the term is used in the Danish legislation on the issue, I will nevertheless apply it, reluctantly, in accordance with this when appropriate in what follows.

The legal foundation for testing recreational athletes in Danish gyms

As in many other countries, the handling and distribution of anabolic steroids is illegal in Denmark (Retsinformation 1999), and, as in many other countries, Denmark has had educational campaigns directed against the use of anabolic androgenic steroids and other muscle-building drugs (Anti Doping Danmark 2010b). A unique feature of the Danish anti-doping effort, compared with that of other countries, is, however, that ADD, apart from testing elite athletes, since 2005 has also been required by law to perform doping tests in fitness centres and gymnasia (hereafter, 'gyms') that have signed up to a national anti-doping scheme.

Gyms pay a fee of approximately €1,600 (12,000 DKK) a year to be part of the scheme. They then receive a sticker with a happy smiley reading: '☺We test for doping in collaboration with Anti Doping Denmark', which they are required to display on the entrance door. Gyms that do *not* sign up for the testing scheme receive a sticker with a sulky smiley reading: '☹We do *not* test for doping in collaboration with Anti Doping Denmark', which they are also required by law to make visible to their customers at the entrance. In June 2010, 50 per cent (n = 230) of all commercial gyms in Denmark (n = 459) were part of the scheme, embracing approximately 80 per cent of all Danish gym members (n = approximately 550,000) (Steele *et al.* 2010). As more gyms have joined the scheme, testing has increased, while the percentage of positive tests has stayed at around 20–25 per cent. It is important to note, however, that testing is targeted, and so one cannot make direct inferences as regards the prevalence of doping in the general population of gym members from these figures. The latest estimate from 2010 suggests that 44,000 Danes have experience with using what are referred to as 'muscle-building drugs' (Singhammer and Ibsen 2010).

The Danish 'Act on Promotion of Doping-Free Sport', which is the juridical base of the testing scheme, was passed in 2004. The Act embraces all sports,

Table 8.1 Number of tests conducted and positive tests in commercial Danish gyms

Year	*Number of tests*	*Number of positive tests*	*Percentage of positives*
2005	106	24	23
2006	216	46	21
2007	243	51	21
2008	463	111	24
2009	751	151	20

Source: Anti Doping Danmark (2010a)

and likewise the testing is intended to embrace all sports. According to paragraph 9 in the Act:

> Anti Doping Danmark, shall endeavour to enter into collaborative agreements on the fight against doping in sport with the following parties: 1) owners of relevant businesses and others offering sports or related activities, including public bodies, and 2) groupings of athletes not affiliated to the sports organisations.
>
> (Retsinformation 2004: paragraph 9)[2]

However, the application of this simple policy soon becomes trickier than first envisaged, for 'the collaborative agreements [. . .] shall ensure that the parties concerned implement doping control and sanctions in such a way as to comply with the guidelines applying to the sports organisations'. In line with this, the collaborative agreements are therefore obliged to define doping in accordance with the substances and methods on the World Anti-Doping Agency's (WADA) prohibited list, and the regulations on doping control and sanctions shall also be in accordance with the World Anti-Doping Code (WADC) (Retsinformation 2009: paragraph 3). Hence, it is not merely anabolic steroids that are the focus of attention when testing in gyms but – ideally – all drugs on the list. Further, the procedure for the tests in gyms must follow the international standards for testing and sanctioning of athletes, as laid out in the WADC. Therefore, any Danish citizen training recreationally in a commercial gym that has a happy smiley at the entrance is subject to the WADC, the list of banned substances and the associated sanctions.

Testing non-competitive, recreational athletes in Danish gyms thus follows a practice developed for international elite sport. This is also the case regarding the sanctions. A recreational athlete who uses anabolic steroids (or another drug found on WADA's list of banned substances) and tests positive in a control is excluded from the gym in question for 2 years, and from all other gyms that are part of the scheme. Moreover, if the Act is to be taken at face value, the person is also excluded from *all* organised sports in Denmark for the 2-year period. As in elite sport, a refusal to be tested is counted as a positive test.

In order to evaluate this legislation, we need first to consider its foundation. Recently, the chair of ADD, Jens Evald (who is also a Professor of Law), has given such an account. Although the point of departure for his analysis is elite sport and the whereabouts system, it is the Danish legislation that is his focus of attention. After a thorough analysis of the legal foundation of anti-doping work in Denmark, Evald states:

> The purpose of doping control, as it is stated in the preliminary work to the Act on promotion of doping-free sport, is to strengthen the fundamental values of sport and secure the health of the athletes. To this is added the prospect to affect the sale of doping drugs, which are often

> imported and distributed illegally, especially in environments in and around gyms. There is no doubt that doping control pursues legal purposes. Neither is there any doubt that doping control is a necessity, if the legal purposes should be realised.
>
> (Evald 2009: 81–2)

There are thus two main arguments for conducting doping controls: (1) 'to strengthen the fundamental values of sport' and (2) to 'secure the health of the athletes'. In order to evaluate the solidity of this foundation, we need to have an idea of what is actually meant by 'the fundamental values of sport'. This phrase seems to be related to what WADA calls 'the spirit of sport', which is encompassed by eleven so-called core elements, among which 'ethics, fair play and honesty' are represented (WADA 2009b: 13). The notions of the *spirit of sport* and the *fundamental values of sport* are meant to be the normative foundation for sport and are thus often referred to in after-dinner speeches where sport is praised, but they are never defined in any applicable way. I will not go into a lengthy discussion on the exact meaning of the notion of the 'fundamental values of sport' here. It is safe to say that, in this context, it means something along the lines of 'fair play' or 'the good competition'. This is obviously only a cursory and tentative interpretation, as these notions themselves are not carved in stone, but for the present discussion it will suffice.

Four problems concerning the testing regime

In the elite-sport context of Evald's analysis, it is probably correct that doping control does pursue legal purposes and is necessary if the legal purposes are to be realised. Yet the use of performance- and image-enhancing drugs in gyms is a different thing from doping in elite sport, and it is therefore necessary to evaluate the rationale for, and possible consequences of, applying a law created for elite sport in a setting of non-competitive recreational exercise. I will do this by addressing four problems regarding the application of the Act on Promotion of Doping-Free Sport in the gym environment.

The first problem is that the foundation for doping control in gyms seems to rest solely on the health argument. I will therefore argue that imposing sanctions on individuals by excluding them from training might be counter-productive. The second problem relates to some possible objections to the first and lists and discusses some of the possible *intended*, but not official, purposes of the testing scheme. The third problem is concerned with the fact that a consequence of the law is that drugs that are often used by girls and women in the gym environment are not tested for. This results, not only in gender bias, but also a contradiction at the heart of the policy, which makes problematic the idea that health is the core rationale for testing in gyms. The fourth problem addresses the prospect that the act may not only exist to fight doping but also to affect the sale of illegal drugs.

Are the consequences of the act counterproductive?

As noted above, Evald emphasises two arguments for conducting doping controls: (1) to strengthen the fundamental values of sport and (2) to secure the health of the athletes. As it is these arguments that constitute the foundation for the anti-doping work – also in gyms – we have to assess what happens to the strength of this foundation if one of the two arguments is irrelevant.

Insofar as achievement sport involves competition, a hierarchical structure and an institutional framework and is governed by a set of written rules, training recreationally in a gym cannot be considered to be sport (Møller 2010). Further, we know that the great majority of individuals training in gyms never compete. Therefore, non-competitive recreational athletes using performance- and image-enhancing drugs cannot be said to be breaching the principle of 'fair play', nor that of 'good competition', nor 'the fundamental values of sport'. The primary foundation for conducting doping tests on these individuals must then be to 'secure the health of the athletes'. This leaves us with a delicate situation that prompts the following argument: a doping violation by a recreational drug user in a Danish gym cannot be considered a sporting infringement. A doping violation in a gym is nevertheless governed by rules developed for sport. A doping sanction that follows as a consequence of such a violation will seriously affect an individual's opportunity to participate in organised sport, training or exercise, as the associated sanction involves exclusion, not only from the gym where the individual holds his or her membership and all other gyms that are part of the scheme, but from *all* organised sport in Denmark. Having a positive test from a gym thus also has, as a consequence, the situation where the individual is not allowed to play, for example, badminton for a 2-year period. If, however, participation in sport, exercise or training is regarded as a prerequisite for good health, then excluding an individual from sport participation is counter-productive for promoting good health. However, as the performing of doping controls in gyms has health as its apparent primary legal foundation, the testing can be considered a contradictory practice.

There are, of course, objections to this argument. The second problem addresses one such likely objection.

Intended consequences of the testing scheme

In connection with the 2nd Nordic Conference on Anabolic Steroids, in Hamar, Norway, in May 2009, I presented the above view for ADD's adviser on information and education, Jakob Berget. He made me aware of the fact that there might be intended consequences of doping controls in gyms that are not mentioned in the Act, in the executive order or in the preliminary work to the Act. I took note of this. To ensure that I had understood him correctly, I asked Berget, in an email, to confirm that the controls, in his view, can also have the following effects:

- people will abstain from using drugs out of fear of being excluded from their gym owing to a positive test;
- gyms with control will have fewer negative role models, resulting in fewer new users; and
- testing in (most) gyms will concentrate drug users in (the few) gyms where testing does not take place; this makes it easier to contain and control the problem.

Berget was kind enough to confirm this. For the last of the three propositions he specified that, in gyms that do not have a drug-testing agreement, 'there is an opportunity to meet others who use steroids, but this of course also makes the task of locating and controlling the problem correspondingly easier'. To this he added that, 'It is however important to remember that just because a gym has no doping control, this doesn't mean that there is doping in the gym'.[3]

With these three propositions in mind, one could argue that what is meant by 'the health of the athletes' is open to misconstrual. Thus, if these intended consequences of the testing scheme are to be realised, the purpose of protecting the athletes' health could still be served. For this reason, the above propositions deserve close attention.

The fear of exclusion

The idea that people will abstain from using performance- and image-enhancing drugs out of fear of being excluded from their gym builds on two assumptions:

1. increased control and surveillance will make people behave in accordance with the norms and values of the controlling body in order not to get sanctioned; and
2. for individuals who have the potential to be tempted by banned substances, belonging to a specific gym is more important than using the drugs that can help them build the body they desire.

These assumptions might be correct, but, in order to have any impact, they are both dependent on a certain degree of intensity in the control scheme. In order to be feared, the power of the surveillance system needs to be present.

The data in Table 8.1 indicate that, although testing has increased over the years, the percentage of positive tests has been fairly constant. From this, one might think that people have not been deterred by the occasional (though rare) presence of control officers in their gym. The fairly constant figures could, of course, also indicate that the control officers have become better at picking subjects for testing, and that they thereby maintain a high percentage of positive tests, although the absolute number of drug-using individuals has decreased.

Recent research, however, suggests that the primary concern among users of anabolic steroids in Danish gyms is not the risk of having a positive test, but rather the negative health effects of their drug use. Thus, in an analysis of the anonymous questions ADD's enquiry service received over an 18-month period, less than 10 per cent of enquirers who used anabolic steroids and other WADA-banned substances reported concerns with respect to having a positive doping test and the concurrent ban, whereas 58 per cent expressed health concerns in relation to drug use. Also, among enquirers who considered using anabolic steroids and other WADA-banned substances, less than 5 per cent expressed concerns about having a positive doping test as a result of such usage, whereas more than 80 per cent were asking questions related to adverse effects and the potential health risks (Bojsen-Moller and Christiansen 2009).[4] Thus, when addressing enquiries to ADD ,the primary concern for those using or considering using anabolic steroids was not the risk of a potential ban, but rather considerations to do with their health.

One reason why the controls might not deter users of performance- and image-enhancing drugs could be that they are too few to have the expected effect. Gyms that are part of the scheme can only expect to have two control visits per year, with two individuals being tested per visit (Anti Doping Danmark 2010b). In a large gym with maybe 2,000 members, four tests per year (where, on average, one is positive) might be insufficiently comprehensive to act as a deterrent.

Negative role models

From both cross-sectional and longitudinal studies on substance use, it is known that adolescents whose peers use substances are more likely to use drugs and use them more frequently, than youths whose friends are non-users. It has also become clear that peers play a greater role in drug-using behaviour than parents do (Needle *et al.* 1986; Jenkins 1996; Oetting and Donnermeyer 1998; Bahr *et al.* 2005). Some studies have shown, however, that the influence of peers is more likely to be due to social selection than to social influence (Bullers *et al.* 2001). There is, however, little research on the effect of role models specifically regarding the use of anabolic steroids (Backhouse *et al.* 2007), but it can be assumed that the influence here is somewhat similar to that of other illicit substances. At any rate, such an assumption is in line with what has been observed in qualitative studies on drug use in the fitness and gym environment (Klein 1993; Barland 1997; Pope *et al.* 2000; Monaghan 2001; Bach 2005; Gray and Ginsberg 2007). Senior gym members and the peer group's attitudes and drug-using behaviours can thus be expected to be an important factor affecting the drug use of young people.

This general assumption needs to be balanced by other considerations. In contrast to the use of such drugs as tobacco, alcohol, marijuana or cocaine that are the focus of attention of most studies examining the influence of peers and parents, the use of anabolic steroids often takes place in settings with an otherwise high awareness of a healthy lifestyle. Thus, people in strength-training environments often pay more attention to their diet, exercise, alcohol and sleep patterns than do either young people taking the substances mentioned above or the general population.

Furthermore, one cannot reject out of hand the idea that, for younger individuals who have made the decision to begin using, for example, anabolic steroids, the presence in the gym of senior users could make their decisions more informed, by exploiting the potential access to relevant information about proper dosages and sufficient attention to adverse effects. In other words, to the extent that they are responsible, the sharing of their experience by senior users can also play a role in minimising the potential harm of the drugs for the callow user.

As a general rule of thumb, it might be true that gyms without steroid-using bodybuilders as role models will have fewer new users. Yet, the impact of this connection is dependent on the degree of testing being sufficiently significant that it makes steroid users go elsewhere. Further, such an argument can also be used to support the alternative point of view. If excluded individuals do turn to gyms with no controls, the role-model effect will be reinforced in such gyms, whereby only little is won. Ultimately, the only way to test the hypothesis that fewer gyms with negative role models will lead to fewer new users is to collect reliable prevalence data that can document a decline in the number of new steroid-using individuals as the testing scheme expands to most Danish gyms.

Containing the problem

Some gyms outside the scheme are reported to have more drug users than before the testing scheme was introduced.[5] Following the above argument, the consequence is that the negative impact of role models in these gyms must be heavy. Nevertheless, Berget's suggestion that the potential concentration of users in such gyms makes it easier to control the situation implies that there is some sort of control in these gyms. It is difficult to see how this can be the case, however, as ADD is only allowed to conduct controls in gyms with which it has a collaborative agreement. Gymnasia owners themselves do not and cannot perform controls in these gyms, and there are no 'outreach workers' in Denmark to make contact with members of such 'high-risk gyms'. The problem might thus be isolated in fewer gyms with more users, but how this helps to 'secure the health of the athletes' is not clear.

The idea could, of course, be that the concentration of users would give the police better opportunities to intervene. To examine this possibility, I contacted Per Sandau, from the Danish National Police's Centre for Prevention. Sandau is concerned with the preventive effort relating to anabolic steroids and explained that, with the available resources, the fight against anabolic steroids in the gym environment is not the police's highest priority. Neither do the police have any plan of action for a specific scheme to investigate gyms that are not part of ADD's testing scheme. He further expressed concern about the idea of isolating users in fewer gyms: 'In a prevention perspective, it is inexpedient to concentrate users in fewer gyms. It might kick in as negative advertising,' he said.[6]

Further, if the intention of the act is fulfilled, *all* gyms – including those where steroid users are thought to be concentrated – will eventually be part of the scheme, and users of performance- and image-enhancing drugs will either be driven underground to private basement gyms or stop exercising, owing to their being banned from all Danish sport under the Act. This will lead to a situation where even less can be controlled; where steroid users are further criminalised; where contact with steroid users and the application of harm-reduction strategies are further complicated; and where the argument about the Act's counter-productivity on health will therefore be even more relevant.

To sum up: of the three propositions, only the role-model argument seems to have some strength. Whether it is enough to reject the argument that the testing regime can be regarded as being counter-productive in relation to its own foundation – namely to secure the health of the athletes – is doubtful. This, however, can only be determined by empirical data that are not yet available.

Testing for drugs used by girls and women

If the aim of the Act is to eradicate or diminish the use of performance- and image-enhancing drugs in gyms, owing to their detrimental effects on health, does the Act then allow for all such drugs to be included in the testing scheme? The answer is 'no'. A consequence of the Act's adherence to the WADC is that testing recreational athletes in gyms is done in accordance with the regulations for out-of-competition testing. Therefore, stimulants that, in the context of elite sport, are only rational to use in competition are not tested for. This, however, is irrational in the context of fighting drugs in gyms, as many stimulants on the list – primarily ephedrine, but also amphetamine and cocaine – are used by girls and young women (as well as by bodybuilders) in their pursuit of burning off fat.[7] And the adverse health effects of these drugs are not any less serious than those of anabolic steroids. Ephedrine is the mildest of these three commonly used stimulants; however, the US Food and Drug Administration reports that the adverse effects of ephedrine alkaloid-containing dietary supplements include 'elevated blood pressure, rapid heartbeat, nerve damage, muscle injury, and psychosis and memory loss. More serious effects have also been reported, including heart attack, stroke, seizure and death' (McClellan 2003). The adverse effects of amphetamine and cocaine are worse (WHO 2004).

However, a consequence of the Act being bound to the WADC is that the regime does not target such drugs that are sometimes used by women to enhance their physical image. This means that the Act's purpose of 'securing the health of the athletes' in reality only means securing the health of male athletes, which indeed is a contradiction at the heart of the policy. The idea that public health is the core rationale behind the testing scheme is thus undermined.

The fact that this inequality has not been addressed in general, nor by the gyms specifically, might be because the gyms' primary interest is not health but a *healthy image* and a well-ordered gym environment. In the gym, women slimming down on stimulants are less visible than their male counterparts 'beefing up' on steroids. They make less noise and are less intimidating to other customers. It is therefore understandable (albeit still unacceptable) that neither the gyms nor their professional organisation have focused on women in their efforts to contribute to the fight for clean gyms. Although such public relations motives might be dominant for a commercial gym owner, however, they cannot be the rationale for a state campaign against drugs in gyms, as they have little to do with public health, but more to do with the enhancement of the gyms' image.

The prospect of targeting the sale of illegal drugs

Nevertheless, the argument of securing the health of the athletes seems to constitute the basis for the Act. However, as Evald notes: 'To this is added the prospect to affect the sale of doping drugs, which are often imported and distributed illegally, especially in environments in and around gyms' (Evald 2009: 82). With this, the Act juxtaposes two levels of intervention: a sporting level (based on securing athletes' health) and a policing level. From the police's perspective, drugs should be fought because of their criminal status. Fighting criminal activity is clearly a legitimate purpose. But it then also follows that it is *illegal drugs* that should be the focus of the campaign, and not drugs banned by WADA or other sporting authorities. It further follows that the campaign against steroids must then be an issue for the police rather than for the sporting bodies (in this case ADD). Consequently, the Act, with its adherence to the WADC, should be withdrawn, and the campaign (and its funding) should perhaps be assigned to the police, who could work from the basis of the existing legislation on illegal drugs, which already embraces anabolic steroids, testosterone, human growth hormone and other hard-core performance enhancers (Retsinformation 1999: paragraph 1).

As was noted above by Sandau, in the present context of resource limitations, the police do not prioritise the illegal distribution of drugs in and around gyms. When the police occasionally do find and confiscate quantities of tablets, ampoules and liquids, such findings are not a result of targeted hauls at gyms, but most often side effects of searches in relation to other crimes (Moberg and Hermansson 2006).[8]

We have established that the primary intended purpose of the Act is the need to secure athletes' health. We have further seen that the way the legislation is designed and practised means that it only meets this purpose to – at best – a limited extent. It is therefore difficult, in the context of drug use in the gym environment, to substantiate (as Evald does for the elite sport context) that doping control is necessary in order to pursue the legal purpose of the Act. The question remains, however, whether the test procedure itself presents a potential problem.

Does the testing violate privacy rights?

As noted above, one consequence of the Act is that everyone training in a gym that is part of the scheme is subject to the WADA list of banned substances and the associated sanctions. The same goes for the actual testing procedure as laid out in the WADC. When an individual is chosen for control, he or she must undress in front of the doping control officer. The person is asked to roll their trousers down to the knees and lift their T-shirt up to the waist, making the genitals clearly visible, thus ensuring 'an unobstructed view of the *Sample* leaving the *Athlete*'s body' (WADA 2009b: 78, Annex D). If a gym member refuses to submit to this procedure, it counts as a positive test, and he or she will be sanctioned accordingly.

It is not surprising that the procedure does not meet with universal acceptance. In relation to my research, I interviewed a young man who trains four or more times per week and who has a well-developed physique but has never used banned substances. He gave this personal account of how he experienced being tested:

> It wasn't nice. We can all pee when we are at the pub. But it isn't easy when someone is watching. And it isn't easy when you're also under suspicion and therefore nervous too. And you stand there with that f—g little cup and need to hit the target and it can all be such a mess. It was unpleasant. He stood close behind me with his chin over my shoulder so he could look down at my willy while I urinated. It was necessary for him to stand like that to see if I had a rubber tube with false urine or wanted to cheat in some other way. I am not even sure if they are allowed to do that? Isn't that indecent exposure? And at the same time the other officer, who is a lady, sits in the changing room next to us. It's not that she can see anything, but her room is not separated by doors from where I am. So she can hear all what's happening.

He obviously did not like the process and felt intimidated. He even felt the procedure amounted to enforced 'indecent exposure'. His discomfort with this issue is relevant, and it must be asked whether this is a fair and reasonable practice to be forced to submit to, just because you are exercising (or training hard) in your local gym. Can it perhaps be considered a breach of an individual's privacy rights to have to accept total strangers into the bathroom to watch your genitals while you urinate?

Initially, it can be observed that the WADC does not contain rules limiting doping controls for reasons of privacy. However, both the Danish Constitution (§ 71) and the European Convention on Human Rights (Article 8) contain provisions for protection of privacy, and the laws and conventions that are in force in Denmark do also embrace sport (Evald 2009). One can further argue, as Evald does, that

> when considerations of privacy and integrity protection of citizens can be derived from constitutional provisions, laws and international conventions, then standards about this must be conferred significant weight in a democratic constitutional state – including in the formulation of rules on doping control and management of these rules.
>
> (Evald 2009: 72)

If we look to the European Convention for the Protection of Human Rights, Article 8 says that, 'Everyone has the right to respect for his private life'. And in Section 2 it is added that: 'There shall be no interference by a public authority with the exercise of this right except such as is in accordance with the law and is necessary [. . .] for the protection of health or morals' (Council of Europe 1950: paragraph 8). Because the Danish state is the primary contributor of funding for ADD, and because the chairman of the board of ADD is appointed by the minister of culture, it is fair to say that the Danish state plays a significant part in doping control and, hence, is responsible for ensuring that ADD's doping controls conform to the European Convention on Human Rights, Article 8 (Evald 2009). What are the consequences of this? Again, Evald's work is helpful:

> It follows from article 8. 2 that the state may only encroach on citizens' privacy, if there are substantial reasons for doing so, and at the same time there must be proportionality between the nature of the interference and the aim pursued. The requirement of proportionality means that the state must choose a less intrusive form of restriction rather than a more intrusive and that the measure must be proportionate to the stated purpose.
>
> (Evald 2009: 82)

The question then is whether, in this case, there are substantial reasons, i.e. the protection of health or morals, for the interference in citizens' privacy that is caused by doping controls in gyms? Further, is there 'proportionality between the nature of the interference and the aim pursued'? As we have seen, the purpose of the testing in gyms is not clear (is it to secure male drug-using athletes' health, to secure non-drug-using athletes' health, to limit the number of potential bad role models, to secure a healthy image of the fitness industry or to affect the sale of illegal drugs?). If we adhere to securing athletes' health as the primary purpose, as we have done hitherto, it is clear that requiring gym members to urinate in a cup under surveillance *is* to encroach on that citizen's privacy. What is not clear, however, is whether it genuinely serves the stated purpose. Neither is it clear that this purpose is served by the exclusion from participating in sport that follows from a positive test. It could, of course, be argued that individuals who oppose this kind of testing could choose to exercise in a gym that is not part of the scheme. But, with the scheme's expansion, there are many towns where this choice does not exist. Hence, individuals living in those areas have no choice but to accept to be tested and be subject to this procedure, if they want to work out in a gym.

It is possible to argue – as Evald does – that the interference that an ordinary doping control constitutes in elite sport is not in breach of the European Convention on Human Rights, Article 8. It does not follow that the same is true for doping controls in gyms. The problem is that, although doping controls in gyms are in accordance with the law, the objectives that are pursued seem to be poorly defined. Furthermore, there is no evidence to verify that the control, with its current intensity and its gender bias, can meet the stated objectives (securing athletes' health). Thus, it is not clear in what ways the controls benefit either citizens' health or morals. Finally, there does not seem to be sufficient proportionality between the intensity of the interference and the objectives pursued. Against this background, it appears that doping controls in gyms are contrary to the European Convention on Human Rights, Article 8. Hence, the mandatory control of individuals in gyms is a violation of those individuals' right to privacy.

This conclusion has further implications for the analysis above. As was emphasised in the sections on 'The fear of exclusion' and 'Negative role models', it is necessary that there is a certain degree of intensity in the pattern of testing if the scheme is to fulfil its purpose of lowering the prevalence of drug-using individuals by imposing fear of a positive test. However, increased intensity adds to the argument concerning privacy. Increased intensity might thus solve one side of the problem, while paradoxically increasing another, no less important, side.

Conclusion

This chapter has taken doping control in Danish gyms as its case study, but the problems that have been highlighted point to more general issues concerning the fight against drugs in and around gyms that is of relevance also outside the Danish context. Initially, I noted that the guidelines for testing in Danish gyms are identical to those practised in elite sport, which is a consequence of the legislation's affiliation to the WADC. I also highlighted the fact that the use of performance- and image-enhancing drugs in gyms has a different character and a different purpose from the use of doping in elite sport. This indicates that the use of the same terminology – 'doping' – for the two phenomena is infelicitous. As a media phenomenon, doping in the public domain is perceived as an evil to be combated. Hence, when the concept is transferred directly from elite sport to describe the use of drugs in gyms, decision-makers have naturally used it to tackle the phenomenon with the same punitive approach as is done in sport, which is what the Danish legislation is designed to do. However, the assumption that doping controls in gyms are necessary if the legal purpose of the Act, promoting doping-free sport, is to be realised is unwarranted.

This points towards the more fundamental problem, namely that a clear and consistent objective of the effort has not been formulated. Nor is there any clear identification of precisely what it is that is to be combated. The authorities have not identified substances or groups of substances that are of particular concern in the gym environment, but instead have uncritically adopted the WADA list, which gives rise to the system's absurd neglect of some harmful substances sometimes taken by girls and women. Furthermore, the means that will most likely lead to fulfilment of the (not very clearly) listed objectives have not been identified. Once again, the authorities have simply transferred the elite sports practice, which has resulted in the implementation of offensive doping controls that gym members cannot decline. Instead of making thorough considerations of the objectives that should be pursued and what means should be employed to reach them, a system created to combat doping in elite sport with the aim of ensuring athletes a level playing field has been taken over in an uncritical and potentially harmful manner.

The Danish case illustrates the pitfalls lurking when one wants to tackle a complex social problem by simplistic means. The politicians responsible know that fighting 'doping' is an easy way to raise their profile with the electorate. They also know that the model of mandatory testing in gyms has wide appeal in the general population (Steele *et al.* 2010) and, with the Act's punitive approach, they can therefore demonstrate initiative and drive. I have tried to show that the legislation and the test system, in their present form, have serious unintended consequences and potential for more harm than good. There are therefore good reasons to revise them.

Notes

1 This is clear from e-mail correspondence with the ADOs in Norway, Sweden and Finland, where I have queried the organisations' view of the Danish model (January 2010).

2 English language versions of the Danish anti-doping Act and the accompanying executive order can be found on WADA's website at: www.wada-ama.org/en/World-Anti-Doping-Program/Legal-articles-case-law-and-national-laws/National-Laws/ (accessed 4 December 2009).

3 Author's email correspondence with adviser on information and education in ADD, Jakob Berget, 11 January 2010.
4 A total of 1,398 enquires were analysed; 15 per cent (n = 208) of enquirers used anabolic steroids or other WADA-banned substances, and an additional 15 per cent (n = 205) considered using such drugs.
5 The TV channel TV2 Fyn reported, on 25 May 2009, on how steroid users frequented certain gyms in Denmark's third largest city, Odense, after several of the city's other gyms were enrolled in the scheme.
6 Author's telephone and e-mail correspondence with Per Sandau of the Danish National Police's Centre for Prevention, 30 November 2009.
7 For a list of substances and methods *not* tested for in gyms, see 'Substances and methods prohibited in-competition' (WADA 2009a: 7).
8 Taken from personal interview with Per Sandau of the Danish National Police's Centre for Prevention.

References

Anti Doping Danmark (2010a) *Kontrolstatistik*. Available online at: www.steroids.dk/da/Dopingkontrol/Kontrolstatistik.aspx (accessed 31 March 2010).

Anti Doping Danmark (2010b) *Steroids.dk*. Available online at: www.steroids.dk/ (accessed 31 March 2010).

Bach, A.R. (2005) *Mænd og muskler: en debatbog om styrketræning og anabole steroider* (*Men and muscles*), København: Tiderne Skifter.

Backhouse, S., McKenna, J., Robinson, S. and Atkin, M. (2007) 'International literature review: attitudes, behaviours, knowledge and education – drugs in sport: past, present and future'. Prepared for World Anti-Doping Agency.

Bahr, S.J., Hoffmann, J.P. and Yang, X. (2005) 'Parental and peer influences on the risk of adolescent drug use', *Journal of Primary Prevention*, 26(6): 529–51.

Barland, B. (1997) *Gymmet: en studie av trening, mat og dop* (*The gym: a study of training, diet and dope*). Ph.D., NIH, Oslo.

Bojsen-Moller, J. and Christiansen, A.V. (2009) 'Use of performance- and image-enhancing substances among recreational athletes: a quantitative analysis of inquiries submitted to the Danish anti-doping authorities', *Scandinavian Journal of Medicine & Science in Sports* (e-publication ahead of print).

Bullers, S., Cooper, M.L. and Russell, M. (2001) 'Social network drinking and adult alcohol involvement: a longitudinal exploration of the direction of influence', *Addictive Behaviors*, 26(2): 181–99.

Council of Europe (1950) Convention for the Protection of Human Rights and Fundamental Freedoms (ECHR).

Evald, J. (2009) '*Retlige grænser for dopingkontrol* (Legal boundaries for doping control)', in A.V. Christiansen (ed.), *Kontrolsport – Big brother blandt atleter og tilskuere*, Odense: Syddansk Universitetsforlag, pp. 71–88.

Gray, J. and Ginsberg, R. (2007) 'Muscle dissatisfaction: an overview of psychological and cultural research and theory', in J.K. Thompson and G. Cafri (eds), *The muscular ideal: psychological, social, and medical perspectives* (1st edition), Washington, DC: American Psychological Association, pp. 15–39.

Jenkins, J.E. (1996) 'The influence of peer affiliation and student activities on adolescent drug involvement', *Adolescence*, 31(122): 297–306.

Klein, A.M. (1993) *Little big men: bodybuilding subculture and gender construction*, Albany: State University of New York Press.

McClellan, M.B. (2003) *Ephedrine alkaloid-containing dietary supplements*, US Food and Drug Administration.

Moberg, T. and Hermansson, G. (2006) Mandom, mod och morske män: anabola androgena steroider – medicinskt, rättsligt och socialt (Manhood, courage, and contentious men), Göteborg: Mediahuset.

Møller, V. (2009) 'Conceptual confusion and the anti-doping campaign in Denmark', in V. Møller, M. McNamee and P. Dimeo (eds), *Elite sport, doping and public health*, Odense: University Press of Southern Denmark, pp. 13–28.

Møller, V. (2010) *The ethics of doping and anti-doping: redeeming the soul of sport?*, London: Routledge.

Monaghan, L.F. (2001) *Bodybuilding, drugs, and risk*, London: Routledge.

Needle, R., Mccubbin, H., Wilson, M., Reineck, R., Lazar, A. and Mederer, H. (1986) 'Interpersonal influences in adolescent drug-use – the role of older siblings, parents, and peers', *International Journal of the Addictions*, 21(7): 739–66.

Oetting, E.R. and Donnermeyer, J.F. (1998) 'Primary socialization theory: the etiology of drug use and deviance', *Journal of Substance Use & Misuse*, 33(4): 995–1026.

Pope, H.G., Phillips, K.A. and Olivardia, R. (2000) *The Adonis complex. How to identify, treat, and prevent body obsession in men and boys*, New York: Free Press.

Retsinformation (1999) '*Lov om forbud mod visse dopingmidler* (Act on the prohibition of certain doping drugs)'.

Retsinformation (2004) '*Lov om fremme af dopingfri idræt* (Act on Promotion of Doping-free Sport)'.

Retsinformation (2009) '*Bekendtgørelse om fremme af dopingfri idræt* (Executive Order on Promotion of Doping-free Sport)'.

Singhammer, J. and Ibsen, B. (2010) *Motionsdoping i Danmark: en kvantitativ undersøgelse om brug af og holdning til muskelopbyggende stoffer (The use of doping among recreational athletes in Denmark)*, Odense: Center for forskning i Idræt, Sundhed og Civilsamfund, University of Southern Denmark.

Steele, R., Bang, S., Brandt, H. H. and Kirkegaard, K. L. (2010) *Indsatsen mod motionsdoping i kommercielle motions – og fitnesscentre – en evaluering af mærkningsordningen (The fight against doping in commercial fitness centers – an evaluation of the labelling scheme)*, København: IDAN (Danish Institute for Sport Studies).

WADA (2009a) 'The 2009 Prohibited List. International Standard. World Anti-Doping Code'. Available online at: www.wada-ama.org/rtecontent/document/2009_Prohibited_List_ENG_Final_20_Sept_08.pdf (accessed 1 April 2010).

WADA (2009b) *World Anti-Doping Code*. Available online at: www.wada-ama.org/rtecontent/document/code_v2009_En.pdf (accessed 15 July 2010).

WHO (2004) *Neuroscience of psychoactive substance use and dependence*, Geneva: World Health Organisation.

9 Steroids in the court of public opinion

Roger Clemens versus the Mitchell Report

Rob Beamish

Introduction

In the conclusion to one of the most high-profile investigations into steroid use in sport, US Senator George Mitchell wrote: 'There has been a great deal of speculation about this report. Much of it has focused on players' names: how many and which ones' (2007: 310). Although he was fully aware of the history of 'naming names' in American history (see Navasky 1980), Mitchell decided it was appropriate and necessary. At the same time, he hoped that the media and the public would 'look beyond the individuals to the central conclusions and recommendations of this report' (2007: 310). That turned out to be wishful thinking.

Mitchell's report identified eighty-nine players. Within hours of its release, journalists had compiled and published the entire list of names (see Associated Press 2007; ESPN.com 2007). Of all the names, one name stood out in particular: Roger Clemens. Clemens, arguably the most dominant pitcher in baseball history, had a reputation for his outstanding work ethic, an 'American pie' image of 'down home Texas' wholesomeness and success based on his intense competitive spirit. Steroids had not been tied to his name before.

Clemens immediately denied the allegations concerning his use of steroids and HGH, leading to what ultimately became a 'trial' in 'the court of public opinion'. That trial and its significance in the protection of citizens' fundamental legal rights, including due process, is the central focus of this chapter. To address the event properly, however, there is considerable background information one must know to fully appreciate why Clemens's adamant denial of steroid use threatened to undermine the Mitchell report, and how the ensuing events impacted upon the House Committee on Oversight and Government Reform's (CoO&GR) integrity.

'Naming names' is always fraught with difficulty, particularly in the United States, where the tactics of the House Committee on Un-American Activities (HUAC) and McCarthyism still cast an ominous shadow over first and fifth amendment constitutional rights and the rule of law (see Navasky 1980).

Indeed, as Republican Representative Dan Burton noted, the principle that 'until a man is proven guilty, he's innocent' is seriously undermined when names are released and there is a 'trial by media' (CoO&GR 2008b: 103).

Like the HUAC hearings in the mid twentieth century, there was far more involved in the investigation into steroids in Major League Baseball (MLB) than what one may read in the House Committee's transcripts or find in the Mitchell report. The Mitchell report and Clemens's challenge are simply the visible aspects of a complex process, where particular individuals wanted 'justice', no matter how it was achieved. Ultimately, the standards of American jurisprudence were bypassed because a victory in the court of public opinion seemed preferable and ironically appropriate.

Behind the Mitchell Report: Novitzky, Bonds and BALCO

Although steroid use in baseball occurred well before 1994, Mitchell began his investigation with the 1994 strike (see Mitchell 2007: 41–5, 60–111). In the years since free agency began, players' salaries had increased dramatically because some owners offered extravagant contracts to 'buy' championship teams. To control costs, the majority of owners supported a proposed salary cap, which led to the 12 August 1994 player walkout (Staudohar 1997). Fans were offended and blamed 'greedy millionaires' for the cancellation of the World Series.

Although owners realized their goal of capping salaries, the fans remained angry, and attendance plummeted. The home run exploits and physiques of players such as Barry Bonds, Jose Canseco, Mark McGwire and Sammy Sosa rekindled fan interest and became baseball's new image. McGwire quickly took centre stage, smashing Roger Marris's longstanding single-season home run mark in 1998. It was Bonds' new record of 73 that caught Jeff Novitzky's attention.

Novitzky, an agent with the Internal Revenue Service's Criminal Investigations (IRS CI) unit, began to focus on Bonds because Greg Anderson – Bonds' personal trainer – was associated with the Bay Area Laboratory Cooperative (BALCO) and the steroid guru, Victor Conte (see Assael 2007: 220–1; Fainaru-Wada and Williams 2006: 165–7). Sifting through BALCO's garbage in September 2002 for evidence, Novitzky found material linking Conte to several professional and world-class athletes. Using a subpoena to search BALCO's medical waste, Novitzky found material that appeared to link Bonds and Anderson to what seemed to be Conte's underground steroid network – a discovery that dramatically changed the nature of Novitzky's investigation and, ultimately, the Mitchell report (see Novitzky 2003; Fainaru-Wada and Williams 2006: 157–60).

Steroids are a Schedule III substance, and the penalties for their non-authorized use and distribution are relatively light. As a result, there is normally little incentive or reward to pursue the users and distributors of Schedule III substances. The high profile of the users in the BALCO case, however, was different. In fact, as the BALCO investigation proceeded, the search for guilty parties became the reverse of normal drug investigations. Rather than actively encouraging users to give up the pushers and distributors higher up the chain of command, in the MLB investigation, distributors were pressured to give up the direct users, because their names would yield the greatest payoff to federal agents.

On 3 September 2003, Novitzky and armed federal agents raided BALCO (Novitzky 2003; see also Thompson *et al.* 2009: 63–5). Conte quickly agreed to cooperate and began implicating fifteen track and field athletes, seven National Football League (NFL) and five MLB players, including Bonds. The agents seized Conte's ledger, which listed athletes, their drug regimens and blood and urine test results (Fainaru-Wada and Williams 2006: 175–80). Under testimony, secured on a separate warrant, Anderson admitted to supplying 'the little guys' on his MLB client list with BALCO substances but denied giving them to Bonds.

At the end of September, a federal grand jury convened to investigate BALCO. Three-dozen MLB, NFL, Olympic track and field athletes, swimmers, cyclists, boxers and bodybuilders gave sworn, sealed testimony. With few exceptions, they admitted to steroid use (Fainaru-Wada and Williams 2006: 195–7). At his appearance, Bonds denied taking steroids knowingly (see Fainaru-Wada and Williams 2006: 199–206).

The sealed grand jury testimony provided two critical leverage points for Novitzky and his investigation. First, although the list of athletes testifying was supposed to be secret, media personnel swarmed the Phillip A. Burton Federal Building where the proceedings were taking place. The sports pages across the nation reported the names of athletes subpoenaed to appear. More important, even though the list was incomplete, athletes, through word of mouth, knew exactly who had testified before the grand jury.

The second point of influence concerns Section 1001 of Title 18 of the *United States Code* (2006), which makes it a criminal offence, punishable by fine and imprisonment up to 5 years, for anyone who 'knowingly and wilfully falsifies, conceals, or covers up by any trick, scheme, or device a material fact' or makes a 'materially false, fictitious, or fraudulent statement or representation' to a federal agent. With the grand jury testimony sealed, none of the people Novitzky subsequently investigated knew exactly what information he already had. As a result, any misrepresentation that he could substantiate with information gathered previously could mean federal prosecution. This proved a decisive lever in all the ensuing investigations – including the Mitchell report.

Following the BALCO revelations, the alleged connection to Bonds, and controversy over McGwire's use of androstenedione, President Bush linked steroids to America's war on drugs in his 2004 'State of the Union' address (see Beamish 2009). To make good choices, children need good examples, Bush noted, and sport should provide them. 'The use of performance-enhancing drugs like steroids in baseball, football and other sports is dangerous, and it sends the wrong message' he continued, calling on owners, coaches and players to 'get tough' on steroids (Associated Press 2004).

With the BALCO story continuing in the *San Francisco Chronicle* and the president's comments, the focus on steroids in baseball intensified. Rushed into publication to capitalize on the breaking events, Canseco's *Juiced: wild times, rampant 'roids, smash hits, and how baseball got big* (2005a) increased the pressure for an investigation into steroids and baseball. Tom Davis, chairman of the Committee on Government Reform (CoGR), took the next steps (see CoGR 2005: 1–4; Thompson *et al.* 2009: 85–6).

From the House Committee on Government Reform to the Mitchell Report

On 17 March 2005, the CoGR (2005) convened televised hearings with a carefully scripted agenda. Hall of fame pitcher and conservative Republican Senator Jim Bunning testified first. Bunning represented the established values of baseball's 'golden age'. Bunning embodied the proceedings' key theme – integrity. 'As a member of the Hall of Fame, as someone who helped found the Players Association, and as a lifelong fan', Bunning began, 'protecting the integrity of our national pastime is a matter that is near and dear to my heart' (2005: 1).

In panel two, the Garibaldis' (Garibaldi 2005: 2) stark claim – 'There is no doubt in our minds that steroids killed our son' – and Don Hooton's summary statement – 'On behalf of Taylor Hooton, Rob Garibaldi, Efrain Marrero and other kids around the country who have lost their lives to steroids, let me implore you to clean this mess up' (2005: 3) – provided the riveting testimony that hung over the next two panels.

Panel three was the centrepiece. Canseco (2005b), McGwire (2005a), Rafael Palmeiro (2005a, 2005b) and Sosa (2005) were chosen to represent the dirty ballplayers, while Curt Schilling (2005) and Frank Thomas (2005) stood for the integrity of the game. Canseco's (2005b) hulking, physical presence said more than his prepared statement. Sounding more like one of the Hollywood Ten before HUAC than a home run king, McGwire (2005a: 4) stated that, following legal advice, he would not 'answer questions about who took steroids in front of television cameras'. His frequent response to Committee questioning – 'I'm not here to talk about the past' – left a lasting, negative impression on viewers (see McGwire 2005b).

Panel four included MLB commissioner 'Bud' Selig and MLBPA executive director Don Fehr. They faced probing questions and critical commentary as the Committee performed for the voters back home (see CoGR 2005: 330–78). The grilling allowed Selig to unilaterally launch MLB's own investigation into steroid use on 30 March 2006, resulting in the *Report to the Commissioner of Baseball of an independent investigation into the illegal use of steroids and other performance enhancing substances by players in Major League*

Baseball. The report created headlines but left many questions unanswered, including those related to behind-the-scenes intrigue that shaped the report decisively.

While cowed by the CoGR, Selig remained in control of the ensuing events. Selig kept the investigation of baseball internal. He also chose a chairman who was beyond reproach but nevertheless sympathetic to MLB and its owners. Selig (2006: 2–3) emphasized Mitchell's extensive investigative experience; he had, to echo the CoGR's dominant theme, an 'impeccable reputation for integrity' (see Mitchell 2007: A1–A2). Despite his credentials, Mitchell's investigative power was severely limited. As a private investigation, Mitchell had no power of subpoena, and witnesses did not supply sworn testimony.

Mitchell (2007: SR6, B1–B6) poured over 115,000 pages of documents from the Commissioner's Office and thirty MLB clubs and 20,000 electronic documents and he conducted over 700 interviews with witnesses, more than 550 with current or former MLB officials, managers, coaches, team physicians, trainers or resident security agents. The task force also attempted to interview almost 500 former players, though only 68 agreed. The MLBPA, Mitchell (2007: SR7) maintained, 'was largely uncooperative', rejecting requests for relevant documents and, through a memorandum, 'discouraged players from cooperating' (see also Mitchell 2007: B7–B10).

Despite the scope of the documentation Mitchell reviewed, it becomes clear upon reading the report that there were really only three sources for the most critical material it contained: the information supplied by Radomski and Clemens's personal trainer, Brian McNamee, owing to their particular plea agreements with Novitzky; IRS affidavits and memoranda related to the BALCO raid; and a series of Fainaru-Wada and Williams' articles in the *San Francisco Chronicle* that used illegally leaked testimony from the BALCO grand jury hearings (see Radomski 2009: 174–5; Mitchell 2007: 112–17, 138–9, 167–8, SR19–SR21; Thompson *et al*. 2009: 137–9, 142–3). Without Novitzky's involvement, the Mitchell report would have been little more than a whitewash.

Radomski was a trainer for the New York Mets when Novitzky and a team of federal agents raided his home with a warrant on 15 December 2005 (Radomski 2009). Informed that he faced charges of possession, distribution and money laundering – the last alone could lead to 25 years in a federal penitentiary – and told by his lawyer it would cost 'a couple of million dollars, maybe even more' to fight the charges, Radomski agreed to plead guilty and cooperate with investigators (see Radomski 2009: 143–6).

Radomski's plea bargain was particularly significant. In addition to cooperating with federal investigators, Novitzky also required Radomski's cooperation with the Mitchell investigation (see Radomski 2009: 174–5; Mitchell 2007: 138–9, SR19–SR20). The same condition applied to McNamee – whom Radomski had identified to Novitzky (see Mitchell 2007: 167–8, SR20-SR21; Thompson *et al*. 2009:137–9, 142–3). Novitzky's assistance to Mitchell would help Mitchell, while also assisting Novitzky's efforts to put pressure on those with inside information on steroid use in baseball, in general, and Bonds' use, in particular, to come forward.

In his final report, Mitchell indicated that, although the investigation was prompted by revelations of player involvement with BALCO, the evidence it uncovered showed that steroid use was not isolated among just a few players or clubs (see Mitchell 2007: SR1, SR5, SR17). 'For more than a decade', Mitchell emphasized, 'there has been the widespread use of anabolic steroids and other performance enhancing substances by players in Major League Baseball' (2007: SR1).

After explicitly indicating why steroid use was a major issue, Mitchell (2007: 60–111) outlined 'The steroids era' – a discussion almost fully indebted to Radomski's materials and meetings with Mitchell. Radomski's testimony and evidence helped identify 'dozens of current or former players' who had possessed or used performance-enhancing substances (Mitchell 2007: 147–8). Although none of it had been tested in court, Mitchell (2007: 149–229) used Radomski's information to discuss fifty players, ranging in stature from high-profile all-stars such as Lenny Dykstra, David Justice, Mo Vaughn and Eric Gagné, through journeymen such as Larry Bigbie, Jack Cust, Gregg Zaun and Ryan Franklin, to career minor leaguers such as Phil Hiatt, Cody McKay and Bart Miadich. Mitchell (2007: 147–8) also identified McNamee as 'a direct eyewitness and participant' in the alleged illegal use of steroids by Clemens, Andy Pettitte and Chuck Knoblauch, whom he served as a personal trainer.

The Mitchell report had two outcomes of major importance for this discussion. The first was the CoO&GR (2008a) reconvening to discuss the report with Mitchell and question Selig and Fehr about its findings. The second was the standoff between Clemens and McNamee.

Committee on Oversight and Government Reform and the Mitchell Report

Regarding the first outcome, the new Committee chair, Henry Waxman (CoO&GR 2008a: 3), began the 15 January 2008 session by informally setting a rather open agenda, which included aspects of steroid use that he felt the media had overlooked and Mitchell underemphasized. He set the main context of his agenda with a calculated, opening statement:

> When our committee held its first hearing 3 years ago on Major League Baseball's steroid scandal, I talked about how the culture of Major League clubhouses trickled down to become the culture of the high school gym.

Later that same day, Dan Hooten and Denise and Raymond Garibaldi proved that connection with their powerful testimony about the deadly impact that steroids had on their sons. 'The starting point for addressing any scandal is in the facts', Waxman argued, and the Mitchell report took, 'a hard look at baseball's steroid era' and, while it 'didn't tell us everything . . . it told us enough'. 'And what it tells us is damning' (CoO&GR 2008a: 4).

Waxman argued that the report made it clear that everyone in baseball holds some responsibility for steroid use in baseball (CoO&GR 2008a: 4). 'Despite that shared responsibility', he continued, 'most of the media attention over the past month has focused on the players. They are the face of the game, and they are the ones our kids emulate' (CoO&GR 2008a: 4–5). But, Waxman emphasized, 'the steroid scandal is not just about ball players' (CoO&GR 2008a: 7). Not enough attention had been paid to those who run baseball. After citing two specific examples, Waxman noted: 'It is a dismal record and it needs to be put front and center; not hidden' (CoO&GR 2008a: 8).

Following a review of some of the changes to drug testing that MLB had instituted since the report's release, Waxman returned to his opening theme – steroid use in MLB filters down to the youth of America. A statement from Efrain Marrero's parents was entered into the Committee record, asking for 'simple, honest accountability' (CoO&GR 2008a: 9–10). No family, the Marreros wrote, should have to endure the anguish they had suffered, and yet thousands of children remained at risk. 'For them we ask you to dig deep, find the unvarnished truth and report it fairly.' 'To Mr. and Mrs. Marrero, and Mr. Hooton', Waxman concluded, 'and to all the concerned parents around our nation, I want you to know we're trying to do just that.'

Former Committee Chairman Davis's opening statement contrasted with Waxman's. He saw the Committee's task in very precise terms: 'Let's be clear about our purpose' he began:

> We're not self-appointed prosecutors trying the claims of the Mitchell report. This is not a court of law. And the guilt or innocence of the players accused in the report of steroid abuse is not our major concern. Our focus is on Senator Mitchell's recommendations more than his findings. We're here to save lives, not ruin careers. We want steroids and other dangerous drugs out of sports, period.
>
> (CoO&GR 2008a: 11)

Mitchell echoed Davis's statement:

> I urge everyone involved in Major League Baseball to join in a well planned, well executed and sustained effort to bring the era of steroids and human growth hormone to an end and to prevent its recurrence in some other form in the future
>
> (CoO&GR 2008a: 2)

In the statements and questions that followed, Mitchell received various queries about the mechanics of the investigation, the lack of support from the

MLBPA and the 'dangers of steroid use by young people' (see CoO&GR 2008a: 30–6, 37–40, 68–70, 85–6). There were, however, two points that committee members probed more deeply.

One issue concerned the limitations Mitchell faced in collecting information (see CoO&GR 2008a: 55–62). Republican Mark Souder (CoO&GR 2008: 55–6) noted that Mitchell had no subpoena powers and could not grant immunity to players, and so there were no major breakthroughs in his collection of evidence. Democrat Stephen Lynch pursued the issue further. Lynch (CoO&GR 2008: 59–60) noted that Mitchell was required to carry out what amounted to an investigation into the Federal Controlled Substances Act, without the proper tools – he had no power of subpoena and could not engage in any plea bargaining. The most important information relied on Radomski and McNamee's information, which was not voluntary but part of their plea agreements.

Whether by design or not, Mitchell (CoO&GR 2008) avoided the issue by saying that he did not think it was an investigation into the Controlled Substances Act and did not address how much credibility one could put into a report that was simply a voluntary investigation.

The second issue foreshadowed the other major outcome of the Mitchell report – Clemens versus McNamee – and the aggressive partisan split that would ensue in the Committee's February meeting. Democrat Eleanor Norton (CoO&GR 2008a: 71) asked Mitchell to outline the standard of evidence he had used in his decision to name or not name specific players.

After Mitchell explained his process in detail, Norton continued: 'Now we see Mr. Clemens coming out and strongly denying these allegations and doing so publically' – Clemens had already used his own website, YouTube, an interview with Mike Wallace on *60 Minutes* and the print media to adamantly deny Mitchell's statements about his use of steroids and HGH (see Clemens 2007; *60 Minutes* 2008a, 2008b). 'Why do you think he refused your invitation to talk to you before the release of the report?' (CoO&GR 2008a: 72–3). 'I do not know why', Mitchell replied. As he began to explain the legal process he had followed, Norton (CoO&GR 2008a: 73) cut in: 'Obviously, he hasn't told you and he hasn't told us. That's why I wondered' – suggesting Mitchell's standard of evidence trumped any basis for Clemens's repeated and vigorous public denials.

Norton followed with questions about the credibility of McNamee's testimony, which Mitchell answered at length. When Norton had finished, Waxman re-emphasized Norton's main points: 'Senator Mitchell, in other words, despite the public presentation by Clemens that the testimony was not accurate, you continue to feel comfortable with Mr. McNamee's credibility?' Mitchell responded: 'We believe that the statements provided to us were truthful' (CoO&GR 2008a: 73–6).

Norton and Waxman had used Mitchell's integrity and credibility to publicly undermine Clemens; they emphasized the circumstances under which McNamee had given his information, thereby affirming why the CoO&GR

could be confident his statements were truthful. The Committee would move on to question Selig and Fehr, but the stage was already being set for the strongest test the Mitchell report would face – the Clemens/McNamee showdown.

Committee on Oversight and Government Reform: Clemens versus McNamee

Clemens adamantly denied the allegations that he had used steroids and HGH. In a 1 minute 48 second video, Clemens (2007) was emphatic:

> And let me be clear the answer is no! I did not use steroids, human growth hormone and I have never done so. I did not provide Brian McNamee any drugs to inject into my body . . . This report is simply not true.

In a 60 *Minutes* interview, Clemens was equally categorical. He expressed anger that, after all he had done for baseball, 'I don't get the benefit of the doubt'. 'It's hogwash for people to assume this', he continued and rhetorically asked, 'How can you prove your innocence?'. 'Never happened', Clemens stated emphatically (60 *Minutes* 2008b; see also 60 *Minutes* 2008a).

Clemens's protest was a direct challenge to the Mitchell report's accuracy, and it would quickly politicize the investigation, as many Republicans viewed Clemens as one of their own, being placed under attack. It would take considerable courage for a politician from a Republican state to risk his or her reputation by questioning a man President Bush had identified as a close friend and fellow Texan.

Few in the CoO&GR wanted the February hearing, because, once it began, there would be no doubt that one was either with Clemens or with McNamee. The transcript of the hearing indicates the extent to which the bipartisan attack on steroids in baseball became politicized and partisan as the focus shifted to Clemens and McNamee. The session became a high-profile public 'trial', where Mitchell, Clemens, McNamee and the members of the CoO&GR would all be judged.

Waxman (CoO&GR 2008b: 2–8) opened the session by emphasizing the hearing's unusual nature. He justified it as a test of the report's integrity (CoO&GR 2008b: 2–3). Davis echoed Waxman's position:

> It gives me no joy to have joined you in calling this hearing. We were faced with an unenviable choice: Allow a strenuous challenge to the Mitchell Report to stand without review, or open ourselves up to criticisms that we were grandstanding, that we are acting like self-appointed prosecutors trying the claims of that report.
>
> (CoO&GR 2008b: 15)

Determining whether the Mitchell Report could stand was critical, Davis emphasized. 'Today, we will let the American people judge who is to be believed in this unfortunate battle of wills, memories and reputations'.

Both sworn in before the Committee, Clemens (CoO&GR 2008b: 19–77) and McNamee (CoO&GR 2008b: 78–85) read prepared statements. Clemens read an abbreviated version of the full statement he had submitted to the Committee earlier. The submission included a 49-page analysis of his career by Hendricks Sport Management, which sought to establish that Clemens's late career successes were no different from comparable, hard-throwing, all-star pitchers such as Nolan Ryan, Randy Johnson or Schilling (CoO&GR 2008b: 29–77).

Why Clemens read a shorter statement is unclear – particularly because the submission was superior to his oral presentation – although the shorter, folksier statement may have seemed more authentic (see Clemens 2008; CoO&GR 2008b: 20). 'Thank you for allowing me to tell you a little bit about myself and how I have conducted my career for the past 25 years', Clemens (2008) began.

> I have always believed that hard work and determination were the only ways to be successful and to reach goals. Shortcuts were not an option. This was instilled in me since I was a young boy by my mother and by my grandmother.

His conclusion was equally informal:

> No matter what we discuss here today, I am never going to have my name restored, but I have to try and set the record straight. However, by doing so, I am putting myself out there to all of you, knowing that because I said that I didn't take steroids that this is looked as an attack on Senator Mitchell's report. Where am I to go with that?
>
> I'm not saying Senator Mitchell's report is entirely wrong. I am saying Brian McNamee's statements about me are wrong.
>
> Let me be clear. I have never taken steroids or HGH. Thank you.

The statement the Committee had received earlier began: 'I appreciate the opportunity to tell this Committee and the public – under oath – what I have been saying all along: I have never used steroids, human growth hormone, or any other type of illegal performance enhancing drug' (CoO&GR 2008b: 22). Clemens's statement then drew upon his history as one of baseball's most dominant pitchers in a carefully crafted manner that would have allowed him to speak directly to the American people: 'I have tried to model my baseball career, and indeed my entire life, on the premise that "your body is your temple"'. His statement (CoO&GR 2008b: 23) continued: 'The suggestion that I would use steroids or other illegal drugs is totally incompatible with who I am and what I stand for'. Clemens's statement touched on how he had grown up poor, the values his mother instilled, his work ethic and the toil he had undertaken. He then spoke about his own family and his charity work (in the subsequent questioning, Clemens brought out some of these themes – see CoO&GR 2008b: 128, 152–3). 'At the end of the day', the precisely worded conclusion began:

> I have been accused of doing something that I did not do. I have been asked to prove that I did not do it. How in the world can I prove a negative? No matter what we discuss here today, I am never going to have my name restored. I know that a lot of people want me to say that I have taken steroids and be done with it. But I cannot in good conscience admit to doing something that I did not do; even if it would be easier to do so. That's not the type of person I am. Instead, I will try to set the record straight, and I will do so directly to Congress and under oath. I have been told that by doing this, I am subjecting myself to possible criminal prosecution. I know that some people will still think I am lying no matter what I say or do. And I know that because I've said that I didn't take steroids, it will look like an attack on Senator Mitchell's report. I am not saying Senator Mitchell's report is entirely wrong and I am not trying to convince those who have already made up their minds based only on an allegation. For those with an open mind, however, I am saying that Brian McNamee's statements about me are wrong. Once again, I never took steroids or human growth hormone.
>
> (CoO&GR 2008b: 26)

McNamee (CoO&GR 2008b: 81) had to establish his credibility. After noting that the Mitchell report documented 'the pervasiveness of steroids' in MLB, admitting he was 'part of that problem' and apologizing to 'the Committee, and to the American people' for his conduct, McNamee indicated that his testimony would now let him 'be part of the solution'. McNamee (CoO&GR 2008b: 81) noted: 'I am not proud of what I have done, and I am not proud to testify against a man I once admired'. He emphasized that he found no satisfaction 'in bringing down Roger Clemens. Let me assure you that **<u>nothing</u>** could be further from the truth' (CoO&GR 2008b: 83; underlining and bold in original). McNamee made all of the points he needed to make about his specific actions and their veracity while dispelling any doubts about his motivation for telling the truth.

McNamee began the most critical section of his statement thus:

> **<u>Make no mistake</u>**: When I told Senator Mitchell that I injected Andy Pettitte with performance enhancing drugs, I told the truth. Andy Pettitte – who I know to be honest and decent – has since confirmed this.
>
> **<u>Make no mistake</u>**: when I told Senator Mitchell that I injected Chuck Knoblauch with performance enhancing drugs, I told the truth. Chuck

> Knoblauch, I believe, will confirm this as well [Knoblauch had already testified to this under oath in a deposition to the Committee (CoO&GR 2008b: 3)].
>
> **And make no mistake**: when I told Senator Mitchell that I injected Roger Clemens with performance enhancing drugs, I told the truth. I told the truth about steroids and human growth hormone . . . Unfortunately Roger has denied this and has led a full court attack on my credibility . . .
>
> I have no reason to lie, and **every reason not to**. If I do lie, I will be prosecuted. I was never promised any special treatment or consideration for fingering star players. I was never coerced to provide information against anyone. All that I was ever told, was to tell the truth to the best of my ability, and that is what I have done.
>
> (CoO&GR 2008b: 82–3; underlining and bold in original)

In the ensuing questioning, the Democrats forcefully and critically interrogated Clemens, while the Republicans focused on McNamee (see, for example, CoO&GR 2008b: 129–30, 156–7). The substance mattered less than form, and each side struck blows where their target was weakest or jumped to the rescue of the man they were supporting.

Democrat Elijah Cummings (CoO&GR 2008b: 86–90) spoke first, establishing Pettitte's credibility by quoting Clemens's lawyers and referring to Pettitte's religiosity. Reminding Clemens he was under oath, Cummings (CoO&GR 2008b: 87) asked, 'do you think Mr. Pettitte was lying when he told the committee that you admitted using human growth hormones'? Clemens (CoO&GR 2008b: 87) responded with his now famous 'I think Andy has misheard' and 'Andy misremembers'. Clemens was forceful in his responses.

Following a second response that Pettitte 'misremembers', Cummings (CoO&GR 2008b: 88) emphasized the credibility of Pettitte's version further, but Clemens (CoO&GR 2008b: 89) deflected it all by conceding that Pettitte is 'a fine gentleman' and a very close friend, but 'I think he misremembers'. Cummings (CoO&GR 2008b: 157) was most successful in forcing his point later in the hearing:

> As I said before, I have listened to you very carefully and I – I take you at your word. And your word is that Andy Pettitte is an honest man and his credibility pretty much impeccable. Your lawyer says the same thing. But suddenly – and the committee gave him time after time after time to clear up his testimony and he consistently said the same thing under oath. Not only that, his wife, he goes and tells his wife everything and she says the same thing. But suddenly he misunderstood you. All I'm saying is it's hard to believe, it's hard to believe you, sir. I hate to say that as – you're one of my heroes. But it's hard to believe.

Republican Tom Davis (CoO&GR 2008b: 91–6) followed Cummings's opening questions by focusing on the inconsistencies in the information McNamee had given authorities. Davis also probed a telephone conversation that Clemens had taped. In it, Clemens stated: 'I just need you to come out and tell the truth'. 'And you didn't respond', Davis asserted. 'Why didn't you just tell Mr. Clemens during the course of that conversation, Roger, I did tell the truth' (CoO&GR 2008b: 92).

McNamee (CoO&GR 2008b: 92) appeared reluctant to respond directly: 'I realized that it was being taped, and I also didn't know if anyone else was listening', he said (see *New York Daily News* 2008). At the time of the call, according to Thompson, Vinton, O'Keeffe, and Red (2009: 159–61), McNamee was still trying to protect Clemens. McNamee stated, 'if you listen to it and you know my jargon, I did say that. It is what it is'. Although the Republican, Davis, had made McNamee seem as though he was evading the truth to viewers watching on television, Democrat Mark Souder (CoO&GR 2008b: 151) tried later to establish McNamee's credibility by having it entered into the record that 'it is what it is' is 'a New York expression for telling the truth'.

Davis (CoO&GR 2008b: 93–4) also focused on McNamee's assertion that Clemens had attended a June 1988 barbecue at Canseco's residence. Davis cited affidavits from Canseco and his wife that Clemens was not there. Davis (CoO&GR 2008b: 95–6) also established the fact that Clemens could distinguish a B-12 injection from one with steroids or HGH by the different colour of the fluids, lending support to Clemens's claim that McNamee had injected him with B-12.

Democrat John Tierney began by questioning McNamee, but then turned forcefully to Clemens and the contention that Clemens had not talked to McNamee about HGH. Referring to Clemens's earlier sworn deposition to the Committee, Tierney's (CoO&GR 2008b: 97–8) persistent questioning brought out apparent inconsistencies in Clemens's claim and the facts related to McNamee injecting Debbie Clemens with HGH. Tierney (CoO&GR 2008b: 98) questioned how Clemens could reconcile three statements that he had not spoken with McNamee about HGH but 'when somebody specifically finally asks you about your wife, you have a recollection of two very distinct and memorable conversations'.

Republican Dan Burton directed an aggressive ad hominem attack at McNamee, portraying him as a chronic liar (CoO&GR 2008b: 100–3). With his time running down, Burton emphasized his main points. 'You're here as a sworn witness. You're here to tell the truth. You're here under oath'. Conflating past and present, he continued: 'And yet we have lie after lie after lie after lie of where you – you've told this committee and the people of the country that Roger Clemens did things, and I don't know what to believe'. 'I know one thing I don't believe', he noted with a great flourish, 'and that's you'.

Democrat Stephen Lynch (CoO&GR 2008b: 103–8) focused on some physical evidence – a 28 July 1998 MRI of 'a palpable mass' in Clemens's right buttock. Lynch cited the conclusion of an independent analysis conducted by Dr Mark Murphy from the Armed Forces Institute of Pathology indicating that it was his 'opinion that the history and the MRI imaging descriptions are more compatible with a Winstrol injection, as the inflammatory component is prominent by report' (see also CoO&GR 2008b: 105). One of Clemens's lawyers tried to intervene but was ruled out of order. Lynch chose his words carefully: 'Given the – given the physical testimony – the physical evidence that we've had there that seems to be consistent with much of what Mr. McNamee is saying'. He asked Clemens how the physical evidence could be wrong.

Davis (CoO&GR 2008b: 109), the former Committee chair and a Republican Committee member, interjected: 'We ask unanimous consent to insert into the record a report by Dr. Burt O'Malley, professor and chair of molecular and cellular biology, who comes to a much different conclusion.' The report, provided by Clemens's attorneys, did not actually address the MRI or the abscess (see CoO&GR 2008b: 110–11) but, at that moment, it seemed to counter Lynch's argument.

Davis was recognized and came to Clemens's defence. Davis noted that Clemens was not a doctor and should not be expected to respond to questions about a report he had not seen. He maintained that the physician who had ordered the MRI would submit a deposition that afternoon indicating he had not reached the same conclusion as Murphy. 'And there is zero evidence at that point', Davis (CoO&GR 2008b: 115) continued, 'or even suspicion that drugs or anything had caused this.' He then tried to dismiss Lynch's questions by calling them 'a new definition of lynching'.

In his summary statement, Davis (CoO&GR 2008b: 160–1) argued that the Mitchell report 'remains largely intact', while minimizing the day's events as a mere 'bone of contention'. Claiming the real goal was to eliminate steroids from baseball, Davis tried to redirect attention away from Clemens's struggle with credibility.

Waxman (CoO&GR 2008b: 161) was more definitive and openly partisan. Echoing Davis's comment that each member and 'perhaps everyone in the audience' will reach his or her own conclusion, he emphasized what he had learned:

> Chuck Knoblauch and Andy Pettitte confirm what Brian McNamee told Senator Mitchell. We learned of the conversations that Andy Pettitte believed he had with Roger Clemens about HGH. And even though Mr. Clemens says his relationship with Mr. Pettitte was so close that they would know and share information with each other, evidently Mr. Pettitte didn't believe what Mr. Clemens said in that 2005 conversation.

Waxman apologized to McNamee for the way some committee members had treated him, before concluding that steroids had to be taken out of professional sports 'because we're seeing the culture of the clubhouse become the culture of the high school gym'.

Deliberation

Roger Clemens's trial in the court of public opinion emphasizes two key issues. First, there is a widespread feeling among those who support a banned list that the current system of detection is failing. Their behaviour suggests they support more aggressive action, where the end justifies the means. In this case, Novitzky played a critical role in providing Mitchell with information that he could not normally have obtained. McNamee's and Radomski's unique plea bargains ensured that Mitchell had information that appears to provide bona fide insight into steroid use in MLB and has far greater legal credibility than anything else Mitchell was able to gather. Mitchell then chose to use that information in his report. From a legal perspective, both those decisions proved significant.

The rule of law guarantees two fundamental rights. First, the accused has the right to discovery – the right to see all the evidence arrayed against the accused. The accused has the right to cross-examine that evidence and face and cross-examine those who testify against him/her. Clemens, and other players named in Mitchell's report, did not have that opportunity before they were identified – or after. Similarly, Clemens did not have the opportunity to cross-examine McNamee or systematically question the 'evidence' that different committee members used when questioning him during the February hearing. The report itself and the ensuing February hearing allowed Mitchell and various Committee members to make uncross-examined assertions of largely uncontested, putative fact.

Second, the legal standard for conviction in a matter of the magnitude that Clemens faces is very high – beyond a reasonable doubt, according to a judge or jury. Clemens and others have not only been denied the opportunity to contest the evidence brought against them, they have not had the weight of all the evidence, following cross-examination, weighed and considered by an appropriate legal body. While calling the proceedings, as Davis (2008: 3) did, 'a nationally televised show trial' might be too strong, it certainly indicates that Novitzky's, Mitchell's and the CoO&GR's actions took their case directly to the public, without concern for the rule of law.

This moves directly into concerns over the politicization of due process. The HUAC's actions in the 1940s and 1950s remain among the more notorious government actions in American history. The HUAC's legacy should serve as a constant reminder of the dangers that exist when individuals are condemned for political gain or in aid of a particular cause – no matter how just the cause may appear. At the February hearing, the CoO&GR split along partisan lines, defending or pursuing Clemens, and did so before the viewing public and the media. Rather than positively contributing to the debate on steroid use in MLB or among American youth, the Committee members undermined their role as political leaders and sank to the level of partisan opportunists seeking a conviction in the court of public opinion. Sadly, the final verdict cannot be a positive one for anyone involved in the hearings on the Mitchell report.

References

Assael, S. (2007) *Steroid nation: juiced home run totals, anti-aging miracles, and a Hercules in every high school – the secret history of America's true drug addiction*, New York: ESPN Books.

Associated Press (2004) 'Text of President Bush's State of the Union Address', 21 January. Available online at: www.post-gazette.com/pg/04021/263842.stm#drugs (accessed 22 October 2006).

Associated Press (2007) 'List of names in Mitchell Report'. *SportingNews*, 13 December. Available online at: www.sportingnews.com/mlb/article/2007-12-13/list-names-mitchell-report (accessed 23 June 2009).

Beamish, R. (2009) 'Steroids, symbolism, and morality: the unintended consequences of the social construction of a social problem', in V. Møller, P. Dimeo and M. McNamee (eds), *Elite sport, doping and public health*, Odense: University of Southern Denmark Press.

Bunning, J. (2005) 'Statement by U.S. Senator Jim Bunning, House Government Reform Hearing on Steroids and Major League Baseball, March 17, 2005', in Committee on Government Reform, *Restoring faith in America's pastime: evaluating Major League Baseball's efforts to eradicate steroid use*, pp. 55–60. Available online at: http://ftp.resource.org/gpo.gov/hearings/109h/23038.pdf (accessed 6 December 2010).

Canseco, J. (2005a) *Juiced: wild times, rampant 'roids, smash hits, and how baseball got big*, New York: HarperCollins.

Canseco, J. (2005b) 'March 17 Opening Statement to House Committee on Government Reform', in Committee on Government Reform, *Restoring faith in America's pastime: evaluating Major League Baseball's efforts to eradicate steroid use*, pp. 208–14. Available online at: http://ftp.resource.org/gpo.gov/hearings/109h/23038.pdf (accessed 6 December 2010).

Clemens, R. (2007) 'Denial of steroid use as claimed in Mitchell Report', 22 December. Available online at: www.youtube.com/wrclemens (accessed 23 June 2009).

Clemens, R. (2008) 'Roger Clemens, MLB Player, Opening Statement', 13 February. Available online at: www.youtube.com/watch?v=_k9v6tgk914&feature=related (accessed 26 June 2009).

Committee on Government Reform (2005) 'Restoring faith in America's pastime: evaluating Major League Baseball's efforts to eradicate steroid use', 17 March. Available online at: www.diamondfans.com/archive/house_hearing_109-8_steroids.pdf (accessed 23 July 2009).

Committee on Oversight and Government Reform (2008a) 'The Mitchell Report: the illegal use of steroids in Major League Baseball', 15 January, preliminary transcript. Available online at: http://oversight.house.gov/images/stories/documents/20080205163114.pdf (accessed 6 December 2010).

Committee on Oversight and Government Reform (2008b) 'The Mitchell Report: the illegal use of steroids in Major League Baseball, day 2', 13 February. Available online at: http://oversight.house.gov/index.php?option=com_content&task=view&id=3605&Itemid=2 (accessed 6 December 2010).

Davis, T. (2008) 'Weighing the Committee record: a balanced review of the evidence regarding performance enhancing substances in baseball'. Staff Report, US House of Representatives, 110th Congress, Committee on Oversight and Government Reform. Available online at: http://hosted.ap.org/specials/interactives/_sports/baseball08/clemens_congress/MinorityReport.pdf (accessed 16 June 2009).

ESPN.com (2007) 'Players listed in the Mitchell Commission Report', 13 December. Available online at: http://sports.espn.go.com/mlb/news/story?id=3153646 (accessed 22 June 2009).

Fainaru-Wada, M. and Williams, L. (2006) *Game of shadows: Barry Bonds, BALCO, and the steroids scandal that rocked professional sports*, New York: Gotham Books.

Garabaldi, D. (2005) 'Oral testimony before the House Government Reform Committee, March 17, 2005'. Available online at: http://ftp.resource.org/gpo.gov/hearings/109h/23038.pdf (accessed 6 December 2010).

Hooton, D. (2005) 'Oral testimony before the House Government Reform Committee, March 17, 2005'. Available online at: http://ftp.resource.org/gpo.gov/hearings/109h/23038.pdf (accessed 6 December 2010).

McGwire, M. (2005a) 'March 17 opening statement to House Committee on Government Reform', in Committee on Government Reform, *Restoring faith in America's pastime: evaluating Major League Baseball's efforts to eradicate steroid use*, pp. 219–26. Available online at: http://ftp.resource.org/gpo.gov/hearings/109h/23038.pdf (accessed 6 December 2010).

McGwire, M. (2005b) 'Mark McGuire Senate testimony'. Available online at: www.youtube.com/watch?v=942HcHKbOno&feature=related (accessed 15 June 2009).

Mitchell, G. (2007) *Report to the Commissioner of Baseball of an independent investigation into the illegal use of steroids and other performance enhancing substances by players in Major League Baseball*, 13 December. Available online at: http://files.mlb.com/mitchrpt.pdf (accessed 16 June 2009).

Navasky, V. (1980) *Naming names*, New York: The Viking Press.

New York Daily News (2008) 'Transcript of the Clemens phone call', 8 January. Available online at: www.nydailynews.com/sports/baseball/yankees/2008/01/08/2008–01–08_transcript_of_the_clemens_phone_call-2.html (accessed 23 July 2009).

Novitzky, J. (2003) 'Affidavit of Sepcial Agent Jeff Novitzky in support of request for search warrants', 3 September. Available online at: www.sfgate.com/chronicle/acrobat/2004/02/13/affidvt.pdf (accessed 23 June 2009).

Palmeiro, R. (2005a) 'Testimony of Rafael Palmeiro before the Committee on Government Reform, United States House of Representatives, March 17, 2005', in Committee on Government Reform, *Restoring faith in America's pastime: evaluating Major League Baseball's efforts to eradicate steroid use*, pp. 227–8. Available online at: http://ftp.resource.org/gpo.gov/hearings/109h/23038.pdf (accessed 6 December 2010).

Palmeiro, R. (2005b) 'Rafael Palmeiro face to face lying'. Available online at: www.youtube.com/watch?v=kAxo4pCITRM (accessed 23 June 2009).

Radomski, K. (2009) *Bases loaded: the inside story of the steroid era in baseball by the central figure in the Mitchell Report*, New York: Hudson Street Press.

Schilling, C. (2005) 'Statement of Curt Schilling', 17 March, in Committee on Government Reform, *Restoring faith in America's pastime: evaluating Major League Baseball's efforts to eradicate steroid use*, pp. 229–35. Available online at: http://ftp.resource.org/gpo.gov/hearings/109h/23038.pdf (accessed 6 December 2010).
Selig, A. (2006) 'Statement of the Commissioner Allan H. (Bud) Selig', 30 March. Available online at: www.dlapiper.com/files/upload/selig_statement.pdf (accessed 23 June 2009).
60 Minutes (2008a) 'Roger Clemens', 8 January. Available online at: www.cbsnews.com/video/watch/?id=3680216n&tag=related;photovideo (accessed 23 June 2009).
60 Minutes (2008b) 'Transcript from Roger Clemens on *60 Minutes*', 8 January. Available online at: www.cbsnews.com/stories/2008/01/03/60minutes/main3671585.shtml (accessed 23 June 2009).
Sosa, S. (2005) 'Statement of Mr. Sammy Sosa', 17 March, in Committee on Government Reform, *Restoring faith in America's pastime: evaluating Major League Baseball's efforts to eradicate steroid use*, pp. 215–18. Available online at: http://ftp.resource.org/gpo.gov/hearings/109h/23038.pdf (accessed 6 December 2010).
Staudohar, P. (1997) 'The baseball strike of 1994–95', *Monthly Labor Review*, March: 21–7.
Thomas, F. (2005) 'Testimony of Frank Thomas before the Committee on Government Reform, United States House of Representatives', 17 March, in Committee on Government Reform, *Restoring faith in America's pastime: evaluating Major League Baseball's efforts to eradicate steroid use*, pp. 236–7. Available online at: http://ftp.resource.org/gpo.gov/hearings/109h/23038.pdf (accessed 6 December 2010).
Thompson, T., Vinton, N., O'Keeffe, M. and Red, C. (2009) *American icon: the fall of Roger Clemens and the rise of steroids in America's pastime*, New York: Alfreed A. Knopf.
United States Code (2006) Available online at: http://frwebgate.access.gpo.gov/cgi-bin/usc.cgi?ACTION=RETRIEVE&FILE=$$xa$$busc18.wais&start=1925859&SIZE=10370&TYPE=PDF (accessed 6 December 2010).

10 It's not about the blood!

Operación Puerto and the end of modernity

Martin Hardie

> This is the west, sir. When the legend becomes fact, print the legend.
>
> (*The Man Who Shot Liberty Valance*)

> If we want things to stay as they are, things will have to change.
>
> (*Il Gatopardo* or *The Leopard*)

> In the history of cycle sport, fabrications crowded out facts from the very outset.
>
> (Benjo Maso 2005)

The end of modernity?

Verner Møller has argued that contemporary anti-doping law and policy signal the end of the spirit of modernity in sports (Møller 2004). Møller's characterisation of such an event appears to be founded upon the view that the challenge manifested by the States' and the World Anti-Doping Agency's (WADA) intrusions into sport's 'long tradition of self-governance' signals a 'growing lack of confidence in and an unease about the very project of modernity itself' (Møller 2004: 145). This unease and the will to impose order that accompanies it exert pressure upon fundamental bourgeois legal principles and ideals of freedom. One of the symptoms Møller immediately identifies with this rupturous passage is the growing incidence and acceptance of trial by media (see Beamish, *passim*). In this situation, the ends are seen to justify the means, and anecdotal evidence replaces evidential standards previously needed in modernist courtrooms. Møller correctly identifies this tendency towards trial by media and anecdotal evidence as gaining acceptance and support in so far as it is 'in the service of the virtuous campaign against doping' (Møller 2004: 148). Møller's position, or fear, is that what we are currently witnessing within sport 'may be a portent of a more general departure from the ideals on which the modern world is based' (Møller 2004: 149). Such a view should not seem far-fetched, especially when the Australian Minister for Sport announced, at the 2009 Australian New Zealand Sports Law Association (ANZSLA) Conference, that the whereabouts scheme was a model for dealing with the drug question within the rest of society.

Møller's assessment of anti-doping policy as the end of modernity for sports immediately raises a number of issues that have ramifications which spread beyond the milieu of the world of sports law and doping. Importantly, what Møller puts on the table for discussion is the end of the modernist idea of the rule of law and the coming of what has been termed the permanent state of exception (Agamben 1998, 2005); it includes the idea of law's rationality becoming law's functionality, and it includes the increasing playing out of these matters within a global society of the spectacle, which adopts the tactics of a just war where 'public pillorying (becomes) unmistakably punishment' (Møller 2004: 149). These three factors – exception, functionality and spectacle, bundled together under the rubric of a 'just war', come together when we look at the case of *Operación Puerto* and its discontents, that is the various responses to it, such as the media circus, the 'Riders' Commitment to a New Cycling' (UCI 2006), the whereabouts system and the biological passport. They herald, as Møller has sensed, a change in the way we do (sports) law in a postmodern age. The factors that Møller highlights are also consistent with many of the symptoms identified by writers such as Hardt and Negri as signalling the end of modernity and the coming of what they have dubbed 'Empire' (Hardt and Negri 2000; 2004; 2009).

If the assumption that we have come to the end of modernity (as a period in history) is correct, the question that we need to consider is 'whereabouts are we now?' *Operación Puerto* assists us in coming to terms with the situation as it exemplifies the manner in which the media crisis and trial by media have taken over from the niceties of modernist law practice. One way of understanding this and of highlighting the points made by Møller is by reference to the ongoing saga of *Operación Puerto*. One symptom of the passage that Møller has highlighted, I will argue, is that all things – law, politics, the economy, science and sport – tend to merge into a zone of indistinction (Agamben 1998, 2005). The boundaries between the old disciplines are no longer distinct, and, in such a situation, it is unhelpful to try and isolate one from the other in a manner in which we may have in modernity. In the age of biopolitical production, or immaterial labour (see Hardt and Negri 2009; Lazzarotto 2002), where what is produced are lifestyles, and where production increasingly becomes the production of affect, what we are able to see is a space where the 'economic' or 'Marxist' critique of the causes of doping can be mapped on to the more individualistic and affective understandings of the problem as put forward by Møller – sacrifice, the communication of intensities becomes what is produced, reproduced, bought and sold in a new economy. Subsequently, if what are produced and sold today are, at their most basic, lifestyles, an analysis of the doping problem that seeks to continue to treat sport as some pure, isolated phenomenon, unconnected with the heady world of global business or politics, is of little use to us. Even if we view professional sport, with its emphasis on results, on *faster*, *higher*, *stronger*, Møller is close to the mark when he remarks that 'there is no valid argument against doping that is not at the same time an argument against sport itself' (Møller 2004: 151; see also Konig 1995).

For many, to even accept the position that things cannot be neatly separated and discretely categorised brings about a form of existential crisis that sends them rummaging throughout their modernist toolbox with even greater zeal. Yet we cannot rewind the clock and return to the safety zone of pure modernity. And if we start by taking the attempts to characterise anti-doping as a form of 'sporting rule', the problems become immediately apparent. That sport is more than sport, that sport is business, and that sport and the politics of the nation state are interlinked, are all truisms within the field in which we work and play. Nevertheless, many still try to describe and justify the types of penalty and other measure meted out for anti-doping infractions as being only sporting penalties, with no ramifications outside the ideal world of pure sport.

The clear point is that sporting rules have real ramifications outside sport and real impacts upon the lives of those subjected to them. As a textbook example, Marco Pantani transgressed, possibly by mistake, a technical rule that said a cyclist should not compete, on health grounds, with a level of haematocrit higher than 50 per cent. As Waddington (2000) has pointed out, this may have been the most successful anti-doping rule that we have ever had, in part owing to the role played by the riders (including Pantani) in instigating it. It was the closest thing we have seen in cycling since *Festina* to a doping penalty that was a pure sporting rule. However, even the infraction of a rule that carried with it the lowest opprobrium of all doping penalties – the resting of a rider for 15 days on health grounds – still triggered a criminal investigation, trial and appeal, which were only finally concluded in the rider's favour after his death in tragic circumstances (Rendell 2006). Pantani is but one example – a whole list can be created of cyclists who fall in one way or another into situations as tragic as Pantani's – but the simple point to be made here is that, in such circumstances, it is increasingly naïve, perhaps deceptive, to speak of mere or pure sporting rules (Hardie 2009).

Before developing further this line of enquiry, or contextualising it within the global processes occurring today, a question must be raised as to whether we are experiencing fundamental changes in the way we 'do' law. If this is the case, then we need also to think about the role and purpose of what might be called 'sport criticism'. Konig has criticised sports ethics as being a 'bad idealism with an antiquated knowledge' (Konig 1995: 257), and, in some ways, this is the point I seek to open up for further investigation. If what we are witnessing is, as Møller has highlighted, the end of modernity, and if we are going to deal with this juncture and all that it portends, we need to go beyond viewing anti-doping policy as just a matter for sport and concerning mere sporting rules. To take Konig seriously, we need to stop playing long enough – or really to play with it some more (Agamben 2005) – and to examine the totality of the situation facing us strategically (Shogan and Ford 2000). We need to locate sport both historically and within existing power relations. Sport and its rules can only be understood against the background of the development and changes occurring within global capital, and not by reference to a set of values that arose in a different place and at a different time (Bryson 1990). By recognising that what is at stake is not the purity of sport but, fundamentally, the control of the athlete, as labour and as commodity, we are able to start to tackle the problem (Kreft 2009). From that point, it may be possible to begin the task of constructing a useful critique of sport and doping policy that seriously takes into account the new conditions sensed by Møller and that seeks to contribute to building a sustainable system as an alternative to the one within which athletes currently find themselves.

Cycling, doping and the media

Cycling has, deservedly or not, a reputation as having an entrenched doping culture existing within a closed community where some bending of the rules has been seen as historically permissible, if not required, in order to cope with the exceptional nature of its events. Whether cycling is unique in this aspect is not entirely clear. The anecdotal position is that cycling is, in reality, no different from other sports in terms of the use of doping practices, but that cycling has been subjected to a greater level of testing than have other sports in the last ten years. What is certain is that, during this period, as cycling has itself become embroiled in the processes of globalisation, the sport has been subjected to a number of internal crises and increasing external scrutiny. Throughout this process, the problem of doping and how effectively to deal with it remains an important and unresolved issue.

The increased scrutiny of professional cycling commenced in a large part owing to the events of the 1998 Tour de France involving *Festina* and other teams. In fact, this event is, in part, credited with the movement towards the formation of WADA (Møller 2004: 146). More recently, other than the ongoing *Operación Puerto* inquiry in Spain, there have been the successive problems associated with the three contests of the Tour de France that were contested during the Armstrong interregnum (2006 – Landis; 2007 – Rasmussen, Vinokourov, Mayo; 2008 – Kohl, Schumacher, Ricco and Piepoli). All of these events have raised questions regarding the effectiveness of current anti-doping policy and its attempts to change behaviour in relation to doping practices within cycling. They also raise, in one way or another, the manner in which matters are *not* dealt with by the strict application of the rule of law, but are played out where the media construction of the problem seems to overdetermine the law.

Schneider (2006) makes the valid point that the history of the nature of the problem of doping in cycling is constructed in large part from the extensive media coverage of it. She correctly raises the question as to how far current anti-doping policy is not a result of research or analysis, but is rather a reaction to these successive media and related crises. The point made by Schneider is not that far removed from the concerns of Møller. While my approach seeks to take a lead from the observations of both Møller and Schneider, it differs from that offered by Carstairs in that I have not formed the view that the value to the 'society of the spectacle' (Debord 1995: 147) and the media crisis surrounding doping in cycling has had a 'bums on seats' or 'ratings' effect (Carstairs 2003). I cannot agree with Carstairs that the playing out of the doping question in cycling has had a marketing value or spin-off in the way that she seems to argue that it has.

People may be fascinated by doping scandals, and this may contribute to selling the sport's media to fans, but, rather than a marketing value, what appears to me is that the crisis of doping in cycling plays a much more profound role as part of the contemporary system of governmentality, discipline and control in a global system. It is, moreover, a matter of discipline, control and biopower in a global system (Foucault 1978, 2003; Deleuze 1992). The crisis concerning doping is, thus, a more significant sign of fundamental changes in the nature of global production and sport's place in the global system than the media portrayal of the crisis ever lets on (Hardt and Negri 2000, 2004, 2009). It may be here that Bryson's comments concerning how drugs have overtaken debates on amateurism in contemporary sport are most relevant (Bryson 1990).

Operación Puerto – it's not about the blood

Operación Puerto (Operation Mountain Pass) is the name given to a criminal investigation conducted by the Spanish *Guardia Civil* (*Guardia Civil* 2006), and it encapsulates the manner in which the reality of the material processes occurring have become hidden and confused by the media crisis (for comment on *Operación Puerto*, see: Hardie 2007; Lippi *et al.* 2007, 2008; Pottgiesser *et al.* 2007; Atkinson and Young 2008; Møller 2008; Rebeggiani and Tondani 2008; Rosen 2008; Strulik 2008). The manner in which the *Puerto* drama has been dragged out and portrayed in the media and by many in positions of power within cycling brings into stark focus the situation that Møller describes concerning trial by media. For administrators and policymakers, their aims – good administration and the making of good policy – appear, at times, to have taken second position behind a perceived need to engage in the sustaining of an ill-informed and self-interested slanging match that seeks to denigrate and override the niceties of the mechanisms of modernist justice. Rather than being a simple black and white question, as it is generally portrayed, polarised around the binaries of 'clean' and 'dirty', or 'fair play' and 'cheating', what *Puerto* reveals is that the issue is one of critical complexity, where the public stances and the media's portrayal of the situation belie the forces and movements at play as cycling's helmsmen seek to transform it into a global commodity in the society of the spectacle. *Puerto* reveals a space of critical opalescence, where rumour, suspicion, media, law and politics all converge into a media-constructed zone of indistinction (Agamben 1998, 2005; Galison 2003; Hardie 2007). *Puerto* reveals a space where the global system in construction pushes forth, utilising the tools of exception, functionality, spectacle and just war to overdetermine modernist values and law. It characterises as a hindrance, as tardy, as dysfunctional, as an outdated formality, the grand institution of modern Spanish justice.

In May 2006, the Spanish daily newspaper *El Pais* published a series of stories concerning the *Guardia Civil* investigation of a network involved in the medical preparation of a number of professional cyclists and other athletes (Arribas 2006; Hardie 2009). At the centre of the storm was the Madrid-based gynaecologist, Dr Eufemiano Fuentes. It is history now that the reporting of *El Pais* subsequently sent the cycling world into turmoil as the extent of Dr Fuentes' preparation programmes was revealed, and the affair quickly took on a life of its own. At first, the focus was on the Spanish team, *Liberty Seguros*, whose title sponsor quickly withdrew their financial support. The riders of the team, directed by Manolo Saiz, were forced to cover up their sponsor's name with tape as they competed in the 2006 *Giro d'Italia* (Hood 2006; Tan 2006). Almost immediately, other famous cycling names began to emerge, such as Ullrich and Basso, with the effect, not of only calling into doubt their performances in that staging of the *Giro*, but also of cutting the list of favourites of that year's Tour de France to shreds (Cyclingnews.com 2006a).

The media's focus since that time has been on the cyclists involved and how they should be punished. This has also been the main focus of the International Cycling Union (UCI) – constantly calling for the riders to be disciplined in a manner that, deliberately or not, misunderstands what *Puerto*, as a criminal and judicial process, is all about. This line of attack is not only reserved for the media. Senior officials of both the UCI and WADA do nothing to shed light on the complexity of the situation (*Cyclingnews* 2009b; Hood 2009; Stokes 2009). However, to begin to understand *Puerto*, one needs to consider why, in the first place, the police had been engaged in the surveillance of Fuentes, Saiz and others.

Piecing together the documents, it appears that this surveillance emerged out of the intersection of two seemingly unrelated concerns in Spain. The first was the ongoing investigation by the Spanish *Guardia Civil* into the importation of prohibited medicines, such as insulin growth factor 1 (IG-F1), from Australia in *Operación Mamut* (Mammoth) (*Guardia Civil* 2004). *Mamut* had uncovered a network of importation and distribution of IG-F1 from an Australian company, Gropep. That company, which is based in Adelaide, South Australia, was originally funded by an Australian governmental authority, the Commonwealth Scientific and Industrial Research Organisation (CSIRO), and the University of Adelaide. At the time of the investigation, Gropep had in fact planned to license the right to manufacture IG-F1 to the *Mamut* suspects (*Cyclingnews* 1998). When the *Guardia Civil* followed the trail of Gropep's IG-F1 to and throughout Spain, its distribution eventually led them to the doors of Dr Fuentes and his cohorts. In the first instance, it was this illegal importation and subsequent supply that the *Guardia Civil* were interested in cracking. Their interest was not Fuentes, Saiz nor their collaborators. Even more clearly, the cyclists were not involved. However, the fact of the matter was that it was the trail of IG-F1 from Adelaide that led the *Guardia Civil* to Fuentes and his collaborators.

During the course of the *Mamut* investigation, the *Guardia Civil* became aware of the declarations of the ex-*Kelme* cyclist, Jesus Manzano, that had been published in the Spanish sports daily, *AS* (AS 2004; Bose 2004). Manzano set out in great detail the system of rider preparation that existed within his former team, *Kelme – Communidad Valenciana*. This system, Manzano claims, was driven, not by the individual cyclists, but by those who managed and ran the team. Included among those were the team's various director sportifs, including the principal director, Vicente Belda. Belda now stands charged alongside Fuentes and Saiz in the *Puerto* process.

In late 2005, the *Mamut* investigation intersected by chance with the disaster that arose for Spanish cycling after Roberto Heras's positive test for EPO in 2005 in the *Vuelta a España* (*El Pais* 2005a, 2005b; Cyclingnews.com 2006b). The repercussions for Unipublic, the race's organisers, sponsors and the Spanish state were enormous. For a complex array of reasons, Spanish cycling was in crisis following Heras' positive test. The Grand Tours have always played a role in marking out and defining a territory, a nation and its people. In that respect, the tours were as much a part of creating the Europe of the twentieth century as was the documentation and administration of life that Michele Foucault describes so very well in his lectures entitled, 'Society must be defended'. The people, customs, fêtes, fairs and fiestas each day, complete with the local version of cheese, chorizo and champagne, are always a part of the backdrop of the tours, but they have been steadfastly created and maintained by an alliance of the state, industrial capital and the media. With its resumption after the Civil War in 1941, Spain's *La Vuelta* covered the longest route in its history, demarcating the victor's territory across the country and particularly the former Republican strongholds. For some years, Franco restricted it to only Spanish participants. In modernity, these races all played their role in reinforcing the status of a unified territory, a people, a nation and its capital. It must be in this broad light, along with the years of American domination of the Tour de France, and the sale of Unipublic to the Tour de France owners ASO, that the positive test of Heras must be understood.

At the end of the 2005 *Vuelta*, Heras was the only real Spanish possibility to conquer the Grand Tours (*Giro d'Italia*, *Vuelta a España* and the Tour de France) in a post-Armstrong world. But he was in disgrace. The loss to Unipublic as a result of Heras' positive test brought into focus the perceived problem of doping in Spain and the alleged attitude of impunity that existed there (Cyclingnews.com 2005). It may be possible to speculate that it was also this loss of credibility, both in the public eye and in terms of possible future sponsorship and television coverage, that drew the hunt of the *Guardia* closer to Fuentes.

The evidence given by *Liberty Seguros*' director sportif, Manolo Saiz, when he was detained by the *Guardia Civil*, provides some insight into both how the *Vuelta* disaster came to be and how the *Liberty* team became entangled in the ongoing investigation into illegal importation (*Guardia Civil* 2006). Saiz had been under video surveillance by the *Guardia Civil* and was arrested with a bag of cash allegedly to pay his team's outstanding account with Fuentes. The cash was in the mixed denominations of euros, Swiss francs and Australian dollars, the dollars supposedly being money left over from the team's per diem payments by the organisers of the Tour Down Under in Adelaide, earlier that year. Saiz has had a long history in professional cycling, but, unlike most other team directors, he was never a professional cyclist. Nevertheless, his contacts extended far and wide throughout the cycling world, and he has been, for many years, one of the most successful and complete director sportifs. Saiz was the mentor (or, at least, inspiration) for Lance Armstrong's director sportif, Johan Bruyneel, who rode and served his cycling apprenticeship with Saiz during the 1990s. Saiz also has close connections with ex-Australian professionals and cycling powerbrokers such as Neil Stephens and Stephen Hodge. In Spain, his followers and contacts are known collectively as the 'Manolo-istas' and they are anecdotally regarded as being closely linked to those that broker the power behind the UCI. It is of no surprise, then, that Saiz was also significantly a prime mover, along with the former UCI president, Hein Verbruggen, and his protégé, Alain Rumpf, in the creation of the Pro Tour model adopted by the UCI.

When he was interviewed in detention, Saiz said that he had known Fuentes since his stint with the Spanish cycling team *ONCE* in the early 1990s, a time when his team was populated by a number of high-profile riders, many of whom are still involved in the sport as administrators or director sportifs (*Guardia Civil* 2006). Saiz said that, after Fuentes left the team, they had occasional personal contact but that it was in 2004, with his signing of Roberto Heras, that the relationship recommenced on a more than friendly level. Saiz said that, on his arrival at *Liberty* from the *US Postal Service* team (*USPS*), Heras had asked that he be able to have Fuentes as his personal doctor. According to Saiz, Heras wanted to deal directly with Fuentes. At first, Saiz had refused the request, as it did not seem to him to be the best way to manage the team. After much insistence on the part of Heras, Saiz gave in, but it seems that he decided to try and manage the relationship as best he could. Saiz was insistent, in his evidence, that it was Heras and other riders in his team, some of whom had also previously been in *Kelme*, who pushed for the Fuentes connection. There was, of course, no love lost between Saiz and *Kelme*'s director sportif, Vicente Belda. During the previous years, Saiz had been instrumental in pushing through the Pro Tour and *Kelme*'s exclusion from it. This exclusion had, in part, been brought about by Saiz's and others' insistence that *Kelme* was still engaged in cycling's old ways (*Bike Radar* 2004; Hardie 2004).

After Heras's positive test, the *Guardia Civil* appear to have thought it worthwhile to see if there was any link between the substances being used by cyclists and their investigation of importation and distribution in *Operación Mamut*. This, of course, was not the only event that had led them to the consulting rooms of Fuentes. The year before, the *Vuelta* had been hit by two positive doping tests for blood transfusions. The first to break was that of Tyler Hamilton, another ex *USPS* rider, who tested positive following his 11 September time-trial victory over his (soon to be again) teammate, Floyd Landis, in Valencia (Hardie 2004a, 2004b; Jones 2004). The second involved the post-race revelations concerning Hamilton's teammate, Santi Perez (Abt 2004). On the road, the *Phonak* team was managed by ex-*Kelme* director sportif, Alvaro Pino (Maloney 2006). The files also suggest another link, from Hamilton to his friend '*Nick*' and '*Nick's friend*' (*Guardia Civil* 2006). This little mystery has not received the attention that the reference to '*Valv Piti*' has received in the cycling world. And, of course, seemingly outside the Fuentes affair, the next doping incident to really rock cycling was that of another ex-*USPS* rider, Floyd Landis (Ballester and Walsh 2006; Canadian Broadcasting Corporation 2006; Cyclingnews.com 2006c; Walsh 2007; *Velocity Nation* 2009). These events involving Heras, Hamilton and Perez drew the *Guardia Civil* closer and closer to their stakeout of Fuentes.

Puertas Abiertas

In May 2006, *Operación Puerto* broke when *El Pais* published details from the leaked *Guardia Civil* files. Not only were *Liberty Seguros* embroiled, but so were Hamilton, Perez, a host of *Kelme* riders and two of the main challengers for that year's Tour de France – Jan Ullrich and Ivan Basso. All of this is old news. Most that follow cycling are now all too familiar with the stories of the blood bags, the nicknames and the speculation that still continues over them. Bags of the evidence have come to light regarding Fuentes and the methods he practised. The riders both implicated and suspected and the subsequent disciplinary and criminal proceedings against many of them have all been in the news (Cyclingnews.com 2009a).

Many seem to believe that there is something else that Spanish justice needs to resolve, other than the prosecution of Fuentes and co., that will assist cycling's renewal. This is the continual line pushed by the media, the UCI and WADA. But the point that is often forgotten in the fog is that, as far as the *Guardia Civil* investigation and the Spanish courts are concerned, the cyclists have never been suspects. Sure, there were bags of evidence implicating various riders in the Fuentes scheme, bringing to light for the first time the details of planning and administration that went on to help produce some 'great' rides (for examples, see Hardie 2004b, 2004c) but no cyclist was ever charged, or likely to be charged, with a criminal offence in Spain as a result of *Operación Puerto*.

In this context, the consistent media reports of riders being cleared of any involvement by the Spanish judiciary are meaningless. The cyclists were always witnesses, and in some ways possibly the victims, of the network focused around Fuentes. The approach of the Spanish courts is abundantly clear, even from the reports in the cycling media. For example, one report has even sets out in detail the questions that Investigating Judge Serrano intended to ask cyclists when giving evidence (Cyclingews.com 2006d). The questions point to the status of the cyclists as victims rather than perpetrators. The questions were:

1 Is the witness still a professional cyclist?
2 For which teams has he ridden since 2002?
3 As a professional cyclist, does he know the doctors Eufemiano Fuentes, Yolanda Fuentes or Alfredo Córdova? Has he received blood transfusions? If so, in what laboratory and with whose authority?
4 During his career as professional cyclist, has he ever been sent by his doctor, manager, or other person to the laboratory of Dr Merino Batres in Madrid?
5 Has he ever ridden for a team for which Manolo Saiz was technical director or manager? Did he receive blood transfusions during that time?
6 Assuming that he had suffered health disadvantages as consequence of the treatment by the doctors Fuentes and/or Córdova and/or the actions of Saiz, has he suffered any damage that he could claim in this process?

Their status as such is further illuminated by the comments made by one of the accused, Merino Batres, who told the police:

> Poor Mancebo, I believe that we swindled him a bit. He didn't need the transfusions for anything. He had such a high natural Haemotocrit that we couldn't do half as much for him that we did for the others.
>
> (Author's translation)

Batres recounts how Mancebo paid Fuentes €50,000 in 2005 alone for – as he indicates – more or less needless doping services. As a result of being caught up in Puerto, Mancebo's income fell from €1,000,000 in 2006, with the French team Ag2r, to a low of €10,000 when he was riding in Portugal during 2008 (Arribas 2009a).

In these circumstances, instead of pursuing the riders, what Spain has sought to do is to deal with the public health issues arising from doping in sports and to deal with the supply of doping substances flowing into that country from what is regarded as a part of the new (and by implication 'clean') cycling world. The interest of the *Guardia Civil* was, and has always remained, the importation of potential doping products and their distribution and administration throughout Spain. The *Guardia Civil* believed that Fuentes was probably in collaboration with other sports doctors implicated in doping practices, and that these doctors and groups that they formed constituted independent but interrelated criminal groups – acting independently, but related through their shared objective of providing medical assistance to cyclists. These groups were interlinked with those seeking to import, manfacture and distribute the substances (*Guardia Civil* 2006). Simply put, Spain has gone after the dealers and the pushers, and not the end users or the victims.

The conclusion reached by the *Guardia Civil* was that Fuentes and his gang developed and were involved in the practice of doping, which they described as the integral preparation of the riders, based on illicit methods using medicines in a manner contrary to Spanish health laws. The preparation methods of Fuentes used products that were imported into Spain without passing the normal controls applied to the importation of medicines; they were using the medicines for purposes other than those for which they were designed; and many of the products used were beyond their use-by date (*Guardia Civil* 2006). The January 2009 appeal decision in *Puerto* has highlighted the grounds upon which the case against Fuentes and his cohort will proceed (Audienca Provincial de Madrid 2009a). These include that the practice endangered public health in that:

- they did not extract blood and conduct transfusions on adequate premises;
- they did not transport blood in adequate receptacles;
- the identities of the donors were not adequately recorded;
- there did not exist a system to guarantee that the blood was stored at the correct temperatures or that the fridges and freezers had adequate back-up electricity in the case of black out; and
- the operation of extracting and transfusing blood was conducted in a clandestine manner.

(Author's translation)

As the story of Pantani's relationship with Fuentes suggests, these practices of preparing cyclists raise other important public health concerns. It is on this basis that the *Guardia Civil* and Spanish justice continue to pursue the charge of endangering public health.

'We don't want to know'

The Spanish judicial process, like any other judicial process, has not been a linear affair, with interlocutory steps and appeals by various parties, including the UCI and WADA, all having their effect on the course of the proceedings. For example, in 2007, the Investigating Judge Serrano shelved the inquiry (Juzgado de Instrucción 2007). His finding was that he did not have enough evidence to obtain a prosecution against anyone involved, as doping was not then a crime in Spain. As well as that, in the Investigating Judge's view, the facts as presented did not fit with the concept of a charge of endangering public health. At that point, it seemed that in Spain, to all intents and purposes, *Operación Puerto* was finished. Nevertheless, the damage rolled on, as the riders who had been implicated, some of whom who had been 'cleared' by their national cycling federations or national anti-doping agencies, found it difficult to obtain a ride in a top-tier team. Some were sanctioned, with Basso being the highest-profile rider involved. Others ended up either retiring, racing in lower-level teams or racing as refugees in places such as Portugal and the United States until things blew over.

In the end, the sanction imposed on most of them has not been that meted out by the courts, nor by their federations. It has, however, been dealt to them by the management and sponsors of the Pro Tour teams and the race organisers. This is evidenced by Mancebo's case referred to above, and, as many of the other cases show, retribution for involvement in *Puerto* is not legal in the way we used to think about such things. Whatever the legal outcome might be, retribution manifests itself in one form as an inability to obtain a contract with a decent team. Both the Australian Sports Anti-Doping Agency (ASADA) and the Royal Spanish Cycling Federation (RFEC), respectively, found that those involved had no case to answer. The comparison between Spain and Australia is telling, as in all the rhetoric one is painted as being 'out of step' and the home of the old ways of cycling, while the other is 'in step' and a home of the new ways of cycling, but both decisions were made on identical grounds.

The issue is complex and defies the simple explanations concerning the old and new cycling worlds. On one hand, there is the position that Judge Serrano had refused formally to release evidence to the relevant sporting bodies until the criminal process against Fuentes and his collaborators had been completed. This order of the Court has itself been highlighted in the media wars as further evidence of Spain not being in step with the new cycling culture. There is no great conspiracy here. It is the simple application of ordinary principles of justice, in which disciplinary proceedings are suspended pending the outcome of criminal hearings. This approach was confirmed by the Provincial Court of Madrid in December 2009 (Audienca Provincial de Madrid 2009b) and is consistent with fundamental principles of law and natural justice; not to be bound by them would place the integrity of the criminal trial at stake. There is ample judicial authority, not only in Spain, but also in Australia, to support such a conclusion (High Court of Australia 1982).

On the other hand, the UCI received a bundle of fifty-six files, encompassing the bulk of the then *Operación Puerto* documents from the *Guardia Civil* (*Guardia Civil* 2006). The UCI retained a consultant to deal with the *Puerto* files and, in early 2006, subsequently passed these on to the respective national cycling federations. It was on this basis that, for example, CONI disciplined Ivan Basso. In the Australian case, of the fifty-six bundles of documents sent to the federations, it appears that only one page actually made it to the independent anti-doping body, ASADA. Without more than this one page, consisting of a calendar accompanied by some handwritten and coded annotations, it is of no surprise that ASADA found that there was no case to answer. The question that must be asked is: Where did the chain of custody for these documents break down? How did Cycling Australia, if that is indeed where the chain broke, fail to pass on all of the relevant documents? Nevertheless, the UCI continues to hold out Australia as one of the representatives of the new cycling culture that have dealt with the *Puerto* problem in a comprehensive way, while Spain is characterised as an example of the old ways.

In February 2008, the Provincial Court of Madrid reopened the case for the first time (Audienca Provincial de Madrid 2008). The three magistrates of the court found on appeal that there was sufficient evidence for the charge of 'endangering public health' to be pursued, and they directed Judge Serrano to reopen his investigation into that charge. However, it may be that an equally important finding of the Provincial Court was that the cyclists had never engaged in fraud in respect of their employers or sponsors. This decision is important, not only for the the riders insofar as they continue to suffer at the hands of administrators and sponsors who fear the sullying of their good names, but also for the continuing schizophrenic and paranoid manner in which *Puerto* and, more broadly, doping policy are dealt with in cycling. The Provincial Court finding suggests, in fact, that these very same sponsors and administrators have been all too well aware of the practices within their respective teams for too long – and thus are not in a position either to have their name sullied or to have been defrauded.

The 2008 Provincial Court decision rejected the argument of fraud as being openly artificial and stated that it was not realistic to try to fit acts such as those in question in *Puerto* within the Spanish law of fraud. Fraud in Spain, as with most jurisdictions, requires either those contracting the cyclists (the teams) or those running publicity campaigns in concert with the cyclists (the sponsors) to be deceived, and to be deceived seriously, hence, the concept and the offence of 'serious fraud'. The court stated that:

> when it is notorious that for many years there has been talk of irregular practices, when there have been cyclists who have died from the consumption of drugs, frequent disqualifications and sanctions, when cycling is the mirror into which other sports look with fear, when it is known that the caravans and logistic premises of cycling teams have been searched for stimulants, when random controls are necessary after each race or stage, and the cycling teams have their own specialist doctors, to affirm that the cyclists have defrauded those who have contracted them is to close one's eyes to reality . . . There is at least an 'I don't want to know' attitude, and that is incompatible with the idea of serious fraud.
> (Author's translation)

The implication of this finding is clear. The Provincial Court felt that the sponsors and the sport's administrators had knowledge of the fact that there had been a number of doping cases in cycling in recent years and that doping existed within cycling. The further and more important implication is that both groups had been happy to turn a blind eye while it was in their interests. This finding undermines somewhat the simplistic rhetoric of cheating and fair play, often repeated by members of both these groups, that pervades the discussion around doping in cycling in contemporary times, and the arguably hypocritical situation whereby it is only the cyclists who are taking the blame for the problem. For all the talk of cultural change in cycling, there is still little acknowledgement from the various levels of the sport's administration and sponsors that, while many of them continue to build their own careers, they too were a part of cycling's old ways.

The *Puerto* files refer to various media reports, those of Roux, Manzano, Heras, Hamilton and Perez in particular. All of this suggests that the widespread use of performance-enhancing substances in cycling was common knowledge. Drugs in cycling have a long history. As we know, it was Simpson's death (Fotheringham 2003) that brought the health and safety of the cyclists into focus as anti-doping controls developed during the 1960s (Houlihan 1999). It was also with Simpson's death – the Englishman who helped start the process of globalising the Tours – that doping first became a political matter, but it still remained an internal issue, something for the sport to deal with. The late 1990s mark the point at which it became a matter for the state, and it was with the *Festina Tour*, with borders being crossed, that we first saw doping becoming criminalised. Even at the time of the *Festina* affair, the ethos behind anti-doping measures was health and safety. Only recently, as the pressures of a global market demanded, has that focus shifted to risk management, backed by the rhetoric of fair play and cheating, to be monitored by a bio-political passport regime.

Puerto also reveals a new post-*Festina*, 'postmodern' approach to the organisation of doping. *Festina* became criminalised because of the seizure of various illegal substances in Willy Voet's team car (Voet 2001). The riders, including Australian Neil Stephens, were held in police detention for days, with the almost blind Swiss rider, Alex Zuelle, even being deprived of his glasses. The *Festina* affair exposed the old team-based practices of preparation, where team doctors themselves were responsible for the team's doping programme. In the aftermath of *Festina*, that system began to break down, and it seems that it was replaced by a more networked and outsourced preparation system. *Operación Puerto* exposes the outsourced network model that came into existence in cycling in great detail (*Guardia Civil* 2006). It also suggests that *Liberty* returned to a more team-based approach, as Saiz was aware of the dangers to his riders' health, not to say the team's reputation, if they were left alone and allowed to do their own thing. Journalist and ex-professional Paul Kimmage has recently argued that, rather than dealing with its history and the problem of doping, in a post-*Festina* world, these practices only became further perfected (*Velocity Nation* 2009).

Fuentes, Pantani and Chaba

The effect of Fuentes' practices on the health of the riders is one of the issues raised by the continuing, post-appeal *Guardia Civil* investigation. Although there have been suggestions that the *Guardia Civil* may have investigated the links between Fuentes and Marco Pantani and Jose Maria Jimenez, the references to these two riders in the *Puerto* files have not been widely speculated about in the media (*Guardia Civil* 2006). What the files (*Guardia Civil* 2006) do call into question is the assumption by Matt Rendell in his book, *The death of Marco Pantani* (Rendell 2006), that, in his final year, *Il Pirata* (as Pantini is referred to) was not doping.

Rendell documents Pantani's life during his last year in some detail: the plastic surgery, the outcome of the criminal and disciplinary trials and appeals, the visits to the psychiatrist and his doctors in Italy, the hospitalisations, the crack and cocaine binges, on to his retirement and final death on 14 February 2004. During this time, it was thought that Pantani was, for racing purposes, clean, although he used crack and cocaine after his retirement. Rendell recounts how doctors in Italy had warned him that racing itself might not be the best thing for his mental or physical health, but that racing doped was far more dangerous.

Nevertheless, it was in this same period, painstakingly documented by Rendell, that the *Puerto* investigation tells us Pantani was also visiting Madrid and Dr Fuentes (*Guardia Civil* 2006). During Pantani's last season on the bike, the one immediately before his death, commencing late January 2003, Fuentes equally painstakingly records an intense calendar of preparation, including EPO (almost daily for over a month), IG-F1, T3 Levothroid (a hormone used in the treatment of menopause) and insulin. The programme lasted from late January until Pantani's retirement in June 2003 (*Guardia Civil* 2006).

The coincidence between this programme and Pantani's documented incidents of mental instability during his final year raises significant causes for concern as to the health implications of doping. In the context of the investigation into the charge that Fuentes endangered public health, it will be interesting to see if this coincidence or mis-incidence of events in Pantani's last year of life comes to light. And it should not be forgotten that another Fuentes patient who also suffered from depression and instability, Jose Maria Jimenez, died a little over 2 months before Pantani.

Functionality, spectacle and exception

Spain and Australia, in the guise of Valverde and Davis, were the unfortunate focus of another *Operación Puerto* sideshow that was played out in advance of the 2007 World Cycling Championships in Stuttgart (Cyclingnews.com 2007a, 2007b, 2007c). Although, at that point, there was only speculation and rumour as to Valverde's involvement in *Puerto*, the Stuttgart organising committee decided that they did not want Valverde to compete in the 2007

World Championships to be held in that city, owing to this rumoured involvement with Dr Fuentes. This involvement, they said, was sufficient to exclude Valverde, as his presence was not consistent with the city's plans to give cycling a new start. The UCI quickly fell into line with their hosts and announced that, not only were they prohibiting Valverde from riding, but also that they would commence disciplinary proceedings against him. The problem for the UCI and Stuttgart was that they had opened a can of worms, in that other riders who had been listed to start at the World Championships were in a similar or even worse position than Valverde in relation to their documented *Puerto* involvement.

The UCI quickly realised this apparent inconsistency and decided that the cases of Davis and Valverde were the same and that both, along with the Czech, Rene Andrle, would be excluded from the race (McQuaid 2007). It did not matter that the court in Spain had restricted the use of the *Puerto* evidence until that case was concluded, nor that the RFEC and ASADA had found no case to answer. The law was now being simultaneously made, interpreted and applied by the UCI, the Stuttgart race organising committee and sponsors of the World Championship. Eventually, the UCI agreed to the RFEC suggestion that they mediate the dispute in the CAS, rather than seeking an injunction in a civil court. Davis also commenced proceedings in the CAS, and the matters were effectively resolved, with the CAS arbitrator considering:

> that a ban imposed on a cyclist, not yet recognised as guilty of doping, from participating in the World Championships constituted a form of advance sanction . . . The UCI was prevented from implementing the type of procedure which would allow it to pronounce such a severe sanction whilst maintaining in an adequate manner the rights of the cyclist.
>
> (Cyclingnews.com 2007d)

In short, the organising committee and the UCI had sought to deny the riders natural justice. Unimpressed by this, the German interior minister froze the government's subsidy to the organisers of the race (Bike Radar 2007). Functionality, spectacle and exception again overdetermined modernist law.

Why us?

Despite the outraged claims to the contrary (Audienca Provincial de Madrid 2009b; Cyclingnews 2009b, 2009c), *Puerto* is now proceeding towards a trial of those involved in the network of supply and administration, including Dr Fuentes and his team, along with team directors Saiz and Belda. Beyond media discussion, however, every conversation about *Operación Puerto* raises the questions, 'Why cycling?', 'Why us and not all those other sports that dope?'. Equally universal is the protest: 'cyclists are the most tested athletes', and so on. Whether details of other athletes were ever found by the *Guardia Civil* we may never know (Arribas and Hardie 2009; *Bike Radar* 2006; Cyclingnews.com 2006e; *Le Monde* 2006). On this matter, one can only speculate. Nevertheless, what can be said is that those other sports are far more established, on a global scale, than cycling is. And they have a different institutional sporting tradition to that of cycling. Unlike other sports, cycling now finds itself in the midst of a crisis of its globalisation: the shift from a relatively small, European-based trade into a global international media spectacle.

In reality, cycling was always professional. The Tour grew out of the media's need to sell newspapers, and doping quickly became the way that the 'convicts of the route' (Mignion 2003; Londres 2009) managed to perform the impossible task set for them. Not only was cycling always linked to selling something else, it was also tied intimately to the new science of physiology and hormone research from the very beginning (Hoberman 1992). Doping became a part of cycling culture, as it operated outside the ethos of the amateur sporting world. Drugs became, as one old Aussie pro put it to me once, the 'tools of the trade'. Like truck drivers on amphetamines, it was simply a way of getting the job done.

Additionally, cycling has always been run at a grass-roots level, itinerant small groups, riders, managers, directors, like nomadic bands of gypsies. It was never big business – only recently did that occur. The Armstrong years saw cycling develop into a global media product, and, with it, a new level of scrutiny grew, as the struggle to control the emerging global commodity intensified. Cultural change in cycling is being driven by the fight over global cycling TV rights and who will control this new commodity. This is what is at the heart of the battle between the Grand Tours and the UCI – a potential multimillion-dollar TV product, where the Tours wish to retain their control over their races, and the UCI seemingly wishes to integrate them into one grand package, under its control. In this situation, rumour and suspicion serve as the cipher with which the battle is played out, as points are scored against the other side. Caught in the middle of this power struggle between the sport's 'owners' are the riders, who become isolated scapegoats.

In this context of 'cultural change', it is only the riders being subjected to scrutiny, and not those who have managed the sport for many years and who, it seems, have known what was happening the whole time. It is still only the cyclists who are risking losing their livelihood, the exceptions being Fuentes or the odd director, but even they might come back in one way or another. True cultural change within cycling depends upon it being accepted that it was not just the cyclists involved in doping. It involves recognition that the practice was widely known about and accepted, even in some cases promoted by those in the know – administrators, sponsors and the media. At present, riders are criminalised, while others involved in the sport are mouthing the mantras of 'zero tolerance' and 'cultural change'. Against a backdrop where policy is developed upon the basis of a media crisis, genuine reform is impossible.

Puerto exists within the framework of the abandonment of old notions of law and the construction of a new functional, global system. Anti-doping, as it has been played out so far in relation to *Operación Puerto* and its discontents, exemplifies Møller's fear – this is the end of modernity, and law is made in the media as much as it is made in the courts. *Operación Puerto* is a perfect example of the distance that exists between the rhetoric of the media crisis surrounding doping and pro cycling and the actual reality of the material processes that are occurring as cycling goes through the process of global structural readjustment. If one is serious about developing a sustainable anti-doping policy, there is a need for a genuine evidential basis, rather than improvised reactions to a media crisis. In the case of *Puerto*, it is the media crisis that has driven sports policy: it is this media crisis that has defined what *Puerto* is about for the purpose of reactive policymaking. It is a circular operation, fraught with pitfalls for a sober policy framework, where currently the rigours of the law and justice seem to have no place.

Those engaged in the rhetoric surrounding *Operación Puerto* have painted a picture of Spanish justice being slow and out of step with the cultural change that the purported 'new cycling world' is trying to embrace. For example, the UCI president, Pat McQuaid, has often criticised the Spanish authorities for being 'too lenient in their approach to doping' (Deutsche Presse-Agentur 2008). This rhetoric is not only simplistic, it is misleading. One focus of this rhetoric has been the 'fact' that the Spanish cycling federation itself has not properly dealt with the riders involved. As noted above, the same criticism could also be levelled against those countries, such as Australia, that are said to represent the new cultural change within cycling.

Fixation on the allocation of blame is not the answer. It is more important to register the complexity of the processes occurring and to highlight that, in a world of policy congestion, driven by media crises, it is difficult to develop coherent responses (Green and Houlihan 2005; Houlihan 2005). Rather than creating scapegoats or engaging in witch-hunts, a policy of engagement on all sides, based upon a thorough and sober assessment of the relevant issues, should be pursued. But all of this seems to have become lost in the current evangelising character of anti-doping, which only results in a moral condemnation worthy of a medieval inquisition, rather than the mores of modernity. One can't get rid of the feeling that, more than anti-doping, more than fair play and cries for justice, what is being played out here is the construction of the new global cycling cartography, where legitimacy is made through the management of crisis and events – exception, functionality and spectacle – under the guise of the just war against the evil of doping.

References

Abt, S. (2004) 'Pérez of Phonak is accused', *International Herald Tribune*, 1 November 2004. Available online at: www.nytimes.com/2004/11/01/sports/01iht-phonak_ed3_.html (accessed 25 November 2009).

Agamben, G. (1998) *Homo Sacer, sovereign power and bare life*, Stanford: Stanford University Press.

Agamben, G. (2005) *The state of exception*, Chicago: The University of Chicago Press.

Arribas, C. (2009a) '*Mancebo hace sufrir a Armstrong*'. Available online at: www.elpais.com/articulo/deportes/Mancebo/hace/sufrir/Armstrong/elpepidep/20090217elpepidep_7/Tes (accessed 25 November 2009).

Arribas, C. (2009b) '*Queremos llegar al fondo de la trama*'. Available online at: www.elpais.com/articulo/deportes/Queremos/llegar/fondo/trama/elpepidep/20090212elpepidep_6/Tes (accessed 14 July 2010).

Arribas, C. and Hardie, M. (2009) '*En la Operación Puerto también había tenistas y futbolistas*'. Available online at: www.elpais.com/articulo/deportes/Operación/Puerto/habia/tenistas/futbolistas/elpepidep/20090118elpepidep_12/Tes (accessed 25 November 2009).

AS (2004) '*El lado oscuro del ciclismo: El escándalo destapado por Jesús Manzano y el Diario AS contado capítulo a capítulo*'.

Atkinson, M. and Young, K. (2008) *Deviance and social control in sport*, Illinois: Human Kinetics.

Audienca Provincial de Madrid (2008) Sección no. 5, Rollo 566/2007, Organo Procedencia: JDO Instrucción N. 31 de Madrid, Proc. Origen: Diligencias Previas Proc. Abreviado no. 4293/2006, Auto Numero 496/08, Ilmos Magistrados D. Arturo Beltran Nunez, D. Jesus Angel Guijarro Lopez, D Paz Redondo Gil, dated 11 February 2008.

Audienca Provincial de Madrid (2009a), Sección no. 5, Rollo 702/2008, Organo Procedencia: JDO Instrucción N. 31 de Madrid, Proc. Origen: Diligencias Previas Proc. Abreviado no. 4293/2006, Auto Numero 63/09, Ilmos Magistrados D. Arturo Beltran Nunez, D. Jesus Angel Guijarro Lopez, D Paz Redondo Gil, dated 11 January 2009.

Audienca Provincial de Madrid (2009b), Sección no. 5, Rollo 395/2009, Organo Procedencia: JDO Instrucción N. 31 de Madrid, Proc. Origen: Diligencias Previas Proc. Abreviado no. 4293/2006, Auto Numero 3734/09, Ilmos Magistrados D. Arturo Beltran Nunez, Da. Pascual Fabia Mir, D. Paz Redondo Gil, dated 26 November 2009.

Ballester, P. and Walsh, D. (2006) *LA confidential*, Paris: Points.

Bike Radar (2004) 'Saiz and Belda fall out over Valverde'. Available online at: www.bikeradar.com/news/article/saiz-and-belda-fall-out-over-valverde-9981 (accessed 14 July 2010).

Bike Radar (2006) 'Conspiracy of silence?'. Available online at: www.bikeradar.com/blog/article/conspiracy-of-silence-10980 (accessed 25 November 2009).

Bike Radar (2007) 'Valverde; Sinkewitz implicates Bettini; Minister freezes funds'. Available online at: www.bikeradar.com/news/article/valverde-sinkewitz-implicates-bettini-minister-freezes-funds-12592 (accessed 25 November 2009).

Bose, M. (2004) 'Tour cyclist claims drug caused'. Available online at: www.telegraph.co.uk/sport/othersports/cycling/2375552/Tour-cyclist-claims-drug-caused-collapse.html (accessed 14 July 2010).

Bryson, L. (1990) 'Sport, drugs and the development of modern capitalism', *Sporting Traditions*, May, 2: 135–53.

Canadian Broadcasting Corporation (2006) *Cycle of denial implicated on the Internet*. Available online at: www.cbc.ca/sports/indepth/landis/instantmessage.html (accessed 25 November 2009).

Carstairs, C. (2003) 'The wide world of doping: drug scandals, natural bodies, and the business of sports entertainment', *Addiction Research & Theory*, 11(4): 263–81.

Cyclingnews.com (1998) 'Australian press report'. Available online at: http://autobus.cyclingnews.com/results/1998/sep98/sep2.shtml (accessed 25 November 2009).

Cyclingnews.com (2005) UCI press release May 2005. Available online at: www.cyclingnews.com/news/the-uci-responds-to-the-spanish-affair (accessed 14 July 2010).

Cyclingnews.com (2006a) 'Ullrich and Basso deny involvement with Fuentes'. Available online at: www.cyclingnews.com/news.php?id=news/2006/may06/may26news (accessed 14 July 2010).

Cyclingnews.com (2006b) 'Beating the cheaters', News feature, 11 October. Available online at: www.cyclingnews.com/features/?id=2006/epo_protease (accessed 14 July 2010).

Cyclingnews.com (2006c) 'Speculation catches fire over Tour de France positive'. Available online at: www.cyclingnews.com/news.php?id=news/2006/jul06/jul27news2 (accessed 25 November 2009).

Cyclingnews.com (2006d) '51 witnesses for *Operación Puerto*'. Available online at: http://autobus.cyclingnews.com/news.php?id=news/2006/dec06/dec22news (accessed 25 November 2009).

Cyclingnews.com (2006e) 'Spanish soccer clubs linked to Fuentes?'. Available online at: www.cyclingnews.com/editions/first-edition-cycling-news-for-december-8–2006 (accessed 25 November 2009).

Cyclingnews.com (2007a) 'Valverde's defence optimistic, Davis fights to save Worlds spot'. Available online at: www.cyclingnews.com/editions/latest-cycling-news-for-september-21–2007 (accessed 25 November 2009).

Cyclingnews.com (2007b) 'Zabel, Valverde not welcome in Stuttgart'. Available online at: www.cyclingnews.com/news.php?id=news/2007/aug07/aug15news (accessed 25 November 2009).

Cyclingnews.com (2007c) 'UCI says no Worlds for Valverde and initiates proceedings'. Available online at: www.cyclingnews.com/news.php?id=news/2007/aug07/aug30news (accessed 25 November 2009).

Cyclingnews.com (2007d) 'Valverde cleared by CAS to ride World Championships'. Available online at: www.cyclingnews.com/editions/cycling-news-flash-for-september-27–2007 (accessed 25 November 2009).

Cyclingnews (2009a) 'Complete coverage of "*Operación Puerto*"'. Available online at: http://autobus.cyclingnews.com/news.php?id=news/puerto_complete (accessed 25 November 2009).

Cyclingnews (2009b) 'WADA frustrated by Spanish Courts in Operación Puerto case'. Available online at: www.cyclingnews.com/news/wada-frustrated-by-spanish-courts-in-Operación-puerto-case (accessed 14 December 2009).

Cyclingnews.com (2009c) '*Operación Puerto*: case closed'. Available online at: www.cyclingnews.com/news/Operación-puerto-case-closed (accessed 14 December 2009).

Debord, G. (1995) *The society of the spectacle*, New York: Zone Books.

Deleuze, G. (1992) 'Postscript on the societies of control', *October*, 59(Winter) Cambridge, MA: MIT Press: 3–7.

Deutsche Presse-Agentur (2008) 'McQuaid: Spaniards are "too lenient in their approach to doping"'. Available online at: www.earthtimes.org/articles/news/224947,mcquaid-spaniards-are-too-lenient-in-their-approach-to-doping.html (accessed 9 December 2010).

El Pais (2005a) '*Roberto Heras, positivo por EPO*'. Available online at: www.elpais.com/articulo/deportes/Roberto/Heras/positivo/EPO/elppordep/20051108elpepudep_1/Tes (accessed 25 November 2009).

El Pais (2005b) 'Heras: "Estoy completamente seguro de que soy inocente"'. Available online at: www.elpais.com/articulo/deportes/Heras/Estoy/completamente/seguro/soy/inocente/elpepudep/20051108elpepudep_7/Tes (accessed 25 November 2009).

Fotheringham, W. (2003) *Put me back on my bike: in search of Tom Simpson*. London: Yellow Jersey Press.

Foucault, M. (1978) *The history of sexuality*, London: Vintage, pp. 135–45.

Foucault, M. (2003) *Society must be defended*, London: Penguin.

Galison, P. (2003) *Einstein's clocks and Poincaré's maps: empires of time*, New York: Hodder and Stoughton.

Green, M. and Houlihan, B. (2005) *Elite sport development: policy learning and political priorities*, London: Routledge.

Guardia Civil (2004) '*Sección de Consumo y Medio Ambiente de Guardiia Civil*', Dilegencia de Exposicion de Hechos, March.

Guardia Civil (2006) '*Jefatura Información y Policia Judicial, Unidad Central Operativa, Sección de Consumo y Medio Ambiente*'. Dilegencia de Exposicion de Hechos, 23 May.

Hardie, M. (2004a) 'Belda takes aim'. Available online at: http://autobus.cyclingnews.com/news.php?id=news/2004/sep04/sep25news2 (accessed 14 July 2010).

Hardie, M. (2004b) 'Tyler starts the fight club on September 11', Cyclingnews.com. Available online at: http://autobus.cyclingnews.com/road/2004/vuelta04/?id=results/vuelta048 (accessed 25 November 2009).

Hardie, M. (2004c) 'Liberty trifecta', Cyclingnews.com. Available online at: http://autobus.cyclingnews.com/road.php?id=road/2004/jun04/euskalbizikleta04/euskalbizikleta043 (accessed 25 November 2009).

Hardie, M. (2007) 'Deleuze: "Had I not done philosophy I would have done law"', *International Journal for the Semiotics of Law*, 20(1/March).

Hardie, M. (2009) 'An open letter'. Available online at: http://velocitynation.com/content/features/2009/open-letter (accessed 25 November 2009).

Hardt, M. and Negri, A. (2000) *Empire*, Cambridge, MA: Harvard University Press.

Hardt, M. and Negri, A. (2004) *Multitude*, Cambridge, MA: Harvard University Press.

Hardt, M. and Negri, A (2009) *Commonwealth*, Cambridge, MA: Harvard University Press.

High Court of Australia (1982) *Hammond* v. *Commonwealth of Australia*, (1982) 152 CLR 188, 206, per Deane J., citing *Huddart, Parker and Co Pty Ltd* v. *Moorehead* (1909) 8 CLR 330, 379–80, and *Melbourne Steamship Co Ltd* v. *Moorehead* (1912) 15 CLR 333, 346.

Hoberman, J. (1992) *Mortal engines: the science of performance and the dehumanization of sport*, Free Press.

Hood, A. (2006) 'Velonews, Liberty pulls plug on sponsorship', 25 May. Available online at: http://velonews.com/article/9913 (accessed 24 November 2009).

Hood, A. (2009) 'The scandal that just keeps on giving: *Puerto* investigation faces another delay', *Velonews*, 16 October. Available online at: http://velonews.competitor.com/2009/10/news/the-scandal-that-just-keeps-on-giving-puerto-investigation-faces-another-delay_99302 (accessed 25 November 2009).

Houlihan, B. (1999) *Dying to win: doping in sport and the development of anti-doping*, Strasbourg: Council of Europe Publishing.

Houlihan, B. (2005) 'Public sector sport policy: developing a framework for analysis', *International Review for the Sociology of Sport*, 40: 163.

Jones, J. (2004) 'Hamilton fails blood tests'. Available online at: www.cyclingnews.com/news.php?id=news/2004/sep04/sep21news3 (accessed 14 July 2010).

Juzgado de Instrucción Num. 31 (2007) Madrid, DPA 4293?06 H, Autosobreseimiento, dated 8 March 2007.

Konig, E. (1995) 'Criticism of doping: the nihilistic side of technological sport and the antiquated view of sport ethics', *International Review for the Sociology of Sport*, 30(3–4): 247–60.

Kreft, L. (2009) 'The elite athlete – in a state of exception?', *Sport, Ethics and Philosophy*, 3(1/April): 3–18.

Lazzarotto, M. (2002) 'From biopower to biopolitics', *Pli, The Warwick Journal of Philosophy*, 13(100). Available online at: www.warwick.ac.uk/philosophy/pli_journal/vol_13.html (accessed 25 November 2009).

Le Monde (2006) '*Des footballeurs ont été vus chez le docteur Fuentes*'. Available online at: www.lemonde.fr/cgibin/ACHATS/acheter.cgi?offre=ARCHIVES&type_item=ART_ARCH_30J&objet_id=969121&clef=ARC-TRK-D_01 (accessed 25 November 2009).

Lippi, G., Franchini, M. and Cesare Guidi, G. (2007) 'Tour de crisis, Doping in sport should be addressed by prevention rather than prosecution', *British Journal of Sports Medicine*, 41: 625–6.

Lippi, G., Franchini, M. and Cesare Guidi, G. (2008) 'Switch off the light on cycling, switch off the light on doping', *British Journal of Sports Medicine*, 42: 162.

Londres, A. (2009) *Los Forzados de la carretera – Tour de Francia 1924*, Barcelona: Editorial Melusina.

Maso, B. (2005) *The sweat of the gods*, Norwich: Mousehold Press.

McQuaid, P. (2007) Personal communication. UCI President Pat McQuaid, 20 September 2007.

Maloney, T. (2006) 'Six years, 11 doping scandals: the Phonak legacy'. Available online at: www.cyclingnews.com/news.php?id=features/2006/phonak_legacy (accessed 14 July 2010).

Mignion, P. (2003) 'The Tour de France and the doping issue', in H. Dauncey and G. Hare (eds), *The Tour de France, 1903 2003: a century of sporting structures, meanings, and values*, London: Frank Cass, p. 230.

Møller, V. (2004) 'The anti-doping campaign – farewell to the ideals of modernity?', in J. Hoberman and V. Møller (eds), *Doping and public policy*, Odense: University Press of Southern Denmark.

Møller, V. (2008) *The doping devil*, International Network of Humanistic Doping Research, vol. 1, Copenhagen: Books on Demand GmbH.

Pottgiesser, T., Umhau, M., Ahlgrim, C., Ruthardt, S., Roecker, K. and Schumacher, Y.O. (2007) 'Hb mass measurement suitable to screen for illicit autologous blood transfusions', *Medicine & Science in Sports & Exercise*, 39(10/October): 1748–56.

Rebeggiani, L and Tondani, D. (2008) 'Organizational forms in professional cycling – efficiency issues of the UCI Pro Tour', *International Journal of Sports Finance*, 3.
Rendell, M. (2006) *The death of Marco Pantani: a biography*, London: Weidenfeld & Nicolson.
Rosen, D.M. (2008) *Dope: a history of performance enhancement in sports from the nineteenth century to today*, Westport: Praeger.
Schneider, A.J. (2006) 'Cultural nuances: doping, cycling and the Tour de France', *Sport in Society*, 9(2): 212–26.
Shogan, D. and Ford, M. (2000) 'A new sport ethics: taking Koenig seriously', *International Review for the Sociology of Sport*, 35(1): 49–58.
Stokes, S. (2009) 'Operación Puerto delay scandalous, says McQuaid', Cyclingnews.com, 16 October. Available online at: www.cyclingnews.com/news/Operación-puerto-delay-scandalous-says-mcquaid (accessed 25 November 2009).
Strulik, H. (2008) 'Riding high – success in sports and the rise of doping cultures'. Leibniz Universitat Hanover Discussion Paper No. 372. Available online at: http://ssrn.com/abstract=1009826 (accessed 14 July 2010).
Tan, A. (2006) 'Liberty Seguros terminate contract', Cycling News Flash for 25 May, 2006. Available online at: www.cyclingnews.com/news.php?id=news/2006/may06/may25news3 (accessed 14 July 2010).
UCI (2006) 'Riders' commitment to a new cycling'. Available online at: www.uci.ch/Modules/BUILTIN/getObject.asp?MenuId=MTI1NDg&ObjTypeCode=FILE&type=FILE&id=MzIwMzA& (accessed 25 November 2009).
Velocity Nation (2009) 'Interview with Paul Kimmage, *Fighting the good fight*'. Available online at: http://velocitynation.com/content/interviews/2009/paul-kimmage (accessed 25 November 2009).
Voet, W. (2001) *Breaking the chain, drugs and cycling – the true story*, London: Yellow Jersey Press.
Waddington, I. (2000) *Sport, health and drugs: a critical sociological perspective*, London: Routledge.
Walsh, D. (2007) *From Lance to Landis, inside the American doping controversy at the Tour de France*, New York: Ballantine Books.

11 'A prison of measured time'? A sociologist looks at the WADA whereabouts system

Ivan Waddington

Writing in the late 1970s, the Marxist physical educationalist, Jean-Marie Brohm, argued that sport in 'bourgeois capitalist societies' had become a 'prison of measured time' (Brohm 1978). By this he meant that, under capitalism, sport has developed in such a way that it has come, for elite athletes, to represent constraint rather than freedom, with the removal of all creative spontaneity and playful impulses, characterized by the sterile worship of the stop-watch. Sport was, he argued, 'one of the strongest factors removing the element of play from bodily activity' (Brohm 1978: 41) and he cited his fellow French writer, Ellul, to the effect that we 'are witnessing a process whereby playfulness and joy . . . improvisation and spontaneity are disappearing: all these things are abandoned in favour of obedience to strict rules, efficiency and record times' (Ellul, cited in Brohm 1978: 41).

Of course, it is not difficult to criticize Brohm's arguments from a more detached sociological perspective for, like the work of many Marxists, his writing is highly ideological and, at times, his ideology appears effectively to have predetermined the results of his analysis. But, if Brohm's analysis was in some respects problematic, might it nevertheless be the case that his description of modern sport as a 'prison of measured time' may not be entirely inappropriate, even if in a rather different sense from that intended by Brohm? This is a question that I wish to raise in relation to the whereabouts system, introduced by WADA in 2003 and extended in 2008.

I should make it clear at the outset that I do not wish to argue that the whereabouts system either can or cannot be justified, for this is a philosophical or moral issue, rather than a properly sociological one, and my main concern here is to look at the whereabouts system through the eyes of a sociologist. In this regard, I want first to locate the whereabouts system within the context of broader social processes, including changing practices and ideas concerning surveillance and control, personal liberty, privacy and democracy. Such an approach will, I hope, highlight some of the characteristics of what is – at least within liberal democratic societies – an extraordinary system of surveillance and control of people who have committed no offence. Second, I want to examine the impact of the introduction of the whereabouts system on the relationship between elite athletes and WADA. It is my hope that this will help in understanding some of the opposition to, and the major difficulties associated with, this system.

The WADA whereabouts system

Under the WADA code adopted in 2003, all international and national sport federations were required to establish a registered testing pool of elite athletes and to carry out in-competition and out-of-competition testing (WADA 2003a). In order to facilitate out-of-competition testing, all anti-doping organizations (ADOs) were required to collect, as a minimum, the following information from athletes in the testing pool: name, sport/discipline, home address, contact telephone numbers, training time and venues, training camps, travel plans, competition schedule and any disability that might affect the testing process (WADA 2003b).

The WADA code stipulated that athletes who receive three warnings within an 18-month period for failing 'to provide accurate whereabouts information . . . or a combination of failure to provide whereabouts information and missed tests, may be subject to an anti-doping rule violation', which could result in a suspension of between 3 months and 2 years. The whereabouts system was revised in 2008, and the obligations on athletes were extended; under the new rules, which came into operation in January 2009, athletes in a registered testing pool had to provide: a complete mailing address; details of any disability that might affect the sample collection; for each day during the following 3 months, the full address where the athlete would be staying (e.g. home, temporary lodgings, hotel etc.); for each day during the following 3 months, the name and address of each location where the athlete would train, work or conduct any other regular activity; their competition schedule for the next quarter, including the name and address of each location where they were scheduled to compete and the day(s) on which they would be competing (WADA 2008). In addition, each athlete had to indicate, for each day during the following quarter, one specific 60-minute time slot between 6 a.m. and 11 p.m. when s/he would be available for testing. Under the new system, the minimum period of suspension for breaching these rules was also extended from 3 months to 1 year.

The whereabouts system, civil liberties and privacy

Writing in 2001, the sports philosophers Schneider and Butcher noted that it 'has become apparent to those involved with doping control that, despite some "in-competition" positive tests, the only effective way to test for banned substances is to introduce random, unannounced out-of-competition testing'. However, they argue that the 'demand that athletes be prepared to submit to urine testing at any time, with no notice, is a serious breach of their civil and human rights in North America'. They go on to suggest that,

> that sort of intrusive intervention in people's lives could only be warranted by the need to protect others from serious harm. It is questionable whether the depth of harm required to warrant such extreme interference with personal liberty can be established at the present time.
>
> (Schneider and Butcher 2001: 130)

It should be noted that the comments by Schneider and Butcher were made *before* the introduction of the WADA whereabouts system, which has intruded into the lives of elite athletes in a much more significant way. It should also be noted that, within liberal democratic societies, there is no longer any serious debate about whether drug testing involves a breach of privacy; as Teetzel has noted, as long ago as 1992, the Canadian privacy commissioner bluntly acknowledged that drug testing constitutes an invasion of privacy, noting 'the principle [sic] privacy issue flowing from drug testing is not whether it is intrusive. It is' (cited in Teetzel 2007: 166). In terms of privacy, the key question is therefore, not whether drug testing in general and the whereabouts system in particular constitute invasions of privacy – they clearly do – but rather, whether such invasions of the privacy of athletes can be justified. Again, I emphasize that I am not seeking to answer that question directly, but rather to locate the ongoing debate within the context of broader social processes; particularly relevant in this regard, as a basis of comparison with the WADA whereabouts system, are recent policy developments relating to the surveillance and control of those who have committed serious breaches of the criminal law.

It is a sobering thought that there is only one other group of people who immediately come to mind as being required regularly to report their whereabouts to the authorities: they are convicted criminals who have been released from prison early on parole, and criminals who are considered particularly dangerous, such as those who have been convicted of sexual offences against children. In the case of convicted criminals released on parole, the moral basis for monitoring their whereabouts and the associated restriction of their liberties is clear and generally accepted and lies precisely in the fact that they have been convicted of particularly serious offences, which in most people generate a deep sense of revulsion. But elite athletes who are required to provide information about their daily whereabouts have not committed any criminal offence; indeed, they will be regarded by many people as being involved in a worthwhile and socially valued activity, and many of them will have represented their countries, sometimes with great distinction, in international competition.

Given these differences in the social status and public perception of elite athletes and convicted criminals, a comparison of the surveillance and control of these two groups is particularly revealing. We have already noted the requirement on elite athletes to report and update their whereabouts. But how does this system compare with the surveillance and control of, for example, convicted paedophiles? In Britain, those who have been convicted of sexual offences against young children are, under the Sex Offenders Act of 1997, as amended by the Sexual Offenders Act of 2003, required to register with the police within 3 days of being released from prison, and they must re-register with their local police on an annual basis. They must also inform the police if they change their name or permanent address, if they intend to spend 7 days or more away from home, or if they intend to travel abroad (Batty 2006). Convicted paedophiles – who, it should be noted, constitute one of the most reviled groups in modern societies – are thus required to provide less information about their whereabouts to the police than elite athletes are required to supply about their whereabouts to ADOs. Given this situation, one can perhaps understand the recent comment of Yves Kummer, the president of the European Elite Athletes Association, that 'paedophiles and criminals on probation have more rights than athletes' (Kummer 2009). There is little doubt that most people would find this situation quite extraordinary.

As we noted earlier, unlike convicted paedophiles and criminals released on parole, most athletes have not been convicted of any wrongdoing. It should also be borne in mind that, while convicted criminals who are subject to police reporting have been found guilty of serious breaches of the criminal law, even an athlete who tests positive for performance-enhancing drugs will not normally have broken any criminal laws, but will simply have broken the rules of sport. It is difficult to see any obvious basis for the use of more intrusive methods of surveillance and control to enforce the rules of sport than are used to ensure the protection of young children against sexual predators.

But this is not the only extraordinary aspect of the system of surveillance and control established by WADA, for WADA has successfully claimed for itself powers that are not normally available to any other organization, not even the state, in liberal democratic societies. As Schneider (2006: 152) has pointed out, in 'most countries, the state is not permitted to subject its citizens to random tests for the use of illegal drugs unless there is some direct risk of harm to others (e.g. pilots)'; it might be added that, even where the state does claim the right to subject specific groups of workers to drug testing on grounds of public safety, those workers, unlike elite athletes, are not subject to drug testing 365 days a year, but only during their working hours. In this regard, Schneider (2006: 152) has suggested that we are entitled to ask if there are 'compelling reasons why sports organizations have a power denied to the state?'.

The athletes' response

The first systematic survey of athletes' views – in this case, of all athletes in the Norwegian registered testing pool – was undertaken by Hanstad and his colleagues in 2006, the results of which were published in 2009 (Hanstad *et al.* 2009; Hanstad and Loland 2009). Norway and its athletes have long enjoyed a reputation as being particularly supportive of anti-doping policies, and it is therefore perhaps surprising that,

> when [Norwegian] athletes are asked about the justification of the whereabouts system, they report considerable scepticism and raise a number of objections, in particular that the system is not implemented for all athletes [in other countries] and therefore is unfair, and that the system requires information about their whereabouts every day, all year round which is seen as an intrusion and violation of individual privacy.
>
> (Hanstad and Loland 2009: 6)

A quarter of all athletes in the Norwegian survey regarded the WADA system as a 'Big Brother' system, and particularly revealing in the light of Brohm's work is the fact that one in four of the athletes reported that 'the joy of elite sport is reduced by anti-doping surveillance and measures such as this one' (Hanstad and Loland 2009: 7). This view was most clearly expressed by one athlete who said that, with the new regulations, it would be a relief to quit:

> Anti-doping work is very important, but the requirement to report, and the risk of a doping verdict when the doping control officer shows up and you are not there, I think is wrong. It will be a relief to escape this the day I retire.
>
> (Hanstad *et al.* 2009: 40)

The authors note that 'the expressed views of the athletes may go some way towards explaining why just 43% agreed that the whereabouts system was necessary to carry out efficient doping controls' (Hanstad *et al.* 2009: 40).

A survey of British elite athletes carried out in 2007 similarly indicated widespread dissatisfaction with the WADA whereabouts system. Although the questions were rather different from those in the Norwegian survey, there were many similarities in the attitudes of Norwegian and British athletes. Like the Norwegian athletes, the British athletes were in favour of doping controls, but felt that the system introduced by WADA was unacceptable in several respects. In particular, British athletes felt strongly that they should not be required to be available for testing on 7 days of the week, with just 12 per cent supporting this idea. British athletes also echoed the view widely held by Norwegian athletes that the system was not fair because it was not effectively implemented in many other countries, and 66 per cent of the British athletes felt that the whereabouts system was not the most effective way to catch/deter drug users (British Athletes Commission 2007).

It is important to note that both these surveys were carried out before the revised whereabouts system, which places even more obligations on athletes, came into effect in January 2009, and it is a reasonable assumption that, if these surveys were to be repeated, they would reveal even higher levels of hostility in athletes towards the new system. That this is so is indicated by the fact that, since the new system came into operation, there has been an outpouring of protest from athletes from numerous countries and from a wide range of sports.

Central to these criticisms has been the claim that the whereabouts system constitutes a violation of athletes' privacy and many athletes, in an echo of Brohm's argument, also indicated that it is a constant source of anxiety that reduces their pleasure in sport. Just one month after the new WADA system was introduced in January 2009, Raphael Nadal, then the world's no. 1 tennis player, said that the rules showed 'a lack of respect for privacy' and, drawing a parallel between the treatment of elite athletes and the treatment of criminals, he added, 'we are humans and we do not have to feel like criminals just because we do sport' (*Independent Online* 2009). More recently, Nadal has renewed his criticism of the whereabouts system, saying: 'It's too much to have to say where you are every day of your life' (BBC Sport 2009a). The British no. 1, Andy Murray, similarly claimed that the 'new rules are so draconian that it makes it almost impossible to lead a normal life'. Murray added:

> I may miss a flight or a flight may be delayed, yet I have to let WADA know exactly where I will be, even when I am resting. They even turned up at my hotel in Miami while I was on holiday.
>
> (BBC Sport 2009b)

In objecting to the system of surveillance and control, the US hurdler Lolo Jones said, 'Maybe in the future they will find a tag they can put on us like dogs have' (*Sports Illustrated* 2009a), thus echoing a comment by Carolina Klüft, the Swedish Olympic heptathlon champion who, in an interview with a Swedish newspaper, 'half jokingly . . . suggested having a data chip implanted into her body so that the doping controllers could monitor her at all times!' (Hanstad and Loland 2009: 7). In February 2009, sixteen British world and Olympic rowing medallists published an open letter in which they expressed 'grave reservations about the principles underpinning the "Whereabouts" regime, and its implementation' and they added: 'We spend our days panicking: having always to think about when our nominated hour is on that day' (rowingservice.com 2009).

Objections from individual athletes have also been echoed by many organizations within sport. The British rowers' criticisms were supported by the International Rowing Federation (Around the Rings 2009), while the Professional Players Federation, an umbrella group of professional player associations in the UK, described the WADA system as a 'fiasco' (BBC Sport 2009b). In football, the chairman of the FIFA medical committee asked, 'Is this the time of the inquisition, or what?' (*Sports Illustrated* 2009a). The official view of both FIFA and UEFA is that 'both on a political and juridical level, the legality of the lack of respect of the private life of players, a fundamental element of individual liberty, can be questioned' (FIFA 2009). Shortly before the new code came into effect, the European Elite Athletes Association, representing some 25,000 elite athletes, issued a lengthy statement in which it said: 'The new code seriously undermines the rights of professional athletes as both European citizens and employees. Furthermore, some of the key areas of the new WADA Code are of questionable legality' (European Elite Athletes Association 2008).

The legality of aspects of the code has also been questioned by the European Union. In August 2008, the EU's Data Protection Working Party considered a draft of the WADA code and expressed concern about the degree to which the code met EU standards in relation to privacy and personal data protection; on this basis, and acting in their capacity as members of WADA's Executive Committee and Foundation Board, European governments tried, without success, to get WADA to postpone the introduction of the whereabouts system (European Union 2009a). In April 2009, the EU Working Party, in a second opinion, expressed regret that WADA had not fully taken into account its comments on the earlier draft code and indicated its continuing concern about 'matters which the Working Party believes continue to be problems in the context of European requirements for privacy and personal data protection' (European Union 2009b: 2–3). In its conclusion, the Working Party emphasized that it was aware of the importance of the fight against doping, but added that it 'insists on pursuing this fight with respect for the fundamental rights of athletes and their entourage, particularly for the right to protection of their privacy and personal data' (European Union 2009b: 18).

The legal basis of the code, and in particular the question of whether it breaks European Union privacy laws, is set to be challenged in a Belgian court. The action has been brought by sixty-five athletes who have been brought together by Sporta, the organization representing professional sportspeople in Belgium. The solicitor representing the athletes has claimed that the whereabouts system is 'a draconian measure' that 'gives WADA a pass to invade the privacy of athletes' and amounts 'to putting the whole town in prison to catch one criminal' (BBC Sport 2009c; ESPN 2009).

Protests against drug testing in sport are, of course, not new. In 1966, when the first drug tests were introduced into professional cycling, they triggered a riders' protest strike (Mignon 2003: 241) and, more recently, riders staged a sit-down protest against the police investigation into drug use in the 1998 Tour de France. However, such protests have, previously, been limited to particular sports, notably cycling, which has from the earliest days of professional cycling been characterized by a culture of acceptance of drug use (Waddington and Smith 2009). What is striking about the current criticisms of the WADA code is that they have been made by such large numbers of athletes, from many disciplines and many countries. As the *New York Times* observed, 'never before has there been so much protest regarding out-of-competition testing', adding that athletes 'in nearly every sport . . . have publicly criticized the doping agency's regulations' (22 March 2009). *Sports Illustrated* similarly noted that 'hardly a day goes by without more athletes or groups complaining about the system' and it added: 'From Raphael Nadel to Serena Williams to Michael Ballack, from athletics to skiing, it seems no one is happy' (*Sports Illustrated* 2009a). Most recently, the chief executive officer (CEO) of the anti-doping authority of the Netherlands referred to the 'unprecedented number of objections from individual elite athletes and athletic organizations' (Ram 2009). It is both the huge number and the diversity of sources of such objections to the WADA code that mark this out as a distinctive development in the history of anti-doping policies and, perhaps, also in terms of the relationship between elite athletes and ADOs. But how have WADA and associated ADOs responded to critics of the code?

WADA's response to its critics

We have already noted that WADA rejected a request from European governments to postpone the introduction of the whereabouts system and that, in their second opinion, the EU's Data Protection Working Party expressed regret that WADA had not fully taken into account its comments on the draft code. WADA rejected all the criticisms of the EU Working Party in an almost contemptuous manner, dismissing their opinion as 'incorrect' and 'inaccurate', and accusing the Working Party of making objections based on a 'flimsy pretext', of using 'petty examples', of having 'unrealistic expectations' and making 'unrealistic requests' and of lacking 'any grounding in reality'. WADA also, rather surprisingly, suggested that 'the aim of the [EU] opinion is less to offer a balanced and accurate assessment . . . and more to promote other agendas', though the nature of these alleged 'other agendas' was not clear (WADA 2009). Given the choice of words used by WADA, it is perhaps surprising that it should also have accused the EU Working Party – whose report is written throughout in very considered and restrained language – as being 'overtly confrontational'!

WADA has shown a similar lack of empathy with all its critics. In January 2009, following the early outpouring of criticism of the new system, David Howman, WADA director general, claimed in a press interview that athletes who criticized the system simply did not understand the rule and undiplomatically suggested that they should 'Find out something more before you open your mouth' (*Sports Illustrated* 2009b). In February, Howman visited London, where he met with critics of the new system; afterwards, Howman made it clear that this 'was not a negotiation' and 'Nothing is about to change' (*Daily Telegraph*, 17 February 2009). Howman appears to have made no attempt to address athletes' many publicly expressed concerns about privacy, civil liberties and the practical difficulties of providing in advance 3-months' whereabouts information, but dismissed these as 'some people . . . just reacting negatively to change' (UK Sport 2009). Within Britain, bodies charged with anti-doping responsibilities have been equally dismissive of athletes' objections. Thus, criticisms of the earlier whereabouts system, revealed in the survey by the British Athletes Commission, were claimed by UK Sport to indicate 'a lack of understanding of procedures, and particularly why such procedures are in place' (UK Sport 2007a), while, at a conference on doping sponsored by UK Sport and held at Loughborough University in March 2009, the director of regulatory and legal affairs at British Swimming dismissed athletes' objections to the system as a 'no brainer' (Gray 2009). Perhaps most indicative of the communication gap between regulatory bodies and elite athletes was UK Sport's earlier description of the whereabouts system as 'athlete-friendly' (UK Sport 2007b).

But perhaps the athletes' objections are not important. Perhaps the bottom line is, as Howman uncompromisingly put it, 'a lot of people complain about changes but these are the rules of sport' (*Daily Telegraph* 17 February 2009). Of course, whether athletes simply have to accept that these are the rules of sport will depend partly on the judgement in the court case being brought by the sixty-five Belgian athletes. But even if the court decides that the WADA system does not break EU privacy laws, there are other, non-legal, issues that may be no less important in terms of the relationship between athletes and WADA. These issues relate to consent and associated issues relating not just to the legality but, perhaps more importantly, to the perceived legitimacy of WADA policy and, by implication, of WADA's authority. Let us explore these issues further.

Legitimacy and consent as problematic

As the WADA regulations may be both challenged and enforced in law, it might be suggested that they constitute, in effect, a contract between WADA and elite athletes. However, as the French sociologist Emile Durkheim observed over a century ago, not everything in the contract is contractual, for the effective enforcement of contracts is dependent on a number of non-contractual elements that underpin and give meaning and legitimacy to the contract. In this regard, Durkheim noted that it is not enough 'to desire that engagements contracted for be kept; it is still necessary . . . that they be spontaneously kept. If contracts were enforced only by force or through fear of force, contractual solidarity would be very precarious' (Durkheim 1933: 382). A similar idea has recently been expressed, specifically in relation to anti-doping policy, by Hanstad *et al.* who point out that it is important to understand how athletes view the whereabouts system, 'if it is assumed that the effectiveness and efficiency of the system will, to some degree, be dependent on the co-operation and compliance of athletes' (Hanstad *et al.* 2009: 32). There is good evidence that such an assumption is valid.

In this regard, a brief examination of the development of anti-doping policy in professional cycling is useful. The longstanding existence of what may be called a 'culture of tolerance' in relation to drug use in cycling has been documented in detail elsewhere, and it is clear that, for very many years, the widespread acceptance of this culture within cycling effectively undermined attempts to control the use of drugs in the sport (Waddington 2000; Waddington and Smith 2009). As we noted earlier, the first attempts to introduce drug testing in 1966 were met with riders' strikes and, as Hoberman has noted, when the Tour de France came under attack during and after the 1998 drug scandal, its organizers, team managers and riders reacted as a 'closed community' that sought to defend 'what many members of the cycling subculture regard as a utilitarian doping regimen that is no one's business but their own' (Hoberman 2003: 107, 111). The degree to which those involved in cycling were able to render drug testing more or less ineffectual was clearly demonstrated by the fact that, although the police investigation in the 1998 Tour established beyond doubt that drug use was widespread, systematic and highly organized within teams, not a single rider tested positive for any drugs as a result of drug tests carried out by the Tour organizers.

However, at a time when drug use was both widespread and generally tolerated within cycling, the international governing body of cycling, the *Union Cycliste Internationale* (*UCI*), successfully introduced, in 1997, a blood test of riders, which has proved extremely effective as a means of controlling the use of erythropoietin (EPO). It has been argued elsewhere that this may well be the most effective policy that has ever been introduced to control the use of drugs in sport; certainly, the new policy has resulted in the exclusion from racing of many more riders than have ever been excluded as a result of failing a conventional drug test for EPO (Waddington and Smith 2009: 227). How then, can we account for the successful introduction of this test, even in a climate of hostility to conventional drug testing in cycling?

In this regard, it is important to note that, even though riders had long resisted conventional drug testing in cycling, the new test was introduced with the support of riders and teams. Although the UCI could not, at that time, compel riders to provide a blood sample, riders voluntarily cooperated in providing the blood samples required for the test and there is no doubt that the riders' acceptance of, and support for, the policy has been critical to its success; in short, the test was, from the outset, accepted as legitimate by those at whom the tests were targeted. This legitimacy rested on several key aspects of the test, but central to its acceptance by the riders was, first, the fact that it was introduced as a health check rather than a conventional drug test and, second, the fact that it was seen as an appropriate response to what was recognized, not just by those responsible for organizing the testing but, more importantly, by the drug-using cyclists themselves, as a serious health concern, namely the dangerous side effects of EPO use.

Clearly, the consent of those who are subject to drug testing may have important consequences for the effective implementation of anti-doping policies. On a general level, there is no doubt that anti-doping policies are likely to be more effective if they have the support of the athletes themselves. Houlihan has recently suggested that athletes will be more effectively motivated to comply with an anti-doping programme if the moral basis for that programme is clear; more specifically, he noted that the motivation to comply will be stronger if there is a perception by those subject to the regulations that those regulations are reasonable, that they are reasonably implemented and that they are enforced fairly (Houlihan 2009). The available data on athletes' perceptions of the whereabouts system suggest that it is problematic – and therefore lacks legitimacy in the eyes of many athletes – on all three grounds identified by Houlihan.

A broadly similar point has recently been made by the CEO of the Netherlands Anti-Doping Authority who, in the context of the problems associated with the WADA whereabouts system, observed that 'making anti-doping policies more democratic also makes them more effective' (Ram 2009). But here again, WADA policy, as it currently stands, faces major problems. Although Hanstad and Loland have pointed out that WADA policy has the support of the Athletes' Committee within WADA, it is clear that the Athletes' Committee can hardly claim to be the legitimate representative of athletes in general. In its statement on the WADA code, issued in November 2008, the European Elite Athletes Association stated:

> The WADA Athletes Committee is not a representational body but is made up of 12 individuals who are appointed, given a certain status by WADA and then are asked to give their personal opinions regarding doping regulations. A review of the Athletes Commission's 'meeting outcomes' reports reveals that the Athletes Commission is involved in and gives input regarding many important decisions and consultations without any mandate from other athletes to do so. EU Athletes has no confidence in the independence of the WADA Athletes Committee or in its ability to negotiate the necessary protection of the privacy and data protection rights of professional players. In no way can this structure be substituted for social dialogue or collective bargaining with independent and truly representative athletes associations.
>
> (European Elite Athletes Association 2008)

Yves Kummer, the president of the association, has recently said that the WADA Athletes Committee has 'no constituency' and that elite athletes 'do not feel seriously represented' (Kummer 2009). In this regard, it might be noted that, when those who are subject to a body of regulations have no representation on the body that frames those regulations, then – particularly when those regulations are generally acknowledged to be intrusive – the legitimacy of those regulations is likely to be called into question.

Implicit in much of the previous discussion is the issue of consent, which is also raised in the examination of the whereabouts system by Hanstad and Loland (2009). Hanstad and Loland were the first researchers systematically to document elite athletes' views of the WADA whereabouts system, but, despite the fact that, as we have seen, they documented widespread criticism of the system by athletes, they nevertheless concluded that the system could be conditionally accepted as justifiable anti-doping work. I do not wish to examine here their general conclusion, which clearly falls within the field of moral philosophy, but I do want to focus on one thread of their argument, which relates to the key issue of athletes' consent. In this regard, they suggest that, if athletes do not agree with the whereabouts system, they 'can withdraw from the surveillance' by withdrawing from sport; in this regard, they suggest that the 'point argued by, among others, Rune Andersen of the WADA, of sport as a voluntary practice . . . is a relevant one' (Hanstad and Loland 2009: 8).

This argument, like many other aspects of WADA policy, is based on a highly individualized conceptualization of the elite athlete, who is presented as an asocial, isolated individual who is able to make a more or less free and unconstrained choice about whether or not to participate in sport and therefore in the surveillance that goes with it. But such a conceptualization is fundamentally flawed. It reflects what Norbert Elias called a '*homo clausus*' conceptualization of the elite athlete (significantly, conceptualized in the singular) as a 'closed man' or 'closed personality', rather than a more adequate conceptualization of athletes (in the plural) as '*homines aperti*', that is 'open people', bonded together with others in various ways and degrees and whose choices are constrained, sometimes very severely, by those bonds with others (Elias 1970).

The idea that athletes have a free choice about whether to participate in sport has, perhaps, some limited applicability in relation to young people who may be deciding whether or not to play sport, though even here we know that the choices of young people are heavily constrained, particularly by parents and peers (Coakley and White 1999; Smith 2006; Smith *et al.* 2009). However, the suggestion that elite athletes who are subject to the WADA whereabouts system can freely choose to withdraw from athletics if they dislike that system is simplistic and misleading. Let us reflect on some aspects of the careers of elite athletes.

Elite athletes will have taken the key decision to participate in sport many years prior to attaining elite status. In order to attain that status, they will have shown a very high level of continuing commitment and dedication to improving their sporting performance over many years. They, and sometimes also their parents, will often have made a huge emotional investment – and perhaps also financial and other forms of investment – in their sporting careers. In many cases, they will have sacrificed other opportunities in relation to education or training and employment in order to concentrate on their athletics careers. Many will have struggled to overcome pain and injury in the pursuit of athletics success. Their lives – including their friendships and even their marital and other family relationships – will for many years have been structured around the demands of training and competition. Becoming a successful athlete will have become, for many, an increasingly important part of their self-identity and an increasingly important source of a positive self-image. And, after many years, they will have attained elite status and, in many cases, enjoyed the celebrity status and huge financial rewards enjoyed by successful athletes, which greatly exceed the very modest rewards that are all that most could expect to earn outside the sporting context. It is clear that withdrawing from elite sport would involve such huge costs and sacrifices that it could not, in any meaningful sense, be considered a realistic option for most elite athletes.

The EU Working Party, in its second report on the whereabouts system, showed a much greater understanding of the constraints on elite athletes and, as a consequence, it was quite unambiguous about the issue of consent. The Working Party expressed regret that WADA had not taken into account its earlier remarks about the validity of the participants' consent and it pointed out that, under an EU directive, consent was defined as 'any freely given specific and informed indication of his wishes by which the data subject signifies his agreement to personal data relating to him being processed'. They added that the

> sanctions and consequences attached to a possible refusal by participants to subject themselves to the obligations of the Code (for example by providing whereabouts filings) prevent the Working Party from considering that the consent would be, in any way, given freely.
>
> (European Union 2009b: 11)

Conclusion

By way of conclusion, let us return to the question raised at the beginning of this paper: in what sense, if any, can it be said that the WADA whereabouts system constitutes a 'prison of measured time'? In the sense in which Brohm used the term 'prison', it was meant to imply several things: that modern athletes were increasingly regulated, constricted and constrained by what he regarded as the 'despotism', the arbitrary rule and the bureaucratic management of modern sport and that, as a consequence, much of the spontaneous and playful enjoyment of sport has been lost. The data from the two national surveys of athletes' attitudes towards the whereabouts system, together with the almost innumerable criticisms of the WADA system from individual athletes and from athletes' federations, indicate that many elite athletes do indeed perceive the WADA system in terms not very dissimilar to those described by Brohm.

But what of the second part of Brohm's description: in what sense might the WADA system be considered a prison *of measured time*? Brohm used the phrase 'measured time' to refer to the pursuit of record times as part of what he saw as the sterile worship of the stop-watch, a process that involved increasing demands on elite athletes for ever greater efficiency in the application of science and technology and ever greater demands on athletes' bodies. The WADA system, in contrast, involves a much more direct constraint on athletes' bodies and one that is clearly associated with measured time, for the whereabouts system is explicitly designed to ensure that all elite athletes are available for drug testing in a measured time slot – 1 hour – on every single day of the year, and it is this, of course, that has led to the widespread criticisms of the WADA system by athletes.

It should also be noted that the movement towards increasingly draconian social control of athletes, and the restriction of their civil liberties that this entails, is not an accident, but rather it is the *inevitable* outcome of the inexorable logic of the 'detect and punish' philosophy on which anti-doping policy has always been overwhelmingly based (Waddington and Smith 2009: 207–8). Thus, when drug testing was first introduced in the 1960s, it was confined to testing in-competition. When it became clear that this was largely ineffective, out-of-competition testing was introduced, but this had only limited effectiveness because ADOs often had difficulty contacting athletes outside competition. This led to the establishment of the first WADA whereabouts system in 2003, but this in turn was felt by WADA to be inadequate and, hence, additional constraints were placed on athletes by the revised code of 2008. But what if the new whereabouts system is also found to be inadequate? What is the next logical step for WADA? This is a question that has recently been raised by the president of the European Elite Athletes Association, Yves Kummer, who, at the Play the Game Conference in Coventry in 2009, asked 'What is the next step?'. Kummer echoed the view expressed by some athletes, cited earlier, who have suggested that athletes, like dogs and some criminals, might in future be tagged; the solution, suggested Kummer, might be 'transponders up the bottom' (Kummer 2009). The transponders might not be placed up the bottom, but the attachment of transponders to athletes might indeed be the next logical policy step, if the current system is judged to have only limited effectiveness.

But let us conclude by returning to Brohm. Writing about drug use – which he saw as an inevitable aspect of the '*manipulation of human robots* [sportspeople] by doctors, psychologists, bio-chemists and trainers' in the pursuit of record times (Brohm 1978: 18; italics in original) – Brohm argued that, in the fight against doping:

> the sports authorities are introducing more and more preventive measures, threats, surveillance of athletes, blood tests, urine tests, new techniques for detecting banned substances and of course disciplinary measures. In other words, within the institution of sport, generally described as educative, liberating and fulfilling, we see the outbreak of the same contradictions to be found in the police-style regimentation of hearts and minds in capitalist society in general – a society haunted by the totalitarian dream of absolute control over people's private lives.

> The sports and medical authorities, reigning hand in hand over a system governed by the logic of competition and productivity, inevitably give birth to a strengthened judicial and police apparatus.
>
> (Brohm 1978: 22–3)

And he cited a key question from an article published in *Le Monde* in 1976:

> Do we have to face more and more supervision, all year round, both of the competitions themselves and of training? That would mean turning the world of athletics (and of all other sports events) into a huge police operation area, and would seriously infringe on the athletes' private life.
>
> (cited in Brohm 1978: 23)

As we noted at the outset, Brohm's work is, in many respects, problematic, not least because his analysis is obviously coloured by his Marxist ideology; for example, very few social scientists would accept his characterization of capitalism as 'a society haunted by the totalitarian dream of absolute control over people's private lives'. However, one does not have to share Brohm's Marxist framework, nor its associated ideology, to recognize that the questions that he raised about sport in the 1970s remain very relevant today.

Acknowledgement

I would like to thank Andy Smith for his comments on an earlier draft of this paper.

References

Around the Rings (2009) 'Rowing appeals for changes to WADA rule'. Available online at: www.aroundtherings.com/articles/view.aspx?id=31547 (accessed 21 September 2009).

Batty, D. (2006) 'Q&A: the sex offenders register'. Available online at: www.guardian.co.uk/society/2006/jan/18/childrensservices.politics1 (accessed 6 July 2009).

BBC Sport (2009a) 'Doping rules too strict – Nadal'. Available online at: http://news.bbc.co.uk/sport1/hi/tennis/8353208.stm (accessed 10 November 2009).

BBC Sport (2009b) 'Wada hits back in doping rule row'. Available online at: http://news.bbc.co.uk/sport1/hi/olympic_games/7874306.stm (accessed 25 June 2009).

BBC Sport (2009c) 'Legal threat to anti-doping code'. Available online at: http://news.bbc.co.uk/sport1/hi/front_page/7844918.stm (accessed 20 April 2009).

British Athletes Commission (BAC) (2007) *Anti-doping and athlete whereabouts questionnaire*, Marlow, Buckinghamshire: BAC.

Brohm, J.-M. (1978) *Sport – a prison of measured time*, London: Pluto Press.

Coakley, J. and White, A. (1999) 'Making decisions. How young people become involved and stay involved in sports', in J. Coakley and P. Donnelly (eds), *Inside sports*, London: Routledge, pp. 77–85.

Durkheim, E. (1933) *The division of labor in society*, Glencoe: Free Press.
Elias, N. (1970) *What is sociology?* London: Hutchinson.
ESPN (2009) 'Belgian group challenges WADA rule'. Available online at: http://sports.espn.go.com/oly/news/story?id=3863905&campaign=rss&source=OLYH (accessed 16 April 2009).
European Elite Athletes Association (2008) 'EU athletes position statement on anti-doping'. Available online at: www.euathletes.info/issues/ (issued 28 November 2008; accessed 8 December 2010).
European Union (2009a) *Report from the EU Working Group on Anti-Doping*, Second meeting, Brussels, 14 January 2009.
European Union (2009b) Article 29 Data Protection Working Party, *Second opinion 4/229 on the World Anti-Doping Agency (WADA) International Standard for the Protection of Privacy and Personal Information, on related provisions of the WADA Code and on other privacy issues in the context of the fight against doping in sport by WADA and (national) anti-doping organizations*, Brussels.
FIFA (2009) 'FIFA and UEFA reject WADA "whereabouts" rule'. Available online at: www.fifa.com/aboutfifa/developing/releases/newsid=1040455.html (accessed 21 September 2009).
Gray, A. (2009) 'From new WADA Code to new NADO: the national governing body perspective'. Presentation at ESRC Research Seminar Series: *Anti-Doping Policy*, Loughborough University, UK, 31 March.
Hanstad, D.V. and Loland, S. (2009) 'Elite athletes' duty to provide information on there whereabouts: justifiable anti-doping work or an indefensible surveillance system?', *European Journal of Sport Science*, 9(1): 3–10.
Hanstad, D.V., Skille, E.A. and Thurston, M. (2009) 'Elite athletes' perspectives on providing whereabouts information: a survey of athletes in the Norwegian registered testing pool', *Sport und Gesellschaft – Sport and Society*, 1: 30–46.
Hoberman, J. (2003) '"A pharmacy on wheels": doping and community cohesion among professional cyclists following the Tour de France scandal of 1998', in V. Møller and J. Nauright (eds), *The essence of sport*, Odense: University Press of Southern Denmark, pp. 107–28.
Houlihan B. (2009) 'Implementation and compliance in anti-doping policy: how much compliance is enough?'. Presentation at ESRC Research Seminar Series: *Anti-Doping Policy*, Loughborough University, UK, 31 March.
Independent Online (2009) 'Nadal rebels against new Anti-Doping Code', 28 January. Available online at: www.int.iol.co.za/index.php?set_id=6&click_id=30&art_id=nw20090128211610864C280941 (accessed 22 September 2009).
Kummer, Y. (2009) 'Professional athletes views on anti-doping policy'. Presentation at *Play the Game Conference*, Coventry, UK, 11 June.
Mignon, P. (2003) 'The Tour de France and the doping issue', in H. Dauncey and G. Hare (eds), *The Tour de France 1903–2003*, London: Cass, pp. 227–45.
Ram, H. (2009) 'Democratic values and the global fight against doping'. Presentation at *Play the Game Conference*, Coventry, UK, 11 June.
Rowingservice.com (2009) 'WADA letter'. Available online at: www.rowingservice.com/RowingWADAletter09.pdf (accessed 21 September 2009).
Schneider, A. (2006) 'Privacy, confidentiality and human rights in sport', in R. Giulianotti and D. McArdle (eds), *Sport, civil liberties and human rights*, London: Routledge, pp. 147–64.

Schneider, A. and Butcher, R.B. (2001) 'An ethical analysis of drug testing', in W. Wilson and E. Derse (eds), *Doping in elite sport: the politics of drugs in the Olympic Movement*, Champaign, IL: Human Kinetics, pp. 129–52.

Smith, A. (2006) 'Young people, sport and leisure: a sociological study of youth lifestyles'. Unpublished Ph.D. thesis, University of Liverpool.

Smith, A., Green, K. and Thurston, M. (2009) 'Activity choice and physical education in England and Wales', *Sport, Education and Society*, 14: 203–22.

Sports Illustrated (2009a) 'WADA, athletes clash over privacy', SI.com, 23 February. Available online at: http://sportsillustrated.cnn.com/2009/more/02/23/wada-athletes.ap/index.html (accessed 25 June 2009).

Sports Illustrated (2009b) 'WADA seeks special meeting to discuss new drug-testing rules', SI.com, 29 January. Available online at: http://si.printthis.clickability.com/pt/cpt?action=cpt&title=WADA+seeks+special+me (accessed 30 January 2009).

Teetzel, S. (2007) 'Respecting privacy in detecting illegitimate enhancements in athletes', *Sport, Ethics and Philosophy*, 1(2): 159–70.

UK Sport (2007a) 'British athletes back whereabouts system'. Available online at: www.uksport.gov.uk/news/british_athletes_back_whereabouts_system/, 29 March, (accessed 13 February 2009).

UK Sport (2007b) 'UK Sport welcomes WADA's athlete friendly whereabouts procedures'. Available online at: www.uksport.gov.uk/news/uk_sport_welcomes_wadas_athlete_friendly_where (accessed 25 June 2009).

UK Sport (2009) 'WADA: Whereabouts here to stay', 25 February. Available online at: www.uksport.gov.uk/news/wada_whereabouts_here-to_stay/ (accessed 27 February 2009).

WADA (2003a) *The World Anti-Doping Code*, Lausanne: World Anti-Doping Agency.

WADA (2003b) *The World Anti-Doping Code. International standard for testing*. Montreal: World Anti-Doping Agency.

WADA (2008) *The World Anti-Doping Code. International standard for testing*. Montreal: World Anti-Doping Agency.

WADA (2009) 'WADA comments (full version) on the European Working Party advisory opinion dated April 6, 2009, on the International Standard on the Protection of Privacy and Personal Information'. Available online at: www.wada-ama.org/rtecontent/document/WADA_comments_WP29_Opinion_FINAL.pdf (accessed 22 September 2009).

Waddington, I. (2000) *Sport, health and drugs*, London: Spon.

Waddington, I. and Smith, A., (2009) *An introduction to drugs in sport. Addicted to winning?* London: Routledge.

12 The expulsion of Michael Rasmussen from the Tour de France 2007

A manifestation of the ideal of a level playing field?

Verner Møller

Discussions about doping tend to be formed around the question of whether one is for or against the ban on performance-enhancing means and methods in sport. Critics of the current campaign against doping are often accused of being libertarians who advocate free doping, which some indeed do.[1]

The pro–con framing of the problem is, however, unfortunate, and not merely because it has made it too easy to shrug off critique of anti-doping as irresponsible libertarianism. In its crudity and oversimplification, this posture obstructs unprejudiced discussions about how the problem of doping can be approached efficiently, *while at the same time* respecting both the dignity of athletes who are subjected to the anti-doping regime *and* the rationale that anti-doping is based upon: namely, the protection of the athletes' health and the idea of competition on a level playing field. Doping in sport has a long history, and, in certain sports, doping cultures are so ingrained that they will be very difficult to change. In contrast, the worldwide anti-doping campaign run by the World Anti Doping Agency (WADA) is a rather new enterprise, and it takes time and experience to mature and develop proper standards and strategies.

So it is understandable if anti-doping officials and others with vested interests in clean sport have become increasingly frustrated by the constant flux of doping cases, which suggest that the traditional in-competition-test system is little more than a paper bullet, and consequently have called for more powerful weapons such as out-of-competition testing and the obligation to submit whereabouts information, which have been used with groups of top-ranked athletes since 2004 (WADA 2004). In cycling, perhaps the most tarnished sport of all, the international cycling federation (UCI), the Pro-Tour teams and the private organizers have added extra sanctions and launched new initiatives: such as 'the riders commitment to a new cycling' and the so-called biological passport, where the riders, through regular blood testing, have their blood profiles measured as a means of finding indications of blood doping. All in all, it appears that the answer to the apparently endless problem is unimaginative: further tightening of the rope. Protection of the athletes' privacy rights seems too easily to be sacrificed for the sake of the good – the good of sport, or even the athletes' own good.

The aim of this chapter, based on a case study of the expulsion of Danish cyclist Michael Rasmussen from the 2007 Tour de France, is to demonstrate that the way anti-doping is currently governed in some jurisdictions is significantly lacking transparency and efficacy. In fact, it exposes athletes to random judgements from officials who have been equipped with quasi-legal powers with the potential to destroy professional athletes' careers (Soek 2006). Moreover, because there is no clear distinction in sport between legislative, executive and judicial powers, it is not certain that anti-doping rule violations, even when they are clear, will lead to prosecution where other interests intervene.

Anti-doping: between idealism and realism

Before I start presenting facts about the Michael Rasmussen case, let me make it clear from the outset that I share the fundamental values that anti-doping is based upon: the protection of athletes' health, and the protection of a level playing field. I am of the opinion that fair play and sporting integrity are values worth fighting for. Ideally, I agree with Mike McNamee's view that the task of anti-doping is both admirable and necessary (McNamee 2008). But it is also my opinion that athletes – even if they have committed an anti-doping rule violation – should still be treated equally, fairly and humanely. I find it disheartening and contrary to the spirit of sport to see athletes treated as hardboiled criminals because – spurred by extreme ambition – they have broken a sporting rule. If athletes' support for anti-doping is to continue, it is crucial that those who lead the anti-doping campaign understand that they have not been recruited as crusaders, but rather have been appointed to act on behalf of the athletes. The rationale for anti-doping is ideally sound. However, as Ross Coomber poignantly points out, 'An unintended effect of existing policy may be that it works against some of the principles upon which it is based and seeks to maintain' (Coomber 1999: 103). In relation to the present chapter, we can note that WADA was founded with the purpose of preventing medical health hazards and securing fair competition. But, as the battle against doping has intensified, the initial motives, fair play and health, seem to have been cast aside, which ought to be a matter of serious concern, because it could prove detrimental to athletes' faith in the anti-doping system and, consequently, their general support for anti-doping work. In recent years, more athletes have begun to criticize the system for being overzealous.

In 2009, a group of sixty-five Belgian athletes from soccer, volleyball and cycling even went so far as to challenge the rule requiring athletes to notify drug testers of their whereabouts, contending that it violates privacy (Associated Press 2009). The case, which was filed with Belgium's Council of State high court, shows that athletes' acceptance of anti-doping is not complete, nor without limits. In light of this, there is reason to believe that athletes' opposition to the system will increase if they begin to notice that the anti-doping measures seem disproportionate in relation to the problem they are enforced to oppose and, worse still, that the powers anti-doping agents are handed are administered unfairly.

Hence, as former WADA president Dick Pound poignantly expressed, anti-doping officials carry great responsibility as role models:

> Officials must demonstrate that accountability starts at the top. Their own conduct in the management of sport must be, and like Caesar's wife, be seen to be, above reproach. They have a responsibility to act fairly, impartially and within the letter and spirit of the governing rules [. . .] If the officials show no respect for the sport, how can the athletes and the public be expected to observe higher standards?
>
> (Pound 2004: 272)

In the summer of 2008, I was contacted by Danish cyclist Michael Rasmussen, who invited me to examine his case and offered full access to his files. Even at first glance, I realized that the warnings he had received for whereabouts information failures and missed tests, which were the catalysts for his expulsion from the Tour de France 2007, were produced in an amateur way. Further scrutiny made it obvious that the anti-doping system is far from ideal. In fact, the Michael Rasmussen case alarmingly exemplifies that the anti-doping system does not fulfil Pound's 'ideal'. In what follows I shall argue why.

Leaked information

While placed as overall leader in the Tour de France 2007, Rasmussen was expelled from his team, Rabobank, and removed from the race because he allegedly had lied to the team management about his whereabouts in the month before the start of the event. This was the culmination of a media campaign, unprecedented in the world of cycling. While Rasmussen was wearing the yellow jersey (as is the overall leader's privilege), it was leaked to the press that he had received warnings in relation to the whereabouts system. It is not uncommon that athletes received warnings for filing failures or missed tests. What was unusual was that the name of one specific athlete, who had received warnings, was leaked to the press.

We do not know who leaked this information. Three organizations knew about them: the UCI, Anti Doping Denmark (ADD) and the Danish Cycling Federation. Therefore, the leak must stem, either from one of these organizations, or from Rasmussen's own team management. When Danish television made it public that they had learned that Michael Rasmussen had warnings from anti-doping authorities, my initial thought was that a trusted person had 'spilled the beans'. This is always a risk. Given that confidentiality is a cornerstone of the acceptance of the whereabouts system, this was of course regrettable and disturbing, yet, to a certain extent, understandable, as part of the media circus that surrounds elite sport generally and the Tour de France in particular.

As part of my study, I interviewed Niels Christian Jung, the journalist who launched the story about Rasmussen's warnings. Over many years, Jung has built up a reputation as a persistent investigative journalist dedicated to anti-doping goals. The fact that the information was only leaked to Danish media suggested that the information either came from ADD or the Danish Cycle Federation, and, given that the latter organization, prior to the Tour, had informed Rasmussen that he would no longer be in the frame for the Danish national team because of the warnings he had received, it seemed to have a prima facie motive for leaking the information. Hence, I asked Jung about his source and whether he had received the information about Rasmussen's warnings from a source within the Danish Cycle Federation. It is, of course, a principle of investigative journalism that one does not reveal one's sources, and so I was fully aware that his first response would be to protect his source. The question nevertheless produced a stunning reply:

> Well, I won't tell who my source was in this particular case, but for your background and for quotation: I have especially good sources in WADA and in the UCI. It becomes pretty obvious if you see whom I have access to. I have access to the President and all the other decision makers. So, I guess, my information does not come from where you think, just to set that straight from the outset.

Jung indicates that, as a matter of course, people at the highest level in the sports organizations actively use privileged journalists in the pursuit of their goals by providing confidential information off the record. The media theorist Marshall McLuhan has labelled it 'government by news leak' (McLuhan 2001 (1964)). Although it is a longstanding and common practice in political organizations, its practice is less commentated upon in sports politics. Moreover, it could prove detrimental to athletes' faith in the whereabouts system if it becomes known that this improper practice is also at work in sports governing bodies.

When I asked Jung why he found the information about Rasmussen's warnings relevant in the first place, given that warnings were not uncommon, and that the number of warnings he had received did not amount to an anti-doping rule violation, his response was once again out of the ordinary: '*I already knew in 2006 that there were problems with [Rasmussen's] whereabouts*', he explained. This means that, when Rasmussen received his first warning from the UCI, a mole in the system must have brought this to the journalist's attention.

The fact that there are moles in the anti-doping system is a serious problem, but, to my knowledge, no attempt has been made to find the leak. Even more disconcerting is that sports leaders are not subject to sanctions, even when they openly admit they do not respect the rules, as the director of the Danish Cycle Federation, Jesper Worre, did when confronted, during a live television broadcast, with the claim that Rasmussen had received warnings from the anti-doping authorities. He openly confessed: 'When we receive this information [about his warnings] from the UCI and from Anti Doping Denmark then it is actually confidential information. But we have decided . . . We will not lie about this.' Moreover, he did not restrict his proclamation to the confirmation of the information. He proceeded to give the exact number of alleged violations. Although this statement had serious consequences for the athlete in question, Worre still holds his position as director and was not even given a warning for his misconduct. The Danish Cycle Federation defended its position by reference to an internal ethical code that – notably – has never been published nor presented to the athletes who are subject to it.

Today, the Danish Cycle Federation still privileges its own so-called ethical code over the WADA rules, which say that whereabouts information is strictly confidential. This became apparent when the facts of the Rasmussen case were presented at an international conference on *Doping and legal rights* in Aarhus in August 2009, where the organization was challenged by media for its failure to observe the duty of confidentiality. The chairman of the federation, Tom Lund, denied that the organization had done anything wrong, arguing that it simply refused to lie when quizzed about athletes' warnings (*Politiken* 2009). The conclusion appears to be this: every time UCI or ADD inform the Danish Cycle Federation that a rider has received a warning, it is prepared, potentially, to violate Danish riders' right to confidentiality.

After the expulsion of Rasmussen, the head of the UCI Anti Doping Commission, Anne Gripper, provided a response to the Danish Cycling Federation's misconduct:

> In the UCI we are disappointed that Michael Rasmussen's case became public and find it wrong. I fully understand that it creates a feeling of inequality and a request for all warnings to be made public, but that would be unfair. We have a clear rule, which says that potential doping cases shall not be public, and these warnings are at a level below that. In fact one shall have three warnings before we are dealing with a potential doping case. Therefore we shall of course not make the warnings public. (*Jyllands-Posten* 2007a)

These reasonable words give a strong impression of integrity. They are not congruent, however, with Jung's final argument as to why he thought Rasmussen's warnings were a story worth pursuing. Jung maintains that UCI had indicated that Rasmussen was suspected of doping. Prior to the Tour de France 2007, UCI made public that there were six or seven riders they watched particularly, because they trained at remote places in anonymous outfits, and so they were difficult to find for out-of-competition testing. This group of riders were labelled 'men in black'. A Danish journalist wanted to know if Rasmussen was one of these riders, and so he called UCI's Anne Gripper, who informed him: 'We know that he has been in Mexico for a period of time. He is one of the riders we pay close attention to because he travels to various places to train' (Jyllands-Posten 2007b).

With this remark, the head of the UCI anti-doping commission clearly violated her duty of confidentiality, because she can only have known about Rasmussen's whereabouts from the whereabouts information he provided. This information should be kept confidential according to the rules: 'The UCI shall maintain whereabouts information in strict confidence at all times and shall use it exclusively for purposes of planning, coordinating or conducting testing' (UCI 2004: paragraph 92).

The fact that Gripper contravened the UCI's privacy policy contributed directly to mounting pressure on Rasmussen. The UCI itself (personified by Gripper) also played an indirect part in increasing the pressure on Rasmussen, not only by issuing him with a recorded warning less than a week before the Tour, but also by sending a letter reminding him about recent warnings from UCI and ADD, although ADD was the only national ADO that had informed the UCI about warnings they had issued riders. This letter caused a crisis meeting in the Rabobank team management, the outcome of the meeting being that the then leading sports director, Theo de Rooij, issued Rasmussen with a €10,000 fine. The fine itself is somewhat curious, as the team management and the riders had a mutual understanding that two recorded warnings were no problem whatsoever, as noted by the independent Vogelzang commission, whom Rabobank appointed to investigate the Rasmussen case (Vogelzang *et al.* 2008). de Rooij used the strong wording of the UCI letter as his explanation for issuing the fine. This fine was the final piece of the picture that inspired Jung to research Rasmussen's whereabouts.

From the information given above, it is safe to conclude that the treatment of the whereabouts information Rasmussen provided and the warnings he received from the governing bodies was not according to the rulebook. For those who believe in the system, it is perhaps tempting to suggest that the Rasmussen case was an unfortunate one off. So let me just note, in passing, that Michael Rasmussen is not alone. The following year, the Belgian cycling sprinter Tom Boonen was tested out of competition and found positive for cocaine. Why he was tested out of competition for a drug that was only regarded as a doping drug in competition seems unusual in itself. Even more disconcerting, however, was the fact that the result of the test was leaked to the press, which had the consequence that the Tour de France refused to accept his participation in the 2008 race. Most disheartening, perhaps, was that WADA did not challenge the Tour de France management's decision, although it was an extraordinary sanction, out of line with the idea of a level playing field.

Thus far, we have seen that there is no guarantee that the athlete's right to confidentiality is respected. Were athletes' rights a top priority then violations of them might have had severe consequences. It sends a message of approval when the director of the Danish Cycle Federation, Jesper Worre, and the head of UCI's Anti Doping Commission, Anne Gripper, were not penalized for their misconduct and maintained their respective positions. In light of this, it may come as no surprise that the sanction system that caused Rasmussen's problems is not impeccable either. This will become clear when we turn our attention to the warnings he received.

Rasmussen's warnings

For the purposes of evaluating the governance of Michael Rasmussen's case, it is necessary to articulate current policy. The correct whereabouts procedure demands that the athletes first receive a written warning that draws attention to a potential whereabouts violation: this may either be a filing failure or a missed test. The athlete then has 10 days from receipt of the written warning to provide an explanation. After evaluation of the explanation, the written warning is either cancelled or confirmed and recorded. If an athlete receives three recorded warnings in a rolling period of 18 months, this amounts to an anti-doping rule violation, and disciplinary proceedings will follow.

Rasmussen was included in the registered testing pool on 1 October 2005, after he had won the Tour de France's polka-dot jersey – the symbol of the winner of the king of the mountains competition. He received his first warning from the UCI on 26 March 2006 for a filing failure. This warning, against the stated procedure, was issued as a recorded warning without any previous written warning. In December, he had received whereabouts forms for the year 2006 – four 'athletes' location forms' for four quarters. He filled in the form for the first quarter – January, February and March – and set the three other forms aside. Thus, the UCI was informed about his whereabouts until 31 March. According to the rules, he should, however, have submitted forms for the next three months by 15 March. He did not receive a reminder telling him that he was late and had to update his whereabouts. In consequence, the UCI sent him a recorded warning on 26 March, five days before the whereabouts information he *had* provided expired. He found the letter in his mailbox on 3 April, when he returned from a trip with his team, and responded immediately – as if it was a written warning – and sent the required whereabouts information for April, May and June. He wrote:

> I, Michael Rasmussen have received your letter today April the 3rd. There is only one reason why I haven't filled in the Athlete location form, and that is a simple and pure slip of my memory. I therefore request that this written warning will be erased from my record.
>
> (Quoted from copy of letter to the UCI Anti-Doping Commission)

Rasmussen alleges that he never received an answer to his request. He says he called the UCI and was informed by a secretary that the person he should talk to was in Canada. After this, the matter was not taken up again by UCI, so Rasmussen understood that they had accepted his explanation. However, the warning had been recorded and stayed in his files. UCI admitted to the Vogelzang commission that recording this warning was a mistake (Vogelzang *et al.* 2008). He should only have received a written warning. *Notably*, five of his teammates had also forgotten to submit their whereabouts for April, May and June. It is surprising, then, that none of them received a warning for their forgetfulness (Vogelzang *et al.* 2008).

The second recorded warning he received from the UCI was dated 29 June 2007, which resulted in the aforementioned fine. It came after a written warning issued on 11 June, with the explanation that he had provided updates too late for his stay in Mexico from 4 to 12 June (which we know today was incorrect information, as in reality he trained in the Italian Dolomites in that period). UCI only knew about this pretended change of plans on 11 June. Moreover, at first glance, the update appeared to be sent from Italy on 8 June. This situation must have been puzzling, because, if he left on 4 June, what would the point be in having the update sent from Italy on 8 June? This anomaly invited a warning.

One perfectly naturally thing to do would be to take a closer look at the envelope. If Gripper had done that, she would have found two postmarks, one dated 8 June from Verona and the other dated 4 June from Bardolino, which suggests that he posted the letter 1.5 kilometres from his home in Lazise, after which, for some unknown reason, it was transported to the post office in Verona, where it got a new postmark before it was sent off to the UCI's headquarter in Aigle, Switzerland (see Figure 12.1).

Gripper, who may have thought Rasmussen deserved a warning, decided not to dwell on the circumstances of the situation. Instead, she sent him a written warning, claiming that:

> You are responsible for providing accurate information to the UCI and to provide it before any modification in your planning occurs. Concerning

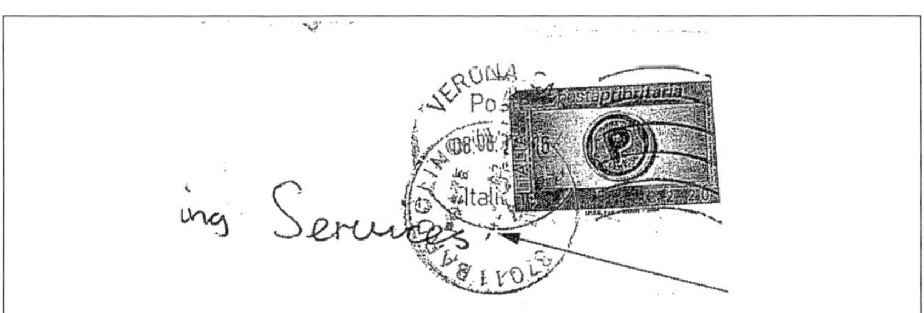

Figure 12.1 Double postmarks

> your stay in Mexico from June 4th til June 12th, the UCI only knew about it on June 11th· *Moreover, the letter providing the UCI the information was posted from Italy on June 8th.*
>
> (Italics added)

Rasmussen responded to the written warning insisting that the letter was sent on 4 June. The person who reviewed his explanation was Anne Gripper – the same person who issued the written warning. Obviously, this is not the highest standard of impartiality. It is understandable if the UCI anti-doping commissioner became frustrated, or perhaps even furious, when she received the late update, which rightly may have invoked the impression that Rasmussen was abusing the system and that he deserved to be punished for it. Maybe that was the reason why she issued him with a recorded warning immediately after the reception of his explanation and neglected to check the postmark, which meant that she did not see that he had posted his update on time, on 4 June. Whatever the reasoning, she added that:

> There are many ways to inform UCI concerning any modification in your planning. Fax, emails, phones. *In the future*, we require you to be more cooperative in using means of communication that will guarantee our knowledge of your change of plans <u>before</u> the change occurs.
>
> (Italics added, underlining in original)

The fact that she requires him to be more cooperative in the future is a clear indication that she understands that his update by regular mail may have been justified according to the guidelines UCI sent out with the athletes' location forms, which said:

> The duly completed forms, as well as all updates, should be sent, preferably by E-mail, to whereabouts@uci.ch, by fax to + 41 24 468 59 13, *or by regular mail* to the UCI Anti-Doping Services (Aigle – Suisse). N.B. We draw your attention to the fact that the forms must be returned on time.
>
> (Italics added)

The wording 'returned on time' is open to interpretation. Rasmussen claims that he understood 'returned on time' to mean that he was allowed to post the letter the day he changed his whereabouts.

Gripper refused to accept his explanation. Moreover, she made it sound as if he was on the verge of a doping violation, by not only reminding him about *the wrongly issued* UCI warning, but also – as noted above– reminding him of the two warnings he had received from ADD. In hindsight, what made this even more frustrating for Rasmussen was that the ADD warnings, which were justified by the rules, exemplified that the system works inconsistently.

The first recorded warning he received from ADD came after a missed test on 6 April 2007. When he received the written warning, he explained that he had decided to depart for a race in Spain one and a half days earlier than he had declared on his location form. He says he forgot to update his whereabouts. Effectively, then, he lived out-of-step with his whereabouts information for 36 hours. As evidence to support his claim, he attached a flight ticket with his name on it. ADD did not accept this explanation, and so the missed test resulted in a recorded warning. The letter contained no reason why his explanation was not accepted, other than a reference to paragraph 14.3 in the WADA code, which stresses the obligation on athletes in the registered testing pool to provide precise and updated whereabouts information. The letter seemed to imply that every filing failure or missed test should result in a recorded warning, even though this is not the case. A problem arises from the fact that ADD has no clear principles by which they can decide whether a written warning should be recorded or not.

This became clear when I interviewed another rider who had experienced a situation comparable to Rasmussen's. The anonymous rider, who like Rasmussen lives in a foreign country, had decided to return to Denmark for an event 2 days later than announced in his whereabouts. Therefore, he was not present when the doping control knocked on the door at the address where he was supposed to be. The rider explained that he had decided to stay at home for training for 2 days more than originally planned. Therefore, he had lived out of step with his whereabouts for 48 hours. He had kept neither his flight ticket nor his boarding pass. All the evidence he had to support his story was an impersonal parking ticket from the airport he claimed to have departed from 2 days later than stated on his location form. This rider's justification of his whereabouts violation was accepted by ADD, who subsequently withdrew the written warning.

The contrasting outcomes of the two riders' missed tests suggest that ADD does not live up to the principle of equality before the law. The impression of inequality of treatment of athletes subjected to the whereabouts system was further strengthened by the Vogelzang commission's observation that a rider under another national ADO, who had received a written warning for a missed test, had also had this written warning withdrawn after he had provided an explanation identical to Rasmussen's (Vogelzang *et al.* 2008). Thus, the principle of equal treatment under the law was compromised, not only by ADD, but also by the whereabouts warnings system as such, because of international variations in compliance. When confronted with the different outcomes under his auspices, the chairman of ADD, Professor of Law Jens Evald, defended the inequality by stating that 'Every case is different therefore every case is treated differently'.[2] But Evald refused to explain the difference in principle between the two situations, and yet implicitly condoned opaque and apparently unfair decision-making behind closed doors, which leaves athletes' rights unprotected.

The second warning issued to Rasmussen by ADD resulted from a missed test that occurred in the period that was covered by the recorded warning for a filing failure that he received from UCI. If Rasmussen had been treated by the same standard as every other rider in the registered testing pool, his second warning from UCI would not have caused Rabobank's leading sport director, Theo de Rooij, to fine him, because, as previously mentioned, riders and management shared the understanding that two warnings were no problem whatsoever (Vogelzang *et al.* 2008). Moreover, if his right to a fair hearing had been protected by an independent review panel, it seems doubtful that even this written warning would have been upheld at all, as it is unlikely that an independent review panel would choose to neglect the fact that he actually had returned the letter on time.

Of course, now that it has been revealed that Rasmussen speculated on the imprecision of the whereabouts rules and provided incorrect information to the UCI, it is tempting to argue that he deserved to be penalized. Even so, from a legal rights perspective, it appears to be problematic that the same person who issues the written warning is one and the same person who evaluates the athlete's explanation (i.e. appeal) and decides whether or not to accept it and so whether or not the athlete is given a recorded warning. One might reasonably expect some degree of independence here, in order for due process to be carried out, with a nod to Richard Pound, for its being seen to be justly effected.

Ironically, the Tour de France director, Christian Prudhomme, pointed to the legal principles in general when he was asked to explain why Bjarne Riis, the first Dane to win the Tour de France, was erased from the winners' list when, in the spring of 2007, he admitted to using doping during the Tour in 1996, which he won. Notably, French riders such as Bernard Thevenet (who openly admitted to having used doping in the 1970s) were not erased. 'For us it is important that you are not just indicted on rumours but on proof or confession. It is just like it is in real life', Prudhomme argued (*Ekstra Bladet* 2007a). But, only a few weeks later, when the credibility of the Tour de France's main symbol, the yellow jersey, was threatened by the media frenzy that surrounded Rasmussen, Prudhomme decided to protect the Tour de France's brand by abandoning the same legal principles. After Rasmussen was withdrawn from the race by his team, Rabobank, Prudhomme proudly remarked that the Tour management had pressed for the discriminatory decision: 'We cannot say that Rasmussen cheated but his negligence and lies had become unbearable' (*Ekstra Bladet* 2007b).

Now, if Rasmussen had not been included in the registered testing pool, he would not have received any warnings and would have won the Tour without any furore, because he never tested positive, nor had his name implicated in any of the character-compromising doping cases.

With this in mind, I asked WADA director David Howman, at the *Play the Game* conference in Coventry in June 2009, how WADA reconciled the idea of a level playing field with the invention of a registered testing pool, which means that some athletes are obliged to submit whereabouts information, whereas many of their competitors are not? Howman's response beggars belief: 'Well this is one of the misunderstandings of the system. The registered testing pool does not mean that those outside are not being tested. They are.' By this, Howman attempted to convince the audience that those who are subjected to the whereabouts information system are not disadvantaged in comparison with those who are not. But, if the testing system is equally efficient without whereabouts information, then that would imply that the whereabouts system is superfluous, and it is difficult to imagine that Howman was really of that opinion. If not, however, he appeared to obfuscate the fact that those outside the registered testing pool had been granted an advantage by WADA, against his better judgement. The situation was another indication that WADA has sacrificed the idea of sporting equality in the service of a greater good.

To sanction or not to sanction . . .

When the 2007 Tour de France was over, there was clearly a need to sanction Rasmussen. Otherwise, his exclusion from the Tour would seem unjustified, and the image of cycling's anti-doping effort would be in tatters. According to the rules, however, it was not a straightforward matter. He had received warnings from the anti-doping authorities, but they did not amount to a doping rule violation. If so, he would not have been allowed to start in the race.

The crucial information that ended Rasmussen's Tour dreams was Italian television commentator David Cassani's public claim that he had seen Rasmussen train in the Dolomites on 13 June when, according to his whereabouts information, he should have been in Mexico. When Cassani's statement was published, de Rooij confronted Rasmussen, who confirmed the meeting with Cassani had taken place. This made the sports director, de Rooij, who was already under pressure because of the media storm, assess it would be hazardous to continue supporting his team captain. After negotiations with representatives from the sponsor, Rabobank, it was decided to protect the integrity of the team by axing Rasmussen (*NCR Handelsblad* 2007). Accordingly, de Rooij announced to the press that Rasmussen was now withdrawn from the Tour, claiming that Rasmussen had lied to him and thereby committed a breach of trust. Clearly, this argument, if true, is sufficient for termination of a working relationship. However, with regard to a sporting sanction, it was useless, insofar as there was no rule stating that a rider had to be truthful. Besides, Rasmussen had been issued with a recorded warning for providing unsatisfactory whereabouts information, which summed up his violations during the month of June as follows:

> We regret to inform you that the written warning that was sent to you on June 11th 2007 is not withdrawn. It has been recorded despite the explanations you sent to the UCI by fax on June 27th. You are responsible

> for providing accurate information to the UCI and to **provide it before any modification in your planning occurs**. Concerning your stay in Mexico from June 4th till June 12th, the UCI only knew about it on June 11th. Moreover, the letter providing the UCI the information was posted from Italy on June 8th. [This she maintains despite his explanation that the letter was posted on time 4 June and she had the envelope in her possession to confirm it.] Finally, on June 12th, you posted a letter from Mexico to inform the UCI that you would stay in Mexico till June 28th. The UCI has received the letter today on June 29th and this is not acceptable. Moreover, the information you provided was not correct as you were back in Italy at least on June 26th. There are many ways to inform the UCI concerning any modification in your planning. Fax, emails, phones. In the future, we require you to be more cooperative in using means of communication that will guarantee our knowledge of your change of plans before the change occurs.
>
> (Emphases in original)

The wording of the letter leaves little doubt that he had been punished for his whereabouts merry-go-round, pursuant to the whereabouts rules. The rules did not distinguish between 'incorrect information' and 'intentionally incorrect information'. So, to sanction him once more for the same rule violation would appear to collide with the legal principle *ne bis in idem* ('not twice for the same').[3] In an attempt to put an end to the negative impact upon Rabobank's reputation, which had deteriorated with Rasmussen's claim that he did not lie to his team and that the management had known about his whereabouts all along, Rabobank initiated an independent investigation, which resulted in the above-mentioned Vogelzang report. Rasmussen decided to collaborate with the commission and put his cards on the table. His lawyer, acting upon his behalf, also proposed a meeting with the UCI, hoping that, if Rasmussen was cooperative, they could find a solution that was satisfactory for the UCI as well as for him. In hindsight, this was a bad mistake for Rasmussen. If Rasmussen had denied meeting Cassani and denied he privately confirmed to de Rooij that this meeting took place, the UCI would have been unable to prove that he actually had provided false whereabouts information.

On 24 August, the UCI sent Rasmussen a letter with the heading: 'Potential anti-doping violation', which suggests that the UCI was looking to sanction him. The letter begins as follows: 'The UCI has completed a full review of the whereabouts information which you provided during the month of June. We have also reviewed the statements made by yourself and others relating to your location during June.' This introduction bears witness to a doping rule violation made by the UCI itself, insofar as paragraph 92 about confidentiality states that:

> The UCI shall maintain whereabouts information in strict confidence at all times and shall use it exclusively for purposes of planning, coordinating

> or conducting Testing. The UCI shall destroy the whereabouts information after it is not longer relevant for these purposes.
>
> (UCI 2004)

Rasmussen's whereabouts information for April, May and June were no longer relevant for planning, coordinating and conducting testing on 1 July and should therefore have been destroyed on that date. But apparently they were not. So, the UCI was able to evaluate the information in August – which it did, although the rule clearly declared that the information should exclusively be used for testing purposes.

The evaluation led to two observations: namely, that the UCI and ADD had been unable to locate him for out-of-competition testing during most of June; and, second, that the information that he provided to the UCI was in conflict with statements made by himself and others during the month of June. The letter went on:

> Based on these two observations, the UCI has reason to believe that you have been deliberately evading sample collection. We have therefore opened an initial investigation to assess whether you have committed an anti-doping rule violation of *evading sample collection* under Article 15.3 of the UCI Anti-Doping Rules.

This was alarming news for Rasmussen, who thought that violations of the whereabouts rule would be sanctioned by warnings. Now he realized that another article had come into play, which could lead to 2 years' suspension. Moreover, he was informed that he was expected to incriminate himself, insofar as article 185 suggested: 'Before taking a decision, the Anti-Doping Commission may order additional investigations. National Federations shall be obliged to conduct such investigations as the Anti-Doping Commission may deem appropriate. **All License Holders are obliged to assist**' (bold in original letter). In line with this, Rasmussen was required to provide 'full and complete evidence that [he was] located in Mexico during the two periods advised to the UCI via updates to [his] whereabouts information'. 'The nature of evidence [the UCI] was seeking included entry and exit stamps for Mexico in [his] passport or airline tickets.'

What the UCI apparently did not know was that Mexico did not stamp visitors' passports. Rasmussen, whose wife is Mexican and so has travelled between Italy and Mexico numerous times, has plenty of stamps in his old passport, which expired in 2008 – I have seen them – but not one of them is from Mexico. So he could not provide the first form of evidence, because such evidence did not exist. He did, however, have airline tickets to cover his story and he could have sent these to Aigle as 'evidence', along with recent pictures of himself in identifiable Mexican surroundings. In that case, the UCI may have also requested his boarding passes, which could have been a problem, but if he maintained he had thrown them out, it is hard to see what the UCI could have done, as this is a perfectly normal action. Moreover, because the UCI is not a state authority, it would not have been in a position to ask for passenger lists. So it is difficult to see how the UCI could penalize him if he had not cooperated with the Vogelzang commission, and – uncertain of the Rabobank-appointed commission's conclusion – as it transpired he had decided to be proactive. On 14 November 2007, Rasmussen held a press conference at which he admitted that he had provided the UCI with incorrect whereabouts information regarding his pretended stay in Mexico. Rasmussen felt that he had a good case to have his ban reduced, as he was ready to cooperate with the UCI.

However, because of the obligation to self-incrimination declared in article 185, he was not eligible for such a ban reduction. When he admitted that he had provided inaccurate whereabouts information, on 1 July 2007 he was banned for 2 years on the grounds that his whereabouts violations were also a violation of article 15.3 – evading sample collection – and 15.5 – tampering with doping control. As if the UCI wanted to bring attention to the fact that they had no legal justification for banning him prior to his confession, they proposed the ban be brought into effect only from 14 November 2007, rather than from the time of his suspension on 26 July 2007.

All animals are equal . . .?

It is understandable, given the strict liability principle and the obligation to self-incrimination contained in the UCI regulations, article 185, that Rasmussen did not deserve a reduction for his admission. The surprising thing was that he did not get any reduction for providing evidence that the Rabobank team management was informed about his whereabouts during June. If Rasmussen had committed an anti-doping rule violation under articles 15.3 and 15.5, then Rabobank had committed a rule violation according to UCI's anti doping regulations, article 15.8, which referred to: 'Administration or Attempted administration of a Prohibited Substance or Prohibited Method to any Rider, or assisting, encouraging, aiding, abetting, *covering up or any other type of complicity involving an anti-doping rule violation or any Attempted violation*' (UCI 2004, italics added).

The day after UCI confirmed Rasmussen's 2-year ban, he won a civil court case against Rabobank. He convinced the judge of his evidence that the Rabobank team management had known his whereabouts all along. As soon as the verdict was reached in the civil court, in the Rasmussen–Rabobank case, UCI therefore should have brought charges against Rabobank for covering up its knowledge of his whereabouts. In light of the strict liability principle in sport, it is hard to see how Rabobank could have been let off the hook, if UCI had taken the opportunity to start disciplinary proceedings. UCI could have used Rasmussen as witness. His evidence in the case is overwhelming. But UCI chose not to. So Rabobank escaped disciplinary proceedings and continued its role as generous sponsor of cycling.

The reason for the unfortunate development of the anti-doping movement is that spectacular doping cases, such as the Festina affair in 1998 and *Operación Puerto* in 2006,[4] have caused moral panic that has increased concurrently with the realization that the traditional methods of attacking the problem do not work properly. Hence, as Erich Goode and Ben-Yehuda suggest, the thinking among agents of social control is that 'new situations need new remedies . . . and this entails suspending rights and liberties previously enjoyed' (Goode and Ben-Yahuda 2006: 27). This is one disconcerting conclusion that must be drawn from the Michael Rasmussen case, which alarmingly exemplifies that the anti-doping system is far from fulfilling Pound's request that 'Officials must demonstrate that accountability starts at the top and have a responsibility to act fairly, impartially and within the letter and spirit of the governing rules' (Pound 2004). Another, no less crucial, conclusion is that, if the indispensable anti-doping work is not to lose credibility, it is urgent that the legal procedures behind the sanction system are thoroughly evaluated and revised accordingly.

Notes

1 See http://sportsanddrugs.procon.org/viewresource.asp?resourceID=002352.
2 'Doping and legal rights', Aarhus University, Denmark, 20 August 2009.
3 For a detailed discussion about legal principles in sport, see McNamee and Tarasti (Chapter 1) in this volume.
4 For a thorough presentation of the *Operación Puerto*, see Hardie (Chapter 10) in this volume.

References

Associated Press (2009) 'Belgian group challenges WADA rule', 27 January. Available online at: http://sports.espn.go.com/oly/news/story?id=3863905 (accessed 3 January 2010).

Coomber, R. (1999) 'Controlling drugs in sport: contradictions and complexity', in Nigel South (ed.), *Drugs – cultures, controls & and everyday life*, London: SAGE.

Ekstra Bladet (2007a) 'C'est la vie', 15 July.

Ekstra Bladet (2007b) '*Kyllingens nedtur: Tourchef Prudhomme: Løgne blev ubærlige*', 27 July.

Goode, E. and Ben-Yahuda, N. (2006) *Moral panics – the social construction of deviance*, Oxford: Blackwells.

Jyllands-Posten (2007a) 'UCI jagter dopingspøgelser', 23 June.

Jyllands-Posten (2007b) 'DCU vil af med fortroligheden', 16 August.

McLuhan, M. (2001(1964)) *Understanding media – the extension of man*, London: Routledge.

McNamee, M. (2008) *Sports, virtues and vices – morality plays*, London: Routledge.

NCR Handelsblad (2007) 'The Rasmussen Schandal'. Available online at: www.nrc.nl/international/Features/article1858787.ece/The_Rasmussen_schandal (last updated 13 July 2009; accessed 14 July 2010).

Politiken (2009) 'Forsker: Rasmussen snydt for Tour-sejr', 20 August.

Pound, D. (2004) *Inside the Olympics: a behind-the-scenes look at the politics, the scandals and the glory of the Games*, London: Wiley.

Soek, J. (2006) *The strict liability principle and the human rights of athletes in doping cases*, The Hague: T.M.C. Asser Press.

UCI (2004) *UCI Cycling Regulations; Part 14 Anti-Doping Rules of the UCI*, Aigle: UCI.

Vogelzang, P., Langevoort, G., Olfers, M. and Geraets, J. (2008) *Vogelzang report on the Michael Rasmussen Case*, Amsterdam: Rabobank.

WADA (2004) *The World Anti-Doping Program – Guidelines for athletes' whereabouts information*, version 2, June, Montreal: WADA.

13 Governance and the whereabouts system

A Norwegian case study

Dag Vidar Hanstad

Introduction

Since its introduction in 2004, and even more so since the introduction of the revised version in 2009, the World Anti-Doping Agency's (WADA) whereabouts system, which requires athletes to report their whereabouts and to be available for drug testing on 365 days a year, has proved controversial. Although some form of reporting is a necessity for effective doping controls in competition or out of competition (Hanstad and Loland 2009), many commentators have focused on the general issues of principle raised by the system and, in particular, whether the system may be considered to breach the civil rights and privacy of athletes (Møller 2009a, 2009b; Waddington and Smith 2009; Waddington, 2010). Such studies have raised a number of important issues in terms of the implications of the whereabouts system for athletes. However, the system also has a number of important implications, not just for those who are subject to the system (i.e. elite athletes), but also for those organizations that are charged with the responsibility of organizing and implementing the whereabouts system at a national level (i.e. national anti-doping organizations).

The central object of this paper is to focus on the managerial difficulties and problems that national anti-doping organizations (NADOs) face in implementing the whereabouts system. In order to highlight these problems, the paper focuses on a case study of the Norwegian beach volleyball player, Vegard Høidalen, and the disciplinary action that was brought against him by Anti-Doping Norway (ADN) and the Norwegian Olympic and Paralympic Committee and Confederation of Sports (NIF).

In 2008, Vegard Høidalen was judged by the NIF to have violated the anti-doping regulations regarding whereabouts information. During Høidalen's appeal, he revealed weaknesses in the procedures of ADN. Among other things, the Høidalen case focused attention on a formal error committed by the doping control officers and on poor procedures by ADN, and highlighted other discriminatory procedures. He was subsequently cleared by NIF's Appeals Committee.

As we noted above, the aim of this paper is to examine the 'Høidalen case' and to draw out some of the implications of the case for anti-doping organizations (ADOs). In particular, issues of practical challenges, the requirements for accuracy, issues relating to the rule of law, the use of discretion and questions of possible discrimination will be discussed. It will be argued that the complexity of the WADA rules creates difficulties for NADOs that WADA had almost certainly not foreseen and, by highlighting the problems created for ADN – generally regarded as one of the most effective NADOs (Council of Europe 2008) – the managerial problems facing NADOs in general are brought into sharp focus.

Before we discuss the whereabouts system and its problems as illustrated in the Høidalen case,[1] it is necessary to say a few words about the central character of the story. Høidalen has been a professional beach volleyball player since 1994, winning the European Championship with his partner in 1997. One year later, he won one of the tournaments on the World Tour. Later, he won medals in European and World Championships and participated in the Olympic Games in 2000 and 2004. He has been highly critical of the whereabouts system ever since it was introduced. He has characterized the system as pathological and expressed doubts about its legality (Jarlsbo 2005) and, like other athletes, has claimed that the system deprived him of a private life and reduced the pleasure of being a top-level athlete (Kise Karlsen 2007). He has publicly stated that the system should be abolished immediately (Grøndal 2009).

Whereabouts information

In 2004, the demand for athletes to submit whereabouts information to their national or international federation was introduced as a new tool in the fight against doping in the World Anti-Doping Code. In 2009, a revised version came into force. According to the code, international and national sports federations have to establish registered testing pools of elite athletes and carry out in-competition and out-of-competition testing as set out in the International Standards for Testing (WADA 2008a). International federations and NADOs are required to define (and publish) criteria for athletes to be included in the testing pools (WADA 2008b). Athletes belonging to these pools have to be available for testing 24 hours a day. For one specific 60-minute time slot every day, athletes have to specify a location for testing (WADA 2008b). The athlete can choose the location for the 60-minute slot, for example the place of residence, training or work/school. It is the athlete's responsibility to ensure that the information provided enables the doping control officer to find the location, to gain access and to find the athlete at the location.

Athletes who fail to file required whereabouts information and/or cannot be found by the doping control officers at the reported meeting point (missed test) may receive a warning. Any combination of three missed tests and/or filing failures within an 18-month period constitutes an anti-doping rule violation (WADA 2008a). The sanction is a period of ineligibility of between

1 and 2 years (WADA 2008a). This is an increase from the 2004 version, in which 3 months was the minimum sanction (WADA 2004). This earlier version was applicable in Vegard Høidalen's case, because he received all his three warning before the revised version came into force.

Among the most high-profile athletes to have been sanctioned for violations of the whereabouts information system are the (then) British Commonwealth 400 meter champion, Christine Ohuruogu (BBC 2006), who subsequently won Gold in Beijing, the Olympic medal-winning Greek sprinters Katerina Thanou and Kostas Kenteris (IAAF 2006) and the Danish cyclist Michael Rasmussen (Ferdinand 2008).

The system has generated a great deal of controversy among athletes (Hanstad and Loland 2007; Broadbent 2008; European Elite Athletes Association 2008; Associated Press 2009a; Hansen 2009; Hanstad *et al.* 2009), sports organizations (Associated Press 2009b), intergovernmental organizations (Article 29 Data Protection Working Party 2009) and scholars (Kreft 2009; Møller 2009a, 2009b; Waddington and Smith 2009, Waddington, 2010). A survey among the Norwegian athletes in their registered testing pool in 2006 showed resistance to some parts of the system (Hanstad and Loland 2009; Hanstad *et al.* 2009). Many athletes had experienced technical problems with the system, with just over one third (34.7 per cent) indicating that they had been unable to update their whereabouts information owing to technical problems. Most also disagreed with the statement that three warnings in 18 months should be regarded as a doping offence, with only a very small minority (10.6 per cent) agreeing with the statement. Further, they found it unfair that, because the WADA system was not fully implemented in many countries, competitors from other nations were not subject to the same regime regarding whereabouts information. The uneven implementation of the WADA whereabouts system in many countries was confirmed in a study carried out among NADOs in 2008 (Hanstad *et al.* 2010).

Hearing process and sanctions

According to the code, every athlete has the right to a fair hearing. WADA has set out the principles for a hearing process that include, among other things, the right to be represented by counsel, to present evidence, to call and question witnesses, and to be given a timely written, reasoned decision (WADA 2008a). The decision may be appealed, both by athletes and sport/anti-doping organizations. For international-level athletes, the decision may be appealed directly to the Court of Arbitration for Sport (CAS), while national cases may be appealed to an independent body, in accordance with rules established by NADOs (WADA 2008a).

There are a variety of practices regarding hearing processes. In what follows, the hearing process in Norway at the time of the Høidalen case will be described (2006–8). After each warning, an evaluation process was undertaken by ADN staff (the whereabouts adviser, the chief of doping controls and the general director), and the athlete was given the possibility to respond.[2]

According to the result management system of ADN, three warnings within 18 months means that the case is sent to a *prosecution committee* for determination of whether a violation of NIF's provisions regarding doping should be brought before NIF's tribunal. Members of the prosecution committee, consisting of a chairman and two other members, are independent in relation to the activities of the foundation (Anti-Doping Norway 2009). The current chairman is also the commissioner of the Oslo Police.

The prosecution committee may either dismiss the case or, alternatively, report a breach of the anti-doping regulations to the NIF's *adjudication committee*, with a proposed time period of suspension. The adjudication committee organizes a hearing. Both the athlete and ADN may appeal the judgment to the *appeals committee*.[3] A competence requirement is that members of both the adjudication and appeals committees are not current members of the control committee or the NIF's executive committee (or the athlete's national association) (NIF 2008b). The appellate body organizes a hearing and reaches a new judgment, which may either confirm or reject the earlier judgment.

The Høidalen case

Vegard Høidalen received three warning within 18 months, as follows:

- Warning 1: Missed test, 14 December 2006. The doping control officers were unable to find Høidalen at the location (his own residence) at which he had indicated he would be present between 6 and 7 a.m.
- Warning 2: Failure to file whereabouts for 7 days, 1–7 February 2007.
- Warning 3: Failure to file whereabouts for three months, 1 February to 29 April 2008.

The ADN staff decided to forward the case to the prosecution committee, which, on 25 June 2008, reported a violation of the anti-doping regulations to the NIF's adjudication committee, with a proposal that Høidalen should (1) be suspended from participating in sport for 9 months and (2) immediately be given a provisional suspension. He was alleged to have violated NIF's doping rules that deal with whereabouts information: 'To violate guidelines concerning athlete information or not to be available for doping control according to the guidelines' (NIF 2008b: art.12.2d).

Høidalen was given a provisional suspension for 2 months. After 2 months, the prosecution committee forgot to renew the suspension, until it became aware of it as a result of TV coverage some days after Høidalen was allowed to train and compete again. The adjudication committee then refused to extend the suspension pending its own hearing, thus allowing the athlete to train prior to the hearing into his case, which was held on 11 October 2008. Following the hearing, the committee announced, on 29 October 2008, that the athlete would be suspended for 4 months. Høidalen decided to appeal the judgment to the appeals committee. The appellate body organized a hearing for 13 January 2009 and announced a new judgment on 30 January 2009, in which Høidalen was acquitted.

General implications of the Høidalen case

This particular case raises a number of more general issues, which indicate some of the managerial problems associated with the implementation of the whereabouts system. More particularly, the Høidalen case raises issues relating to the practical challenges facing NADOs, the requirements for accuracy, issues relating to the rule of law and the use of discretion and possible issues of discrimination.

Practical challenges

There are a number of challenges, both for athletes and the ADOs. For athletes, these include technical issues regarding reporting (e.g. access to the Internet, use of a laptop), difficulties of providing information 3 months in advance and reporting sudden changes in their schedules. For ADOs, the challenges include the need to give athletes the necessary training to handle the system, getting access to the athletes without advance notice, managing a testing pool with several hundred athletes and carrying out controls in accordance with the information given by the athletes.

Høidalen had given his private residence in Oslo as his meeting point. This is a house with three units, including two flats and a business office, all owned by Høidalen. At the time of the missed test (14 December 2006, which gave rise to warning 1), he had, according to his own testimony, temporarily moved to another part of the house. As a result, the door to the building was opened by another person, who said that Høidalen had moved to another part of the city. In his testimony, this person said that the doping control officers (DCOs) had not introduced themselves, and his answer was an attempt to get rid of the DCOs.

Høidalen did not have any doorbell or name on the door. A witness from ADN said, during the testimony in the appeals committee, that Høidalen had told the ADN that the DCOs instead should have knocked on a window to get access to the building. This was denied by Høidalen during the hearing, but it illustrates the kind of practical challenges ADOs may have in gaining access, even when the athlete has indicated a meeting point.

It is clear that Høidalen did not make it easy for the DCOs, because he did not have his name on the door or a doorbell. In its revised testing standard (2008b), WADA now emphasizes that athletes are responsible for providing information that enables the DCO to find the location, to gain access and to find the athlete at the location. However, this may present challenges for many DCOs. In South Africa, for example, this is a common problem and is not linked to athletes' attitude towards the system. In another study (Hanstad and Loland 2005), the then chief executive officer in the South Africa Institute for Drugfree Sport (SAIDS), Daphne Bradbury, said:

> We sometimes have problems tracking down an athlete for out-of-competition testing, as there are areas where the streets are not indicated on street maps and, in fact, may not even have street names or house numbers. In this respect, it is probably a lot easier to find someone in a country in Europe than it is in a country in Africa.
>
> (Hanstad and Loland 2005: 44)

The Høidalen case shows that, even in Europe, it can be difficult to find athletes. What is interesting here is that Høidalen was given a warning from ADN, even though he, according to his own testimony, was present at the address he had reported, but not in the particular flat to which the DCOs tried to gain access.

Others fear they will receive warnings for similar reasons. The new system (the revised Code and the International Standard for Testing, which came into force on 1 January 2009) is more comprehensive and, from the perspective of the athletes, more demanding. Athletes in the registered testing pool are now required to indicate a potential meeting point for 1 hour each day, the whole year around, which for many athletes involved a change from 5 days to 7 days a week (though not for Norwegian athletes, who had a 60-minute slot, 7 days a week, even before 2009). Athletes have to be available for the whole period (1 hour), the window for this meeting point is between 6 a.m. and 11 p.m. (not from 5 a.m., as for example had been the case in the UK until 2009), and they have to report their whereabouts on a quarterly basis for the forthcoming 3 months.

For professional athletes travelling around the world, this may present a real practical challenge. In tennis, the world no. 16, the Belgian Yanina Wickmayer was, in November 2009, banned for 1 year (she appealed to a Belgian court, and her ban was lifted). Wickmayer said that the failure to follow procedure was due to her not being able to log on to the relevant website, not being able to contact the right people when needed, and not being in the country when written admonitions arrived by mail at her home address (NZPA 2009). Others, such as Britain's no. 1, Andy Murray, have criticized the new regime as unworkable. He told *The Times* that, 'these new rules are so draconian that it makes it almost impossible to live a normal life' (Eason 2009). Sixteen world and Olympic rowing medalists published an open letter branding the rules 'an impractical and unworkable regime' (Quarrell 2009), while Olympic pole vault champion Yelena Isinbayeva said that it would be impossible for athletes such as herself to know where they will be in 2 months: 'this is unfair, it does not work', she told the BBC (2009).

Requirements for accuracy

The requirement for accuracy is important for both athletes and ADOs. In the revised version of the International Standards for Testing (WADA 2008b), no fewer than 36 pages describe the requirements of the whereabouts system. These include the procedures for establishing the registered testing pool, whereabouts filing, testing, results management and responsibilities of the ADOs. In the Høidalen case, ADN – and here it is important to repeat its status among the best in the world – failed to follow its own procedures in at least two respects. First, ADN forgot to apply for an extension of the ban on Høidalen after he had finished serving his 2-month provisional suspension, which it wanted to last until the time of the hearing. A spokesman for the committee responded that 'if so we have lost just a week and think we will survive it' (Stabrun Smith 2008). ADOs do not tolerate such laxity from athletes. The adjudication committee later recognized weaknesses in ADN's procedures by stating that it 'will not praise ADN for the proceedings at every stage in this case' (NIF 2008a: 11).

The other error by ADN was crucial in the decision to uphold Høidalen's successful appeal. In accordance with the requirements by ADN, Høidalen had initially reported 'in the night' as the meeting time (understood as between midnight and 6 a.m.), but this had been changed to a 60-minute slot between 6 and 7 a.m. before the doping control on 14 December 2006, when two DCOs arrived to carry out an out-of-competition test. In their report, the DCOs stated that the athlete had reported the wrong address. They also indicated that the time when they arrived for the test was 7.05 a.m. For Høidalen, this was a core issue during the hearing in the adjudication committee. ADN claimed that the time for testing was not important, because Høidalen was not present at the location at all. It was also claimed that the 60-minute slot was not stipulated in the NOC statutes at the time of the test. This is correct, but in the handbook for athletes belonging to the registered testing pool, dated 4 October 2006, it was stated that athletes had to make themselves available for doping control each day for a limited period of at least 1 hour. Similar information was also given in newspaper articles on the topic (Bugge 2007; Johannessen and Prestvik 2007).

Nevertheless, the adjudication committee supported ADN's explanation and concluded as follows:

> Sure it is stated in the report from the doping control officers that they explored the address at 07.05 a.m. The Adjudication Committee's view is that such insignificant deviations cannot be given decisive importance for the actual question in this case: whether Høidalen had made himself available for the doping control officers.
>
> (NIF 2008a: 7)

The committee suspended Høidalen for 4 months, and he decided to appeal. Høidalen limited the grounds of his apppeal to the meeting time

(7.05 a.m.). After a hearing in January 2009, the appeals committee announced that it did 'not share the assessment of the Adjudication Committee that 7.05 a.m. is an insignificant deviation' (NIF 2009: 5). Høidalen won his appeal, and he was acquitted.

This example shows the need for very precise accuracy on the part of ADOs. More generally, the implementation of the whereabouts information system, with its rigorous recording and monitoring requirements, has generated a complex series of administrative tasks for ADOs. These include monitoring the athletes' registrations, carrying out doping controls in line with the correct procedures, following up athletes who failed to provide the required information and allowing athletes to explain in relevant cases why they had not provided the correct information or had not provided any information. ADN's annual report from 2004 states: 'Collecting and systematizing whereabouts information is time consuming and has occupied many personnel resources in its administration, in terms of both coordinating this with Norwegian and international sport federations and providing information about the system' (ADN 2004: 7).

Use of discretion

ADN has to decide, in each case of a possible breach of regulations, whether or not to issue a warning to the athlete concerned. The use of discretion will inevitably be part of the process, for example regarding sickness, technical problems, lack of access, familiar circumstances, weather conditions, conditions beyond the athlete's control, periods of training (on the system), phase of change and mistakes by the ADN. When the system was new in Norway, there were several examples where ADN decided not to give warnings to athletes because of technical problems.

Another example of discretion involves the use of the telephone when the DCO is unable to find the athlete. When the DCOs could not find Høidalen ('warning 1'), the obvious solution, in his opinion, would have been to have called him on the phone. During the case, he and his lawyer called attention to a lack of consistency in relation to the use of phones by ADN. Even though ADN stated that they do not phone athletes as a matter of principle,[4] DCOs had, over the previous two and a half years, occasionally phoned athletes in what ADN regarded as 'extraordinary circumstances'. But what is an 'extraordinary circumstance'? On one occasion, a mobile phone call had been made in order to arrange a test for a ski jumper. In the adjudication committee, the ADN representative said that this had been done because the ski jumper was on his way out of the country (to a training camp). This claim was rejected in evidence presented by Høidalen and his lawyer. The ski jumper received a warning, but the point here is that the principle of not using the phone had been broken.

Other NADOs did not follow the same tough line as ADN. In a study by the author one year prior to Høidalen's first warning, some other well-organized ADOs replied that they 'called the athletes and told him/her to arrive at the test station within two hours', or they 'called the coach or other support personnel to inform them that the athlete must be back within 24 hours at the latest – preferably as soon as possible' (Hanstad and Loland 2005: 40). Another (anonymous) representative said:

> Phone calls in 2004 were used just in ten percent of completed tests so it is not happening all that often. Our position is that it's still a no-notice test. Within two hours there is little, if any, opportunity for manipulation. That's our opinion. We track phone calls so we know how often phone calls take place. We can go back and search and say 'OK, of the last four attempts on you, this is how many times phone calls were made'.
>
> (Hanstad and Loland 2005: 43)

This was confirmed in a study of members of the Association of National Anti-Doping Organizations (ANADO) in 2007 (Hanstad *et al.* 2010). Seven out of twenty-one NADOs stated that they phoned the athlete to carry out the doping control. In Høidalen's hearing, he cited the case of a Norwegian sailor training abroad who was phoned when the DCO could not find him/her at the specified location. The sailor was preparing the boat and did not receive any warning. This was a control carried out by a Norwegian DCO, but on behalf of the International Sailing Federation.

To sum up, there is no consistency among ADOs around the world regarding how they implement key aspects of the whereabouts system, with each organization using its discretion to determine whether or not a warning should be given. In other words, each case is treated individually. However, it can be asked whether the discretion *can* lead to discrimination against some athletes. Let us return to the Høidalen case.

From discretion to discrimination?

The Høidalen case revealed what may seem to be lack of consistency regarding what was accepted in terms of explanations given by the athletes in their responses after warnings were considered. Both for filing failures and missed tests, other athletes had their explanations accepted and were not given warnings. Consider the following examples.

Late one night in November 2008, Olaf Tufte, the Olympic champion in rowing in 2004 and 2008 and a very popular athlete in Norway, was on a long drive in his car. He felt very tired and decided not to drive home to his residence. Instead, he stayed overnight at the Top Sport Centre (*Olympiatoppen Sport Hotel*), 45 minutes away from his home. The following morning, he was absent from his home (his specified location for drug testing) when DCOs arrived to conduct a drug test. ADN accepted Tufte's explanation, namely that he had been afraid of falling asleep while driving his car under difficult conditions (Kvamme 2009), even though, despite his tiredness, he could have phoned or sent an SMS to change his whereabouts for that night.

Another athlete avoided a warning because he was making preparations for his wedding. Høidalen presented several similar examples during the process (Eriksen 2009). ADN representatives used professional confidentiality as a reason not to explain these examples, but the rower Tufte later said to a Norwegian national daily newspaper, *Dagbladet*, that Høidalen had good reason to protest (Kvamme 2009).

Høidalen claimed that he had been treated more severely than other athletes who had missed tests. In particular, he responded strongly to an earlier decision made by the prosecution committee regarding a cyclist. First, it turned down a notification by the ADN management after a cyclist had received his third warning in December 2006. The argument was that the committee questioned whether the cyclist had actually received his second warning, after the cyclist's lawyer had denied this and criticized ADN's procedures (in a letter dated 17 February 2007). Høidalen also claimed that he had not received 'warning no. 2'. Six months later, the cyclist again received a warning, and ADN forwarded a notification to the prosecution committee. The committee found that the athlete had violated the regulations for whereabouts information but added: 'The consideration of the regulations regarding whereabouts information is to prevent athletes from slinking away. The facts in this case do not indicate any such motive' (document from the prosecution committee, dated 10 September 2007). Høidalen commented on the decision during the hearing in the appeals committee: 'Nor did I attempt to slink away'.

I do not argue that Høidalen was subjected to discrimination, but it is clear that, based on the hearings and information from other cases, his warnings could have been treated differently. During the hearing, the leader of the Athletes' Commission expressed the view that, based on her knowledge about other cases, Høidalen had been subject to discrimination.

The rule of law

The anti-doping regulations follow the general principle that an accused person is 'innocent until proven guilty'; more specifically, the code states that, 'the anti-doping organization shall have the burden of establishing that an anti-doping rule violation has occurred' (WADA 2008a: 26). However, athletes can be subject to a provisional suspension without a hearing (WADA 2008a: 45–7), for example as a result of an adverse analytical finding during an event. Then, the principle is reversed and he/she is considered guilty until proven innocent. For Høidalen, this process had major consequences. Without any hearing, he was suspended in the middle of the season and lost the chance to qualify for the Olympic Games in Beijing. Høidalen was on the World Tour in beach volleyball and, because of the suspension, he lost prize money and, more importantly, ranking points, which made it more difficult for him and his partner when he was back on the Tour circuit after the acquittal (lower-ranked teams meet the best players in the preliminary rounds). Again, this would have had potentially serious economic consequences for the player.

However, this is not only about financial loss. A doping case that lasts for more than half a year and includes a suspension may affect the athlete's reputation and integrity, which is difficult to correct, even after an acquittal.

It seems clear that a basic principle of the rule of law – that a person is innocent until proven guilty – was not followed in this case. Høidalen lost the possibility to train and compete as a result of a case in which he was later acquitted. This had no consequences for ADN or NIF. In sports organizations, there are no procedures for compensation in such cases, even where a professional player such as Høidalen might suffer serious financial loss. Høidalen considered litigation in the courts to obtain compensation, but at the time of writing he had not succeeded in raising enough money to pursue the case. Possibly an athlete in a sport with much higher rewards may have been in a position to bring such a case, but it may also be the case that, in such a situation, the prosecution committee might have been more reluctant to impose a temporary suspension without any hearing.

Planned and unplanned outcomes

As we have seen, the Høidalen case illustrates some of the managerial problems involved for NADOs in implementing the whereabouts system. Although many athletes have publicly supported the system, among them the tennis champion Roger Federer (Harman 2009), the Olympic swimming champion Rebecca Adlington (Roughley 2009) and the Olympic javelin champion Andreas Thorkildsen (Krug 2009), WADA has come under attack from leading sportspersons and representatives of powerful sporting organizations. What originally appeared to be an isolated critique from a few individuals has, after the implementation of the revised code, developed into an organized campaign by groups of athletes, with support from international federations, lawyers, athletes' organizations and, not least, media representatives, some of whom are harshly critical of the new WADA requirements.

This critical reception had almost certainly not been anticipated by WADA. The chapter will conclude with a broader discussion about the outcome of the whereabouts system.

WADA's objectives in introducing the whereabouts system are obvious. Athletes can no longer just disappear for days or weeks prior to championships – actions that were common before the system was established (Hanstad *et al.* 2009). If they do so, they will receive warnings for failure to submit necessary information and/or missed tests. It is also easier to carry out effective out-of-competition testing, because the ADOs have (or should have) a specified meeting point for the athletes every day.

However, this chapter has shown that there are some outcomes of the system that could hardly have been planned or intended by WADA, such as, for example, that the system is so difficult to administer that even a best-practice NADO such as Norway made mistakes. Planned policy developments, such as the whereabouts system, are always likely to have a number of unplanned outcomes, because they are a 'logical outcome . . . of the complex interweaving of planned and unplanned social processes' (Dunning *et al.* 2004: 199).

Of particular concern, for the ADOs, must be that the whereabouts system has become the focus for discontent. As pointed out elsewhere (Hanstad *et al.* 2009), criticisms of the system, among other things, are related to:

1 the technical challenges faced by athletes in sending and amending the required information if they are to avoid violating the whereabouts requirements;
2 athletes' perceptions of the system as unfair because of what they perceive as the discrepancy between an infringement and the resulting sanction; and
3 athletes' perceptions of the system as being unfair because there is too much variation in how the system has been implemented in different nations.

This was hardly planned by WADA. Waddington (2010) points out that a policy that was presumably designed to support what WADA calls the 'spirit of sport' appears to have had the effect of actually undermining what is considered one of the four fundamental values of sport.

> In a word, the introduction of the whereabouts system, one justification for which relates to the desire to create a 'level playing field', has actually given rise to a new and 'unlevel' playing field by requiring athletes in some countries to meet requirements which are not operative in other countries. Given the central value of the concepts of fair play and the 'level playing field' within sport, this must be seen as the most ironic of the unplanned outcomes of the whereabouts system.
>
> (Waddington 2010)

Such unplanned outcomes indicate the need for continuous monitoring of policies to see whether they are achieving the desired goals or whether they are having consequences that were not only unintended but that, from the perspective of the policymakers, may actually be judged undesirable.

Concluding remarks

It is reasonable to assume that it was not WADA's intention that 'clean' athletes should be labelled 'guilty' for a doping offence when the system was established.

Vegard Høidalen attacked the system and won his appeal because of mistakes by ADN. This chapter has illustrated some of the organizational problems facing organizations charged with implementing the whereabouts system and has focused on the practical challenges, the requirement for accuracy, the use of discretion and the possibility of discrimination, and rule of law. Fortunately for Høidalen, the hearing process within the national sports organization in Norway functioned satisfactorily because he had the right to appeal his case.

Notes

1 The author sat through hearings in the adjudication committee and appeals committee. The meeting in the adjudication committee, held on 11 October 2008, lasted for nine and a half hours (from 10 a.m. to 7.30 p.m.). The participants were the athlete and his lawyer, staff in ADN (n = 3), ADN's lawyer, one witness, members of the adjudication committee (n = 3) and its secretary. The meeting in the appeals committee, on 13 January 2009, lasted for seven hours (from 10 a.m. to 5 p.m.). The participants were the athlete and his lawyer, staff in ADN (n = 2), ADN's lawyers, witnesses (n = 4) and five members of the appeals committee. This chapter is also based on archival material, which included documents from the prosecution committee and the appeals committee; warning letters and warnings regarding whereabouts information from ADN to several athletes (n = 10); other documents presented during the case (n = 20); and the whole decisions of the adjudication committee (NIF 2008a) and the appeals committee (NIF 2009).

2 In 2009, after the Høidalen case, ADN established a new panel consisting of six elite athletes. It is the panel's responsibility to consider each alleged warning before it is given to the athlete.

3 The adjudication committee is elected by the NIF's general assembly and comprises a chairperson, deputy chairperson, one member and two deputy members. The adjudication committee organizes a hearing and makes a decision. Both the athlete and ADN may appeal the judgment to the appeals committee, a committee elected by the NIF's general assembly and comprising a chairperson, a deputy chairperson, three members and two deputy members.

4 By calling the athlete, he/she may have time to manipulate some blood parameters (haematocrit/concentration in haemoglobin), super hydration (possibility to urinate and drink a lot, which will make the detection of substances harder, as the urine will be very diluted (as has happened with respect to EPO)) or obtain a urine sample from somebody else and substitute it (Hanstad *et al.* 2005).

References

Anti-Doping Norway (2004) *Årsrapport Antidoping Norge 2003* (*Annual Report Anti-Doping Norway 2003*), Oslo: Antidoping Norge.

Anti-Doping Norway (2009) 'Articles of Association'. Available online at: www.anti-doping.no/en/t2.asp?p=42006 (accessed 28 November 2009).

Article 29 Data Protection Working Party (2009) 'Second opinion 4/2009 on the World Anti-Doping Agency (WADA) International Standard for the Protection of Privacy and Personal Information, on related provisions of the WADA Code and on other privacy issues in the context of the fight against doping in sport by WADA and (national) anti-doping organizations'. Data Protection Working Party. Available online at: http://ec.europa.eu/justice_home/fsj/privacy/docs/wpdocs/2009/wp162_en.pdf (accessed 15 July 2010).

Associated Press (2009a) 'Belgian group challenges WADA rule', *ESPN*. Available online at: http://sports.espn.go.com/oly/news/story?id=3863905 (accessed 28 November 2009).

Associated Press (2009b) 'FIFA, UEFA criticize WADA doping rules', *USA Today*. Available online at: www.usatoday.com/sports/soccer/2009-02-18-3612847778_x.htm (accessed 28 November 2009).

BBC (2006) 'Ohuruogu banned for missing tests'. Available online at: http://news.bbc.co.uk/sport2/hi/athletics/5251180.stm (accessed 28 November 2009).

BBC (2009) 'Drug test rules upset Isinbayeva'. Available online at: http://news.bbc.co.uk/sport2/hi/athletics/7901743.stm (accessed 28 November 2009).

Broadbent, R. (2008) 'Testing idea comes under fire', *Times Online*. Available online at: www.timesonline.co.uk/tol/sport/more_sport/athletics/article5328109.ece (accessed 28 November 2009).

Bugge, M. (2007) '*Utøvere skremmes til å melde seg*' ('Athletes scared to sign up'), *Aftenposten*, 2 October: 28.

Council of Europe (2008) *Anti-Doping Convention (T-DO): Project on compliance with commitments respect by Norway of the anti-doping convention*, Strasbourg: Council of Europe.

Dunning, E., Malcolm, D. and Waddington, I. (2004) 'Conclusion. Figurational sociology and the development of modern sport', in E. Dunning, D. Malcolm and I. Waddington (eds), *Sport histories: figurational studies of the development of modern sport*, London: Routledge, pp. 191–204.

Eason, K. (2009) 'Andy Murray criticises new anti-doping rules', *Times Online*. Available online at: www.timesonline.co.uk/tol/sport/tennis/article5671975.ece (accessed 28 November 2009).

Eriksen, K. (2009) '*Høidalen hevder norske stjerner slapp "billig"*' ('Høidalen claims Norwegian sports stars got easy'), *VG Nett*. Removed from VG online.

European Elite Athletes Association (2008) 'EU athletes position statement on anti-doping'. Available online at: www.euathletes.info/news/news/?no_cache=1&tx_ttnews%5Btt_news%5D=218&tx_ttnews%5BbackPid%5D=91 (accessed 14 April 2010).

Ferdinand, P. (2008) '*To års karantæne til Rasmussen*' ('Two years suspension for Rasmussen'), *Ekstra Bladet*. Available online at: http://ekstrabladet.dk/sport/cykling/article1028273.ece (accessed 28 November 2009).

Grøndal, K.-I. (2009) 'Meldepliktsystemet må avskaffes' ('The whereabouts system must be abolished'), *Stavanger Aftenblad*, 27 June: 28.

Hansen, P.Ø. (2009) 'How do a group of elite level athletes evaluate and interpret the whereabouts information system?' Master's thesis, Norwegian School of Sport Sciences, Oslo.

Hanstad, D.V. and Loland, S. (2005) 'What is efficient doping control?' Report. Norwegian School of Sport Sciences, Oslo.

Hanstad, D.V. and Loland, S. (2007) '*Meldeplikt for toppidrettsutøvere: Forsvarlig antidopingarbeid eller uforsvarlig overvåkning?*' ('Elite level athletes' duty to provide information on their whereabouts: justifiable anti-doping work or an indefensible surveillance regime?'), *Nytt Norsk Tidsskrift*, 24: 314–22.

Hanstad, D.V. and Loland, S. (2009) 'Elite level athletes' duty to provide information on their whereabouts: justifiable anti-doping work or an indefensible surveillance regime?', *European Journal of Sport Science*, 9: 3–10.

Hanstad, D.V., Skille, E.Å. and Loland, S. (2010) 'Harmonization of anti-doping work: myth or reality?', *Sport in Society*, 13: 418–30.

Hanstad, D.V., Skille, E.Å. and Thurston, M. (2009) 'Elite athletes' perspectives on providing whereabouts information: a survey of athletes in the Norwegian registered testing pool', *Sport und Gesellschaft*, 6: 1–16.

Harman, N. (2009) 'Roger Federer defends strict new doping rules', *Times Online*. Available online at: www.timesonline.co.uk/tol/sport/tennis/article5679526.ece (accessed 28 November 2009).

IAAF (2006) 'Kenteris and Thanou accept anti-doping rule violations'. Press release from International Association of Athletics Federation. Available online at: www.iaaf.org/news/Kind=512/newsId=35111.html (accessed 28 November 2009).

Jarlsbo, Ø. (2005) '*Høidalen har fått doping-advarsel*' ('Høidalen has received a doping warning'), *Verdens Gang*, 25 July: 16.

Johannessen, B.A. and Prestvik, J. (2007) '"Føler meg forfulgt"' ('"I feel persecuted"'), *Verdens Gang*, 23 March: 2.

Kise Karlsen, T. (2007) 'Sterk uenighet om meldeplikten', *Dagsavisen*, 9 March: 24.

Kreft, L. (2009) 'The elite athlete – in a state of exception?', *Sport, Ethics and Philosophy*, 3: 3–18.

Krug, M. (2009) 'Olympian backs WADA rules', *Aljazeera*. Available online at: http://english.aljazeera.net/sport/2009/03/2009311194225828766.html (accessed 28 November 2009).

Kvamme, S. (2009) '"Jeg var redd for å sovne bak rattet"' ('"I was afraid of sleeping when driving"'), *Dagbladet.no*. Available online at: www.dagbladet.no/2009/01/15/sport/antidoping/olaf_tufte/hoidalen/4386245/ (accessed 28 November 2009).

Møller, V. (2009a) *Løgn over løgn* (*Lies over lies*), København: People's Press.

Møller, V. (2009b) 'Whereabouts – en demoraliserende regel' ('Whereabouts – a demoralizing regulation'), in A.V.Christiansen (ed.), *Kontrolsport. Big brother blandt atleter og tilskuere*, Odense: Syddansk Universitetsforlag.

NIF (2008a) *Domsutvalget. Protokoll. Sak 11/08: ADN mot Vegard Høidalen. Anmeldelse for brudd på dopingbestemmelsene*, Oslo: Domsutvalget Norges idrettsforbund og olympiske komité.

NIF (2008b) *Lovhefte*, Oslo: Norges idrettsforbund og olympiske og paralympiske komité.

NIF (2009) *Appellutvalget. Protokoll ankesak 11/08: Vegard Høidalen mot Stiftelsen Antidoping Norge*, Oslo: Appellutvalget Norges idrettsforbund og olympiske komité.

NZPA (2009) 'Banned Wickmayer slams tennis officials', *Sydney Morning Herald*. Available online at: http://news.smh.com.au/breaking-news-sport/banned-wickmayer-slams-tennis-officials-20091229-li1r.html (accessed 12 April 2010).

Quarrell, R. (2009) 'Olympic rowers call new WADA "whereabouts" drug-testing system "unworkable"', *Telegraph*. Available online at: www.telegraph.co.uk/sport/othersports/drugsinsport/4699721/Olympic-rowers-call-new-Wada-whereabouts-drug-testing-system-unworkable.html (accessed 28 November 2009).

Roughley, G. (2009) 'Rebecca Adlington calls for drug testers to get tough on footballers', *Guardian*. Available online at: www.guardian.co.uk/sport/2009/mar/25/rebecca-adlington-drugs-in-sport-premier-league-football (accessed 28 November 2009).

Stabrun Smith, A. (2008) '*Glemte å forlenge suspensjonen*' ('Forgot to extend the suspension'), *NRK*. Available online at: www.nrksport.no/1.6215282 (accessed 28 November 2009).

WADA (2004) *World Anti-Doping Code*, Lausanne: World Anti-Doping Agency.

WADA (2008a) *World Anti-Doping Code 2009*, Montreal: World Anti-Doping Agency.

WADA (2008b) *The World Anti-Doping Code. International Standard for Testing*, Montreal: World Anti-Doping Agency.

Waddington, I. (2010) 'Surveillance and control in sport: a sociologist looks at the WADA whereabouts system', *International Journal of Sport Policy*, 2: 255–74.

Waddington, I. and Smith, A. (2009) *An introduction to drugs in sport. Addicted to winning?*, London: Routledge.

14 A critique of the contemporary trend towards severe anti-doping sanctions

Changing directions

John Gleaves

Introduction

Despite evidence suggesting reasons for doubt, the popular consensus still holds that doping seriously harms athletes' health, contradicts sport's fundamental values, and constitutes what some consider an intolerable immoral action. These beliefs, it seems, are driving a trend towards harsher punishments. For example, the sport of cycling, which has a long history of doping violations, sanctions first-time doping offenders with automatic disqualification from the competition, a two-year suspension, and a fine equal to the rider's current yearly salary (UCI 2009a). Additionally, many professional teams now levy their own fines for doping, fines sometimes upwards of five times an athlete's annual salary (Agence France Presse 2009). Others now believe that only extreme measures can save the sport, calling for measures such as immediate lifetime bans (Associated Press 2008) following an athlete's first doping offense or increasing criminal punishments for doping offenses (Reuters 2007).

The current trend towards stronger punishments shows no signs of slowing. Nevertheless, there must be a limit as to how far a sport can go in punishing its athletes for doping. And, while it may be argued that some sports may have already arrived at that limit, most sporting organizations appear willing to continue stiffening their doping sanctions in the name of clean and fair competition. Yet these sanctions are not only ethically questionable but also harmful to the overall state of sport. Unless sporting organizations change their attitudes towards those who dope, and the manner in which they sanction them, I believe that they will eventually become the victims of their own harsh policies.

Thus, in the following, I hope to accomplish two things. First, I will provide three reasons for the rejection of the current trend towards harsher doping punishments, reasons that support a new approach towards sanctions for anti-doping violations. Second, I attempt to show how sanctioning doping in the same manner as other rule infractions may generate punishments that better preserve fairness and accomplish their goal of deterring doping. I conclude by providing just such an example of the type of game-based punishments that sports ought to consider when reconfiguring their own policies towards doping. By using a sport-specific approach, sports can continue punishing users who violate anti-doping rules, while preserving the integrity of their contests.

Part I: Rejecting the current approach

In this section, I will argue that the current approach to punishing doping in sport is unjustifiable. I provide three reasons for rejecting this approach. First, I argue that the common view of doping—a view that influences the majority of anti-doping policies—misunderstands the nature of doping. Second, I question whether the science used to convict athletes of doping can justify the severity of current punishments. Finally, I argue that harsh punishments may unnecessarily harm innocent athletes, fans, and the quality of the very competition that they seek to protect. Taken together, these three arguments demonstrate the need for a reconfigured approach to sanctioning doping offenses.

Recontextualizing doping in elite sport

Currently, sporting organizations such as the World Anti-Doping Agency (WADA) and the International Olympic Committee (IOC), the media, and a large portion of the general public often express a view of doping that scholars have termed "anti-doping fundamentalism" (Møller 2008). Perhaps well intentioned, but certainly misguided, anti-doping fundamentalism places doping in an immoral category, separate from other rule infractions. Unlike the widespread and more readily accepted professional or strategic foul (which indicates the athlete's game intelligence), the common view holds that doping points to an athlete's character flaw or lack of moral rectitude. When justifying their opposition to doping, members of these groups often cite WADA's official position that doping is unfair, harmful to an athlete's health, and contradictory to the spirit of sport (WADA 2009). To resolve the problem of doping, holders of the common view support the aggressive punishment of doping transgressors, with the intention of dissuading future athletes from the temptation of tasting the forbidden fruit.

The view that doping has no place in elite sport is, to my mind, neither historically nor philosophically justifiable. As most scholars who study the history of performance-enhancing drug use in elite sport now understand, sports initially tolerated athletes' use of such substances. In fact, as Hoberman (1992) points out, almost from its inception in the late nineteenth century, high-performance sport has had an ongoing relationship with the method of enhancement now known as "doping."[1]

Although the simple fact that athletes historically used doping does not necessarily justify permitting athletes to dope, it does undermine the assumption that doping inherently conflicts with sporting values. Athletes' common use of stimulants —and the general public's knowledge of such use— suggests that doping contradicts neither sporting traditions nor an implied "spirit of sport." Thus, historical practices conflict with the assumption that pharmacological performance enhancement cannot ever be justified, as past sports have tolerated just such a practice.

Additionally, scholars such as Møller (2008, 2010) and Miah et al. (2005) have illustrated philosophical inconsistencies in assuming that doping conflicts with the values of elite sport. The common claim that doping is wrong because it is cheating is question begging. Additionally, the claim that doping contradicts the spirit of sport is flawed, as many desirable aspects of sport—such as training hard and pursuing excellence—are furthered by an athlete doping. Moreover, the fact that elite sport inherently carries health risks undermines the force of the argument that doping potentially harms an athlete's health. Last, the libertarian claim for individual freedom persuasively asserts that doping prohibitions constitute an unjustifiable form of paternalism, because they deny individuals the ability to make free and informed choices. In a less radical sense, such philosophers have argued that sports have no justification for banning doping if athletes are only harming themselves and they are fully competent to make that choice.

To be sure, I am not arguing that we should permit the widespread use of performance-enhancing drugs in sport. Instead, I am criticizing the assumptions that underlie the trend towards severe sanctions. Such philosophical criticisms provide reasons to doubt anti-doping fundamentalism's intense moral vehemence towards doping. Despite sport's legitimate desires to punish those who gain an unfair advantage by violating anti-doping rules, the common attitudes towards prohibited methods of enhancement have neither a historical nor a philosophical basis. To believe, as some have argued, that doping presents a moral crisis is to misunderstand the nature of anti-doping rules and, for that matter, the larger debate over performance enhancement. Yet it is these same zealous beliefs in the immorality of doping that have resulted in today's overly severe sanctions. As we shall see, altering these views of doping plays a large role in creating more effective and more justifiable punishments.

The pseudoscience behind certain severe sanctions

While anti-doping fundamentalism appears philosophically challenging to justify, so to, I believe, are the methods sporting organizations use to sanction athletes for doping. I will argue that such evidence cannot justify sporting organizations applying 2-year suspensions or significant financial fines, let alone lifetime bans. To justify such punishments, sporting organizations would need much stronger standards of evidence than those used today. Without more certain evidence against dopers, sporting organizations should refrain from using severe punishments.

From a scientific perspective, the quality of evidence used to convict riders of doping remains insufficient for justifying such harsh punishments. Although hotly debated, scientists have begun openly questioning the science behind anti-doping tests (Berry 2008; Sottas et al. 2008). Pointing to the probability of false positives, some scientists argue that the reliability of these tests is uncertain at best (Pitsch 2009). In other instances, tests indicate violations, only to prove inconclusive later. According to the United Kingdom Anti-Doping Quarterly Update, in 41 percent of doping charges, it was later found that there was no case for the athlete to answer (UK Sport 2009). This indicates many that many tests initially indicate doping despite not conclusively proving an athlete has doped.

Moreover, the secrecy surrounding the science used by organizations such as WADA frustrates independent scientists who wish to evaluate the methods employed by the WADA-accredited laboratories to analyze the tests. That many athletes also admit to regularly beating doping tests further calls into question testing accuracy (Kröner 2009). Given the number of doubts raised about doping tests, the sporting world should be cautious about imposing penalties that could end an athlete's career or dramatically affect their financial status.

Additionally, some doping violations rely primarily on circumstantial evidence. Occasionally, sporting organizations use evidence such as out-of-competition drug tests or count missed drug tests as a positive to charge riders with doping, although that evidence does not even show that an athlete ever actually competed while benefiting from doping. Finding an athlete guilty of doping without proving they ever entered a competition while using prohibited performance-enhancing drugs is akin to finding someone who drinks guilty of "drunk driving," even though they had never actually gotten behind the wheel of a car. In both cases, a person is charged before having actually committed the infraction. Although a result of the nature of the substances used to dope, the use of out-of-competition tests raises serious ethical questions about the severity of anti-doping punishments. If sporting organizations wish to use such indirect evidence, then the punishments based on that evidence ought to reflect the evidence's limited degree of certainty.

Last, the UCI's adoption of the "biological passport" system—whereby the UCI records a rider's tests and suspends the rider if the test results show minor fluctuations that indicate doping—further illustrates the trend towards using indirect evidence to justify harsh doping sanctions (2009b). In 2009, the CAS upheld the International Skating Union's (ISU) suspension of German speed skater Claudia Pechstein (CAS 2009). The ISU used twenty-seven blood samples collected from Pechstein between October 2007 and April 30, 2009. Based solely on fluctuations in her reticulocyte values, the ISU charged Pechstein with "having used a prohibited substance and/or a prohibited method, i.e., some form of blood doping, which would constitute an anti-doping violation" (CAS 2009).

While the scientific evidence indicates a likelihood that Pechstein did indeed use doping products/processes, the case also illustrates the flaw in the biological passport's approach. Biological passports cannot show what substance an athlete has taken, nor actually demonstrate that the athlete ever took a banned substance. The biological passports, in short, produce no direct evidence of doping. The passports can only circumstantially indicate the likelihood of doping.

With the burden of proof placed on the accused athlete, demonstrating one's innocence becomes quite challenging. How does an athlete refute the charge of using a substance when there is no substance to dispute? Using such indirect evidence should give sporting organizations pause for thought, if only to consider what other areas of life we would apply similarly harsh punishments using such levels of evidence.

How harsh punishments harm sport

The fact that sporting organizations use questionable evidence and methods as the basis for severe punishments is not the only problem with their approach. Severe punishments have also caused innocent athletes to miss competing in important sporting contests, or to have their performances undeservingly discredited. Although anti-doping advocates often claim that strict sanctions can help to create fairer competition, there also exist instances where harsh sanctions harm sport. Both the potential and the real negative effects of harsh sanctions provide a third reason to reject harsh punishments.

One of the effects of harsh doping sanctions is that quality athletes often find themselves on the sidelines simply because of a cloud of controversy. In cycling, superstar riders such as Tom Boonen, Alessandro Petacchi, and Michael Rasmussen have all been suspended for "doping," despite the absence of evidence that any of the riders had intentionally doped. Moreover, in 2008, the 2007 Tour de France champion, Alberto Contador, could not defend his title, as the Tour de France organizing company, Amaury Sports Organization (ASO), decided to ban him and his team, Astana, from that year's race owing to Astana's past doping problems. Because Contador and many of Astana's coaches, managers, and other riders transferred to the team in the off-season, they had no connection with Astana's past doping offenses and arguably did not deserve to be the victim of such penalties. Although cycling claims to be doing everything in the fight against doping, these cases indicate how its policies are preventing innocent athletes from ever having a chance to compete.

On the other hand, innumerable athletes have been found to have committed doping violations, despite their lack of intention to do so. Many of these cases involve over-the-counter medications, or medicine prescribed by a doctor to treat an illness that contains small amounts of banned substances. Such was the case with British alpine ski racer Alain Baxter, who, while in the United States for the 2002 Salt Lake Winter Olympics, purchased an unfamiliar over-the-counter inhaler (BBC 2002). After winning the bronze medal in the Men's Slalom, traces of methamphetamine from Baxter's inhaler, which were too low to have been of any performance-enhancing benefit, triggered a positive test. Under WADA's "strict liability" clause, Baxter was stripped of his medal and given a 3-month suspension.

While cases such as Baxter's or Contador's are accidental consequences of sporting organizations' efforts to "clean up" sport, the fact of the matter remains that harsh policies and zero-tolerance sanctions can harm the overall quality of sport. That innocent athletes are deprived of access to participate in sporting competitions, or are being wrongly stripped of successes, shows the reality of the overly-harsh sanctions' effects on sport: doping controls have not created a fair playing field. Moreover, sporting organizations appear to accept this inequality as the collateral cost of creating the perception of drug-free sport. Yet, having athletes wrongly sit out competitions is not only unfair to those athletes, but diminishes the quality of the competition that their policies aim to protect. Thus, the second part of this chapter examines how we can improve the policies for punishing riders charged with doping.

Part II: Establishing a new approach

In the previous section, I provided three reasons for rejecting the current approach to doping violations in sport. In this section, I attempt to provide a better context for doping violations based on each sport's internal game logic. First, I will distinguish between sports' use of two different kinds of sanction—penalties and punishments—for addressing rule violations. Then, I illustrate that, when it is viewed as a simple rule violation, sporting organizations have a plethora of tactics available for sanctioning doping without needing to resort to extreme sanctions. Last, I show how such a view of doping violations opens the door to new and more effective punishments, punishments that preserve fairness while deterring doping.

An important distinction: penalties and punishments

In order to create better anti-doping sanctions, sporting organizations ought to examine how sanctions are intended to work. Although various scholars such as Meier (1985), Morgan (1995), and Loland (2002) have put forward extended discussions on the infrastructure of game rules, for these purposes we can simply view the sanctions for rule violations in two forms: penalties and punishments. Penalties are sanctions that restore fairness to competition when certain rules are broken. For example, in association football, if a player fouls an opponent, the officials penalize the player by awarding the opponent a free kick. We assume that this free kick restores a reasonable degree of fairness to the competition. Usually, a sport's governing body applies penalties to infractions that it considers to be an acceptable part of the game—either accidental violations or benign varieties of strategic foul. If, for example, the football community wished to eradicate the practice of fouling altogether, it would not use penalties but would instead employ punishments.

Sporting communities add punishments to their penalties to prevent undesirable behaviors from occurring during the competition. Punishments often incorporate penalties so as to restore fairness, but are more severe and, thus, go beyond the function of restoration. An example of a punishment is football's red card. Red cards are given for objectionable behavior such as fighting or malicious tackling. If a player receives a red card, the player must exit the field, and his/her team must play with one fewer member. Unlike penalties, punishments seek not only to restore fairness but also to prevent unwanted behavior. Ideally, the punishment's severity deters players from breaking that rule. The lower the sport community's tolerance for an infraction, the harsher the punishment it imposes.

Simply another rule violation?

As noted above, the prevailing popular view of doping sees it as a moral problem. This view of doping has led to the increase in harsh sanctions and unjustifiable punishments, but also has placed doping violations in a different context than other rule violations. Granting, as I previously argued, that this common view of doping is incorrect, and that this incorrect view of doping has influenced the trend towards harsh punishments, perhaps sport can benefit by adopting a different perspective of the doping issue. Following this, I describe a new approach to doping, one that hopefully retains the desire to prevent athletes from doping but avoids the pitfalls that resulted in today's severe sanctions. Rather than treating doping as a moral problem and creating a special set of severe anti-doping punishments, I propose viewing anti-doping rules as part of a sport's overall game logic. In other words, the rules that prohibit an athlete from using performance-enhancing drugs ought simply to be viewed as some among the many rules that establish a game's desirable challenges, and the sanctions for their violation should mirror the same pattern of penalties and punishments that sports use for other infractions.

Before describing doping's place in game rules, however, it is necessary to provide some background as to the nature of games, drawn from the philosophy of sports and, in particular, the writing of Bernard Suits (2005). Suits explains that games create artificial problems by setting out rules that prohibit certain efficient methods for completing a test (2005). For example, the game of golf involves getting one's ball in a hole using as few strokes as possible. Getting the ball into the hole is golf's artificial problem. However, the rules of golf prohibit certain efficient methods for moving one's ball. These rules range from prohibiting one from simply picking the ball up and placing it in the hole, to the types of club and the composition of the balls that a player may or may not use.

Although arbitrary, the rules are not random. The gamewrights for each game determine the degree of efficiency a player is permitted. The rules that limit a player's efficiency affect the challenges players face when overcoming a game's artificial problem. In the sport of cycling, the construction, weight, and design of a bicycle are regulated in a way that prevents athletes from using new technology to avoid the sport's artificial challenges. In an extreme example, if a cyclist attached a motor to his/her machine, then he/she would no longer face the challenge of propelling his/herself over a set distance. Essentially, a cyclist who used a motor would have failed to confront the sport's artificial problem.

In the instance of doping, sports' governing bodies can argue that doping allows athletes to undesirably avoid a sport's testing and contesting challenges. Rule-makers can justifiably assert (in the sense that it is not logically contradictory) that doping removes an important element of a sport's test. If doping removes an important element of the test—like using a motor in a cycling race or one's hand to move one's golf ball—then the artificial problem central to the test transforms into a weaker version of itself. Gamewrights who believe doping transforms sports into weaker versions of the tests that they originally instantiated (or, at least, as they instantiated them prior to doping) can then create rules prohibiting its use in order to preserve the test's artificial problem.

Once a sport creates rules that prohibit certain efficient means for completing its test, it then often creates penalties and punishments for those who violate them. As penalties and punishments have different effects on how players play the game, rule-makers must consider the impact of the rule violation on the game before determining if a specific rule violation receives a penalty or punishment. This decision is not arbitrary, as it can directly impact the nature of the test.

In the case of anti-doping rule violations, it makes sense to sanction dopers by punishment. There are two arguments to support this position. First, given the way that doping affects many competitions, it appears very difficult, if not impossible, to undo the effect of an illicitly enhanced athlete on a competition's outcome. During a race, a doped cyclist can attack the peloton, causing opponents to expend extra energy to chase them down. In weightlifting or certain track and field events, a doped athlete may set marks that influence the efforts of their competitors. In events with qualifying heats, a doped athlete may eliminate an athlete who followed the rules, thus excluding that athlete from competing in the finals. Essentially, a doped athlete's effects radiate far beyond their placement on the results sheet.

As, in most cases, officials can only catch a doped rider following a competition, the finely honed penalties that sports often use for other infractions are not useful when it comes to doping. The restoration of fairness from unearned advantage cannot typically be effected during a contest. Thus, in most sports, punishments—not penalties—seem to be the order of the day. If it is difficult to restore fairness once behavior X has taken place, the next best option is to prevent behavior X. This is the function of punishments.

Second, the cultural views held by a sporting community about doping further justify sanctioning doping with punishments. Although the cultures of many sports initially accepted doping (Hoberman 1992; Dimeo 2007), in the twenty-first century this is no longer the case. As it stands now, the vast majority of sports have not only chosen to prohibit doping to enhance performance, but also view doping with a certain level of moral disapproval.

If a sporting community's view of doping results in a desire to prevent doping rather than to tolerate it, the community should choose to sanction those who violate that rule with punishments as well as with penalties. As argued previously, there exists a degree of arbitrariness to the rules that prohibit doping. Nonetheless, a sporting community's desire to prevent the violation of its doping rules justifies its use of punishments for the rule violation.

Now, critics may argue that doping is a more serious problem than a simple rule violation and thus merits a much harsher sanction. However, while I admit that doping is undesirable, a form of cheating, and illegal outside the boundaries of cycling, it is actually not much different than other types of behavior we tolerate but punish in sports. Fighting in hockey is a case in point. If two people brawled outside a bar on a Friday night, they both would likely go to jail. Yet, inside an ice rink, with skates on, these same men brawl on national television and receive only a few minutes in the penalty box.

The action's illegality and the related societal disapproval of fighting are an insignificant factor in hockey's determination of the *fairness* of the sanction for the rule infraction. Sport regulations provide punishments for immoral behaviors such as fighting, spitting on an opponent, and using abusive language, but these rules are designed to deter these behaviors more because they harm the game in certain ways rather than because they violate the law or a sense of morality. Sports provide punishments with the goal of preventing those behaviors because those actions detract from fair and enjoyable contests. Thus, the point of punishing doping is not to address issues of civic decency or civil legality—other avenues are available for addressing those issues.[2] The point of punishing is to prevent behaviors that harm the sport or the players.

By viewing doping as a rule violation rather than a moral failing, sporting communities can focus on creating fair punishments that prevent doping but also fit within the context of their specific sport. A sport's rules should prescribe punishments for the violation of its doping rules with the same rationale or game logic that they would use to punish the actions of those who attempt to gain an advantage by intentionally breaking the other rules of the sport. In order to prevent damaging a sport with overly harsh punishments, sporting organizations should design just punishments for dopers who cheat. Even if it believes a behavior such as doping is immoral, a sport's punishments should aim to restore fairness or promote enjoyable competition and not moral instruction.

Effective punishments

Once sports begin to view a doping violation as just one among many rule violations, the trend towards severe doping sanctions—sanctions that have no equivalent in sport—may be replaced by sport-specific punishments. These sanctions ought to be consistent with the same game logic that a sport uses for punishing other types of behavior that it wishes to prevent. Just as each sport punishes unacceptable behavior according to its own internal structure, so the punishments for doping infractions should seek to restore fairness to the competition but also work to prevent the undesirable behavior.

The sport of soccer provides an excellent example of just such a punishment that many sports can use to sanction doping violations. In soccer, when a player commits a particularly egregious infraction, he/she receives a red card. The red card not only removes the player from the game, but also forces the team to play down a player for the rest of the match. Additionally, in severe instances, the offending player may receive a suspension from a set number of future matches.

Given the way a doped athlete affects the outcome of many team sports, the implementation of a "doping red card" can provide a useful punishment. Not only can organizations make teams forfeit matches and suspend athletes following positive doping tests, but it can also force teams to compete "minus a player" in future competitions. In the case of repeated, severe, or systematic doping within a team, officials could extend punishments to the point where teams can face increased punishments. In this way, the doping red card acts as a punishment rather than a penalty, as it does nothing to restore the fairness of the competition, but acts as a significant deterrent in a place where penalties cannot restore fairness.

Such an approach to doping has two positive benefits. First, having punishments that affect entire teams helps puts more pressure on teams to police themselves, by creating an internal climate whereby athletes discourage other teammates from doping, as others' use would negatively impact their career. Also, the sense that one's choice to dope would harm one's teammates may dissuade others from doping. In the case where the entire team agreed to dope, applying sanctions to the whole team would be especially effective, as it was a team effort in the first place.

Additionally, team punishments fix a flaw in the current system. As it stands now, teams can simply sack the offending athlete and continue without further punishment.[3] For example, in the 2008 Tour de France, two athletes from the Saunier Duval team—Riccardo Ricco and Leonardo Piepoli—tested positive for doping. These athletes were removed from the race, but the rest of their team carried on, with no repercussions. Yet, arguably, these doped athletes provided their teammates with advantages. Moreover, this system allows teams to benefit from doped athletes and then simply cut ties once an athlete is caught. If the team benefits from doping, then the team should also be punished for gaining an unearned advantage over its opponents.

By dispersing the punishment between the individual and the team, and shortening the individual's suspension, less of the burden falls on the individual athlete. Considering the quality of evidence used to convict athletes of doping, such a punishment more closely matches the level of certainty in the doping tests. In fact, lowering the length of suspension may prevent the long-drawn-out legal battles that often prevent sports from determining the final results of a competition. Take the case of 2006 Tour de France winner Floyd Landis, who launched an aggressive legal appeal against his doping conviction. The appeal lasted so long that, at the start of the 2007 Tour de France, the winner of the 2006 race still remained unknown. Shorter and more targeted punishments can more quickly allow sports to restore fairness and punish the offending parties.

Critics of the position developed here may argue that the teammates of a doper are innocent and thus should not be punished. However, this criticism is wrong on two levels. First, a doped athlete's contribution, although in some sports this is more ambiguous, certainly benefits his/her teammates. If the team benefits from doping, then the team should also be punished for having benefited from one of its players who violated the rules. Second, often sports punish entire teams when one athlete commits an infraction. In soccer, the red card penalizes the entire team by making it play with one player fewer, despite the fact that only one player committed the infraction. Holding an entire team accountable for its player's decisions is in line with many other punishments sports currently use.

While team punishments present a new mode of punishment for doping, sports should also continue to punish the individual caught doping. At the very minimum, sporting organizations should ban a doped athlete from competition until the physiological benefits from doping have disappeared. For example, when a distance runner boosts his/her hematocrit using erythropoietin (EPO), he/she should at least be banned until the hematocrit returns to normal levels.[4] The same applies to other drugs such as testosterone, steroids, or human growth hormones. Moreover, it makes sense that a sporting organization should increase its scrutiny of athletes caught doping by subjecting them to more rigorous screening.

Conclusion

Those who claim that severe anti-doping punishments can save sport fail to see that harsh anti-doping sanctions may actually harm their sports more than help them. Indeed, more measured punishments may actually prove fairer and reduce the infraction's occurrence. As long as doping is against the rules, there must be sanctions for athletes who break those rules. Yet, rather than treating doping as a morally deviant act and punishing it with "extreme remedies," sporting organizations should view doping as similar to other forms of rule-breaking that need to be dealt with through the employment of restorative penalties and measured punishments.

By moving from unduly severe to more measured and better targeted punishments, we can take a step towards dissolving the current strife caused by doping. Although the rules should punish doping so as to prevent it from occurring, I have argued that they can become too harsh. I have also shown a new way forward that continues to punish athletes who dope, but in an ethical manner that works to prevent doping.

If sporting communities ignore the risks of harsh sanctions, it may be that sport ultimately loses in the end. As Verner Møller warns, "the greatest danger to sport are the many people of good will who do not seem to understand that their helping hands have sport in a stranglehold that will eventually choke the life out of it" (2008: 192). Rather than promoting longer bans and harsher fines, sport should embrace a new approach towards punishing doping, one that fairly punishes the infraction, while reducing its occurrence.

Notes

1 News reports indicate marathon runners and professional pedestrians doped with brandy and strychnine as early as the 1900s, and the popular six-day track racers in the 1910s and 1920s openly doped during their competitions. Even famed Tour de France founder Henri Desgrange believed doping was acceptable, "in a case of absolute necessity to give you for a period artificial vigor." Before World War II, amphetamines, cocaine, heroin, and strychnine would have been but a few of the drugs in most professional athletes' toolkits (Thompson 2008).

2 I believe that extra-sport legal actions are appropriate in addition to sanctions levied by the sport community. Athletes should not be exempt from the law because they violated the law playing a sport. Yet, prosecuting athletes is not the responsibility of a sporting organization. Instead, sporting organizations should cooperate with legal investigations into an athlete's violation of civic law, but should not attempt to sanction the athlete in the sport because they violated a law.

3 In fact, the CAS recently ruled that riders must compensate their former teams for any financial damages caused by their doping (Cyclingnews.com 2010). Such a decision further strengthens the teams' hands by placing them in a win–win situation: use doped riders to help win races and receive a payout if the rider is caught.

4 Hematocrit is a measure of red blood cells. Red blood cells carry oxygen to working muscles and, in endurance sports, increasing the number of one's red blood cells provides a distinct advantage. The drug EPO boosts an athlete's hematocrit, thus athletes who have doped using EPO should not compete until any advantage gained from drug use has disappeared.

References

Agence France Presse (2009) "Three top Katusha riders oppose team rules," Agence France Presse. Available online at: http://velonews.competitor.com/2009/06/news/three-top-katusha-riders-oppose-new-team-rules_92918 (accessed July 14, 2010).

Associated Press (2008) "Italian cycling group suggests lifetime bans needed to combat doping."

BBC (2002) "British skier stripped of bronze." Available online at: http://news.bbc.co.uk/winterolympics2002/hi/english/alpine_skiing/newsid_1882000/1882870.stm (accessed July 14, 2010).

Berry, D.A. (2008) "The science of doping," *Nature*, 454(7205): 692–3.

CAS (2009) "Case Pechstein: The 2-year ban confirmed by the Court of Arbitration for Sport," Press Release, Lausanne: The Court of Arbitration for Sport.

Cyclingnews.com (2010) "Beltran must pay Liquigas damages for positive doping." First Edition. Available online at: www.cyclingnews.com/news/beltran-must-pay-liquigas-damages-for-doping-positive (accessed July 14, 2010).

Dimeo, P. (2007) *A history of drug use in sport 1876–1976. Beyond good and evil*, New York: Routledge.

Hoberman, J. (1992) *Mortal engines: The science of performance and the dehumanization of sport*, New York: The Free Press.

Kröner, H. (2009) "Kohl tells all about doping," Cyclingnews.com.

Loland, S. (2002) *Fair play in sport: A moral norm system*, New York: Routledge.

Meier, K.V. (1985) "Restless sport," *Journal of the Philosophy of Sport*, XII: 64–77.

Miah, A., Kayser, B., and Mauron, A. (2005) "Legalization of performance-enhancing drugs," *Lancet*: 521.

Møller, V. (2008) *The doping devil*, International Network of Humanistic Doping Research, vol. 1, Copenhagen: Books on Demand GmbH.

Møller, V. (2010) *The ethics of doping and anti-doping: Redeeming the soul of sport*, New York: Routledge.

Morgan, W.J. (1995) "The logical incompatibility thesis and rules: A reconsideration of formalism as an account of games," in W.J. Morgan and K.V. Meier (eds), *Philosophic inquiry in sport*, Champaign, IL: Human Kinetics, pp. 50–63.

Pitsch, W. (2009) "'The science of doping' revisited: Fallacies of the current anti-doping regime," *European Journal of Sport Science*, 9: 87–95.

Reuters (2007) "IOC calls on Britain to criminalize doping." Available online at: www.reuters.com/article/idUSSP15795820070724 (accessed July 14, 2010).

Sottas, P. et al. (2008) "Doping: a paradigm shift has taken place in testing," *Nature*, 455(7210): 166.

Suits, B. (2005) *The grasshopper: Games, life and utopia*, Peterborough, ON: Broadview Press.

Thompson, C. (2008) *The Tour de France: A cultural history*, Los Angeles: University of California Press.

UCI (2009a) "Anti-Doping Rules of the UCI," *Union Cycliste Internationale*. Available online at: www.uci.ch/includes/asp/getTarget.asp?type=FILE&id=NDc3MDk (accessed July 14, 2010).

UCI (2009b) "Information on the biological passport." Available online at: www.uci.ch/Modules/ENews/ENewsDetails.asp?MenuId=MjI0NQ&id=NTQzOA&LangId=1 (accessed May 19, 2009).

UK Sport (2009) UK National Anti-Doping Programme Quarterly Update. April–June.

WADA (2009) "World Anti-Doping Code." Available online at: www.wada-ama.org/rtecontent/document/code_v2009_En.pdf (accessed July 15, 2010).

Index

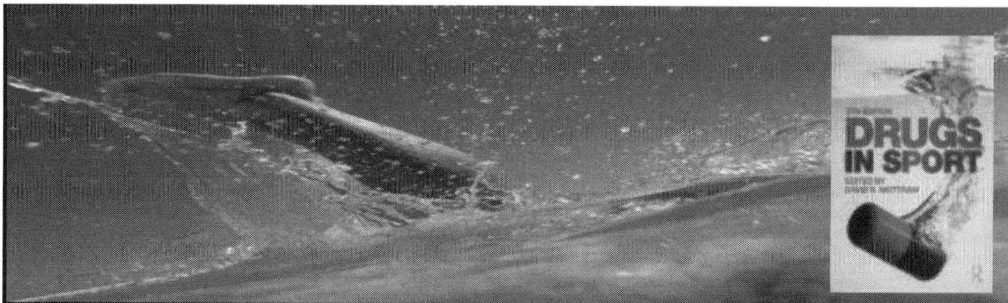
DRUGS
IN SPORT